**transitions**

*General Editor: Julian Wolfreys*

*Published titles*

ORWELL TO THE PRESENT, 1945–1999 John Brannigan
CHAUCER TO SHAKESPEARE, 1337–1580
SunHee Kim Gertz
MODERNISM, 1910–1945 Jane Goldman
POPE TO BURNEY, 1714–1786 Moyra Haslett
PATER TO FORSTER, 1873–1924 Ruth Robbins
BURKE TO BYRON, BARBAULD TO BAILLIE, 1790–1830 Jane Stabler
MILTON TO POPE, 1650–1720 Kay Gilliland Stevenson
SIDNEY TO MILTON, 1580–1660 Marion Wynne Davies

TERRY EAGLETON David Alderson
BATAILLE Fred Botting and Scott Wilson
NEW HISTORICISM AND CULTURAL MATERIALISM
John Brannigan
HÉLÈNE CIXOUS Abigail Bray
GENDER Claire Colebrook
POSTMODERN NARRATIVE THEORY Mark Currie
FORMALIST CRITICISM AND READER-RESPONSE THEORY
Kenneth Womack and Todd F. Davis
IDEOLOGY James M. Decker
QUEER THEORY Donald E. Hall
MARXIST LITERARY AND CULTURAL THEORIES Moyra Haslett
LOUIS ALTHUSSER Warren Montag
RACE Brian Niro
JACQUES LACAN Jean-Michel Rabaté
LITERARY FEMINISMS Ruth Robbins
DECONSTRUCTION•DERRIDA Julian Wolfreys

*Forthcoming titles*

DICKENS TO HARDY 1837–1884 Julian Wolfreys

JULIA KRISTEVA AND LITERARY THEORY
Megan Becker-Leckrone
NATIONAL IDENTITY John Brannigan
HOMI BHABHA Eleanor Byrne
POSTMODERNISM•POSTMODERNITY Martin McQuillan
ROLAND BARTHES Martin McQuillan

(continued overleaf)

*Forthcoming titles (continued)*

PSYCHOANALYSIS AND LITERATURE Nicholas Rand
SUBJECTIVITY Ruth Robbins
POSTCOLONIAL THEORY Malini Johar Schueller
TRANSGRESSION Julian Wolfreys

**Transitions**
**Series Standing Order**
**ISBN 0–333–73634–6**
(*outside North America only*)

You can receive future titles in this series as they are published. To place a standing order please contact your bookseller or, in the case of difficulty, write to us at the address below with your name and address, the title of the series and the ISBN quoted above.

Customer Services Department, Macmillan Distribution Ltd
Houndmills, Basingstoke, Hampshire RG21 6XS, England

transitions

# Modernism, 1910–1945

## Image to Apocalypse

Jane Goldman

palgrave
macmillan

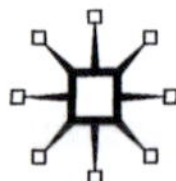



First published 2004 by
PALGRAVE MACMILLAN
Houndmills, Basingstoke, Hampshire RG21 6XS and
175 Fifth Avenue, New York, N.Y. 10010
Companies and representatives throughout the world

PALGRAVE MACMILLAN is the global academic imprint of the Palgrave Macmillan division of St. Martin's Press, LLC and of Palgrave Macmillan Ltd. Macmillan® is a registered trademark in the United States, United Kingdom and other countries. Palgrave is a registered trademark in the European Union and other countries.

ISBN 0–333–69620–4 hardback
ISBN 0–333–69621–2 paperback

This book is printed on paper suitable for recycling and made from fully managed and sustained forest sources.

A catalogue record for this book is available from the British Library.

Library of Congress Cataloging-in-Publication Data
Goldman, Jane, 1960–
Modernism, 1910–1945 : image to apocalypse / Jane Goldman.
p. cm. — (Transitions)
Includes bibliographical references (p. ) and index.
ISBN 0–333–69620–4 (cloth) — ISBN 0–333–69621–2 (paper)
1. English literature—20th century—History and criticism. 2. Modernism (Literature)—Great Britain. 3. American literature—20th century—History and criticism. 4. Modernism (Literature)—United States. I. Title. II. Transitions (Palgrave Macmillan (Firm))

PR478.M6G65 2004
820.9'112—dc21 2003054923

Printed and bound in Great Britain by
Antony Rowe Ltd, Chippenham and Eastbourne

Oh, give me liberty! for even were paradise my prison,
Still I should long to leap the crystal walls

(John Dryden)

For Gus and Roberta, with love

# Contents

# General Editor's Preface

> Transitions: *transition–*, n. of action. 1. A passing or passage from one condition, action or (rarely) place, to another. 2. Passage in thought, speech, or writing, from one subject to another. 3. **a**. The passing from one note to another. **b**. The passing from one key to another, modulation. 4. The passage from an earlier to a later stage of development or formation . . . change from an earlier style to a later; a style of intermediate or mixed character . . . the historical passage of language from one well-defined stage to another.

The aim of *Transitions* is to explore passages and movements in language, literature and culture from Chaucer to the present day. The series also seeks to examine the ways in which the very idea of transition affects the reader's sense of period so as to address anew questions of literary history and periodisation. The writers in this series unfold the cultural and historical mediations of literature during what are commonly recognised as crucial moments in the development of English literature, addressing, as the OED puts it, the "historical passage of language from one well-defined stage to another".

Recognising the need to contextualise literary study, the authors offer close readings of canonical and now marginalised or overlooked literary texts from all genres, bringing to this study the rigour of historical knowledge and the sophistication of theoretically informed evaluations of writers and movements from the last 700 years. At the same time as each writer, whether Chaucer or Shakespeare, Milton or Pope, Byron, Dickens, George Eliot, Virginia Woolf or Salman Rushdie, is shown to produce his or her texts within a discernible historical, cultural, ideological and philosophical milieu, the text is read from the vantage point of recent theoretical interests and concerns. The purpose in bringing theoretical knowledge to the reading of a wide range of works is to demonstrate how the literature is always open to transition, whether in the instance of its production or in succeeding moments of its critical reception.

The series desires to enable the reader to transform her/his own reading and writing transactions by comprehending past developments. Each book in the second tranche of the series offers a pedagogical guide to the poetics and politics of particular eras, as well as to the subsequent critical comprehension of periods and periodisation. As well as transforming the cultural and literary past by interpreting its transition from the perspective of the critical and theoretical present, each study enacts transitional readings of a number of literary texts, all of which are themselves conceivable as having effected transition at the moments of their first appearance. The readings offered in these books seek, through close critical reading, historical contextualisation and theoretical engagement, to demonstrate certain possibilities in reading to the student reader.

It is hoped that the student will find this series liberating because the series seeks to move beyond rigid definitions of period. What is important is the sense of passage, of motion. Rather than providing a definitive model of literature's past, *Transitions* aims to place you in an active dialogue with the writing and culture of other eras, so as to comprehend not only how the present reads the past, but how the past can read the present.

*Julian Wolfreys*

# Preface

*Modernism, 1910–1945: Image to Apocalypse* addresses the main literary transitions in the first half of the twentieth century. It charts and samples the major movements and significant canonical texts of the period; it considers the contexts in which they were written and first published; and points to the important critical and theoretical questions and debates surrounding and emerging from it. This book introduces the reader to major canonical texts by the literary giants of the period alongside key works by a number of its other important and interesting figures. I set out below the (five) main questions this book addresses concerning the period. There follows a brief discussion of the issues of periodisation and the book's selection of material, and a note on the "little magazines" of the period (which provided the first context of publication for many of the works in focus). These questions and issues inform the outline that follows of the formal shape and contents of this book.

## Five introductory questions

**1.** *What are the most important and interesting literary movements and texts of the period 1910 to 1945?*
Broadly speaking, the most important and interesting movements of this period were modernist and avant-garde, according to the argument of this book, and they are located between the Imagist movement at its start and the Apocalypse movement at its close. The most important and interesting texts of this period are energetic and experimental. They pushed (and still push) the "literary" as a genre out of all recognition, and made (make) new transformational languages, forcing new and conflicting models of engagement and interpenetration between art and real life. The "image" becomes a significant semantic and structuring unit, common to all genres, and collage

(or montage, or mosaic) the radical organising principle of many avant-garde texts. What are the major transitions occurring in the literature of this period? The major transitions are in the inventing, the forging, the laying down and recasting of these new, conflicting and transformational, modernist and avant-garde languages. This book will introduce and offer guidance through the main transitions, conflicts and movements of the period and sample a range of its most important avant-garde literary languages.

**2.** *Where was much of the writing of this period first published and read, first theorised, formulated, and reviewed?*
In the international forum of the avant-garde, in the pages of the many "little magazines" that flourished in these decades, and which were issued along with limited editions of individual works, from the many small, independent presses. This was where literary art, in many languages, European, English and American, in many forms, and in both established and new genres, appeared alongside visual (including filmic and photographic) and musical arts, as well as scientific, philosophical, psychoanalytical and cultural, political and social commentary, and aesthetic and political manifestos. This book will introduce the reader to some of the most significant and influential texts of the period, in these important first contexts. Each of the three parts that follow the introduction, therefore, focuses its discussion, in part, on a significant issue (or two) of one important little magazine from the period. Part I looks at *The Egoist,* Part II *Blast,* and Part III *transition.*

**3.** *What are the critical and theoretical questions we should ask of the texts of this period?*
There are many, but the two most important questions that are asked implicitly, and sometimes explicitly, throughout this book are the following: (1) "Who is speaking?" and (2) "Where is she?" The first, "Who is speaking?", is a question I derive from one of the most important and influential critics writing on the literature of this period, Erich Auerbach (see below). This is an excellent question to ask of modernist and avant-garde texts, not only to establish perspectives on their often complex narrative points of view and so on. It is an essential question to ask of such experimental and multi-vocal texts that so often engage in juxtaposing citations and quotations from other sources, and so often give voice to other writers, living and dead, as

well as to discourses and ideologies from such diverse other quarters, social, political, scientific, psychoanalytical, artistic and musical. Is modernity speaking, or is tradition speaking? we might also ask. "Who is speaking?" is also an essential question to ask of experimental texts that seek to explore and produce new models of the self, identity, and subjectivity. Part I, with these questions very much in mind, explores one of the period's major, and formative, manifestos: "Tradition and the Individual Talent", by T. S. Eliot. But the question resonates throughout this book. The second question, "Where is she?", is taken from the influential theorist of gender, Hélène Cixous (see Colebrook). Not only does it supplement the question, "Who is speaking?" with the thought "Is *he* or *she* speaking?", but it also points up the questions of how language itself may be gendered, and how *literary* language may be gendered. If the literature of the period, whether by women or men, is concerned with inventing and developing new, conflicting and transformational, modernist and avant-garde languages, it may well be concerned with how such languages are gendered, and what kinds of gendered subjectivity they record and produce. Part II of this book gives special attention to this question of transitions in gender politics. But again, it is one that resonates throughout.

**4.** *What are the most important and interesting contexts for the literature of this period?*

These contexts may include the historical, political, cultural, and intellectual. The historical and political contexts for the period include: the Great War, the Russian Bolshevik Revolution, the execution of the Russian Tsar (1918), the establishment of the Irish Free State (1922), Mussolini's March on Rome (1922), the establishment of the Union of Soviet Socialist Republics (1923), Hitler's Munich Putsch (1923), the General Strike in Britain (1926), the collapse of the American stock exchange (1929), Hitler's chancellorship of Germany and the burning of the Reichstag (1933), the British abdication crisis (1936), the Spanish Civil War (1936), and the Second World War, culminating in the dropping of atomic bombs on Hiroshima and Nagasaki (1945). The cultural and intellectual contexts for the period's explosion of modern literature and modern art include: the development and accessibility of transport, and huge increases in its speed; the emergence of visible and invisible communications such as photography, the cinema, the telephone, telegraphy and the wireless, which resulted in the rapid transmission of news, ideas, and images on a scale previously unknown; the discoveries of X-rays and radium; the artificial generation of electricity and its use in everyday life; and not least, discoveries and hypotheses about the structure of matter, space, and time, and about the processes of perception, and the understanding of the self. Part I of this book addresses many of these contexts as well as the emergent trajectories of critical and intellectual framing of the period. The Chronology at the back gives a more systematic indication and sampling of such contexts, and the argument throughout the book makes reference to many of them.

**5.** *Who are the most important writers (in English) of this period?* James Joyce, Virginia Woolf, W. B. Yeats, Ezra Pound, Gertrude Stein, T. S. Eliot, H.D., William Carlos Williams, Wyndham Lewis, Wallace Stevens are among the giants who appear in most accounts, including this one. And there are legions more to add to this preliminary list depending on what movements and what critical approaches are emphasised (not all of whom can be, although several are, given detailed attention in this book): Amy Lowell, Katherine Mansfield, Ford Madox Ford, D. H. Lawrence, John Middleton Murray, T. E. Hulme, Wilfred Owen, Siegfried Sassoon, Robert Graves, Laura Riding, Hugh MacDiarmid, Edwin Muir, Ernest Hemingway, F. Scott Fitzgerald, Langston Hughes, Claude McKay, Jean Rhys, Djuna Barnes, Mina Loy, May Sinclair, Dorothy Parker, Aldous Huxley, W. H. Auden, John Dos Passos, Christopher Isherwood, Nathanael West, Stevie Smith, Richard Wright, Muriel Rukeyser, Edith Sitwell, David Gascoyne, Kurt Schwitters, Samuel Beckett, George Orwell, Graham Greene, Stephen Wallace, Rebecca West, Dorothy Richardson. But before this list spills over the page and fills the book, it would be helpful now to consider some of the important factors in the design of this guide, which will both describe the major transitions of the period, as outlined above, and also sample, with close-readings, a significant range of its writing, poetry, fiction, essays and manifestos.

## Periodisation and the selection of material

In charting transitions in this (or any) period, examining the important moments and movements, exploring the works of its significant writers, it would be surprising to find the texts of most interest evenly distributed so that each subdivision of the period (decade or five-year span perhaps) is represented equally. But further complications arise in considering a period that has been roughly defined under the rubric of "Modernism", a retrospectively applied aesthetic order that anachronistically declares itself as a-temporal, or as "the new". It is also a period where the legacy of an apparently arbitrary process of periodisation itself has produced two conflicting aesthetic modes masquerading as historical eras, dividing our task into a consideration of the literature of "the twenties" as high modernist and aesthetic, and of the literature of "the thirties" as realist reportage and politically engaged. Recent critical attempts to rethink and reappraise the literature of these two decades has to some extent undermined their power to signify two distinct sets of aesthetic values, but at the same time the sense is perpetuated, nevertheless, of attributing particular aesthetic values to what remain arbitrary divisions of time.

My choice of dates, 1910 to 1945, however, does indicate, of course, a broad sense of chronological development, and after the Introduction, the book roughly begins with 1910 and ends around 1945. But it soon becomes clear that we have to turn to certain important declarations and developments in the 1920s to begin to understand the significance of the year 1910; and we have to look at other critical moments in the 1930s and well beyond the 1940s to understand how this whole period has been filtered, and how it continues to be filtered by various later and contesting theories (which are often emergent, nevertheless, in the period itself).

If we now consider the two dominant decades in terms of their designation as two aesthetic modes rather than strictly temporal categories, it will be evident to the reader that I have given some priority, in some senses, to material of the 1920s and its antecedents in the 1910s, because this is, without doubt, the most significant material of the period. But it also manifestly exceeds its temporal, historical demarcations. This book gives focus primarily to the works of the 1930s that take forward the founding aesthetics of the earlier avant-garde and modernist pushes. And similarly, the "political" issues of "the thirties" are addressed in terms of their impact on later readings of the 1910s and 1920s. The diverse projects of this period in fact have already been filtered for many post-1945 readers through the dominant critical debates of the 1930s concerning socialist realism and the backlash against "modernism", and through later subsequent Cold War criticism.

My readings from the 1930s may therefore, in places, depart from some representations of "the thirties". This is not because of blind and obvious devotion to "high Modernism" and the "historical avant-garde", although, like George Melly (see Chapter 1), I admit to always carrying on my person the sound poems of Kurt Schwitters (just in case). The most significant work in the 1930s perpetuates and develops from these earlier movements. To dwell on "the thirties" aesthetics would not therefore be representative of the 1930s. It would in fact diminish the power, scope and complexities of continuing avant-garde and modernist projects as they flourished in the 1930s and well after. Unlike some accounts of this period, which read the 1930s as "the thirties", marking the point where the avant-garde and modernism is said to falter and decline, this book shows that the major transitions of the period occur in the 1910s and 1920s; and that the era of the 1930s to mid-1940s marks in fact a period of further flourishing, and of reactions to, and refinements and reassessments of, those first powerful heaves. Furthermore, it is absurd and misleading to try to force an account of the rise of modernism and the avant-garde into neat, linear, chronological order. Many of the movements in this era sought so creatively to interrupt, abolish, conquer or transcend history and time. They do not obey such an impoverished sense of historicism and periodisation. Nor do they afford equal and measured emphasis and space allocated to each decade in mechanical sequence. Such an approach would ignore the very legacy of the period, the very transitions (and gloriously juvenile schismatics) that it wrought. So Blast! all so-called "objective" accounts of the literature of 1910 to 1945. You are dull and irrelevant.

The field of possible material for inclusion, furthermore, is enormous, indeed overwhelming. The Chronology and Bibliography at the back of this book serve as useful quick indices of the significant works of the period. In the course of the book I discuss or mention a great many of them, but inevitably, not all; and nor would I wish to give them the equal emphasis and attention that such tables and lists tend to suggest. The Bibliography and Chronology constitute the closest it is possible to get to an "objective", systematic, and chronological account or reading list for the era. But to extend this approach into continuous prose, focusing on extensive close-readings of texts in relation to contexts of all kinds, is not possible in a book of this length, nor even desirable for the reasons I give above.

## Reading the period through its "little magazines"

In selecting material for close-reading and for constructing the argument, I have included in each chapter material drawn from one or more issues of the three little magazines for particular focus. And I have also found it helpful to take an "image" from visual culture as a springboard to wider discussions. The selection of magazine issues is based first on situating key texts, such as from Joyce's fiction, Eliot's essays, or Wyndham Lewis's manifestos, for example, in this cultural context. A synchronic reading of key moments in the era arises from this practice, and allows an element of chance to dictate what other texts and authors come into focus. In Part I, for example, we turn to *The Egoist* to read one of the era's most influential documents, Eliot's manifesto, "Tradition and the Individual Talent". Turning its pages, we encounter all sorts of bed-fellows and cross-currents: not just the work of other contributors such as Joyce or Dora Marsden, but reviews and advertisements directing us to Pound or Sitwell or Huxley. We are able to visit major canonical authors alongside those less well known, and those who have become of more recent interest in studies of the period. By focusing on the little magazine, then, we already arrive at an understanding of the period that is not available through the more conventional and systematic, genre-based treatment of poetry, novels, plays. The little magazine is a site where these genres explode into each other, and where other genres emerge with new significance – the manifesto and essay in particular.

## Structure and contents

Each main part and each chapter in this book begins with a detailed introduction. What follows below is an overview of the contents, and brief introductions to the main parts: the Introduction, and Parts I to III.

### Introduction: "Make It New" – A Guide to Transitions in the Period of Modernism and the Avant-garde

The Introduction takes its title from Ezra Pound's famous avant-garde slogan "Make It New", the founding impetus for the literature of the period this book covers. Chapter 1, which in fact constitutes the

Introduction, finds an excellent guide to the founding movements of the period, and to their diverse reorientations, in the pages of Nathanael West's cult modernist novel *The Dream Life of Balso Snell* (1931). West's avant-garde guide to the great canonical, avant-garde texts of high modernism (by James Joyce, Marcel Proust, Gertrude Stein, Fyodor Dostoevsky and so on) also enables us to discuss and define the most important critical terms that have emerged in mapping this period: modernism, modernity, the avant-garde, the new, postmodernism, and so on. West's novel arms us with an overview of the scope and range of the period. And from its position in the trajectory of modernist and avant-garde aesthetics, roughly mid-way in the period (1931), is projected a discussion that directs us both back to earlier founding avant-garde texts and languages and forward to their later developments and concerns. Our reading of West's novel provides a set of critical terms and questions, then, for proceeding through the period, and through this book. As well as defining and addressing the terms "avant-garde" and "modernism" and their cohorts, this reading of West also opens up a discussion reflecting on the significance of the other terms, and the dates, in the title of this book: "Image to Apocalypse" and "1910–1945". The rationale and scope of this book is then compared with those of other introductions to the period and to its dominant designated aesthetic mode, "modernism". The chapter closes with a note on the formal, academic study of modernist and avant-garde works.

## Part I to Part III: the tripartite structure

What follows my Introduction is in three parts. And this structure reflects my selection of texts in relation to chronology, from the first heaves in the 1910s and 1920s to the refinements, reactions, regroupings and realignments of the 1930s and 1940s. As for the shape of these three parts, I have modelled them on the structure of Virginia Woolf's, novel *To the Lighthouse* (1927), a structure that Woolf employed specifically to chart, through narrative, the passage of time between two eras. She first outlined this model in a visual image in her notebooks as "two blocks joined by a corridor" (Dick: 44–5), the diagram for the tripartite shape of her novel. The first and third parts of the novel each treat a block of time, while the second, middle part is a corridor in which "Time Passes". Each part, which may also stand alone, as a discrete and distinct piece of work, is subdivided into sections of varying length, sometimes sequential in the argument, sometimes juxtaposed. And, like Woolf's middle section, "Time Passes", the central section of this book is also concerned with the politics of gender and language.

It is not on some whim that I have chosen to follow Woolf's model, but in recognition of her achievement in *To the Lighthouse*, of forging a set of narrative tools for charting and inscribing cultural transitions in the passage of historical time. Erich Auerbach recognises the same achievement in his influential essay on *To the Lighthouse*, the climactic chapter of his classic work on representation and narrative in Western literature from Homer to the twentieth century, *Mimesis: The Representation of Reality in Western Literature* (1946). Here, he offers an impressive reading of a section of *To the Lighthouse* (in terms of point-of-view, narrative voice, time, interior and exterior consciousness, epistemology and fragmentation) and asks of it his famous question: "Who is speaking in this paragraph?" He also makes the point that modern philologists (himself included) share the very technique of modern writers that his final chapter identifies in Woolf. This technique is encapsulated in *To the Lighthouse* by the artist, Lily Briscoe: "The great revelation perhaps never did come. Instead there were little daily miracles, illuminations, matches struck unexpectedly in the dark; here was one" (*To the Lighthouse*, p. 249). Auerbach explains: "interpretation of a few passages . . . can be made to yield more, and more decisive, information . . . than would a systematic and chronological treatment. Indeed, the present book may be cited as an illustration" (Auerbach: 525). And this book too follows this example of representative sampling of key works across the span of the period.

Woolf's structure is also significant for the weighting of emphasis in this book. In this respect it follows the elegiac rhythm of the dactylic pulses in Woolf's three parts (— ^ ^): the first is the longest, followed by two shorter units. And I have replicated that rhythm in the following chapters too in my emphasis on that enormously rewarding and rich "first heave" of avant-gardism of the 1910s and 1920s. The second flourishing (perhaps weakening, perhaps merely disseminating and regrouping), after-echoes of avant-gardism, resonating and retching into the 1930s and 1940s, receive less space. But these after-echoes, I propose, are often robust and of more importance, signifying as they do the continuation of avant-garde and modernist practices beyond the confines of the canonical "period" of modernism, than is the backlash of realism and "political" reportage that is usually foregrounded to characterise the 1930s. The work of this first phase is the image and apocalypse of the era, its theoretical and practical grounding, and its greatest transition. Having survived and regrouped through the trials of the 1930s, avant-garde forces are by the mid-1940s gathering again from dactylic subdual, for the next great creative heave.

### *Part I 1910: Image, Order, War*

Part I, our first block, examines the significance of 1910 and the context of cultural change in the wider period: 1910 is not merely another date on the calendar, an arbitrary historical marker, it is a site of potent cultural myth, the myth of sudden historical and cultural change itself. The "image" that Part I begins with is the Post-Impressionist exhibition of 1910 in London, the first major show of modern art in Britain, but it also touches upon similarly important cultural events and moments elsewhere in the three years that follow: the Armory Show in New York (1913) and the cubist development of collage in Paris (1912). The little magazine of special interest for Part I is *The Egoist,* which comes to focus in the discussion of the period's founding critical works by Virginia Woolf and T. S. Eliot.

Part I addresses three significant essays, from the heart of the period, that have shaped our understanding of literary transitions in this period and since: Virginia Woolf's "Modern Fiction" (1919; 1925) and "Mr Bennett and Mrs Brown" (1924); and T. S. Eliot's "Tradition and the Individual Talent" (1919). In particular, it is in "Mr Bennett and Mrs Brown" that 1910 famously comes to cultural and literary attention as the moment of change, the inception of "the new"; and it is "Tradition and the Individual Talent", first published in *The Egoist* in two instalments, that puts forward a new model of "the new" in art in relation to "traditional" art, both in and beyond time or history. "Modern Fiction" is *the* manifesto of the new from which so many of our ladders of literary modernity start. These essays are considered in dialogue with each other and in relation to other essays and manifestos of the period, as well as in terms of their significance for critical debates on modernism, formalism and the avant-garde. Part I in itself spans and charts many of the intellectual transitions of 1910 to 1945 in focusing, as it does, on canonical modernist manifestos in their immediate published context as well as in a wider cultural context and with reference to their far-reaching critical reception. The rise of the manifesto and essay as an art form in itself may be considered one of the main transitions of the period.

As well as the founding essays of Eliot and Woolf, the work of numerous other authors of the period is touched upon and discussed in Part I, including: Henry Adams, Blaise Cendrars, Ezra Pound, Dorothy Richardson, D. H. Lawrence, James Joyce, Dora Marsden, John Rodker, Edith Sitwell, Osbert Sitwell, Isaac Rosenberg, and Richard Aldington.

### *Part II Image, Gender, Apocalypse*

"Part II: Image, Gender, Apocalypse", our corridor in which "time passes", looks at the currency of the image in a selection of texts from the Imagist movement onwards, and opens up questions of gender, class and war (just as Woolf's "Time Passes" does) as points of transition, opposition, and crisis, and points up montage and collage of the image as the dominant avant-garde aesthetic mode. The springboard "image" is Wyndham Lewis's vortex. The magazine is *Blast* (with a look too at *transition*). The focus is on works, from 1910 into the 1930s, by major "modernist" authors, both male and female: Pound, H.D., Stein, Eliot, Yeats and Woolf. Since the mid-twentieth-century construction of a predominantly male canon of modernist and avant-garde writers, epitomised in Hugh Kenner's, *The Pound Era: The Age of T. S. Eliot, James Joyce and Wyndham Lewis* (1972), several decades of feminist and gender-based scholarship has opened up the field to considerations not only of women writers of the period, but also of the inscriptions of gender and sexuality in both male- and female-authored texts. Part II of this book acknowledges the huge significance of such gender-based work in approaching the period, and shows how gender ultimately in fact provides the metaphorical staging and basis for so many of the wider, and apparently unconnected, concerns of modernist literature and culture.

### *Part III Apocalypse 1945*

"Part III: Apocalypse 1945", our second block, and final part, looks at avant-garde regroupings during the 1930s and 1940s to 1945, in the face of resurgent realism, the nemesis apparent of modernism and avant-gardism, showing that nevertheless modernist and avant-garde practices continue to flourish. The springboard "image" is Picasso's *Guernica*; and the magazine in focus is *transition*. There is discussion too of the Apocalypse movement, and of work by David Gascoyne and

Dylan Thomas and W. S. Graham. I have chosen to emphasise such authors, along with the work of canonical "modernist" writers in the later phase (Joyce, Stein, Woolf, H.D., Stevens and Williams) and of mavericks such as Schwitters and West, more than work by canonical "thirties" and "forties" writers such as W. H. Auden, Christopher Isherwood, Graham Greene, George Orwell and so on. Greene is handicapped, according to Paul Fussell, by "his inability to master English syntax and the fine points of English sentence structure" (1982: 94). He does little for the progress of avant-garde language, and along with Orwell represents a dreary, melancholic residual modernism, in my view, mutilated by liberal guilt, worthiness, and didacticism. Stevens's "The Idea of Order at Key West" (1935), Stein's *Dr Faustus Lights the Lights* (1938; 1949), West's *The Day of the Locust* (1939), Woolf's "Thoughts on Peace in an Air Raid" (1940), Williams's "Paterson: The Falls" (1944), Schwitters's PIN (1946) are the important, and my preferred, landmarks to the 1930s and 1940s. I nevertheless would admit to occasionally balking at that great landmark of late high modernism, Joyce's *Finnegans Wake* (1939), and sometimes in negotiating it have to agree with Orwell's view of Joyce as an "elephantine pedant". But it pains me far more to leave out readings of Jean Rhys, Djuna Barnes, Patrick Hamilton, Muriel Rukeyser, David Jones, or Bessie Smith, or a decent account of the Bahaus and its impact, its transition from Germany to America, than it does to avoid Orwell's and Greene's transatlantic achievements of the period. I choose this sort of route, hardly a "road less traveled by", in the happily biased opinion that what counts here is to mark the indomitable persistence, and sometimes precarious transitions, of avant-garde and modernist practices, in the teeth of the socialist realist backlash and of the rise of fascism, a persistence that Joyce, Gascoyne, Stein, West, Schwitters et al. represent, whether their careers are ending or beginning, more or less, with the dropping of the atomic bomb.

The book's final chapter and final part close with readings of the poetics of Gertrude Stein, Raoul Hausmann and Kurt Schwitters in the mid-1940s. Their words serve as this book's conclusion, marking a post-war place of Apocalypse from which modernism's and the avant-garde's new ladders start. Transitions continue. This book, *Modernism, 1910–1945: Image to Apocalypse*, charts the vast and numerous transitions between two perfect miniature manifestos: between Ezra Pound's injunction to "Make It New", and Rauol Hausmann's and Kurt Schwitters' celebration, "Poetry Intervenes Now"; from "MIN" to "PIN".

# Acknowledgements

This book began with and owes its life to the encouragement and editorial generosity of Julian Wolfreys. It was shaped by many happy years of researching and teaching "Modernism", and by invaluable exchange with colleagues and students, at the Universities of Edinburgh, Glasgow and Dundee, in the Centre for Continuing Education, Edinburgh, and in the Scottish Universities International Summer School. I owe a great deal to formative and illuminating discussions over the years, inside and outside academe, with the following people: Dan Abel, Judith Allen, David Ayers, Hugh Bell, Rachel Bowlby, Claire Brennan, Linda Clare, Claire Colebrook, Hugh Collins, John Coyle, Cairns Craig, Mark Currie, Aidan Day, Peter Easingwood, Paul Edwards, Femi Folorunso, Jonathan Goldman, Martin Hammer, Philip Hobsbaum, David Hopkins, Chris Huxley, Ronnie Jack, Vassiliki Kolocotroni, Gail Low, Alison Lumsden, Paddy Lyons, Mike McIlroy, Gus McLean, Caroline McNairn, John McNairn, Stella McNairn, Niall Martin, Marjorie Metzstein, Andrew Millington, Sara Mills, Drew Milne, Lesley Morgan, Pam Morris, Alan Munton, Ken Newton, Colin Nicolson, Jason Pennells, Michael Phillips, Wayne Price, Geraldine Prince, Faith Pullin, Patrick Reilly, Ian Revie, Andrew Roberts, Wallace Robson, Jack Ross, Louise Rourke, Roger Savage, Dietrich Scheunemann, Susan Sellers, John Seth, Sean Smith, Stan Smith, Lee Spinks, Jane Stabler, Jim Stewart, Randall Stevenson, Kath Swarbrick, Trudi Tate, Olga Taxidou, Geoff Ward, Rob Watt, Archie Webb, Keith Williams, Karina Williamson, Julian Wolfreys, Marion Wynne-Davies. I would also like to thank for their help: Gwen Hunter, Jean Spence and Margaret Swayne in the office of the Department of English at the University of Dundee; Ann Simpson, archivist of the Gabrielle Keiller Collection at the Dean Gallery, Scottish Gallery of Modern Art, Edinburgh; and Valery Rose and Jocelyn Stockley; Sonya Barker and Anna Sandeman at Palgrave. I also thank Peter Kitson, Head of English at Dundee, for finding funds towards the cost of the cover illustration. I am particularly grateful for the constructive criticism of Claire Colebrook, Philip Hobsbaum and Olga Taxidou who read the later drafts of this book. Its ladders start in a childhood spent with painters and lovers of "modern" art, beginning with my parents Joy Sinclair and Robert Goldman. My late father instilled in me a love of visual and verbal art, sharing his energetic pleasure in works by Kurt Schwitters, Gertrude Stein, Wallace Stevens and many other artists and writers who feature in the following pages. This book is dedicated to Gus McLean. I cannot thank him enough for his infectious bibliophilia, for introducing me to the satires of Nathanael West, for placing in my hands many (too many to list) other volumes of consequence, for his support and generosity in so many ways.

# I Introduction: "Make It New" A Guide to Transitions in the Period of Modernism and the Avant-Garde

The Introduction takes its title from Ezra Pound's famous avant-garde slogan (and the title of his book, of 1934) "Make It New", the founding impetus for the literature of the period this book covers. Chapter I, which in fact constitutes the Introduction, finds an excellent guide to the founding movements of the period, and to their diverse reorientations, in the pages of Nathanael West's cult modernist novel *The Dream Life of Balso Snell* (1931). West's avant-garde guide to the great canonical, avant-garde texts of high modernism (by James Joyce, Marcel Proust, Gertrude Stein, Fyodor Dostoevsky and so on) also enables us to discuss and define the most important critical terms that have emerged in mapping this period: modernism, modernity, the avant-garde, the new, postmodernism, and so on. His novel arms us with an overview of the scope and range of the period. And from its position in the trajectory of modernist and avant-garde aesthetics, roughly mid-way in the period (1931), is projected a discussion that directs us both back to earlier founding avant-garde texts and languages and forward to their later developments and concerns. Our reading of West's novel provides a set of critical terms and questions, then, for proceeding through the period, and through this book. As well as defining and addressing the terms "avant-garde" and "modernism" and their cohorts, this reading of West also opens up a discussion reflecting on the significance of the other terms, and the dates, in the title of this book: "Image to Apocalypse" and "1910–1945". The rationale and scope of this book is then compared with those of other introductions to the period and to its dominant designated aesthetic mode, "modernism". The chapter closes with a note on the formal, academic study of modernist and avant-garde works.

## Nathanael West as guide to James Joyce, Ezra Pound, Pablo Picasso et al.

> While walking in the tall grass that has sprung up around the city of Troy, Balso Snell came upon the famous wooden horse of the Greeks. A poet, he remembered Homer's ancient song and decided to find a way in.
>
> On examining the horse, Balso found that there were but three openings: the mouth, the navel, and the posterior opening of the alimentary canal. The mouth was beyond his reach, the navel proved a cul-de-sac, and so, forgetting his dignity, he approached the last. O Anus Mirabilis!
>
> (Nathanael West, *The Dream Life of Balso Snell*)

Searching for an opening to this book, *Modernism, 1910–1945: Image to Apocalypse* (should I start with modernism? or with the dates? or with the image?), I came upon the poet Balso Snell's fumbling entry into the anus of the Trojan Horse, itself the opening passage to Nathanael West's debut novel, *The Dream Life of Balso Snell* (1931), published bang in the middle of the period, and taking us bang into the heart (or bowels) of its dominant mythopoeic, and scatological, imagistic concerns. Balso's graphic declaration, "O Anus Mirabilis!" eloquently compresses the tensions between the chronological and the visceral; and it may be taken to portend the tensions and play between the historicising chronology of my chosen dates, "1910–1945", and the poetic synchronism of the imagery of "Image to Apocalypse". It transpires that "the intestine of the horse is inhabited solely by authors in search of an audience", according to West's advertisement for the novel (West: 398); and Balso's intestinal dreamscape is in fact the terrain of the experimental, avant-garde literatures we have since come to know as "Modernism".

> Disgusted, [Balso] attempts to get out but is tricked into listening to other tales. All of these tales are elephantine close-ups of various literary positions and their technical methods; close-ups that make Kurt Schwitters' definition, "tout ce'que l'artiste crache, c'est l'art" seem like an understatement. (398)

As West indicates, for those engaged in the business of writing in these "various literary positions", no such homogenising label as "Modernism", itself only then emergent (see Smith, *The Origins of*

*Modernism*), or indeed as "avant-garde" (also still evolving as a critical term), would do (they were too busy disagreeing with each other under various factional nomenclatures), and none as yet prevailed – except perhaps "new", or "the new". And Ezra Pound's famous injunction "Make It New" was answered in a myriad of ways.

West's citation of the German avant-garde poet and collagist Kurt Schwitters is appropriate advertisement for his own collagistic novel. His use of Schwitters's declaration "tout ce' que l'artiste crache, c'est l'art" (West seems to have encountered him in French translation), which sounds even more graphic in the original alliterative, onomatopoeic German – *Alles was ein Künstler spuckt ist Künst* – but perhaps less so translated into English: "Everything the artist expectorates [or spits or spews or gobs up] is art" (West: 398), testifies to the erupting diversity and volatility of the period's testing to the limits of the definitions, resources and understanding of Art itself. Schwitters's famous sound poem "Ur Sonata" (1922–32) certainly achieved all of this, one notable performance even furnishing an audience of old Prussian generals with an incredible moment of catharsis (Richter 142). The prelude opens with:

Fümms bö wö tää zää Uu,
pögiff,
kwii Ee.
Oooooooooooooooooooooooooooooooooooo

(Schwitters: 52)

This, the first movement of Schwitters's sound poem, arose not, as one might be forgiven for suspecting, from a particularly guttural case of the "spontaneous overflow of powerful feeling", the traditional Romantic source of poetry, nor even from dabbling in automatic writing, the early experimental habit of avant-garde writers such as Gertrude Stein, but was in fact "partially borrowed" (in the best classical tradition of Imitation), according to Schwitters himself, in "My Sonata in Primal Sounds" (1927), "from a sound poem by [Dadaist] Raoul Hausmann", itself a kind of *objet trouvé* (found object) in the Dadaist manner:

[It] was written down as follows:
FMSBWTCU

PGGF

MÜ

> and . . . was originally nothing more than a type sample for a selection of fonts. With great imagination Hausmann made it into a performance, and as he was originally from Bohemia, he sounded it somewhat like this:
>
> fümms bö wö tää zää uu,
>
> pögiff
>
> mü
>
> (Schwitters: 234–5)

A learned legacy of avant-garde expectoration, then, is behind West's citational work. And *The Dream Life of Balso Snell*, in keeping with such calculated explosive precedents, ends in volatile eruption – not exactly with the poet's expectoration, but his masturbatory ejaculation.

> His body broke free of the bard. It took on a life of its own; a life that knew nothing of the poet Balso. Only to death can this release be likened – to the mechanics of decay. After death the body takes command; it performs the manual of disintegration with a marvellous certainty. So now, his body performed the evolutions of love with a like sureness. (54)

If Balso's journey ends in auto-erotic bliss, it begins as a descent into Hell, and it is no coincidence that Dante's *Divine Comedy* is a key text for many of the writers of this period; and Hell a central trope. Both Homer's and Virgil's foundational accounts of the Trojan War, of course, include episodes describing a descent into, and return out of Hell. But many of the infernal narratives of 1910 to 1945 show little hope of a light beyond; while some wallow in the darkness; or reinvent the place; others plunder its discourses (excuse the pun), even celebrate it. Marion Wynne-Davies follows a heavenly trope common to the writers in her Transitions volume, *Sidney to Milton: 1580–1660* (2002), where although "Heaven was too long a reach for man to recover at one step," it was nevertheless thought mappable if not obtainable (Wynne-Davies, quoting Speed), but this volume's transitions are mainly located in the underworld. Hell now has become mappable, palpable, and inescapable.

Like many students and readers of avant-garde texts, Balso becomes angry and confused on entering the Trojan Horse, and he feels obliged to hire "a philosophic guide who insists on discussing the nature of art" (397), as West explains in his own advertising guide to the novel. Whereas Dante is guided through the inferno by the spirit of Virgil, Balso has to spar with the cryptic rantings of a name-dropping bore:

> "After all, what is art? I agree with George Moore. Art is not nature, but rather nature digested. Art is a sublime excrement."
>
> "And Daudet?" Balso queried.
>
> "Oh, Daudet! Daudet, c'est de bouillabaisse! You know, George Moore also says, 'What care I that the virtue of some sixteen-year-old maiden was the price paid for Ingres' La Source?' Now . . ."
>
> "Picasso says," Balso broke in, "Picasso says there are no feet in nature . . . And, thanks for showing me around. I have to leave."
>
> But before he was able to get away, the guide caught him by the collar. "Just a minute, please. You were right to interrupt. We should talk of art, not artists. Please explain your interpretation of the Spanish master's dictum." (9)

West's favourite inscription for the book was: "From one horse's ass to another". And it is difficult to discern whether *The Dream Life of Balso Snell* is an avant-garde novel or a guide to the avant-garde, or merely a guide to itself. It is of course all of these and a virtuoso parody of high modernism. Such self-conscious complication of categorisation too is a vital component of the art of the period: manifestos, critical commentaries, aesthetics manuals and guides abound to the point where we come to see such documents as "embodying rather than explicating the aesthetic gesture of the new – even while exploding the very category of the aesthetic" (Kolocotroni et al.: xix). And vital too are the interpenetrating influences of the verbal with the visual arts. But by the time his guide begins to prose on about the formative influence of Cezanne – "'Cezanne is right. The sage of Aix . . .'" – Balso manages to escape: "With a violent twist, Balso tore loose and fled" (10). He continues on his journey alone, and, unassisted by the guide, he manages to survive being buttonholed along the way by various other – more entertaining – authors.

## Alternative guides: canonical texts, "little magazines", and anthologies

Whereas my sympathies are all with Balso, I am only too well aware that in undertaking the authorship of this book I have been cast in the unenviable role of Balso's guide. I hope not to drive my readers away just yet. On the other hand, I would strongly recommend that the best guide to the literature of the period (indeed any period) is the literature of the period, and to be read not necessarily in chronological order. But if the prospect daunts of plunging straight into the literature of canonical high modernism – for example, T. S. Eliot's *The Waste Land*, James Joyce's *Ulysses*, Virginia Woolf's *To the Lighthouse*, W. B. Yeats's *The Tower*, Ezra Pound's *Cantos* – then following Balso on his journey, unaided by the likes of me, would constitute a splendid alternative introduction. So too would be a visit to the nearest collection of modern art. So too would be a flick through an anthology of manifestos and critical sources, as Peter Childs also suggests (24–5). I recommend *The Modern Tradition* (1965), edited by Richard Ellmann and Charles Feidelson; *A Modernist Reader: Modernism in England, 1910–1930* (1977), edited by Peter Faulkner; *The Gender of Modernism*, edited by Bonnie Kime Scott (1990); and *Modernism: An Anthology of Sources and Documents* (1998), edited by Vassiliki Kolocotroni, Jane Goldman and Olga Taxidou. Better still, if your library can oblige, would be a glance through some of the period's many – sometimes short-lived – "little magazines", journals, almanachs and reviews, in which much of the significant work of the period first appeared: for example, *The Dial*, Wyndham Lewis's *BLAST*, Guillaume Apollinaire's *Soirées de Paris*, Dora Marsden's and Ezra Pound's *The Egoist* and Margaret Anderson's and Jane Heap's *Little Review* (foreign correspondent: Ezra Pound), Ford Madox Ford's *English Review* and *transatlantic review*, Hugo Ball's *Cabaret Voltaire*, Tristan Tzara's *Dada*, Raoul Hausmann's *Der Dada*, Francis Picabia's *291* and *391*, Marcel Duchamp's *The Blind Man*, Man Ray's *TNT*, Kurt Schwitters's *Merz*, A. A. Orage's *New Age*, John Middleton Murry's *Rhythm*, Grigson's *New Verse*, T. S. Eliot's *Criterion*, and Eugene Jolas's *transition*. In the mean time I will continue to shape my introduction around Balso's journey and, at the same time, try to keep Balso's guide out of my throat.

## Defining modernism and the avant-garde

To return to the title and rationale of this book: in order to explain the use of "Modernism" and of "Image to Apocalypse", I also want to discuss another term that informs my argument. I was initially tempted by the title "Avant-Garde to Modernism", which signals one of the ideological and critical transitions occurring in relation to this period that this book will explore. The French term "avant-garde" suggests the European sources and guiding criticism for much of the literature of this period, and "Modernism", by virtue of its American critical genesis and credentials, suggests its American slant and destination. The tensions and play between these terms inform this book. The term "avant-garde", originally a military one designating the advanced guard, or first troops into battle, emerged, as Paul Wood explains, "in the third decade of the nineteenth century, not in debate about art as such, but in the early socialist tradition as left-wing intellectuals and politicians tried to think through concepts of progress and freedom in emerging modern societies" (Wood; Edwards: 187). Mikhail Bakunin's journal *L'Avant-garde*, founded in 1878, exemplifies the term's purely political usage (Karl: 15). The word "avant-garde", Matei Calinescu points out, "has an old history in French. As a term of warfare it dates back to the Middle Ages, and it developed a figurative meaning at least as early as the Renaissance." But it was not used as a metaphor for "expressing a self-consciously advanced position in politics, literature and art . . . with any consistency before the nineteenth century" (Calinescu: 97). Art came to be seen in this period "as a kind of 'advance guard' for social progress as a whole" (Wood; Edwards: 187). Henri de Saint-Simon, the first critic to use the term in relation to art, rallied artists in 1825, to "unite" and "serve as the avant-garde: for amongst all the arms at our disposal, the power of the Arts is the swiftest and most expeditious" in spreading "new ideas amongst men". He also recognises that the present apparently "limited" role of the arts should be transformed and expanded to achieve this goal (Saint-Simon; Edwards: 187). The concept of the avant-garde, Calinescu concludes, "was little more than a radicalized and strongly utopianized version of modernity", in that, historically, it "started by dramatizing certain constitutive elements of the idea of modernity and making them into cornerstones of revolutionary ethos" (Calinescu: 95).

The sense of a "socially and politically committed 'avant-garde'", Wood explains, "originally stood opposed to the idea of *l'art pour l'art* ('art for art's sake') which emerged at the same time" (187), and which has since shaped definitions of the later, retrospective term "modernism". In the period after the Second World War art criticism, and Anglophone criticism in particular, began to foreground "modernist" as the epithet for the autonomous, "experimental" art of the early twentieth century, a rhetorical manoeuvre exemplified in the work of the American critic Clement Greenberg. At this point, "avant-garde" became interchangeable, even synonymous, with "modernist".

> It is one of those odd twists of history that the dominant understanding of the term "avant-garde" in the years after 1945 should in effect have come to signify the opposite of what was originally intended. This is not because of any sleight of hand on the part of critics and intellectuals, so much as a result of the way art itself evolved in modern western bourgeois societies. These societies have experienced what is widely understood as a "separation of the spheres".... It has been as a part of this widespread social and historical process that modern art has evolved a set of procedures, and references, techniques and assumptions, which add up to something like its own characteristic "language". And it has, further, been as part of this history of development that the notion of being "in advance" came to denote not so much modern art's relationship to society at large, as certain kinds of art's relationship to other, more conventional kinds of art.... In the 1960s this modernist understanding of the idea of an artistic "avant-garde" came under challenge. From what has come to be seen as a constellation of postmodernist points of view, the importance of art's active and explicit relationship to the wider culture beyond art has once more been widely canvassed. As part of this process, the appellation "avant-garde" has been withdrawn by many writers and critics from those "autonomous" art movements with which it was for long identified. . . . The idea of an avant-garde has been returned to those practices which explicitly sought to overcome the separation of art from life, the separation of aesthetics from politics. (Wood; Edwards: 187)

At stake in this shifting semantic terrain between the critical terms, modernism and postmodernism, avant-garde and neo-avant-garde, is the positioning and interpretation of the art of 1910 to 1945 in relation to politics, history, culture and aesthetics. "Postmodernism", a term invented and gaining currency, along with "Modernism", around the mid-century mark, has developed a number of theorised readings of Modernism which seem to confuse as much as clarify, leaving modernism bound up with postmodernist wrangling. Students of Modernism soon become accustomed to conflicting definitions of these terms, which are further complicated by their equally confused relationship to the term "modernity", as Susan Stanford Friedman explores in her very helpful essay "Definitional Excursions: The Meanings of Modern/Modernity/Modernism" (2001). But in considering "modernism" and "postmodernism" in relation to the modern and modernity, she falls shy of offering a similar treatment of the term "avant-garde", which she uses unselfconsciously in her arguments. Fredereck R. Karl prefers to understand the avant-garde as "a form of cannibalism" on modernism, as an extreme of a modernist continuum. Whereas avant-garde aesthetics, I would argue, might be considered at the least transgressive, if not dissident, modernist aesthetics, even under postmodernist auspices, are at most perhaps transgressive. The terms' semantic instability, therefore, and a more complicated critical trajectory than is suggested by "Avant-Garde to Modernism", undermine this title's attraction, but the critical transitions between these two terms nevertheless inform the argument of this book, and are subsumed in the title's "Modernism". The terms "modernism" and "avant-garde" signal the international dialogue in aesthetics, between different critical approaches and between European and American metropolitan centres: Paris, New York, London. While the literary focus of this book is Anglophone literature, and while it is concerned with the cultural contexts of New York and London, its dominant metropolitan pole is Paris, the epicentre of avant-gardism for the first half of the twentieth century.

## From the Imagists to the Apocalypse movement: literary landmarks of 1910 and 1945

I have attempted to preserve the sense of historical heterogeneity and development, indicated in West's advertisement (he is specifying a particular lineage of avant-garde precedents), by using the more specific demarcation, "Image to Apocalypse". Just as "Image" refers to the early international movement of Imagism that came to prominence under the auspices of Ezra Pound, around 1910, so "Apocalypse" refers to the (less well known) English Apocalypse movement, a post-Romantic surrealist group that emerged in the late 1930s and early 1940s, partly taking inspiration from the work of Dylan Thomas. But if 1945 saw the publication of Thomas's *Fern Hill*, it is also the year of Pound's *Pisan Cantos* (*the* literary landmark in post-war poetry), written out of his confinement as a fascist traitor. In a sense, then, my dates take the reader from Pound to Pound (from his aestheticised Imagism to political apocalypse, perhaps), but to enshrine this particular strand of my argument in my title would be too restrictive. It would also be to repeat the errors of personification of other commentaries, most notably Hugh Kenner's nevertheless impressive work *The Pound Era: The Age of T. S. Eliot, James Joyce and Wyndham Lewis* (1972), as well as to ignore the breadth and diversity of the range of authors this volume samples, not to mention their often self-conscious organisation into contesting and *collective* aesthetic and political movements.

## "Image to Apocalypse" as avant-garde technique

As well as referring to the specific avant-garde literary movements embracing the period, "Image to Apocalypse" may also indicate ways of reading avant-garde texts. The image dominates the period, and the juxtaposition of images becomes a dominant aesthetic technique. The power of the image is attested by Pound's much cited definition, in "How to Read" (1928), of the second of three kinds of poetry: "PHANOPOEIA . . . a casting of images upon the visual imagination". The first, by the way, is "MELOPOEIA, wherein the words are charged, over and above their plain meaning, with some musical property, which directs the bearing or trend of that meaning". And the third is "LOGOPOEIA, 'the dance of the intellect among words'", a pleasure not always recognised by first-time readers of avant-garde poetics. Pound explains that this kind of poetry

> employs words not only for their direct meaning, but it takes count in a special way of habits of usage, of the context we *expect* to find with the word, its usual concomitants, of its known acceptances, and of ironical play. It holds the aesthetic which is peculiarly the domain of verbal manifestation, and cannot possibly be contained in plastic or in music. It is the latest come, and perhaps most tricky and undependable mode. (*Literary Essays*, p. 25)

All three modes are important in the period, and Pound's esteemed logopoeia is certainly illuminating in its endorsement of pleasuring the intellect, and actually enjoying the negotiation of densely allusive, difficult texts. But in this period, there is pronounced interest, nevertheless, in the development of phanopoeic writing, not only in terms of the "imagery" of Imagism, say, but also in terms of the visual dimensions of the verbal, particularly where the visual form of writing, and the materiality of the printed word, become vitally celebrated poetic components. This is evident in a whole range of writing, including (to name a few) Imagism, the calligrammes of Guillaume Apollinaire, the cubist poetics of Gertrude Stein, and Dada assemblages.

The reading mode implied by "Image to Aapocalypse" suggests a non-linear, revelatory response to image, where a kind of instantaneous, epiphanic reading occurs in an intense moment of lyric aestheticism or subjective introspection. This approach owes something to the theories of Henri Bergson. His concept of the *durée*, as subjective, psychological, non-spatial, time, and the only site of true freedom, suggests such aesthetic moments constitute an escape from the real, material world. But Bergson's *durée* denies "genuine historical experience", according to Walter Benjamin (*Charles Baudelaire*, pp. 144–5), another important influence on theories of avant-garde art. And it is worth considering how "Image to Apocalypse" might conversely be understood as referring the reader outwards from the image to revelations of historical, political, technological and cultural context. Avant-garde texts may be read, then, as reflecting, and further, as interrupting, disrupting and even *transforming* such contexts, rather than merely escaping them (see Bürger; Eysteinnson).

## Conflicting definitions of the avant-garde: from Baudelaire to Dada

Balso's entry into the Trojan Horse provides a useful analogy here. Is the poet escaping reality by disappearing up the fundament of art into an endless arcade of literary aesthetics (and in this case the fundament is that of the magnificently constructed gift horse the Greeks left at Troy, the central icon of the founding epic text in Western culture, Homer's *Iliad*)? To be avant-garde here means (merely) to be at the cutting edge of art, forging new aesthetics, breaking with – indeed violating – aesthetic tradition while celebrating a release into aesthetic oblivion. Here avant-garde has become synonymous with its earlier antonym, *l'art pour l'art.* And it is with this definition of the avant-garde that many definitions of modernism seem to coincide (see Bradbury and McFarlane). Such release into aesthetic oblivion may be represented by Balso's final erotic oblivion, at the close of West's novel, itself likened to the ultimate oblivion of death. Balso's intense masturbatory fantasy, then, the anal penetration of the Trojan Horse, is an act of self-reflexive literary aesthetics *par extraordinaire.* West's advertisement, "Through the Hole in the Mundane Millstone", certainly encourages the reader to think of Balso's journey as a flight from reality into aesthetics, pointing out "the mechanism used – an 'anywhere out of the world' device [that] makes a formal comparison with Lewis Carroll possible. Just as Alice escapes through the looking glass, Balso Snell escapes the real world by entering the Wooden Horse of the Greeks which he finds in the tall grass surrounding the walls of Troy" (397). The status of the "real world", however, is undermined by the comedic assumption of a real location for the Trojan Horse, and the idea of escape from the world is itself signalled by the citation of Baudelaire's poem "Anywhere Out of this World", presumably already out of this world if we follow this line of logic. Balso is thus already in the long grass of art before entering the horse. Does this reinforce or unsettle the experience of reading *The Dream Life of Balso Snell* as an escape from life into art?

The concept of the avant-garde is also rooted in the attempts of various *historical* European avant-garde movements – German Dadaists such as the photomontagist John Heartfield and satirical artist George Grosz are the most often cited, following the influential *Theory of the Avant-Garde* (1974) by Peter Bürger – to liquidate art itself "as an activity that is split off from the praxis of life" (Bürger: 22), to smash the boundaries between art and life. This is a radically dissident aesthetics deployed to break rather than merely transgress aesthetic, social, cultural and political boundaries. The Trojan Horse, of course, may also be understood as a primary example of this sense of the avant-garde, especially in view of the term's military origins. Misread by the Trojans as a purely aesthetic object, the horse was in fact a cunning instrument of war concealing shock troops. The Trojan War, furthermore, still had powerful cultural resonance in the years following the cataclysmic events of the Great War, which may well have prompted renewed interest in the myths surrounding the ancient conflict. Concealing an army in its guts, the Greeks used the Trojan Horse to penetrate the defences of Troy. The enemy is smuggled into the securest sector. Such military shock tactics are echoed in avant-garde performances where the promise of passive aesthetic enjoyment is dashed by the eruption of transgressive violence – such as the physical attacks on the public advocated by the Futurists: "go out into the street, launch assaults from theatres and introduce the fisticuff into the artistic battle" (Goldberg: 12). Poetry, according to the seventh article of Filippo Marinetti's "Manifesto of Futurism" (1913), "must be conceived as a violent attack" (Kolocotroni: 251), and the ninth article of the manifesto goes beyond the individual skirmish in vowing to "*glorify war*" (Kolocotroni: 251). Tristan Tzara's "Dada Manifesto, 1918" rules that in the work of creative writers "every page should explode" (Kolocotroni: 277). He gives a lyrical account of the revolutionary, and collective, moment of dissolution when the boundaries between art and life are smashed: "a unique fraternity comes into existence at the intense moment when beauty and life itself, brought into high tension on a wire, ascend towards a flash-point; the blue tremor linked to the ground by our magnetised gaze which covers the peak with snow. The miracle. I open my heart to creation" ("Note on Art", 1917; Kolocotroni: 280). Berlin Dadaists, who joined the (real, and doomed) post-war anti-Weimar revolution, declared themselves in 1919 the "Dadaist Headquarters of World Revolution" (Richter: 126).

## The avant-garde, anarchy and political activism

It is difficult to tell sometimes where political activism or anarchism shades into performance art. Think of the British suffragette Emily Wilding Davison, who in 1913 leapt to her death under the horses' hooves at Derby Day, in her fatally dramatic (but not actually clearly suicidal) attempt to disrupt the ritual events of the patriarchal public realm, and publicise "the Cause" (Green: 136). Or think of the American Wobblie troubadour Joe Hill, who joined the American union the IWW (the International Workers of the World – or "Wobblies") significantly enough in 1910, and was author of many of the incendiary lyrics in *The Little Red Songbook* ("songs to fan the flames of discontent"). Before his judicial murder by the State of Utah in November 1915 (he had been framed for murder), at which he wore the standard paper heart for his execution squad to aim at, Hill requested to have his ashes mailed to every state in the Union, bar Utah, not wishing to be caught dead there. The Joe Hill Memorial Committee duly obeyed, and were delighted when some of the packages burst open disrupting the mail (Kornbluh: 157), this accident adding further dada to Hill's avant-garde agenda. Hill's last message to his comrades was: "Don't mourn – Organize!", imperatives to match the "Make It New" of avant-garde aesthetics. Hill recommended in *Solidarity* (December 1911) that "if a person can put a few cold, common-sense facts into a song and dress them (the facts) up in a cloak of humor to take the dryness out of them, he will succeed in reaching a great number of workers who are too unintelligent or too indifferent to read a pamphlet or an editorial on economic science" (Kornbluh: 11). Perhaps this manifesto item is merely a minimal and prosaic version of the ethos of classical literary poetics encapsulated in Horace's dictum, in the *Ars Poetica*, that poetry should both instruct and delight. In fact the "dress" and "facts" – or "Trojan Horse" – of Hill's famous songs are more sophisticated than he makes out. (See, for example, Van Wienen.) They have certainly succeeded in penetrating Western culture over the last century with their rich imagery. "Pie in the sky", for example, is from his most famous song "The Preacher and the Slave"; and the eponymous "Mr. Block" is the *Ur* "blockhead", a semi-reified industrial worker loyal to the bosses, with his own subversive cartoon strip, who may also be an early ancestor of Bob Dylan's "Mr Jones" (neither seems to know what is happening).

Proponents of "art for art's sake", however, would abhor the misuse of art for political effect: propaganda pollutes the purity of aestheticism. We might note that "false Sinon, the Greek from Troy", "the perjurer of the horse", the man who coaxed the Trojans to take in the fatal effigy (an early art critic perhaps), is to be encountered in the putrifaction of the tenth trench of Dante's *Inferno*, a "falsifier in words" squabbling with the "falsifiers in deeds" (*Inferno* XXX.91–9). To smuggle in teaching, or more crudely, political doctrine, or ideology perhaps, is damnable – but is it avoidable? It is not merely a matter of outward dress and content. But, it is in fact difficult to explain or understand how exactly the content of teaching (or dogma or ideology) or delight (or beauty) might be *in* the form of a poem "in the sense that Jeffrey Archer is in jail", to borrow from Terry Eagleton (*London Review of Books*, vol. 24, no. 8, p. 14), or in the sense that Greek soldiers are in the Trojan horse. On the other hand, it is difficult not to miss the shock tactics of a truly avant-garde public gesture! But let us return to the historical avant-garde.

## The historical avant-garde: theory and practice

Avant-garde movements not only dealt in an (anti-)aesthetic of violent intervention; they also, on occasion, incurred violence. Futurist and Dadaist exhibitions and performances frequently attracted or incurred violent attacks, whether from outraged audiences or police raids. But avant-garde art, it should be noted, may also *ward off* physical attacks, as the jazz singer and connoisseur of Dada and surrealism George Melly discovered one dark night in Manchester in the 1950s, when he was set upon by thugs:

> I was anaesthetized by fear. I subconsciously did the only thing that might work and it did. I took out of my pocket a small book of the sound poems of the dadaist Kurt Schwitters, explained what they were, and began to read. . . . Slowly, muttering threats, they moved off. I can't explain why it worked, but I suspect that it was because they needed a conventional response in order to give me a going over. (Melly: 43–4)

We can only wonder what Melly's assailants might have made of a snatch of Eliot, Pound or Woolf. Bürger maintains that the "attack of the historical avant-garde on art as an institution has failed, and art has not been integrated into the praxis of life, art as an institution continues to survive as something separate from the praxis of life" (57). Art, in this post-avant-garde era, he suggests, "can either resign itself to its autonomous status or 'organize happenings' to break through that status" (57). Melly seems to have brought about a spontaneous, if not organised, "happening" that briefly allowed art to penetrate into the praxis of life in a dark backstreet of Manchester. Such happenings, however, cannot achieve the kind of full-scale political and social revolution that Bürger has identified as the aim of the authentic, historical avant-garde. "All art that is not against its time is for it," the German satirist Karl Kraus declared in 1912: "Such art can make the time pass, but it cannot conquer it." He seems to share Bürger's desire for an art capable of root and branch transformation; and he offers language as the medium for the artistic assault on the status quo:

> The true enemy of time is language. Language lives in harmonious union with the spirit in revolt against its own time. Out of this conspiracy art is conceived. In contrast, conformity, in complicity

> with its time, robs language of its own vocabulary. Art can come only from denial. Only from anguished protest. Never from calm compliance. Art placed in the service of consoling man becomes a curse unto his very deathbed. True art reaches its fulfilment only through the hopeless. (Szasz: 158)

Denial, of course, may have many different inflections, incur many different responses, depending upon context. George Grosz, a Berlin Dadaist, is marked in Nazi SS files of 1939 as "one of the most evil representatives of degenerate art who worked in a manner which was hostile to Germany" (quoted Beth Irwin Lewis: 231); but after he had fled to the very different political context of New York in 1932, he dropped his revolutionary style of satirical caricature. "When he illustrated books and articles in America, his drawings were illustrations, nothing more," according to Beth Irwin Lewis. Grosz's avant-gardism was defeated by Nazism:

> Under the impact of totalitarianism, Grosz's pen faltered and became silent. . . . His power of caricature . . . was bound inextricably to the hope and passion of a revolutionary period. George Grosz hated the ruling classes, but he hated in a context that sought to bring revolutionary change. When all possibility of change was denied, Grosz's drawing pen as a weapon of revolution became useless. (Beth Irwin Lewis: 210)

Yet Grosz, while not as extreme or desperate as he was in the context of German culture, and while also attempting an optimistic American outlook (Beth Irwin Lewis: 236), nevertheless seems to have shunned conformity in his American refuge, as is suggested by his editorial of November 1932 for the short-lived journal *Americana*, declaring disaffection with American Republicans, Democrats, Socialists, and Communists alike:

> We are Americans who believe that our civilization exudes a miasmic stench and that we had better prepare to give it a decent but rapid burial. We are the laughing morticians of the present. (Quoted Martin: 215)

*Americana* also published in 1932 extracts from West's *The Dream Life of Balso Snell*, and in August 1933 West joined Grosz as one of its associate editors.

## The transformational languages of the avant-garde

The Trojan Horse is the foundational image of the (pre-Christian) "original sin" in European history and mythology: the Trojan War. It is an appropriate, and common, mythopoeic signifier in the violent years of the twentieth century, marked by two cataclysmic world wars. But West's (ab)use of the Trojan Horse, a violation of a signifier of violation, may also resonate with antagonistic energies of the historical avant-garde, since the horse, according to Deborah Wyrick, is a significant image because it picks up on one of the etymological sources for "Dada", the German word for "hobby-horse" (367). Avant-garde energies also resonate in his choice of military metaphor for his account of Balso's final ejaculation:

> In this activity, Home and Duty, Love and Art were forgotten.
>
> An army moved in his body, an eager army of hurrying sensations. These sensations marched at first methodically and then hysterically, but always with precision. The army of his body commenced a long intricate drill, a long involved ceremony. A ceremony whose ritual unwound and manoeuvred itself with confidence and training of chemicals acting under the stimulus of a catalytic agent.
>
> His body screamed and shouted as it marched and uncoiled; then, with one heaving shout of triumph, it fell back quiet.
>
> The army that a moment before had been thundering in his body retreated slowly – victorious, relieved. (54)

The imagery of Balso's orgasmic release of an army of sperm is not only charged with the mythopoeisis of the Trojan War, then, it is also an homage to more recent avant-garde celebrations of bodily fluids, such as the dictum by Schwitters he cites in his advertisement, as well as more visual examples such as the Dadaist Francis Picabia's blasphemous ink splash entitled *Sainte Vierge* (1920), which was published in his notorious international review, *391* (a publication West, as a disciple of the avant-garde, would probably be familiar with). In undermining the notions of aesthetic and divine transcendence, Picabia's work surely confronts rather than escapes mundanity. "A figuring of the Virgin's defloration in defiant contravention of Catholic dogma" (Hopkins, "Questioning Dada's Potency", p. 317), it challenges the religious pieties of transubstantiation, divine conception, and the afterlife with the visceral reality of ejaculation, and challenges the transcendental pretensions of the aesthetic with the materiality of ink on paper. It "delivers blasphemous and anti-art blows in equal measure" (Hopkins, ibid., p. 317).

The boundaries of West's provocative metaphors are equally unsettled and unsettling. His account of the "catalytic" agency of Balso's orgasm speaks to the transformative as well as confrontational powers of the avant-garde aesthetics he is joyously invoking. By the time West is writing, then, in 1931, there is already available a tradition and a transformational language of "the new", familiar enough to be satirised and yet also supple enough to be stretched and pushed into new locutions, new transformations – aesthetic, cultural, political and historical. And this is one of the major and enabling literary transitions occurring in the period 1910–1945 that this book will chart and explore. The historical avant-garde's assault on the institution of Art transforms all aesthetic and interpretative practices. Any critical appraisal of the period must take account of the position(ing) of specific artists, writers, movements, works and texts in relation to it.

## Transitions in transformational languages

The initiation, the laying-down, and the development of avant-garde transformational languages is, then, *the* major transition occurring in the period addressed by this book. "There is a language of sculpture, of painting, of poetry," acknowledges Benjamin in an essay (unpublished in his life-time), "On Language as Such and on the Language of Man" (1916):

> Just as the language of poetry is partly, if not solely, founded on the name language of man, it is very conceivable that the language of sculpture or painting is founded on certain kinds of thing-languages, that in them we find a translation of the language of things into an infinitely higher language, which may still be of the same sphere. We are concerned here with nameless, nonacoustic languages, languages issuing from matter; here we should recall the material community of things in their communication. (73)

Avant-garde language translates from multiple such sources into another transformational language, if not "into an infinitely higher language". Benjamin recognises that "Language communicates the linguistic being of things", and the art of this period often seems to draw on every kind of language, visual and verbal, in its attempts to forge a new language. Just as Benjamin recognises that "the answer to the question '*What* does language communicate?' is therefore 'All language communicates itself'" (63), so the avant-garde, in a sense, communicates itself. He also alerts us to the idea that the verbal material of poetry is a higher form of everyday language, just as the visual arts transform the material of the everyday object world, itself possessing a kind of language. This thought also informs Kraus's identification of the task facing the contemporary literary artist. Kraus memorably invokes avant-garde practices, and the interpenetration of visual, musical and verbal aesthetics, in his satirical rage against the decline of German language, and the related decline in the understanding of enriching, literary, language, which he saw as concurrent with the rise of right-wing politics in the Weimar period:

> Why do people treat literature so insolently? Because they know the language. They would take the same liberties with the other arts if singing to one another, smearing one another with paint, or throwing plaster at one another were means of communication. The unfortunate thing is that verbal art works with a material that the rabble handles every day. That is why literature is beyond help. The farther it removes itself from comprehensibility, the more importunately do people claim their material. The best thing would be to keep literature secret from the people until there is a law that prohibits people from using language, permitting them to use only sign language in urgent cases. But by the time such a law comes into being, they will probably have learned to answer the aria "How's business?" with a still life. (Kraus: 64)

Kraus points up the differences between literary language and the language of everyday, at the same time as acknowledging their interpenetration. He entertainingly depicts the theatrical gestures typical of avant-garde activism, "smearing one another with paint, or throwing plaster at one another", displacing the language of the everyday; but his closing observation on the absorption of art by capitalist corporate business is simultaneously both an avant-garde gesture and a signal warning to the avant-garde of the ultimate containment and commodification of avant-gardism by the forces it seeks to transform. Yet the historical, transformational languages of the avant-garde, commodified and culturally enshrined, like the Trojan Horse itself, may potentially disclose the forces for continuing resistance and change.

## Gendering modernism and the avant-garde

West's narrative of entry into the Trojan Horse, his imagery of anal penetration and male masturbation and ejaculation, certainly point up the subtexts of homosexuality apparent in many modernist texts, as well as the masculinity and the homosocial nature of many of the movements in the historical avant-garde. But equally, there is a discourse of feminine sexuality and of feminism running through the texts of this period. Several decades of feminist and gender-based scholarship has opened up the field to considerations of the inscriptions of gender and sexuality, in male- and female-authored texts, in ways that suggest these terms provide the image and apocalypse of the modernist period. The middle part of this book addresses these gender wars, and the mythopoeisis of the Trojan War again figures conspicuously. But gender, as we shall see, in fact provides the metaphorical staging and basis for many of the wider, and apparently unconnected concerns of modernist literature and culture. "The alienation from patriarchal discourse that belongs to its creative deviants," Naomi Segal argues, "is . . . . after all the true avant-garde" (p. 249).

## New theories of the avant-garde and new genres

Bürger's theory of the avant-garde has recently been opened up by various critics who have recognised the need both to revise his definition of the term, and to apply it to a wider spectrum of art of the period of the historical avant-garde as well as to the post-war works Bürger identifies as neo-avant-garde (see Murphy; Scheunemann; Karl). It has been argued, further, that Bürger's analysis of the aims of the historical avant-garde is, itself, mistaken. This current critical interest in revising and redefining the term "avant-garde", and in broadening its application, provides this book with a set of theoretical transitions, then, to test in its sampling of the literature of 1910 to 1945. "Image to Apocalypse" carries the freight of these concerns with the avant-garde, and suggests methods for reading and writing avant-garde texts, while also signalling the historical span of avant-garde movements from 1910 to 1945. While "Image" is derived from the particular *poetry* movement, it should be noted that "Imagism" collapses strict generic categorisation, and ushers in a period of exploding old genres colliding with new (such as photography and film). As shorthand for avant-garde aesthetics and methodology, it also transcends distinct genres. The image is the common unit of currency and structuring principle of poetry, fiction, drama, essay, manifesto and so on. The juxtaposition of (broken) images, furthermore, enables the new avant-garde genre of montage or collage that dominates this period. "Image to Apocalypse" thus signals the period's apocalypse of image.

## Modernism and the literary periodisation of 1910 to 1945

Students of the avant-garde and Modernism should find both reassuring and unsettling the choice of dates in my title, each of potent historical, political and cultural significance. The dates go from the death of Edward VII and the political upheavals surrounding the fall of the Asquith government, culturally implicated in all of which is the infamous Post-Impressionist exhibition of 1910 (for which "Image" may stand as shorthand), to the end of the Second World War and the dropping of the Atom bomb ("Apocalypse" indeed). I begin with 1910, itself a familiar topos of modernism, since it is the year (as every novice soon knows) when, according to Virginia Woolf, "human character changed" (*Essays* 3, p. 421); but it is not the year that many surveys of modernism, however enthusiastically they go on to cite it, take as their starting point (although for Peter Faulkner's reader and Critical Idiom introduction, the era of modernism is 1910–30). I conclude with 1945, extending the period beyond its conventionally understood close. The 1930s are often misleadingly treated as a separate and culturally disconnected decade. Modernism is more usually confined by literary commentaries to the period between 1890/1900 and 1930 (for example, Malcolm Bradbury's and James McFarlane's *Modernism*), and has even been narrowed to between 1907 and 1925 (by Frank Kermode) and 1908 and 1922 (by M. H. Levenson in his *Genealogy of Modernism*, although his edited *Cambridge Companion to Modernism* extends the chronology from 1890 to 1939). Peter Childs's recent New Critical Idiom guide, *Modernism*, more vaguely assigns it to the work of authors "who wrote in the decades before and after the turn of the twentieth century" (4). Although two works on women modernists (Gillian Hanscome and Virginia Smyers; Shari Benstock) go to 1940, there are no introductions that go beyond this point – unless it is to go well beyond (the date and sometimes the student) into the realms of postmodernism (Peter Brooker, Brian McHale).

A typical rationale for starting in the mid-/late nineteenth century or turn of the twentieth century is to approach the heights of Modernism gently via the foothills of Symbolism and the Yellow Period, but this gradualist approach tends to defer and diffuse rather than sharply define the specific topics and shock tactics of the various movements in Modernism (see, for example, Peter Nicholls's introduction, which starts with 1845 and with Baudelaire). Starting with Joseph Conrad's *Heart of Darkness* (1899) is also a popular but equally problematic pedagogical and critical strategy: new readers and students of the period often find it difficult, in my experience, to discern the "modernist" aspects of this complex narrative, whereas they benefit enormously, I hope, from the insights gained by plunging into the visually and verbally distinct contours of Imagist poetry of a decade later. Childs opts for "plunging" his readers early into Samuel Beckett's *Murphy* (1938), which he finds "an in some ways exemplary Modernist text, which would actually be sidelined by some definitions of Modernism and by some definitions of Modernist writers" as it was published "supposedly eight years after Modernism started to wane and be replaced by the neo-realism of writers such as Graham Greene, George Orwell and Evelyn Waugh. It is also by a writer who is often cited as the first *postmodernist*" (4–5). I admire this gesture towards an extended boundary for the period and the undermining of "postmodernist" as a useful epithet, but the danger here is that "Modernism" may be seen as shorthand for a fixed category of aesthetic qualities that remain unchanged whatever the context. But whereas Childs's task is to define and explain the term "modernism", mine is to introduce readers to the *transitions* occurring within the period that has been retrospectively categorised as "modernist". "Modernism", it should be emphasised, "comprises numerous, diverse and contesting, theories and practices which first flourished in a period that knew little of the term as it has now come to be understood" (Kolocotroni et al.: xvii). This accounts for our first plunge into *The Dream Life of Balso Snell*, which does in some ways broadly seem to exemplify retrospective definitions of "modernist writing", but which also illustrates, more specifically, the transitions (and regroupings) that have occurred in avant-garde literary practice by 1931.

## Nathanael West: transitions in the avant-garde languages of Marcel Proust, James Joyce and Gertrude Stein

With this in mind, we might explore with Balso a little further what lies beyond "the lips of the mystic portal". What lies around it is graffiti:

> Engraved in a heart pierced by an arrow and surmounted by the initial N, he read, "Ah! Qualis . . . Artifex . . . Pereo!" Not to be outdone by the actor-emperor, Balso carved with his penknife another heart and the words "O Byss! O Abyss! O Anon! O Onan!" omitting, however, the arrow and his initial. (West: 5)

The citation of Nero's dying words, "What an artist is lost with me!" (see West: 820 note), is rhythmically supplemented by Balso's playful and celebratory punning on the lyric exclamation as arsehole, and on this orifice as portal of death ("Abyss"). "O Byss" puns on the Latin verb *obire,* to die, as well as almost suggesting bliss; and the move from Anon to Onan, links the oblivion of authorial anonymity – Eliotic impersonality – with the erotic oblivion of masturbation. Onanism may well be the novel's alpha and omega, for it closes, as we have seen, with an account of Balso in masturbatory ejaculation.

West's novel sports a Proustian epigraph: " *'After all, my dear fellow, life, Anaxagoras has said, is a journey' – Bergotte,*" which sends us on a journey of further citations. Bergotte, himself a fictional construct, "a novelist and Marcel's hero in Proust's *A la recherche de temps perdu*" (see West: 820 note), cites the ancient philosopher Anaxagoras, whose concept of the universe as a "mixture" of "spermata" – seeds "of every qualitatively distinct natural substance, organic and inorganic" (*Oxford Classical Dictionary*) – seems particularly apt for West's onanistic text. If such arcane and obscurantist humour, coupled with West's bizarre and disorientating narration, his Eliotic allusions to classical mythology, and his Joycean wit and sordidity, have not already alerted the 1931 reader to the fact that he is writing in the new, or by now established, avant-garde manner, then Balso's following invocation would surely do so: "O Beer! O

Meyerbeer! O Bach! O Offenbach! Stand me now as ever in good stead" (West: 5). For this synthetic Bacchic (so to speak!) invocation of drink and operatic song also clearly echoes Stephen's famous invocation (of Daedalus) in the concluding lines of one of the major founding avant-garde texts, *A Portrait of the Artist as a Young Man* (1916), by James Joyce: "Old father, old artificer, stand me now and ever in good stead" (213). We might note that *A Portrait of the Artist* itself begins in a conflation of fairy tale, baby talk, colloquialism and song:

> Once upon a time and a very good time it was there was a moocow coming down along the road and this moocow that was coming down along the road met a nicens little boy named baby tuckoo. . . .
>
> His father told him that story: his father looked at him through a glass: he had a hairy face.
>
> He was baby tuckoo. The moocow came down the road where Betty Byrne lived: she sold lemon platt.
>
> *O, the wild rose blossoms*
> *On the little green place.*
>
> He sang that song. That was his song.
>
> *O, the green wothe botheth.*
>
> When you wet the bed first it is warm then it gets cold. His mother put on the oilsheet. That had the queer smell. (5)

It appears that both the opening and closing passages of Joyce's *Portrait*, then, contribute as points of departure for West's opening to *The Dream Life of Balso Snell.* Just as Joyce's text is punctuated by song so West also has Balso break into song as he enters the "foyer-like lower intestine" of the Trojan Horse. Whereas Joyce (just as he cites Ovid, an authentic classical source, in his epigraph to *Portrait*) here uses a snatch of a "real" citation plundered from a "traditional" cultural source (folk song), West, on the other hand, constructs a song from more recent, avant-garde sources:

> To keep his heart high and yet out of his throat, he made a song.
>
> Round as the Anus
> Of a Bronze Horse
> Or the Tender Buttons
> Used by Horses for Ani . . . (5)

Here we find parodied, amongst other things, the sparse syntax of Imagism, the compressed lyric symbolism of Yeats, the perverse somatic humour of Joyce, and the cryptic poetics of Gertrude Stein's volume of cubist poetry, *Tender Buttons.* The "elephantine close-ups of various literary positions and their technical methods" that Balso encounters further down the digestive tract of the Trojan Horse include parodies of Dostoevsky, the Marquis de Sade, Rilke, Rimbaud, J. K. Huysmans, Yeats, Joyce, Proust, Williams, Pound, S. J. Perelman, Dashiell Hammett, Gorky, James Branch Cabell, Rabelais, Voltaire, Aldous Huxley, D. H. Lawrence (see Martin: 129–30).

## Transitions in American and European poetics: from Edgar Allan Poe to performance poetry

As well as pointing up the influence of the maverick Dadaist, Schwitters, West's advertisement also makes clear his debt to French avant-garde sources: "he is much like Guillaume Apollinaire, Jarry, Ribemont-Dessaignes, Raymond Roussel, and certain of the surrealists" (West: 397). West's formative, but relatively brief, pilgrimage to Paris in the 1920s, where he met and mixed with the French Dada/Surrealist crowd, Max Ernst, Louis Aragon and Phillippe Soupault (who befriended him), puts him in the modernist tradition of expatriate Americans in Paris. And out of this experience of the international avant-garde in Europe came *The Dream Life of Balso Snell.* In his satirical portrait of West, S. J. Perelman celebrates his friend's predilections for the life of an American flâneur-writer in Paris:

> Picture to yourself . . . an intellectual vagabond, a connoisseur of first editions, fine wines, and beautiful women, well above six feet in height and distinguished for his pallor, a dweller in the world of books, his keen grey eyes belying the sensual lip, equally at home browsing through the bookstalls along the Paris quais and rubbing elbows in the smart literary salons of the Faubourg St. Honore . . . an intimate of Cocteau, Picasso, Joyce and Lincoln Kirstein, a dead shot, a past master of the foils, dictating his epigrams, aphorisms, and sayings to a corps of secretaries at lightning speed . . . (Perelman: 11)

But we might be wary of casting West, and other writers of the period, as seeking to replicate quite so faithfully the hyper-aesthetics of the fin-de-siècle bibliophile, sensualist, and flâneur. West and Perelman are also in the business of sending up and undermining such stereotypes. West's few statements on his art (for, like many of his heroes, he issued a couple of manifestos) show a particularly American agenda to his avant-garde aspirations, despite his several European calling cards. "Some Notes on Violence" (1932) appeared in the revived *Contact* magazine during his co-editorship with William Carlos Williams (it was co-edited by Williams and Robert McAlmon in the early 1920s). Declaring, "in America violence is idiomatic" (West: 399), it is a defence of the violence at the "core" of modern American writing. In "Some Notes on Miss L." (1933), he shows how the "comic strip technique" of his second novel, *Miss Lonelyhearts* (1932), contributes to his American aesthetic of violence: "Each chapter instead of going forward in time, also goes backward, forward, up and down in space like a picture. Violent images are used to illustrate commonplace events. Violent acts are left almost bald" (West: 401). Here European avant-garde interests in narrative and temporal experimentation and in interartistic exchange meet with the American strip cartoon and American urban violence.

*Contact* magazine, in its new manifestation, was to "attempt to cut a trail through the American jungle without the use of a European compass" (146). This suggests a reorienting of international avant-garde aesthetics toward the development of a new local, in this case American, aesthetic. If the new European lyric novel is represented by Joyce's *Ulysses,* in which epic is recast to account for one day in Dublin as observed from a number of other European locations and over several years (as the novel's closing words tell us: "*Trieste–Zurich–Paris, / 1914–1921*"), then the modern American novelist must "Forget the epic", according to West: "Lyric novels can be written according to Poe's definition of a lyric poem. The short novel is a distinct form especially fitted for use in this country. . . . Remember William Carlos Williams' description of the pioneer women who shot their children against the wilderness like cannonballs. Do the same with your novels" (West: 401).

West's citation of Edgar Allan Poe's manifesto, "Philosophy of Composition" (recommending lyric formalism and brevity), combined with the violent and militaristic imagery of a Futurist manifesto, brings out the complex interrelations and dialogue between European and American literature underscoring this period initiated by Baudelaire's translations of Poe. In "Philosophy of Composition", for example, Poe claims to have forged the compositional foundation to his poem "The Raven" from the refrain of "the long *o* as the most sonorous vowel, in connection with *r* as the most producible consonant" (Poe ); and this primary emphasis on the poem's performance of sound in nineteenth-century American poetics finds strong resonance in the European avant-garde performance of (primal) sound poetry of the early twentieth century. The opening refrain of "O" in *The Dream Life of Balso Snell* sings from both sources.

## *Transition*: the little magazine as international forum

1910–1945 is a period of constant transitions, then, between European and American and between international and local concerns. *Contact* magazine, for example, saw itself in 1930 as the "legitimate successor" (Martin: 144) to Eugene Jolas's aptly named Paris-based journal, *transition*, possibly the most important and influential little magazine of the period. Celebrating, in its famous "Revolution of the Word Proclamation", "the revolution in the English language [a]s an accomplished fact" (Fitch: 19), it was *the* international forum for avant-garde and experimental writing between 1927 and 1939, with a two-year interruption between 1930 and 1932 when *Contact* took up the gauntlet from the other side of the Atlantic. *Transition* published work by James Joyce, Franz Kafka, Samuel Beckett, André Gide, Rainer Maria Rilke, Hart Crane, Ernest Hemingway, William Carlos Williams, H.D., Kay Boyle, Richard Aldington, Djuna Barnes, Dylan Thomas and Gertrude Stein, as well as many leading Dadaists, surrealists and expressionists.

For West, his first novel was both "a very professional book, a play on styles" and "a protest against writing books" (Martin: 129). Such revolutionary experimentalism is in keeping with *transition*'s appeal by and to those "tired of the spectacle of short stories, novels, poems and plays still under the hegemony of the banal word, monotonous syntax, static psychology, descriptive naturalism, and desirous of crystallizing a viewpoint" (Fitch: 19). West's audience, in 1931, was small but select. *The Dream Life of Balso Snell* was published, on the recommendation of William Carlos Williams, by Contact Editions (esteemed publishers in the 1920s of the best experimental writing by authors such as Gertrude Stein and Ernest Hemingway), in a beautifully designed de luxe edition of 500. This impeccable debut into avant-garde letters was "historically fitting", as his biographer points out, "since West would carry out in the thirties the intentions and literary hopes of the twenties" (Martin: 124). Writers such as West, then, were in a position during the 1930s to take up – and discard or adapt – newly forged avant-garde legacies to new ends, and in response to changing cultural contexts and political climates. The example of West's first novel shows a sophisticated dialogue as well as explosive disagreements going on between various avant-garde positions. It also marks a transitional phase in – but not by any means an abandonment of (as some commentators would have it) – avant-garde aesthetics from the 1920s into the 1930s.

## Transitions between aesthetics and politics: genre and periodisation

Modernist literature, according to some still prevalent accounts, is considered to peak as "high Modernism" in the 1920s, then tail off in the "political" 1930s, largely because of the dogmatic influence of the Soviet enforcement of socialist realism, and finally die in the 1940s. But this view, itself a legacy of Cold War criticism of the 1950s, has been undermined by recent scholarship exploring the political engagement of "high Modernism", and the robust life of avant-garde aesthetics during the 1930s and 1940s and beyond. This book will sample and chart some of the many literary transitions –smooth and rocky – occurring in the period 1910–1945, from the so-called "high Modernism" and avant-gardism of the first two decades of the twentieth century to their regroupings and reorientations the 1930s and 1940s. "Literary" is to be understood loosely here, and at all turns to be questioned. And, as argued above, it is not easy, or even just, to divide the literature of this period into distinct genres – drama, poetry, prose, criticism, etc. – for their practice and performance often refuse such easy categorisation, and are in explosive dialogue with the visual arts, with science, with politics, and with new genres such as film, photography and phonography. Indeed, the new method of montage or collage operates, in old and new genres, most basically as the juxtaposition of images. "Image to Apocalypse" signals this collagistic defiance of generic category. Like Balso's collagistically framed journey, this study will involve the digestion of any number of differing literary styles, genres, approaches, materials and influences.

Balso alerts us to such diverse influences in his encounter with the boy in short pants, who is anxious to impress his Russophile teacher, Miss McGeeney, with a Dostoevskyean narrative of perverse Proustian and Freudian overtones "*written while smelling the moistened forefinger of* [*his*] *left hand*" (West: 14) (McGeeney, it transpires, is writing a biography entitled *Samuel Perkins: Smeller*).

## Modernism and the avant-garde inside the academy

Here may be discerned the influence of the Russian canon on Anglophone writers of the period (see also Kaye), alongside that of psychoanalysis and modern French literature. But in seeking academic appraisal of the work penned by his sticky fingers, the boy also alerts us to the sheer and delightful absurdity of actually, formally, *studying* or assessing avant-garde writing. For his apprentice-piece in experimentalism, Balso Snell, named after Walter Snell, West's loathed basketball coach at Brown University (Martin: 55), in fact awards the boy in short pants "B minus and a good spanking" (West: 22). This vignette fondly reinforces Balso's passion for the avant-garde as a strictly juvenile affectation, and one that jeopardises the student's chances of a flying first class degree. On the other hand it portends the apparent fate of all avant-gardes, to be contained by or assimilated back into mainstream, official culture. By the end of the period of "Image to Apocalypse", the academic institutionalisation of its avant-garde literatures was well under way. West's initiation into the perverse disciplines of the avant-garde, however, like that of his heroes, was forged in strictly and gloriously extra-curricular contexts. On the other hand, Joyce was clearly looking forward to establishment in academic canons when he famously boasted that he would put into his work "so many enigmas and puzzles that it [would] keep the professors busy for centuries arguing over what [he] meant" (Richard Ellmann, *James Joyce*, ch. 30). Many bewildered students and readers of this period's highly experimental and often densely allusive texts have taken this playful statement (reducing the status of art to that of a smart crossword puzzle – something academic mediators may, sometimes inadvertently, seem to achieve), along with, for example, Eliot's noted penchant for cryptic footnotes or Pound's virtuoso displays of linguistic genius, as indicative of a certain sense of academic élitism and grave intellectual difficulty pervading its formal study.

"From time to time there appear poets and a poetic audience who prefer [the] refractory haze of allusion to be very dense," Edgell Rickword observes, in "A Fragmentary Poem", his (1923) review of *The Waste Land* for *The Times Literary Supplement* (Rickword: 42). Such preferences are not often noticeable in introductory seminars these days. But, as readers soon discover, any serious examination – or "exagmination" (see Beckett et al.) – of the great works of this period rewards with fantastic education and enormous pleasure in equal measure. I still find it a pleasurable shock to be allowed to study and teach material that so splendidly retains its sense of the illicit, the joyously arcane, the grandly revolutionary and the defiantly experimental. What follows is the fruit of happy years so spent.

# Part I

# 1910: Image, Order, War

On or about December 1910, human character changed.
(Virginia Woolf, 1924)

# 2 Literature after 1910
## Formalism, the Visual Arts and Cultural Change

### Introduction to Part I and Chapter 2

Part I, which begins with this chapter, examines the significance of 1910 and the context of cultural change in the wider period. 1910 is not merely another date on the calendar, an arbitrary historical marker, it is a site of potent cultural myth, the myth of sudden historical and cultural change itself. It also marks the birth of formalist theory for the modern era. Part I goes on, in later chapters, to examine the definitive orders of literary criticism and theory, stemming from the foundational critical work of Virginia Woolf and T. S. Eliot, that emerge in the 1910s and 1920s from this first moment of impact for the aesthetics of modernity in the context of cultural and political upheaval. Part I, indeed, begins and ends with Woolf's famous declaration on 1910: "On or about December 1910, human character changed." It begins with this chapter's considerations of 1910, and closes with considerations, in Chapter 5, of the later context (of the mid-1920s) in which Woolf made the statement.

The "image" that Part I springs from, in this chapter, is the Post-Impressionist exhibition of 1910 in London, the first major show of modern art in Britain, and the occasion for which an influential set of aesthetic formalist theories were formulated and broadly established by Roger Fry and later, Clive Bell. The chapter also points to similarly important cultural events and moments elsewhere in the three years that follow the first Post-Impressionist Show: as well as the second Post-Impressionist Show in London in 1912, there was a similarly ambitious, and even larger, exhibition of modern art in America: the Armory Show launched in New York (1913). Developments in the visual arts in Paris are also discussed, and in particular the groundbreaking cubist gesture, introducing collage to easel painting (1912), an aesthetic mode that came to dominate the construction of literary texts throughout the period 1910 to 1945, and beyond.

Part I addresses three significant essays, from the heart of the period, that have shaped our understanding of literary transitions in this period and since, and whose formulations stem from the break-throughs of 1910: Woolf's "Modern Fiction" (1919; 1925) and "Mr Bennett and Mrs Brown" (1924); and Eliot's "Tradition and the Individual Talent" (1919). These three important, pivotal essays, appearing about a decade after 1910, take stock of literary and cultural change in the intervening years and herald new ways forward. Woolf and Roger Fry were prominent members of the Bloomsbury Group, whose embrace also extended to Eliot. Along with fellow member Clive Bell, they have all contributed to the shaping of Modernist formalist aesthetics. And, considering the way Woolf's and Eliot's essays, in particular, have accompanied the development of Modernist studies, we also need to understand their position in the context of this larger critical trajectory.

Eliot's "Tradition and the Individual Talent" is a key text here, since it both provides a critical vocabulary for thinking about individual texts in larger contexts and has also given shape to a particular critical context in which to read Modernism. And most importantly it seeks to position change and the new firmly back in "tradition", in an unchanging ideal order remote from the specificities of historical change associated, for example, with the date of December 1910. Woolf's "Modern Fiction", on the other hand, is a prime source for modernist critical methodologies and reading practice, and this chapter closes with a detailed analysis of the essay's familiar and less familiar passages.

One aim of this first part is to encourage a less homogenising, or *zeitgeist*, approach to the wider context of change and its relation to literature; and to consider some of the complexities involved in dating and contextualising 1910, this moment of modernism, given the number of historical and critical filters already at work in its reception. The focus of Part II will shift, then, from an account of 1910's formalist credentials, followed by a résumé of cultural changes, via a discussion of Woolf's and Eliot's essays, back to the mythical date of 1910. We will be exploring some of the significant points of critical appraisal of the period that filter our understanding of its dominant theoretical premises, trajectories and apparent teleology. The discussion of Eliot's "Tradition and the Individual Talent", furthermore, puts forward a synchronic methodology for reading his work in the context of the particular issues of *The Egoist*, the little magazine in which it was first published. In this way, the discussion of these formative modernist essays broadens out into a wider sampling of their cultural context. Such insights are not readily available to readers of Eliot's and Woolf's essays as "set texts", reproduced in the Norton anthologies or the collections published by Faber and Hogarth.

The three essays are considered, in the following chapters, in dialogue with each other and in the relation to other essays and manifestos of the period, as well as in terms of their significance for critical debates on modernism, formalism and the avant-garde. Part I in itself spans and charts many of the intellectual transitions from 1910 to 1945 in focusing, as it does, on canonical modernist manifestos in their immediate published context as well as in a wider cultural context and with reference to their far-reaching critical reception. The rise of the manifesto and essay as an art form in itself may be considered one of the main transitions of the period. Woolf's "Modern Fiction" is the manifesto of the new from which our ladders of literary modernity start. It is in Woolf's essay "Mr Bennett and Mrs Brown" that 1910 famously comes to cultural and literary attention as the moment of change, the inception of "the new". And it is Eliot's "Tradition and the Individual Talent", first published in *The Egoist* in two instalments, that puts forward a new model of "the new" in art in relation to "traditional" art, both in and beyond time or history. Our discussion of this essay brings into focus the little magazine of special interest for Part I, *The Egoist*. And Eliot's essay is considered alongside the work of other contributors to this magazine, such as James Joyce, Dora Marsden, and John Rodker, and alongside the work of other writers reviewed and promoted in its pages, such as Ezra Pound, Aldous Huxley and Edith Sitwell. After these informative digressions through the offices of *The Egoist*, Eliot's essay is considered in relation to Woolf's "Mr Bennett and Mrs Brown", which returns us to further thoughts on the literary significance of 1910.

This chapter begins, then, with a discussion of 1910 and the context of cultural and political change, in which we find Roger Fry's landmark exhibition, *Manet and the Post-Impressionists*. While, on the one hand, the impact of the exhibition suggests all the hallmarks of a revolutionary avant-garde event, art sending shock-waves deep into the praxis of life, the critical apparatus, on the other hand, developed by

Fry and fellow critic Clive Bell, to theorise this retrospectively applied term "Post-Impressionism", is recognised as an important foundation for formalist aesthetics. Formalism is a term applied to other theories besides those of Fry and Bell. So there follows, below, a discussion of the different formalisms available to literary criticism, and which should be compared with Bloomsbury formalism. Bloomsbury's formalist theories, however, should also be read in the context of Bloomsbury's avant-garde behaviour, and the group's transgressive activities at the Post-Impressionist Ball and its involvement in the *Dreadnought* Hoax are discussed. Similarly, the discussion of the New York Armory show situates this less theorised event in the context of the avant-garde behaviour of Mabel Dodge, Gertrude Stein and their American circle.

After considering the double cultural impetus of Post-Impressionism, as both radical, avant-garde and formalist modernist, and acknowledging the shifting definitions of formalism, we will then broaden our discussion to consider the major social, political, and cultural shifts and changes in Western culture that form the wider context to these events. The significance of these issues and events for literary aesthetics is discussed with reference not only to Virginia Woolf, whose essay "Modern Fiction" becomes the object of close attention, but also, for example, to Gertrude Stein, Ezra Pound and D. H. Lawrence.

## 1910: the year of cataclysmic change

It was in or about July 1924 that Virginia Woolf declared, in her essay "Mr Bennett and Mrs Brown", that "On or about December 1910, human character changed," and it is as well to consider the cultural and literary context in which this declaration was made, as well as the associations and contexts of the designated date of 1910 itself. But why try to designate a date at all? "If you want a one-sentence example of fatuous stupidity you'll not find a better one than that" (102), opines, with some justice perhaps, a character in William Boyd's recent novel *Any Human Heart* (2002), a fictional journal of the high modernist era. But Woolf was merely articulating a received sense of change felt by many of her contemporaries. In a flash of major cultural and political unrest, 1910 ushers in a period (up to 1945) which will witness the cataclysm of the Great War, the Russian

Bolshevik Revolution, the execution of the Russian Tsar (1918), the establishment of the Irish Free State (1922), the establishment of the Union of Soviet Socialist Republics (1923), Hitler's Munich Putsch (1923), the General Strike in Britain (1926), the collapse of the American stock exchange (1929), Hitler's chancellorship of Germany and the burning of the Reichstag (1933), the abdication crisis (1936), the Spanish Civil War (1936), and the Second World War, culminating in the dropping of atomic bombs on Hiroshima and Nagasaki (1945). In the despondent years after the Great War, 1924 saw the formation of the first Labour government in Britain, headed by Ramsay MacDonald, who in the same year lost the general election to Stanley Baldwin. In the turbulent political context of 1924, then, Woolf looks back over fourteen years of upheaval to 1910, but her statement has only gained in significance in the decades of enormous cultural and political change since it was first published. And 1910 seems to bear the burden of all the upheaval to follow.

This was a period of frequent such annunciations of cataclysmic change. Twelve years after Woolf's declaration, in 1936, George Dangerfield memorably sums up 1910's climate of old order decline and exhilarating cultural change:

> (*Dying!* In the streets of London, the last horse-bus clattered towards extinction. The aeroplane, that incongruous object, earth-bound and wavering, still called forth exclamations of rapture and alarm. Country roads, with blind corners and precipitous inclines, took a last revenge upon the loud invading automobile. There was talk of wild young people in London, more wild and less witty than you would ever guess from the novels of Saki; of night clubs; of negroid dances. People gazed in horror at the paintings of Gauguin, and listened with delighted alarm to the barbaric measures of Stravinsky. The old order, the old bland world, was dying fast . . . ) (63–4)

In drawing attention to the shocked reception of Paul Gauguin's art, Dangerfield is referring us to the event that has become most powerfully associated with Woolf's designation of 1910 as the moment of change: Roger Fry's notorious London exhibition of "modern" art, *Manet and the Post-Impressionists*, which opened in November 1910 and included under Fry's ground-breaking neologism (the first of many "post"s in twentieth-century criticism) work by artists such as Gauguin, Vincent Van Gogh, and Paul Cézanne. Ian Dunlop reminds us of the political upheavals occurring at the time of Fry's historic 1910 exhibition:

> A constitutional crisis over the power of the House of Lords developed, and in the winter of 1910 Asquith dissolved Parliament and called for a general election. In November, a few days after the opening of the Post-Impressionist exhibition, the Home Secretary, Winston Churchill, ordered the troops in to break up the strike of Welsh miners at Tonypandy, an action that was to have lasting effects on labour relations in Britain. Throughout that year the suffragette movement gained momentum. (132)

Retrospectively, 1910 has been understood as the historical gateway to cultural change, cataclysm and catastrophe. But, rather like George Orwell's 1984, it was in fact already marked in advance as an ominous year. Indeed in 1906, four years before it was reached, 1910 was predicted by William Le Queux, in his best-selling shocker *The Invasion of 1910, With a Full Account of the Siege of London,* as the time of "England's grave peril" (x). The book's object was "to illustrate our utter unpreparedness for war, to show how, under certain conditions which may easily occur, England can be successfully invaded by Germany, and to present a picture of ruin which must inevitably fall upon us on the evening of that not far-distant day" (vi). But rather than an invading foreign force, the enemy to England's status quo in 1910, it transpired, came from within, in the form of a range of internal oppositional forces, working class and feminist.

In other parts of Europe, 1910 came to be acknowledged as a year of enormous and turbulent cultural and political change: "1910, that is indeed the year when all scaffolds began to crack", according to the German poet Gottfried Benn; and Thomas Harrison, in his excellent study, *1910: The Emancipation of Dissonance,* has taken Arnold Schoenberg's expressionist painting *The Red Gaze,* of May 1910, as the emblem of the epidemic of suicide and madness among artists and poets that accompanied the unleashing of cultural and political unrest in the Austro-Hungarian empire. But Woolf's optimistic account of 1910 does not communicate this sense of catastrophic disaster.

Eleven years earlier than Woolf's, however, came Charles Péguy's famous declaration, in 1913, that cataclysmic changes had already been occurring for some time: "The Western world has changed less since Jesus Christ than it has in the last thirty years" (quoted in

Shattuck: 1). This suggests the inception of modern experience to be in the 1880s. In considering a period when chronology, linear development and Time itself were under severe scrutiny and question, it is no wonder that coming up with a reliable date for *the* single moment of revolutionary cultural change proves rather tricky. Or is it that every literary period can be represented in terms of revolution in the world and revolution of the word? How is literature – art, aesthetics – to be understood in relation to change? Does (or should, or can) art *reflect* or describe change, or does (or should or can) art actually *produce* change (and on what scale of transformation)?

Wherever the emphasis falls for individual practitioners or movements, it is clear that in the period 1910 to 1945, a period of two cataclysmic world wars, and of massive social upheaval and major political revolution, the very categories of Art or Literature, as eternal, transcendent values, were under considerable assault and transition, undermined by a wide range of oppositional, avant-garde movements. On the other hand, it must also be acknowledged that the revolutionary date of 1910 has become identified as the moment of inception of a dominant strand of formalist aesthetics which is considered to entrench Art and Literature even more firmly in separate (from each other, from life), autonomous disciplines, and which by 1945 had become the modernist critical filter through which to interpret all avant-garde practices.

## A note on defining formalism

"'Mere formalism'", Ann Banfield reminds us, "has long been a term of contempt for the left which is perhaps not aware that, currently, it is the one aspect of aesthetic theory and practice which right and left are agreed in dismissing" (Banfield: xiv). In opposition to this view, she quotes Michel Foucault's observation that "formalist culture, thought, and art in the first third of the 20th century were generally associated with critical political movements of the Left – and even with revolutionary movements" (quoted Banfield: xiv–v). Formalism is the "aesthetic precursor or accompaniment" of such moments, Banfield contends, "regardless of the political affiliations of individual practictioners [*sic*], from Russian revolution to May 68 and even including the neo-classicism of the French Revolution. Only when such revolutionary moments were over – defeated or distorted – did what is more conventionally thought of as political or social literature appear" (xv). This analysis offers a temptingly neat model of transition occurring in the period 1910 to 1945 (and beyond): avant-garde (revolutionary) formalism yields to more overtly political social(ist) realism, just as romanticism yields to classicism. Such transitions may certainly be discerned in the period, but not perhaps in such linear terms: rather, avant-garde (revolutionary) formalism continues also to *contend with* social(ist) realism; romanticism to *contend with* classicism. Political movements in this period variously engage with, develop, reject or retain so-called formalist and realist aesthetics. Banfield's discerned rise of formalist aesthetics in a climate of revolutionary political change in a sense points up the political potency of all form. The rejection of formalism for realism (another form) exemplifies this. Similarly, the emergence and acknowledgement of the avant-garde transforms all aesthetic and interpretative practices. Transitions between the two poles of formalism and realism, in this period, are more fluid and fluctuating than Banfield's model might suggest, but these terms nevertheless provide useful critical insight. Formalism, however, may refer to several different critical movements, and it is worth briefly considering their basic differences before pursuing this line of argument further.

Banfield is introducing readers to the philosophical and aesthetic formalism of Bloomsbury, London – that is, to the work of G. E. Moore, Bertrand Russell, Roger Fry and Clive Bell. Formalism is inflected differently by each of these thinkers, and Banfield helpfully opens up the formalism of Bertrand Russell's logical philosophy for special consideration. Moore's influential work *Principia Ethica* (1903) based his proposition that goodness is indefinable and immeasurable on the principle of organic unity: aesthetic and personal pleasures are good in themselves (Roe: 166). Andrew McNeillie is wary of leaving Woolf's intellectual formation, in particular, "locked in the wooden embrace of G. E. Moore" (McNeillie: 13), and rightly alerts us to many other important influences on her and on Bloomsbury's thinking, not least the classical anthropology of Jane Ellen Harrison. But until Banfield's work, Bell's and Fry's formalism has in any case tended to dominate modernist scholarly interest in Bloomsbury's, and Woolf's, aesthetics. It has as much if not more relevance for reading Eliot's essays, I would suggest, than for readings of Woolf's, in the sense that Eliot is more in sympathy with it whereas Woolf radically transforms it for feminism (see Goldman, *Feminist Aesthetics*).

Fry's and Bell's brand of Bloomsbury formalism may be summarised as a concern with form for form's sake, and with an emotional and spiritual investment in form, which became known through Bell's influential theory of "Significant Form", actually formulated for the catalogue to the second Post-Impressionism exhibition, in 1912. Bell's and Fry's formalism evolved in application primarily to the visual arts, but shows some affiliations with the literary formalism emerging in the early twentieth century which, directly or indirectly influenced by the structural linguistics of Ferdinand de Saussure, "devoted its attention to concentrating on literature's formalism in an objective manner" (Wolfreys, *Encyclopedia*, p. 847), and which shaped emergent English studies. Students are still introduced to formalist methodologies based on the "practical criticism" of the Cambridge scholar I. A. Richards, and of the American New Critics who followed him, all of whom were influenced by Eliot. It is the formalism of New Criticism that is most strongly associated with the emergence of Modernism as an aesthetic and critical category, exemplified in the recent volume (VII) of *The Cambridge History of Literary Criticism: Modernism and the New Criticism* (edited by Litz, Menand and Rainey).

The central tenet of Russian formalism of the same period, on the other hand, whose connections with the Russian Revolution Banfield emphasises, stems from Viktor Shklovsky's theory of *ostranenie* or "defamiliarisation", by which he argues that "the function of art is to 'defamiliarise' one's habitual perception of the world" (Newton: 6). K. M. Newton points out that this initial theory of defamiliarisation became more sophisticated as Russian formalism developed:

> it became less interested in the device as a means of defamiliarising the reader's perception of reality; rather, the emphasis was on the work of literature as an assemblage of devices, some of which would take on a dominating role at the expense of others. Defamiliarisation thus functioned within the literary text and not between text and the reader's habitual mode of perceiving reality. (Newton: 15)

The politically engaged formal experimentation advanced by Bertolt Brecht's theory of epic theatre (1930) owes something to defamiliarisation. The Russian formalists along with the Prague Linguistic Circle, "who continued the work of the Russian formalists after their suppression by the Soviet government during the 1930s", have hugely influenced modern literary and linguistic theory:

> By accenting the structural devices that characterize the literary experience [their] critique of literature and language inevitably strives to highlight the roles of linguistic signs, artistic unity, and literariness that produce our conceptions of narrative. Their discoveries about the nature of linguistics and literary criticism altered the course of twentieth-century textual scholarship and ushered in a new era marked by an interest in narratology and structuralism. (Womack: 119)

The legacy of Soviet socialist realism's antipathy to formalism has been the sometimes crude positioning of formalism almost as the antithesis to politically engaged art. But the spectrum of formalist aesthetics from Bell's significant form to Brecht's alienation technique shows formalism to be highly differentiated and politically nuanced.

Banfield seeks to elucidate the "place of formalism in the life and work of a thinker also interested in changing the world" and suggests that "the fact of Russell's political activity . . . his existence elsewhere, in a separate political sphere . . . is the counterweight to any charge of 'mere' formalism" (xv). This line of argument sits a little oddly with her earlier claim that aesthetic formalism precedes political revolution "regardless of the political affiliations of individual practitioners". In the following account of Fry's and Bell's emergent formalism, however, what is also of interest is the reception of aesthetic formalism in the public sphere as itself inherently political.

## London, 1910: formalism and the first Post-Impressionist exhibition

"On or about" *November* 1910, Roger Fry invented the term "Post-Impressionism" to describe the departure from Impressionism by French-based artists "out of the cul-de-sac into which naturalism had led them". Desmond MacCarthy, the secretary to Fry's notorious exhibition *Manet and the Post-Impressionists*, recalls that here "for the first time the British public saw the works of Cézanne, Matisse, Van Gogh, Gauguin, Seurat, Picasso and other now familiar French painters. No gradual infiltration, but – bang! an assault along the whole academic front of art." This was the great "Art-Quake of 1910" ("Art Quake", p. 123). His choice of language suggests the exhibition to be avant-garde in the sense of breaking with artistic and academic tradition. It also deeply shocked the public. It was "a shock to most people", according to Woolf herself (*Essays*, 1, p. 379). The riotous and shocking explosion of colour happened appropriately enough on 5 November: "A date more favourable . . . for revealing the existence of a wide-spread plot to destroy the whole fabric of European painting could hardly have been better chosen," according to the critic Robert Ross, whose rhetoric suggests that the exhibition was in danger of destroying more than artistic tradition (Bullen: 100). "These sickening aberrations could never have got a footing" but for the "anti-patriotic campaign in favour of anarchism and ultimate chaos" by the "'Modernity' critics" according to Ebenezer Cook (Bullen: 119). These responses suggest the exhibition to be avant-garde in the "Trojan Horse" sense of attempting to liquidate art itself "as an activity that is split off from the praxis of life" (Bürger: 22). The pyrotechnic colourism of this new French art was the point at which the assault was most brutally felt by the many hostile members of the public and outraged critics who came to deride the exhibition. When reactionary critics were not pouring scorn on the primitivism and insanity they saw represented on the walls of the Grafton, they were snorting, with Ross, in disbelief at the most obvious symptom to them of such degeneracy: the "barbaric" (Bullen: 102) colours. The *Daily Express* review is typical in its fury over the depiction of women in exotic and "unnatural" colours:

> In a typical [Gauguin] hideous brown women, with purple hair and vitriolic faces, squat in the midst of a nightmare landscape of drunken palm trees, crude green grass, vermilion rocks, and numerous glaringly coloured excrescences impossible to identify. . . . A revolution to be successful must presumably revolve; but, undeniably clever as they often are, the catherine-wheel antics of the Post-Impressionists are not likely to wake many responsive chords in British breasts. (Bullen: 105–6)

MacCarthy recalls the casual way Fry came to coin the term "Post-Impressionism': "'Oh, let's just call them post-impressionists; at any rate they came after the impressionists'" ("Art Quake", p. 124). Post-Impressionism, then, was not strictly *contemporary* "modern" art. Cézanne, Gauguin and Van Gogh, the most prominently represented artists in the exhibition, were all by 1910 "long since dead" (Bowness,

1979). A smaller sample of work by Fauves and Cubists such as Matisse and Picasso was shown, to indicate the continuation of this newly defined school, but "the whole emphasis was thrown on to the old masters", as Benedict Nicolson observes. The living were not represented by their most recent, avant-garde, achievements; Cubism in fact "was the most serious omission" (Nicolson: 13). The first Cubist painting, Picasso's *Demoiselles D'Avignon*, arguably much more shocking than anything in Fry's show, first shocked the French as early as 1907. Fry's exhibition, nevertheless, marks 1910 as a defining moment in avant-garde aesthetics. It is the moment of European modern art's revolutionary impact on the practices of British artists, but it is also the moment when British formalist theories first emerge and shape the critical apparatus for modernism. Fry's neologism, Alan Bowness remarks, "is unusual, not only because it was invented 25 years after the art it describes, but because it was the invention of an English critic arranging an exhibition of modern French art" (Bowness: 9). Fry's historic exhibition is often cited to explain Woolf's enigmatic statement: "on or about December 1910 human character changed" (Woolf, *Essays* 3, pp. 421, 437). It is worth noting that Bell's theory of "Significant Form" emerged with the second Post-Impressionist exhibition in 1912, but in retrospect has sometimes been conflated with Fry's formalism and anachronistically associated by many critics with the 1910 exhibition.

The 1910 Exhibition Catalogue preface was anonymous, and not in fact directly written by Fry, but ventriloquised through MacCarthy (MacCarthy, "Art Quake", p. 124). It declares the Post-Impressionist artist's individual expression to be at odds with the naturalistic project of the Impressionists. The latter "were interested in analysing the play of light and shadow into a multiplicity of distinct colours; they refined upon what was already illusive in nature" ("Post-Impressionists", p. 8). Impressionism, then, is concerned with pushing analysis of the object world to the limits. The Post-Impressionists use larger, flatter areas of colour in departing from their technique and their naturalism. In Impressionism,

> the "treeness" of the tree was not rendered at all; all the emotion and associations such as trees may be made to convey in poetry were omitted. . . . And there is no denying that the work of the Post-Impressionists is sufficiently disconcerting. It may even appear ridiculous to those who do not recall the fact that a good rocking-

> horse often has more of the true horse about it than an instantaneous photograph of a Derby winner. (8)

## London, 1912: "significant form" and the second Post-Impressionist exhibition

The second exhibition, in 1912, gave space to the work of British artists (including Vanessa Bell, Woolf's sister), inspired by the work of the first exhibition, alongside their continental avant-garde masters. Apart from this, the most obvious shift in emphasis from the first exhibition was from romantic to classic, reflected in the new predominance of Cubism. Nicolson is not surprised "to find that criticism emerging out of the second show differed radically from that emerging out of the first. Whereas the first had popularised the notion that artists were romantic geniuses, the second gave birth to the much more rigid doctrine of significant form" (Nicolson: 13). This new doctrine emphasises an emotional understanding of form for its own sake above everything else. The term "significant form" begins to become almost synonymous with Post-Impressionism.

Clive Bell first uses his famous term "Significant Form" in the 1912 Exhibition Catalogue to introduce the work of English artists converted to Post-Impressionism by the European masters on show in the 1910 exhibition. His opening remarks on the theoretical premises of the second exhibition imply that Post-Impressionism, no longer avant-garde or revolutionary, is now established mainstream art, part of the new status quo:

> Happily, there is no need to be defensive. The battle is won. We all agree, now, that any form in which an artist can express himself is legitimate, and the more sensitive perceive that there are things worth expressing that could never have been expressed in traditional forms. We have ceased to ask "What does this picture represent?" and ask instead, "What does it make us feel?" We expect a work of plastic art to have more in common with a piece of music than with a coloured photograph.

This art is not concerned with depiction, but with the arousal of emotion. Bell makes quite clear that the Post-Impressionist revolution is now over: the English artists are capitalising on the advances already made by the French and "their master, Cézanne".

> What I mean by "simplification" is obvious. A literary artist who wishes to express what he feels for a forest thinks himself under no obligation to give an account of its flora and fauna. The Post-Impressionist claims similar privileges: those facts that any one can discern for himself or discover in a text book he leaves to the makers of Christmas-cards and diagrams. He simplifies, omits details, that is to say, to concentrate on something more important – on the significance of form. ("The English Group", p. 9)

Bell distinguishes the high art of Post-Impressionism from mundanities such as greeting-card illustration or diagram-making; and in his highly influential book *Art*, two years later, he extends his theory of Significant Form to account not just for Post-Impressionist art, but for *all* art:

> There must be some one quality without which a work of art cannot exist; possessing which, in the least degree, no work is altogether worthless. What is this quality? What quality is shared by all objects that provoke our aesthetic emotions? What quality is common to Sta. Sophia and the windows at Chartres, Mexican sculpture, a Persian bowl, Chinese carpets, Giotto's frescoes at Padua, and the masterpieces of Poussin, Piero della Francesca, and Cézanne? Only one answer seems possible – significant form. In each, lines and colours combined in a particular way, certain forms and relations of forms, stir our aesthetic emotions. These relations and combinations of lines and colours, these aesthetically moving forms, I call "Significant Form"; and "Significant Form" is the one quality common to all works of visual art. (*Art*, pp. 7–8)

The qualities of Post-Impressionism as first defined by English theorists to describe French art of the turn of the century are now extended to embrace a universal aesthetic theory. The intervention of new art has served to clarify the definition of all art that precedes it. Bell goes further than this when he develops the notion of the spiritual dimension of significant form into a full-blown religion of art. He closes *Art* with a vision of "aesthetic rapture": "the religion of art will serve a man better than the religion of humanity. . . . What he loses in philanthropy he may gain in magnanimity; and because his religion does not begin with an injunction to love all men, it will not end, perhaps, in persuading him to hate most of them" (*Art*, pp. 292–3).

Fry, consolidating with Bell, closes his contribution to the 1912

Catalogue by disassociating the art on show from the notion of "associated ideas": "All art depends upon cutting off the practical responses to sensations of ordinary life, thereby setting free a pure and as it were disembodied functioning of the spirit" ("Introduction", p. 16). An art that cuts off "practical responses" is of course directly contrary to definitions of the avant-garde as penetrating into "the praxis of life" (Bürger: 22). Yet Fry acknowledges the notion of disassociated spirituality to be an almost impossible ideal. Fry's argument allows for the possibility of "romantic associations", which we might consider the hostile critics of the first exhibition to have lighted upon; but it establishes that these associations are secondary, and passing, compared with the regenerative and eternal aspects of the classic, formal properties of this art. This is behind his oxymoron, the "disinterestedly passionate state of mind" recorded by "classic" art (16–17). It is an art free of literary but also of social, political and historical associations, and therefore it is "disinterested". It is an art of pure emotion. In spite of his protestations, Fry's "classic" art remains close to romanticism. To call the "concentration of feeling" "classic" does not really dispel this. Compare the "dry", "hard" and "fixed" qualities of T. E. Hulme's influential definition of classicism in "Romanticism and Classicism" (1911).

Fry's theory of classic art, then, arises, like Bell's, from the development of his formalist interpretation of Post-Impressionism into a universal formalist aesthetic theory, as the following extract from his *Vision and Design* (1920) illustrates:

> The greatest object of art becomes of no more significance than any casual piece of matter; a man's head is no more and no less important than a pumpkin, or, rather, these things may be so or not according to the rhythm that obsesses the artist and crystallises his vision. Since it is the habitual practice of the artist to be on the lookout for these peculiar arrangements of objects that arouse the creative vision, and become material for creative contemplation, he is liable to look at all objects from this point of view. . . . It is irrelevant to ask him, while he is looking with this generalised and all-embracing vision, about the nature of the objects which compose it. (52)

Fry's formalism and Bell's "Significant Form" furnish formalist-Modernist criticism with the intellectual context in which to explore Woolf's and Eliot's key "modernist" essays, and provide a formalist resonance to Woolf's choice of 1910 as the date of change – a change understood to occur primarily in the history of art. And, as Fry's and Bell's universalising development of their formalist theories shows, if this change was perceived as a shocking rupture of artistic tradition in 1910, it was being presented more smoothly as the continuity of universal formalist values by 1912. But to understand, on the other hand, the full avant-gardiste potency of 1910 as a date, we have to consider how the art in question interpenetrates with the period's history and politics, as Dunlop, quoted above, has shown (132). When Andrew McNeillie glosses Woolf's invocation of 1910 with reference to the Post-Impressionist exhibition and the death of Edward VII (Woolf, *Essays* 3, p. 437), he shows how this art event may be twinned with the end of an era and the start of a new one, eras still designated in terms of the reign of a king. Yet any sense of continuity at this time is severely undermined by the events Dunlop lists. The first Post-Impressionist exhibition was understood as not just symptomatic of, but actually stoking contemporary revolutionary tendencies. By 1912 Bell and Fry are putting forward formalist theories that defuse this avant-gardiste frame of reference.

## Bloomsbury's avant-garde behaviour: the Post-Impressionist Ball and the *Dreadnought* Hoax

But however apologetic, revisionist, and ultimately rather dull, Bloomsbury formalist theories became, Bloomsbury artistic, political, social and sexual practices may be considered avant-garde nevertheless. And Bloomsbury formalism, of course, remains implicated in these practices. Notorious for its heady mix of sexual frankness and experimentalism, promiscuity, bawdiness, homosexuality, pacifism, feminism, liberalism and aestheticism, "'Bloomsbury' behaviour", as Hermione Lee has observed, "looks as if it travesties and sabotages the conventions of Victorian life: the calling card, the morning visit, the marriage market, the polite conversation, the cut, the dressing for dinner, the evening party" (54–5). Virginia Woolf and her sister, Vanessa Bell, for example, outraged decorum when they "gauguinised" themselves for the Post-Impressionist Ball, where they appeared "as bare-shouldered bare-legged Gauguin girls, almost – as it seemed to the indignant ladies who swept out in protest – almost naked" (Quentin Bell, 1, p. 170). Woolf seems to have relished the scandal she created as "a South Sea Savage" (*Letters* 1, p. 455), gleefully exploiting the sexual/racial politics evoked by brazenly donning the Post-Impressionist colours of "native" femininity: "Was I less alarming as a Savage – or as bad as ever?" (*Letters* 1, p. 455). Earlier, in February 1910, she had "blacked-up" and cross-dressed as an Abyssinian Prince for the "*Dreadnought* Hoax" (Quentin Bell, 1, p. 168), when she assisted her brother Adrian Stephen in his conspiracy with the practical-joker Horace de Vere Cole, to impersonate the Emperor of Abyssinia and his entourage and to deceive the British naval high security and the Foreign Office into providing them with a guided tour of the British warship *HMS Dreadnought* (Lee: 282–7). Such transgressive, orientalist masquerades, themselves perhaps suspect reinscriptions of sexual/racial stereotypes, were nevertheless understood to challenge the racialist establishment, as well as to expose the weakness of British military defence rather as Le Queux himself might have predicted.

In the years immediately following the Post-Impressionist exhibitions, London lit up with centres of avant-garde activity. Visitations by Marinetti and the Futurists and the performances of Diaghilev's ballets, for example, were famous attractions for the aficionados of Post-Impressionism. The nightclub and avant-garde arts venue, The Cave of the Golden Calf opened in 1912, and was frequented by the likes of Ezra Pound, T. E. Hulme and Ford Madox Ford. Its interior was designed and decorated by modern artists such as Wyndham Lewis, Jacob Epstein and Eric Gill (Cork: 61–115; Louise Williams: 142). The Rebel Art Centre opened in March 1914 as a venue for meetings and lectures on revolutionary art, where many of these people were regular participants, and it became a centre of the new "Vorticism" (Louise Williams: 142).

## Reactionaries and Post-Impressionism

The racialism of those opposed to Post-Impressionism is apparent in the reviews of Fry's exhibition (see Goldman, *Feminist Aesthetics*, p. 119), and also in Henry Tonks's later satirical portrait of Fry and Bell, entitled *The Unknown God* (exhibited in the New English Art Club, 1923), which shows a ridiculous Fry lecturing on stage as he "holds up a dead cat", according to Dunlop, "a symbol of 'pure form', while Clive Bell rings a bell announcing the new creed: 'Cézannah

Cézannah'." In the front row of the audience are "some of Fry's staunchest opponents: Sickert, MacColl, George Moore and Steer" (Dunlop: 156). Dunlop seems to have mistaken for a dead cat what is in fact a crudely caricatured maquette of an African female nude raised on a plinth. He notes, however, that Sickert for one despised Fry's "elevation overnight [of Cézanne and Van Gogh] into gods, or tribal deities" (Dunlop: 157). Tonks's reactionary satire seems to have something about it of the story of "The Emperor's New Clothes". Fry's and Bell's quasi-religious fervour for the Significant Form of Cézanne's aesthetic legacy, blinds them to what clearly disturbs some of their opponents: not just the deification of Cézanne, Van Gogh, Gauguin and the other Post-Impressionists, but also apparently the glorification of naked African femininity. Whereas Bell and Fry see Significant Form, these disgruntled gentlemen see an object delineated by Tonks for racist and misogynist scorn. Tonks, Slade Professor of Fine Art (1917–30), was also (to give some indication of his own political stance on art), in 1919, artist to the British Expeditionary Force assisting the White Russians at Archangel (Hone: 146). He despised the lasting influence of Fry's "Post-Impressionism" on his students: "They must have it, I suppose, like a puppy and distemper" (Hone: 176).

### New York, 1913: Futurism and Cubism at the Armory Show

Arthur B. Davies and Walt Kuhn caught Fry's second Post-Impressionist show in November 1912, while scouting in Europe for works to stock the huge, ground-breaking American exhibition of Post-Impressionist and Modern art, the New York Armory Show, which opened on 17 February 1913 with suitably explosive impact. The Armory Show was to be "epoch making in the history of American art" and its opening night a "red letter night in the history not only of American, but of all modern art", according to John Quinn, who boasted at its launch that this was "the most complete art exhibition that has been held in the world in the last quarter century. We do not except any country or any capital" (quoted Milton Brown: 43). Public and critical outrage, not without humour, focused on Marcel Duchamp's notorious painting *Nude Descending a Staircase* (1912), which gives a cubistic depiction of successive phases of a figure in motion, and which came with the added cachet of having offended the, by then, orthodox, salon Cubists of Paris (Dunlop: 189). The Cubist room at the Armory show quickly became known as the "Chamber of Horrors" (Milton Brown: 136). American journalists, according to Dunlop, "outdid each other in efforts to describe the work. 'An explosion in a shingle factory,' it was called. 'A pack of brown cards in a nightmare,' was another attempt, and among the wittiest, 'a staircase descending a nude'" (186). But the most vitriolic responses were to Matisse, whose paintings the *New York Times* found "ugly . . . coarse", and "revolting in their inhumanity" (quoted Dunlop: 189). Milton Brown records some of the many verses, some "of good humor and metric felicity" (138), published in press reports, such as Maurice L. Ahern's poem "A Post Impression", which appeared in the *Sun*, on 8 March:

Awful lack of technique
Awful lot of paint
Makes a Cubist picture
Look like what it ain't.

(Milton Brown: 138)

Ahern seems unable to distinguish between Post-Impressionism and Cubism and voices the most common objection to modern art – that it does not resemble what it supposedly depicts. The ordinary, unenlightened person's version of the enlightened, and expert, defence of modern art appears in these lines from the Chicago *Tribune* of 8 February:

I do not say that Futurism
May merely be astigmatism.
I do not urge the Futurist
To hasten to an oculist;
If this or that I can't divine,
It's eight to five the fault is mine.

(138)

The lay spectator thinks the modern artist needs glasses to correct poor eyesight, but it is in fact the lay spectator whose philosophical and aesthetic vision is in need of correction. Once enlightened the laiety will share the aesthetic vision of the cubist poet Gertrude Stein, and be fooled by any cynical perpetrator of "modern art", as the following day's *Tribune* has it:

I called the canvas *Cow with cud*
And hung it on the line,
Altho' to me 'twas vague as mud,
'Twas clear to Gertrude Stein.

(138)

"The naïve doggerel, the sophomoric satires, the puerile jokes at least reflected a certain amount of amiability," Brown notes, "but there were a great many people who were seriously disturbed by the new art. A sense of outrage underlay the hysterical vituperation of many spectators and critics" (140). The exhibition nevertheless made many sales and, as Fry's exhibitions did in England, enabled the beginnings of many important American private and public collections of Post-Impressionist and Modern art. But while "there were many favourable reviews and many enthusiastic defenders of the exhibition and new art", Dunlop points out, "there was no critic capable of giving a comprehensive explanation of modern art and its origins. The show could have done with a Roger Fry, or even someone with Clive Bell's ability to put across an aesthetic argument in a readable and persuasive way" (195). But if the Armory Show lacked the critical apparatus of the English formalists, it could match the Post-Impressionist shows for turbulent social, cultural and political context.

## Mabel Dodge's avant-garde evenings and the workers' pageant

The avant-garde gatherings such as those hosted by Mabel Dodge in New York might readily compare with Bloomsbury bohemianism. Mabel Dodge, a wealthy aesthete and friend of Gertrude Stein, was responsible for bringing together very diverse people in the heady years before and around the time of the New York Armory Show of 1913. While she was involved in the support of this show (see Milton Brown: 95), at her "evenings", Dodge would entertain "a troop of socialists, anarchists, cubists, feminists, reformers, syndicalists, labor leaders, poets and journalists" (Aaron: 13). Big Bill Haywood, a founding member of the IWW (the Industrial Workers of the World, commonly known as "the Wobblies"), was a regular star amongst Dodge's guests, passionately debating with the likes of Max Eastman avant-garde politics and art. Haywood's biography is spliced into the early scenes of John Dos Passos's *U.S.A.* (1930–6), but by the time of this novel's publication the Wobblies were no longer powerful. At the height of their powers in the first two decades of the century, members of this anarcho-syndicalist union got a very rough time from the authorities in the "red scares" of the 1910s and 1920s: many were lynched, some tarred and feathered, or jailed, and some eventually kicked out of America. Perhaps worse, their legends were absorbed and rearranged to fit with the later mythologies of the American Communists. But what brought the two circles of intellectuals and activists together in 1913 was not only the launching of modern art in the Armory Show, but also a major piece of industrial action. According to Daniel Aaron,

> It was not simply coincidence that Haywood and [the anarchists] Alexander Berkman and Emma Goldman attended Mabel Dodge's evenings with representatives of the 'angry idealistic college student generation', or that the rebel artists displayed equal enthusiasm for two important events of 1913: the New York Armory and the strike of the textile workers in Paterson New Jersey. (13)

The strike was organised by the IWW (see Foner) while Mabel Dodge and friends organised a pageant in support of it in Madison Square Gardens, in which the silk workers themselves dramatised their plight. The legendary journalist John Reed, who was to publish his report on the revolution in Mexico, in his book *Insurgent Mexico* (1914), was among Dodge's fellow organisers. This avant-garde cultural event did not, however, assist the workers in any significant way. The interpenetration of Wobbly industrial action and avant-garde art events, although an utter failure as far as the workers were concerned, is nevertheless of significance for understanding the reception of the modern art, which in this context might be thought of as dissident. Like the Post-Impressionist exhibitions in London, the New York Armory Show was understood as politically charged, and left a legacy of modernist and avant-garde aesthetics with this glamorous frisson to be recovered by later generations of "idealistic college student[s]" and "rebel artists". Perhaps over time we have come to think of such art as "transgressive" rather than "dissident" – just as the later American Abstract Expressionism may be seen as "transgressive" rather than "dissident".

But to return to the question of the literary impact of these artistic events: it has been a productive but limited critical strategy to interpret modernist developments in English, and more generally Anglophone, literature in the visual arts terms borrowed from the formalist theories and practices of Post-Impressionism. Writers at the time were sometimes themselves keen to work to such analogies. Woolf, for example, was aware of possible literary analogies to Post-Impressionism, something Roger Fry himself also encouraged (Woolf, *Roger Fry*, pp. 180, 183). Arnold Bennett, of all people, welcomes this possibility in his (at the time, almost uniquely) favourable review of *Manet and the Post-Impressionists*, which Woolf in turn reviewed: "These new pictures, he says, have wearied him of other pictures; is it not possible that some writer will come along and do in words what these men have done in paint?" (*Essays* 2, p. 130) But, before we go on to explore English literary and critical formalism further, it is worth noting another significant development in the visual arts which has shaped literary practice and criticism, and one which occurred about the same time.

## Paris, 1912: the birth of modern collage

Whereas in London, in 1912, English formalist theories were undergoing Fry's and Bell's refinements at the same time as British artists took up their own "Post-Impressionist" practices, in Paris, on the other hand, by 1912 avant-garde practice took an important turn of a different sort. Picasso introduced collage technique into easel painting in 1912, thus marking the transition from Analytical Cubism to Synthetic Cubism. His *Still Life with Chair Caning* (1912) has stuck to its surface a piece of manufactured oil-cloth printed with a caning design. There followed from this a series of works (*papiers-collés*) by Picasso and Braque in which similar, mass-produced printed materials were pasted to the picture surface: fragments and strips of newspapers, advertisements, playing cards, calling cards, wallpaper and so on. This technique greatly enriched the picture surface (Haftmann 2, p. 116), encouraging formalist interpretations suggestive of self-reflexive aesthetics; but it also made the picture surface resonate with references back to the "real world" (Robert Hughes: 32), itself apparently constituted in the detritus of printed matter intruding into the aesthetic realm, and this is properly the crux of its avant-garde status. The technique fed into other art movements, including Russian Constructivism, Surrealism, Dada, Merz and so on. It is worth remembering that, in the hands of some artists, collage could appear seamless. For example, Max Ernst's collage novel *Une Semaine de Bonté* (1933), for which Ernst cut up and re-assembled with "fanatical illusionistic precision" (Robert Hughes: 225) images from Victorian steel-engravings. Collage, and the related technique of montage, of course, greatly influenced literary composition too; and collage has come to be understood as "a general aesthetic principle . . . applied to both pictorial and verbal modes of expression" (Adamowicz: 4). The radically citational texts of Joyce, Eliot, and Pound have all been considered collagistic in their assemblage of diverse cultural and literary materials and discourses. But whereas it is almost a critical commonplace to identify Joyce's collagistic technique in *Ulysses,* for example, or Eliot's in *The Waste Land,* it is the formalist discourse of Fry and Bell that dominates interpretations of Woolf's works, which nevertheless might also very readily be understood as collagistic.

Woolf's sister, Vanessa Bell, who is credited with some of the earliest paintings of pure abstraction in Europe, was also using collage in her paintings around 1914/15, which may have been inspired by her use of *papier-collé* in interior decoration and other design work she did for the Omega Workshops, the progressive design studios set up by Fry in May 1913, employing artists to produce painted furniture, decorated ceramics, screens, murals and printed fabrics. But Bloomsbury also enjoyed sustained and direct contact with many important figures in the French avant-garde, and made frequent and extended visits to France, as Mary Ann Caws and Sarah Bird Wright have shown in *Bloomsbury and France: Art and Friends* (2000). Vanessa Bell bought a cubist Picasso in 1911 (*Letters,* p. 109), and while visiting Paris in January 1914, was taken by Gertrude Stein to meet Picasso in his studio. It was bristling with cubist constructions (Spalding: 126–7), as she writes to a fellow painter, Duncan Grant:

> All the bits of wood and frames had become like his pictures. Some of the newest ones are very lovely I thought. One gets hardly any idea of them from the photographs, which often don't show what is picture and what isn't. They are amazing arrangements of coloured papers and bits of wood which somehow do give me great satisfaction. (*Letters,* p. 160)

Her abstract and collaged paintings represent the brief moment in her career when Bell abandons all representational elements in her work, showing no differentiation between design and fine art. These works may be considered the closest she came to a fulfilment of Fry's and her husband's theories: form, colour and surface relationships are explored for their own sake and refer not to nature but only to themselves. They are self-reflexive and plastic just as Fry might have dictated. Bell's description of Picasso's collage technique emphasises the aesthetic qualities of form, colour and surface, and she seems to understand his aesthetically disrupted and disruptive frames in formalist terms. But the recognition that "the bits of wood and frames had become like his pictures" also shows an awareness of the way collage, in decorating frames while at the same time introducing external, three-dimensional materials into the painting, confuses the boundaries between art and life, and this sense of interpenetration itself may be understood as both formalist, in its sense of self-consciousness, and avant-garde in its sense of transgression.

A month later, in February 1914, Duncan Grant himself was taken by Stein to Picasso's studio, and he took with him at Picasso's request, he told Clive Bell, in a letter dated 26 February 1914, "a roll of old wallpaper which I have found in a cupboard in my hotel" (quoted Caws and Wright: 163) and which Picasso went on to use "in seven collages, now considered to be among his most significant creations", according to Caws and Wright (17). Grant reports that the wallpaper

> excited [Picasso] very much as he makes use of them frequently & finds it very difficult to get. He sometimes tears such pieces off the wall. I think I shall find it difficult to know what to say if I go alone. One wants Roger [Fry]'s tongue and Gertrude's bust to fall back onto. I must say I was very much impressed by his new works.
>
> (Quoted Caws and Wright: 163)

If Grant felt the need of Roger Fry's tongue (to leave aside Stein's bosom) – and therefore presumably his formalist theories – to communicate with Picasso, Caws and Wright still find it useful, along with Saussurean semiotics, for interpreting his collages "where", they find, "the signs no longer refer to the outside world but each other" (163). Yet the introduction of wallpaper sometimes actually torn from the walls, on the contrary, hardly suggests such a semiotic retreat from "the outside world", but rather refers us to wider forms of social and domestic framing beyond easel painting, at the same time pointing up the constructed and manufactured qualities of our environs.

Frances Spalding also finds Bloomsbury's own particular use of collaged paper as indicative of its short-lived flirtation with pure abstraction: "*Papier-collé,* flat and autonomous even when incorporated into a picture, led to experiments with purely abstract shapes" (168). Fry himself made abstract collages such as *Bus Tickets* (*c.* 1913), "in which he incorporated two tickets in a layout similar to the Picasso *Head of a Man* which he owned" (168). These "framed posies of tram tickets", as Sickert dismissed them (Spalding: 199), whether by Fry or Picasso, may be framed, and contained, by Fry's formalist theories, but by intruding onto the picture surface disparate fragments and materials (however flat), garnered from, and still in some sense *of,* the outside world, the collage technique in itself will always challenge such framing.

In the 1920s, Kurt Schwitters was to push collage into the extremes of its directions, collaging words and images and objects, and his aim was "the total work of art" [*Gesamkunstwerk*] (Elderfield: 44). He declared of his collage technique, in 1926, that it made "new art forms out of the remains of a former culture" (Elderfield: 12). The accumulation of detritus, clichés, the second hand, and so on, is the organising principle in his work. Nathanael West later termed this sort of technique "the apocalypse of the Second Hand" (Wisker: 175), and in his satire *A Cool Million* (1934) he has Chief Satinpenny itemise some of the basic materials of the modern collagist unwittingly introduced by the "paleface": "toilet paper, painted boxes to keep pins in, key rings, watch fobs, leatherette satchels". And as "the star of paleface is sinking" ("Spengler has said so; Valéry has said so"), Satinpenny calls for vengeance: "this is the time to run upon his neck and the bosses of his armor. While he is sick and fainting, while he is dying of a surfeit of shoddy" (217). West's satirical collagistic technique, then, attempts to transform America's "surfeit of shoddy".

The term "Merz", which Schwitters came to apply to all his work, originates from an advertisement for a bank, "Commerz und Privatbank" (Elderfield: 12). Schwitters thus fragments and reorganises the discourse of capitalism. Yet he considered his work to be spiritual, abstract, and formalist. His "Manifest Proletkunst" (1923), in the second issue of *Merz,* also signed by Tzara, Arp and Van Doesburg, declares: "Art is free in the use of its means in any way it likes, but is bound to its own laws and to its own laws alone. The minute it becomes art it becomes much more sublime than a class distinction between proletariat and bourgeoisie" (Elderfield: 42). Unlike the

Dadaists from whom he split, Schwitters's goal, according to Serge Lemoine, "was not to eliminate art but to transform it". He points out that Schwitters "did not invent collage as a medium, but he did give it a new moral value" (55). Schwitters's Merz differed from Berlin Dada in seeking to retain Art, albeit transformed by the gleanings of cultural detritus, as a transcendent force. On the other hand, the Berlin Dadaist and photomontagist John Heartfield, for example, declared, in "Der Kunstlump" (1920): "The concept of art and artist is a bourgeois invention, and within the state it can only take the side of the ruling, that is, the bourgeois caste" (Pachnicke and Honnet: 20). In his retrospective account, in 1967, of how he arrived at his innovative photomontage technique, he identifies himself not as an artist but as a soldier:

> I started making photomontages during the First World War. There are a lot of things that got me working with photos. The main thing is that I saw both what was being said and not being said with photos in the newspapers. The most important thing for me was that I intrinsically became involved in the opposition and worked with a medium I didn't consider to be an artistic medium, photography. . . . I was a soldier from early on. Then we pasted, I pasted and quickly cut out a photo and then put one under another. Of course, that produced another counterpoint, a contradiction that expressed something different. That was the idea. It still wasn't all that clear to me where it would lead to, or that it would lead me to photomontage. (Pachnicke and Honnet: 14)

First introduced into art work by Picasso in Paris 1912, collage, then, whether conceived as oppositional and anti-art, as with Heartfield, or as transformational of aesthetics, as with Schwitters, constitutes a truly international and avant-garde aesthetic. Its formal qualities, including the forms taken from disparate sources, provide the pictorial surface (where it remains) with a transgressive, sometimes dissident, hinge onto the real, outside world, at the same time transforming these materials into something new. But how is this outside world itself constituted? It seems appropriate now to broaden our discussion to consider the major social, political, and cultural shifts and changes in Western culture that form a wider context to the artistic practices and theories developing around 1910.

## The new multiverse: cultural shifts and changes

> The child born in 1900 would, then, be born into a new world which would not be a unity but a multiple. Adams tried to imagine it, and an education that would fit it. He found himself in a land where no one had ever penetrated before; where order was an accidental relation obnoxious to nature; artificial compulsion imposed on motion; against which every free energy of the universe revolted; and which, being merely occasional, resolved back into anarchy at last. He could not deny that the law of the new multiverse explained much that had been most obscure.
>
> Henry Adams, *The Education of Henry Adams* (1907)

The "new multiverse" (William James's term) that captivates Henry Adams is, according to a certain vintage of literary commentary, borne of rapid conurbisation, massive industrialisation, and huge and multiple technological and scientific innovations: the development and accessibility of transport, and huge increases in its speed; the emergence of visible and invisible communications such as photography, the cinema, the telephone, telegraphy and the wireless which resulted in the rapid transmission of news, ideas, and images on a scale previously unknown; the discoveries of X-rays and radium; the artificial generation of electricity and its use in everyday life; and not least, discoveries and hypotheses about the structure of matter, space, and time, and about the processes of perception, and the understanding of the self.

In 1901 Max Planck put forward his Quantum Theory exploding the traditional view of the atom as being organised like a miniature version of the solar system, made up of parts in permanent relation to each other. He helped to resolve the phenomenon of radiation: his investigations show that the energy distribution in the atom can only be described by the mathematics of chance. Then 1905 saw the publication of Albert Einstein's *Special Theory of Relativity*, with which Newton's absolute space and time as a necessary framework for physics came to an end. His argument was that no observation of the existence of these is possible; they are ideas given by the mind for the purpose of measuring things and on this special use is nefariously based a theory of their general existence as the framework of the universe. As science was beginning to assert reality as not objectively given but subjectively apprehended through the consciousness, the field of psychology reflected this fundamental shift. Exploration of the mechanisms of consciousness had developed in such influential works as William James's *Principles of Psychology* (1890); Henri Bergson's *Time and Free Will* (1889); and Sigmund Freud's *Interpretation of Dreams* (1900). The intellectual, social and political import of the works of Karl Marx, Charles Darwin and Friedrich Nietzsche was also vigorously explored. This sort of "history of ideas" approach may be supplemented by attention to the political contexts of empire and nation, political upheavals and revolution, the rise and turbulence of the working classes, the emergence of feminism, the flourishing of black urban culture (in America), the campaign for Home Rule in Ireland, the Great War, the Russian Revolution, the General Strike, and so on.

## Writers of the new multiverse: Blaise Cendrars and Ezra Pound

The new multiverse presented to artists and writers the challenge of how effectively to represent and express it, as well as the inspiration and sometimes the means for technical and conceptual innovation. The Eiffel Tower, erected in the late nineteenth century as a temporary construction to commemorate the French Revolution, and remaining for some time as the highest man-made structure, became in the early twentieth century a focus and a beacon for such aesthetic concerns. It was "a symbol", according to Virginia Spate, "of modern man's ability to escape from the earth", giving "those who ascended it a new awareness of the complexity of the city . . . no longer could they isolate a single view of the city, but instead they saw it as an infinity of views each melting imperceptibly into the next" (Spate [3]). She reminds us that in 1912, the Tower "was chosen as the wireless station to broadcast the signals used to co-ordinate time AROUND THE WORLD. Writers and artists soon began to use the Tower as an image for invisible waves of energy, for invisible communications across vast distances and for the radiation of consciousness from individual mind to 'the entire universe'" (Spate [3]). The Eiffel Tower becomes a powerful symbol of an heroic contemporary modernity, then, resonating with the import of such technological advances, and still also signalling its original conception as a celebration of historical revolution; its political, and aesthetic, avant-garde status declared in its amazing girdered form, a veritable homage to form itself, piercing the Parisian skyline, connecting urban humanity with the airwaves. The poet Blaise Cendrars celebrates the Tower in his Simultanist poem *Tower* (1913), and later eloquently recalls, in "La Tour Eiffel" (1924), the Tower's challenge to his generation of artists:

> No formula of art . . . could then claim to express the Tower pictorially. Realism reduced it; the old laws of Italian perspective diminished it . . . when we came close, it bent and leant over us. Seen from the first platform it corkscrewed; and seen from the top, it doubled in on itself, legs spread out, neck drawn in. . . . At midnight we didn't exist anymore, all its lights were for New York with whom it already flirted; at midday, it gave the hour to the ships on the high seas. . . . The first aeroplanes turned around it . . . (Quoted and translated Spate [3])

Cendrars' simultanist optimism was not shared by all of his contemporaries. The Great War has been seen as a great watershed, after which utopian visions of metropolitan and technological advance were dashed. Michael Levenson, for example, whose introduction to the *Cambridge Companion to Modernism* is worth dwelling on here, considers the impact of this "epoch of crisis" on the arts, emphasising how deeply the former is reflected in the latter:

> The catastrophe of the First World War, and before that the labor struggles, the emergence of feminism, the race for empire, these inescapable forces of turbulent social modernization were not simply looming on the outside as the destabilizing context of cultural Modernism; they penetrated the interior of artistic invention. They gave subjects to writers and painters, and they also gave forms, forms suggested by industrial machinery, or by the chuffing of cars, or even, most horribly, the bodies broken in war. (*Cambridge Companion*, p. 4)

Already the energy and optimism of Adams's "multiverse" vision, or of Marinetti's famous homage to "the beauty of speed", the "roaring" motor car (251), for example, are dwindling in this account: Levinson's cars chuff rather than speed. Levinson allows that while "the social cataclysms left traces on modernist art", this reflective function of art was also supplemented by a more interactive one: "so did that art inform and to an extent form the conception of social life within historical crisis" (4). But this is far from endorsing the Trojan

Horse style of "avant-gardiste protest" that Bürger envisions, "whose aim it is to reintegrate art into the praxis of life" (Bürger: 22). This becomes clearer in Levenson's apparently modifying comments on the critical approaches that paint the modernist decades "in unending shades of gray" (Levenson, *Cambridge Companion*, p. 4).

He is wary of leading his readers to the slough of despond in which earlier commentators have wallowed when recounting a doomy modernist *zeitgeist*: "Was modern civilization all a 'Heart of Darkness?' Was it an arid 'Waste Land?'" (4). There are certain foundational readings of Conrad's novella and Eliot's poem that emphasise nihilism, degeneration, and despair, and through which all other modernist texts are read, and which encourage an understanding of the institution of art as an autonomous haven far from the awful praxis of life. Levenson acknowledges that there is some veracity to this view: "It is fair, and indeed important, to preserve memory of an alienation, an uncanny sense of moral bottomlessness, a political anxiety. There was so much to doubt: the foundations of religion and ethics, the integrity of government and selves, the survival of redemptive culture" (5). But Levenson's amendment of this view merely endorses the perpetuation of art as autonomous haven, and suggests a rather stunted set of ambitions for some of the leading writers and artists of the period:

> But if the fate of the West seemed uncertain and shadowy, the struggles with the metrical scheme of lyric poetry or the pictorial space of a cubist painting could seem bracingly crisp. Shining luminously from so much of the work is the happiness of concentrated purpose and the pride of the cultural laborer, believing fully in the task at hand. (5)

Ezra Pound famously declares, in Canto LXXXI, that "the first heave" of his achievement was "to break the pentameter" – in itself suggestive of more than merely (Levenson's) "a *struggle* with the metrical system" – and this declaration should be read in the context of the great "draft" epic work in which it appears. Pound envisages his *Cantos* in terms of a dynamic intersecting of modern and ancient cultures, "a radiant world . . . of moving energies . . . magnetisms that take form, that are seen, or that border the visible, the matter of Dante's *paradiso*, the glass seen under water, the form that seems a form seen in a mirror" (*Literary Essays*, p. 154). These colossal formal achievements are entwined with Pound's political and historical vision of "the fate of the West" as Levinson puts it; for "an epic", according to Pound, "is a poem including history" (*Literary Essays*, p. 86). As well as drawing on such diverse cultural and historical sources as ancient Chinese, Renaissance Italian, and modern American, Pound rails against usury, an obsession of much anti-Semitic propaganda, and pays homage in his poem to the contemporary politics of Benito Mussolini whom he admires because, among other things, he "told his people that poetry is a necessity to the state" (*Guide to Kulchur*, p. 249). The *Cantos* explore and in places propound – as a matter of the poetic business in hand – his extreme right-wing politics, although they cannot be reduced to mere political sloganeering. To "break the pentameter", nevertheless, is to perform a rupture in aesthetics that extends into political and historical life.

## Poetics, politics, gender: Virginia Woolf, Dorothy Richardson and D. H. Lawrence

This is a period when poets' powerful opinions on poetic form were interpenetrating with their powerful and passionate political opinions and activities. Not all writers of the period were as extreme as Pound, but that different kinds of formal experimentalism might be linked to, and interpenetrate with, the current wide and volatile spectrum of politics was a matter of pressing interest to many. Virginia Woolf, for example, raises concerns about politics and aesthetics, in her polemic *A Room of One's Own* (1929), when she comments on the aspirations of the Italian Fascists for a poet worthy of fascism: "We may well join in that pious hope, but it is doubtful whether poetry can come out of an incubator. Poetry ought to have a mother as well as a father. The Fascist poem, one may fear, will be a horrid little abortion such as one sees in a glass jar in the museum of some county town" (134). Her contempt for the forced creation of a patriarchal poetry, however, does not prevent her from contemplating a literary form more suitable to feminist politics: "I went on to ponder how a woman nowadays would write a poetic tragedy in five acts. Would she use verse? – would she not use prose rather?" (100–1). Woolf's feminist opposition to a poetics of fascism seems to counter the fascist anti-feminism explicit in the earlier Futurist manifesto we sampled (in the Introduction), which seeks to "*glorify*" not only "*war* – the world's only hygiene – militarism, patriotism, the destructive gesture of freedom-bringers, beautiful ideas worth dying for" but also "*scorn for women*", as well as vowing to "destroy . . . feminism" (251). Avant-garde and modernist works, it seems, are inescapably shot through with a dissident gender politics interpenetrating with every shade of ideological position.

Woolf seems to confirm her theory of gendered aesthetic form in her (1923) review of Dorothy Richardson's novel *Revolving Lights*: "She has invented, or, if she has not invented, developed and applied to her own uses, a sentence which we might call the psychological sentence of the feminine gender. It is of a more elastic fibre than the old, capable of stretching to the extreme, of suspending the frailest particles, of enveloping the vaguest shapes" (*Essays* 3, p. 367). While many postmodernist-feminist critics, drawing on such statements by Woolf, have found a radical "sexual/textual politics" (the title of Toril Moi's landmark book on the subject) exemplified in the work of modernist writers such as Woolf and Stein, it would be too simplistic to assume "an equivalence", as Rita Felski warns, "between [aesthetic] experimentalism and [political] oppositionality", and in the light of historical and political context, it is also "increasingly implausible to claim that aesthetic radicalism equals political radicalism and to ground a feminist politics of the text in an assumption of the inherently subversive effects of stylistic innovation" (*Beyond Feminist Aesthetics*, p. 161). Such an "ultimately formalist" equation, according to Felski, "fail[s] to theorize the contingent functions of textual forms in relation to socially differentiated publics at particular historical moments" and does not take "into account the changing social meanings of textual forms" (161). Woolf herself, acknowledging that men too have constructed sentences similar to those by Richardson, points out that the difference lies with content and context rather than form alone:

> Miss Richardson has fashioned her sentence consciously, in order that it may descend to the depths and investigate the crannies of Miriam Henderson's consciousness. It is a woman's sentence only in the sense that it is used to describe a woman's mind by a writer who is neither proud nor afraid of anything that she may discover in the psychology of her sex. (*Essays* 3, p. 367)

A woman's sentence, then, according to Woolf, is the fruit of a woman writer's investigation of women's experiences, material and spiritual; and it is therefore defined by content as well as form. Felski's appeal to context actually entails a close attention to text. And it makes sense if we are not to find ourselves making clumsy generalisations about an homogeneous set of "subversive qualities" common to *all* modernist experimentalism, whether by Ezra Pound, John Heartfield or Virginia Woolf, each of whom has evidently created and developed a very different (differently formulated, differently articulated, differently nuanced, and differently mobilised), sophisticated aesthetic and political language.

It is unhelpful, in any case, to think of writers as consistently holding, and working from the same views about the relations between their aesthetics and politics throughout their lives or even during the creation of a particular work. D. H. Lawrence, for example, while in the midst of writing *Women in Love*, composed during the period of the Great War, seems to have understood his writing as an escape from contemporary horrors: "When one is shaken to the very depths, one finds reality in the unreal world. At present my real world is the world of my inner soul, which reflects on to the novel I write" (*Letters* 2, p. 610). If this seems to conform to Levenson's stereotype of the modernist writer's flight into aesthetics, then we can also find Lawrence formulating a more interventionist conception of *Women in Love* as a novel which "knocked the first loop-hole in the prison where we are all shut up" (*Letters* 2, p. 663), suggesting that his writing might be an instrument of social and political liberation. Indeed it might well be argued that his novel contributed to the formation of new approaches to social and sexual relations: "I can only write what I feel pretty strongly about: and that, at present, is the relations between men and women. After all, it is *the* problem of today, the establishment of a new relation, or the re-adjustment of the old one, between men and women" (*Letters* 1, p. 546).

Whatever Lawrence's own conceptions or intentions, his work was certainly received and understood as socially and politically challenging. Woolf, herself, while formulating a somewhat different set of gender politics, nevertheless recognises the import of such revolutionary achievements by Lawrence and other contemporary male writers in her two most cited and anthologised essays, "Modern Fiction" and "Mr Bennett and Mrs Brown", which have become the foundation for much modernist criticism.

## Virginia Woolf's "Modern Fiction" (1919; 1925): a manifesto of "modernism"?

"Modern Fiction", first published in *The Times Literary Supplement* (*TLS*) in April 1919 as "Modern Novels" and revised for Woolf's first collection of essays, the first *Common Reader* (1925: it is the revised, 1925, version of the essay – often misdated 1919 – that is commonly anthologised and cited here), is perhaps Woolf's best known and most frequently quoted essay. Woolf here distinguishes between the outmoded "materialism" of the Edwardian novelists H. G. Wells, John Galsworthy and Arnold Bennett, and the more "spiritual" and experimental writing of her Georgian contemporaries. The tyranny of plot and characterisation afflicts Bennett's work, she contends, along with the obligation "to provide comedy, tragedy, love interest, and an air of probability embalming the whole so impeccable that if all his figures were to come to life they would find themselves dressed down to the last button of their coats in the fashion of the hour". Such writing fails to capture "life", as Woolf's most famous and most quoted passage of criticism explains:

> Look within and life, it seems, is very far from being "like this". Examine for a moment an ordinary mind on an ordinary day. The mind receives a myriad impressions – trivial, fantastic, evanescent, or engraved with the sharpness of steel. From all sides they come, an incessant shower of innumerable atoms; and as they fall, as they shape themselves into the life of Monday or Tuesday, the accent falls differently from of old; the moment of importance came not here but there; so that, if a writer were a free man and not a slave, if he could write what he chose, not what he must, if he could base his work not upon convention, there would be no plot, no comedy, no love interest or catastrophe in the accepted style, and perhaps not a single button sewn on as the Bond Street tailors would have it. Life is not a series of gig lamps symmetrically arranged; life is a luminous halo, a semi-transparent envelope surrounding us from the beginning of consciousness to the end. Is it not the task of the novelist to convey this varying, this unknown and uncircumscribed spirit, whatever aberration or complexity it may display, with as little mixture of the alien and external as possible? (*Essays* 4, pp. 160–1)

This passage is, according to Randall Stevenson, in his introduction to modernist fiction (1992), "one of the most comprehensive and celebrated statements of the priorities of modernism" (59). Woolf's story "The Moment: Summer's Night" (*c.*1929) offers a closer, equally lyrical, account of a luminous "moment of vision", and is often cited in conjunction with this passage (see Guiguet; Harvena Richter):

> Yet what composed the present moment? If you are young, the future lies upon the present, like a piece of glass, making it tremble and quiver. If you are old, the past lies upon the present, like a thick glass, making it waver, distorting it. All the same, everybody believes that the present is something, seeks out different elements in this situation in order to compose the truth of it, the whole of it (*The Moment*, p. 9)

Woolf, it seems, sees the novelist's task as to somehow capture the moment – or life – and give the "truth of it". As if fiction were a contraption to catch butterflies, or the mind a piece of blotting paper with which to soak in life unadulterated. In "Modern Fiction", she continues with almost a call to automatic writing:

> Let us record the atoms as they fall upon the mind in the order in which they fall, let us trace the pattern, however disconnected and incoherent in appearance, which each sight scores upon the consciousness. Let us not take for granted that life exists more fully in what is commonly thought big than is commonly thought small. (161)

Citing "Modern Fiction", and with particular attention to the "luminous halo" passage, David Lodge summarises in his influential book *The Modes of Modern Writing* (1977) the dominant, and enduring, formalist modernist critical credo:

> Modernist fiction is concerned with consciousness, and also with the subconscious and unconscious workings of the human mind. Hence the structure of external "objective" events essential to traditional narrative art is diminished in scope and scale, or presented very selectively and obliquely, or is almost completely dissolved, in order to make room for introspection, analysis, reflection and reverie. A modernist novel has no real "beginning", since it plunges us into a flowing stream of experience with which we gradually familiarize ourselves by a process of inference and association; and its ending is usually "open" or ambiguous. . . . To compensate for the diminution of narrative structure and unity, alternative methods of aesthetic

> ordering become more prominent, such as allusion to or imitation of literary models or mythical archetypes, and the repetition-with-variation of motifs, images, symbols – a technique variously described as "rhythm", "Leitmotif" and "spatial form". Modernist fiction eschews the straight chronological ordering of its material, and the use of a reliable, omniscient and intrusive narrator. It employs, instead, either a single, limited point of view, or a method of multiple points of view, all more or less limited and fallible: and it tends towards a fluid or complex handling of time, involving much cross-reference backwards and forwards across the chronological span of action. (45–6)

In advocating subjective, fleeting, interior experience as the proper stuff of fiction along with the abandonment of conventional plot, genre, and narrative structure, this essay by Woolf has become one of the standard critical sources in the discussion of modernist literary qualities – particularly "stream-of-consciousness" – not least because it includes a (not uncritical) defence of Joyce's work. Woolf cites his *Portrait of the Artist as a Young Man* and the extracts from *Ulysses* recently published in the *Little Review* (1918) to exemplify the new "spiritual" writing. Joyce, she argues, is "concerned at all costs to reveal the flickerings of that inmost flame which flashes its messages through the brain" (*Essays* 4, p. 161). Woolf's alchemical imagery here owes much to Walter Pater's aesthetics (see Meisel), and her concern with subjective temporality – the epiphanic "moment", and the reception of a flow of images, experiences, and emotions – to the philosophy of Henri Bergson (see Kumar). Her "luminous halo" image also echoes an image of an "enveloping . . . misty halo" in Joseph Conrad's *Heart of Darkness* (3). Although Woolf identifies, in "Modern Fiction", a fragment of *Ulysses* ("Hades", extracts of which appeared in the American magazine the *Little Review* in September 1918, and in the British *The Egoist* in July and September 1919 – of which more in Chapter 3) as a "masterpiece" for "its brilliancy, its sordidity, its incoherence, its sudden lightning flashes of significance", she nevertheless finds that it "fails to compare" with the work of Joseph Conrad or Thomas Hardy "because of the comparative poverty of the writer's mind" (161). Woolf is less generous to Joyce in private. On reading *Ulysses*, she notoriously captures him in her diary as "a queasy undergraduate scratching his pimples" (*Diary* 2, p. 188). "Modern Fiction" nevertheless stands as an early and significant defence of his work, and as a manifesto of modernism.

But this complex manifesto-essay is often reduced in critical discussion to the passages cited above. Woolf's injunction to "look within" and her description of the mind as a *tabula rasa*, passively receptive to "a myriad impressions", along with her imagery of luminosity, become perfect fodder for interiorised, *reflective*, impressionistic models of modernist aesthetics where literature becomes the subjective site of an aesthetic haven, removed from the vicissitudes of life and certainly remote from political life. Woolf's rhetorical questions "Is life like this? Must novels be like this?" (*Essays* 4, p. 160), suggest a line of enquiry based on an aesthetics of imitation – that is, art as reflective, imitation of life; and her injunction, "Let us record the atoms as they fall upon the mind in the order in which they fall," suggests the writer as mere reporter from the interface of subjective consciousness and outer reality. But it should be noted that these passages arise from Woolf's meditations on *Joyce's* new fictional methods. Woolf's own "method" in the essay in which they appear is to describe the attractions of her contemporaries' methods and then show their shortcomings. After questioning whether "Mr Bennett has come down with his magnificent apparatus for catching life just an inch or two on the wrong side", she finds: "Life escapes; and perhaps without life nothing else is worthwhile" (159). Having noted the near miss of Bennett's materialist methods, she now turns her attention to Joyce's "spiritual" methods, before moving on to the "influence" of the Russians, and of Chekov in particular. Sympathetic with all of these approaches, she nevertheless exposes their limitations – and this includes the "luminous halo" approach.

Woolf does not leave "the comparative poverty of [his] mind" as her explanation of Joyce's failure: "But is it not possible to press a little further and wonder whether we may not refer our sense of being in a bright yet narrow room, confined and shut in, rather than enlarged and set free, to some limitation imposed by the method as well as by the mind" (161). In referring to the confining space of "a bright yet narrow room", Woolf seems to be opening up for criticism the "luminous halo" passage she has used to introduce Joyce's work, or at the very least suggesting his halo is not big or luminous enough! It may well be the "method" described in that very passage, then, that she seems to be criticising when she asks:

> Is it the method that inhibits the creative power? Is it due to the method that we feel neither jovial or magnanimous, but centred in a

> self which, in spite of its tremor of susceptibility, never embraces or creates what is outside itself and beyond? Does the emphasis laid, perhaps didactically, upon indecency, contribute to the effect of something angular and isolated? Or is it merely that in any effort of such originality it is much easier, for contemporaries especially, to feel what it lacks than to name what it gives? (162)

Here we are alerted to the risk of solipsism and isolation inherent in the subjective methodology of the "luminous halo" approach as practised by Joyce. Joyce's accent – or emphasis – also falls too heavily upon the scatological, Woolf opines. Just as Bennett's materialism misses the mark, so too does the "spiritual" Joyce, however laudable his experimentalism.

Interestingly, Woolf goes on to explore, in later works, a dualistic aesthetic that combines both the material and the spiritual. In "The New Biography" (1927), for example, she describes the art of biography as "that queer amalgamation of dream and reality, that perpetual marriage of granite and rainbow", which corresponds to the combination of "truth" and "personality", and allows us access to "not only the outer life of work and activity but the inner life of emotion and thought", and is concerned as much with the "uneventful lives of poets and painters" as with "the lives of soldiers and statesmen" (*Essays* 4, p. 474). Her dualism, "granite and rainbow", has become helpful critical shorthand for her work's increasing engagement with dualisms, contraries and oppositions. "Modern Fiction" explores both the outer, material, and the inner, spiritual as dialectical positions out of which will emerge Woolf's "perpetual marriage of granite and rainbow".

Critical focus on the "luminous halo" passage has meant a lack of attention to the oppositional energies at work in "Modern Fiction". For example, in pursuing the spiritual aspects of modern literature, Woolf urges us to consider the influence of Russian literature, as a corrective to materialist tendencies in English: "If we want understanding of the soul and heart where else shall we find it of comparable profundity? If we are sick of our own materialism the least considerable of their novelists has by right of birth a natural reverence for the human spirit" (163). Peter Kaye's chapter on Woolf in his stimulating book *Dostoevsky and English Modernism, 1900–1930*, offers a perceptive reading of Woolf's "perhaps tongue-in-cheek" admiration of Russian fiction here: "While recognizing that cultural differences militate against an assimilation of Russian modes of thought or writing, she draws upon their fiction to illustrate the infinite elasticity of the literary imagination" (79). And Kaye recommends that Woolf's essay "The Russian Point of View" (1925) "should be read as a companion-piece to 'Modern Fiction' (both were first published in *The Common Reader*)" (79). Yet her line of argument does not settle with this point. She also sees something in English letters that is missing in the "comprehensive and compassionate" Russian mind:

> But perhaps we see something that escapes them, or why should this voice of protest mix itself with our gloom? The voice of protest is the voice of another and an ancient civilisation which seems to have bred in us the instinct to enjoy and fight rather than to suffer and understand. English fiction from Sterne to Meredith bears witness to our natural delight in humour and comedy, in the beauty of earth, in the activities of the intellect, and in the splendour of the body. ("Modern Fiction", p. 163)

In this stimulating passage, which has escaped the sort of critical attention lavished on the "luminous halo", Woolf points up a distinctly English tradition in a heady mix of dissent, rationalism, humour, materialism, pleasure and sensuousness with which we might temper the spiritual qualities discerned in Russian literature. It seems ironical, if not somewhat provocative, that, in the volatile period after the Russian Revolution, when Woolf was working on this essay, she should choose to characterise Russian culture as long-suffering and stoical, and the English as full of "protest" and "fight". She is, nevertheless, identifying and championing an Enlightenment tradition in English letters overlooked by the many commentators on "Modern Fiction" whose sights remain so tightly locked on the "luminous halo". The passive aesthetic sensibility associated with the "luminous halo", and then passed as the formula for Modernist fiction, should more properly be read alongside the oppositional credo of "protest" and "fight" expressed here in the essay's conclusion. The closing three sentences of this final paragraph are also worth careful consideration.

> But any deductions that we may draw from the comparison of two fictions so immeasurably far apart are futile save indeed that they flood us with a view of the infinite possibilities of the art and remind

> us that there is no limit to the horizon, and that nothing – no "method", no experiment, even of the wildest – is forbidden, but only falsity and pretence. "The proper stuff of fiction" does not exist; everything is the proper stuff of fiction, every feeling, every thought; every quality of brain and spirit is drawn upon; no perception comes amiss. And if we can imagine the art of fiction come alive and standing in our midst, she would undoubtedly bid us break her and bully her, as well as honour and love her, for so her youth is renewed and her sovereignty assured. (163–4)

The essay concludes, not with a recommendation of any one credo for writing fiction ("luminous halo" or otherwise), but with a celebration of "the infinite possibilities of the art". Interestingly, it is in the later version of the essay that Woolf inserts, in her statement that "nothing is forbidden", the parenthetical embellishment " – no 'method', no experiment, even of the wildest – ". Perhaps the appearance, in the intervening years between the 1919 and 1925 versions of her essay, of her friend, Eliot's essay "*Ulysses*, Order and Myth" (1923), is the source of her citation of "method". For it is here that Eliot famously – and dogmatically – pronounces on Joyce's "mythical method" as "a method which others must pursue after him" (Kolocotroni et al.: 373). It is possible that Woolf's 1925 version of "Modern Fiction" opens a critical dialogue with Eliot's 1923 essay (a possibility that is lost when her essay is misdated 1919). Her defence of Joyce is less dogmatic than Eliot's, her manifesto more open. In declaring "everything is the proper stuff of fiction", Woolf departs from Eliot's coded exclusivity (for the "mythical method" is to be achieved by "only those who have won their own discipline in secret" (Kolocotroni et al.: 373). Her later criticism, such as *A Room of One's Own* (1929) and "The Leaning Tower" (1940), shows a commitment to opening up the genre in new ways for women and the working classes both as the writers of, and the "stuff of fiction".

Woolf's closing line in "Modern Fiction" is troubling and intriguing in figuring the art of fiction as a messianic woman seeking transformational violence to her person, as a necessary means for the renewal of her youth and of her beauty. In the earlier version of the essay, "Modern Novels" (1919), this female personification of fiction is even more disturbingly passive and masochistic:

> All that fiction asks of us is that we should break her and bully her,

> honour and love her, till she yields to our bidding, for so her youth is perpetually renewed and her sovereignty assured. (*Essays* 3, p. 36)

Here and in the later version, the writer is positioned with the "three-person'd God" whom the speaker of John Donne's Holy Sonnet 14 beseeches to "batter my heart". In Donne's poem, spiritual renewal and the innocence of chastity are paradoxically made possible through defilement:

> That I may rise and stand, o'erthrow me, and bend
> Your force to break, blow, burn, and make me new.
> . . .
> Take me to You, imprison me, for I,
> Except You'enthrall me, never shall be free,
> Nor ever chaste, except You ravish me. (443)

It is difficult not to read Donne's bullying God and Woolf's bullying writer as masculine, given his imagery of penetration and rape, and her gendering of the victim as feminine. Woolf seems to be making parodic and subversive use of a traditional, mythical and Christian trope that outlines the renewal of masculine sovereignty through the momentary obliteration of violent assault, and violent assault by feminine forces (see Goldman, *Feminist Aesthetics*, pp. 61–3). Renewal through suffering, of course, directs us to the redemptive act of the crucifixion (where the suffering body of Christ might be considered, in keeping with orthodox gender codes, feminine), but it has earlier mythical resonances, as the influential work *The Golden Bough*, by James Frazer, illustrates. In Part Three: *The Dying God* (1911), he describes the ancient cult of the "Kings of the Wood", who "die a violent death" but who may also

> escape from it for a time by their bodily strength and agility; for in several of these northern customs the flight and pursuit of the king is a prominent part of the ceremony, and in one case at least if the king can outrun his pursuers he retains his life and his office for another year. . . . The life of the god-man is prolonged on the condition of his shewing, in a severe physical contest of fight or flight, that his bodily strength is not decayed, and that, therefore, the violent death, which sooner or later is inevitable, may for the present be postponed. (Frazer: 212–13)

The recommendation of shocking violence towards a female figure personifying certain writerly values is also adopted by Woolf, in "Professions for Women" (a paper read to the Women's Service League in 1931, and posthumously published in 1942), against her target, "the Angel in the House", the personification of the anti-feminist forces plaguing the woman writer:

> I turned upon her and caught her by the throat. I did my best to kill her. . . . Had I not killed her she would have killed me. She would have plucked the heart out of my writing. For, as I found, directly I put pen to paper, you cannot review even a novel without having a mind of your own, without expressing what you think to be the truth about human relations, morality, sex. And all these questions, according to the Angel in the House, cannot be dealt with freely and openly by women. (151)

Clearly Woolf is not recommending violence for the sake of vigorous renewal of the angel, although the Angel in the House does not go away so easily: "She died hard. Her fictitious nature was of great assistance to her. It is far harder to kill a phantom than a reality. She was always creeping back when I thought I had despatched her" (153). But it is out of the struggle with this nemesis, that Woolf's preferred model of the woman writer arises. In her figure of fiction for both the 1919 and the 1925 versions of "Modern Fiction", Woolf, at the same time as recommending the renewal of fiction by the violent disruption of tradition, manages both to attack the notion of the feminine as a personifying vehicle; and assert a feminine sovereignty by inverting the gender associations of mythic renewal by violence.

Woolf's mythical personification of fiction here is in some ways the (rainbow-like) antithesis of the mundane (or granite-like) figure of "Mrs Brown", who stands for the elusive fictional object of "life" in Woolf's companion essay, "Mr Bennett and Mrs Brown", which we will consider below. It is useful to note here that these two different feminine aspects of the art of writing anticipate the dualistic model Woolf later puts forward in *A Room of One's Own*, where she outlines a significant discrepancy between women in the real world and "woman" in the symbolic order:

> Imaginatively she is of the highest importance; practically she is completely insignificant. She pervades poetry from cover to cover;

> she is all but absent from history. She dominates the lives of kings and conquerors in fiction; in fact she was the slave of any boy whose parents forced a ring upon her finger. Some of the most inspired words, some of the most profound thoughts in literature fall from her lips; in real life she could scarcely spell, and was the property of her husband. (56)

Woolf here points up not only the relatively sparse representation of women's experience in historical records, but also the more complicated business of how the feminine is already caught up in the conventions of representation itself; how women may be represented at all when "woman", in poetry and fiction, is already a signifier in patriarchal discourse, functioning as part of the symbolic order: "It was certainly an odd monster that one made up by reading the historians first and the poets afterwards – a worm winged like an eagle; the spirit of life and beauty in a kitchen chopping suet. But these monsters, however amusing to the imagination, have no existence in fact" (56). Woolf converts this dual image to a positive emblem for a feminist writing:

> What one must do to bring her to life was to think poetically and prosaically at one and the same moment, thus keeping in touch with fact – that she is Mrs Martin, aged thirty-six, dressed in blue, wearing a black hat and brown shoes; but not losing sight of fiction either – that she is a vessel in which all sorts of spirits and forces are coursing and flashing perpetually. (56–7)

The poetic "vessel" aspect of the feminine as "fiction" is anticipated by the mythical figure personifying "the art of fiction" at the close of "Modern Fiction"; the factual aspect personified as "Mrs Martin" in *A Room of One's Own* is anticipated by "Mrs Brown" in "Mr Bennett and Mrs Brown". This bivalent model, embracing at its extremes prose and poetry, fact and fiction, is of central importance to Woolf's modernist aesthetic, encapsulated in the term "granite and rainbow". In the essay "Poetry, Fiction and the Future" (1927; also known as "The Narrow Bridge of Art"), Woolf acknowledges the different tasks each traditionally performs, but is interested in creating a new form of writing that marries prose and poetry: "[Poetry] has always insisted on certain rights, such as rhyme, metre, poetic diction. She has never been used for the common purpose of life. Prose has taken all the dirty work on to her own shoulders; has answered letters, paid bills, written articles, made speeches, served the needs of business men shopkeepers, lawyers, soldiers, peasants" (*Essays* 4, p. 434). Woolf's personification of poetry as a militant "insist[ing] on certain rights" suggests a politicisation of poetics, but she makes us re-read poetry as an aristocrat clinging to certain traditional privileges when she personifies prose as a servant taking on "all the dirty work". She anticipates a new form of writing in a "prose which has many of the characteristics of poetry", asking whether prose can "chant the elegy, or hymn the love, or shriek in terror, or praise the rose" (436) and so on. This is a celebration of the new lyrical prose of modernism – and indeed of her own novel *To the Lighthouse*, which she famously christened an elegy (see *Diary* 3, p. 34); and it is imbued with the rhetoric of class war: the domain of (courtly) love poetry is to be opened to and transformed by the stevedore of prose. Woolf simultaneously explores the gender implications of this new form of writing and puts it forward as a feminist tool.

By drawing attention to the feminist legacy, apparent in her later work, of these early feminine figures in Woolf's supposedly "high modernist" criticism, I am trying to confirm an implicit feminist subtext at work in "Modern Fiction" and "Mr Bennett and Mrs Brown". It is as if Woolf goes on, in her later work (the overtly feminist and materialist tract *A Room of One's Own*, in particular), to explore more explicitly the gender politics already at work in her earlier essays. But even without the benefit of Woolf's later critical insights, it is evident that Woolf's early formulations on what has become known implicitly as "Modern*ist* Fiction" are bound up with questions of gender, sexuality and feminism, just as the modernist period itself is dominated by them. It is also evident that these early formulations are not rejecting "materialism" out of hand, so much as harnessing it in a dualistic model of aesthetics which does not settle either for spirituality or for materialism, but attempts to keep both in play, and transform, or at times even synthesise, both.

The gender politics touched on here will be more fully explored in Part II. But now, let us turn to Eliot's monumental modernist essay "Tradition and the Individual Talent".

# 3 Tradition, Order, War and the Dead

## Critical and Cultural Contexts for T. S. Eliot's "Tradition and the Individual Talent"

### Introduction

Whereas Woolf's "Modern Fiction" has been an important source for modernist critical methodologies and reading practice, Eliot's "Tradition and the Individual Talent", published shortly after the first version of Woolf's essay ("Modern Novels"), has become foundational in theorising modernism, by providing a general framework and critical apparatus. It has shaped a particular critical context, then, in which we read Modernism. The essay also provides a critical vocabulary for thinking about individual texts in larger contexts, or individual writers within a (or *the*) canon. From this derives a tricky theory of subjectivity, Eliot's anti-Romantic notion of poetic impersonality. Most importantly, Eliot's essay seeks to position change and "the new" firmly back in "tradition", in an unchanging ideal order remote from the specificities of historical change that we have come to associate, for example, with the date of December 1910.

This chapter begins to examine "Tradition and the Individual Talent" in relation to the critical, theoretical, cultural, political and historical contexts in which it has been positioned, and in which it positions itself. It samples the approaches of critics who have emphasised the rise of New Criticism, and the trajectory of Eliot's body of critical work, as the most important contexts to understand his theses, and of those who prefer to look at historical and cultural contexts, such as the Great War, the Russian Revolution, or the rise of fascism. The essay's place in a tradition of formalist, modernist and avant-garde criticism is discussed with special reference to the influential theories of Clement Greenberg, emerging in the 1940s. The essay is also explored for its cultural resonance of memorialising in the era of national mourning after the Great War. There follows a sampling of differing critical approaches to Eliot's "ideal order", and a discussion of his theory of impersonality. It is at this crucial point in the argument that Eliot's essay comes to a stop for its first readers, who had to wait for the next issue of *The Egoist* to read on. This chapter concludes by examining what follows on, in the pages of this journal, after the first instalment of Eliot's essay: the "Hades" episode from James Joyce's *Ulysses,* which itself provides insight into modernist discourses of hell, elegy, mourning and tradition. So the chapter ends, then, by introducing the material, published context in which Eliot's essay first appeared, a context that will provide further food for thought in Chapter 4.

## "Tradition and the Individual Talent" (1919)

Two years after the publication of Eliot's first, ground-breaking volume of poetry, *Prufrock and Other Observations* (1917), and three years in advance of *The Waste Land* (1922), this seminal modernist essay was first published, in two parts, in the journal on which Eliot was assistant editor, *The Egoist* of September and December 1919 (five months after Woolf's "Modern Novels" appeared in the *TLS*). Republished several times in the poet's lifetime, "Tradition and the Individual Talent" has been avidly cited and anthologised by Modernist criticism ever since. More than this, it has been the pedagogical foundation for institutionalising literary canons. The essay's two main propositions concern, first, the mutually adjusting relations between the individual poet or artist and an "ideal order" – or canon – of art (54); and secondly, the status and role of the poet's emotions and "personality" in the production of poetry. It culminates in the identification of "*significant* emotion" (73), which is an aesthetic emotion paradoxically arising from poetic "impersonality": "What happens is a continual surrender of himself as he is at the moment to something which is more valuable. The progress of an artist is a continual self-sacrifice, a continual extinction of personality" (55). This is a dynamic process of repeated cycles of artistic "surrender" to an ideal order of aesthetics and artistic resurrection. More generally, it puts forward a way of thinking about the individual in relation to larger orders or systems. The following discussion will attempt to read the essay in some detail, paying attention to Eliot's framing of his propositions and to some of the contexts in which the essay was first, and then later, published. But it seems helpful and appropriate first to consider some of the different wider contexts – or orders – in which we might think about the essay, given its own special interest in the positioning of individual talents or works in the context of larger orders or systems.

## Orders and contexts: Eliot's essay in literary traditions in historical contexts

Louis Menand, for example, in his chapter on Eliot for *The Cambridge History of Literary Criticism,* places "Tradition and the Individual Talent" in the context of Eliot's critical writing as a whole, and sees it in dialogue with, and indeed as a solution to, "Hamlet and His Problems" (1919), another important and much cited essay, which appeared in the *Athenaeum* in the same month that "Tradition and the Individual Talent" was published in *The Egoist* (Menand: 30). It puts forward Eliot's "objective correlative" thesis: Shakespeare's *Hamlet,* Eliot contends, is an artistic failure because it does not find the appropriate "objective correlative" for Hamlet's state of mind. Menand finds the main propositions of "Tradition and the Individual Talent" refuted in "The Function of Criticism" (1923), published by Eliot in his journal *The Criterion* (Menand: 33). He also helpfully places Eliot's career as critic within the larger context of emergent, modern academic English studies. Indeed, the context of English studies, in which most students first encounter Eliot, is still greatly shaped by his critical interventions, and it is certainly difficult to disassociate him from the wider context of "the modern academy", which, as Menand points out, "at a crucial moment in its history, made a representative figure of Eliot. And this suggests that the answer to the question of Eliot's success [as literary critic] is likely to be found not simply in what Eliot had to say, but in the institutional needs his writing was able to serve" (19–20). Eliot's early critical achievement lies, according to Menand, in his "isolating for criticism the domain of literary values – a strategy that was itself intended as an act of criticism, since he thought that one of the deplorable aspects of modern culture . . . was the adulteration of poetry and the criticism of poetry by the intrusion of extraliterary interests" (18). Eliot's pioneering formalism extends from poetry to criticism: poetry is essentially literary and literary criticism is purely concerned with literature as literary. The achievement of Eliot's literary criticism was, therefore, to answer "a specifically modern need to make literary criticism an autonomous discipline. This need was the consequence of the emergence of the modern university, with its formally defined disciplines and its scientistic organisation of knowledge production" (55). Menand, then, reminds us that the student reading "Tradition and the Individual Talent" in the context of a university English Department is reading in an intellectual environment still shaped by its author's ideas.

Stan Smith, on the other hand, reads "Tradition and the Individual Talent" with attention to a different, and wider historical and political context. He has pointed out Eliot's strangely "persistent mis-dating" of the essay as first published in 1917, the year of the Russian Bolshevik Revolution (*Origins of Modernism,* p. 41). Smith shows how much of Eliot's work may be read as responding to the period of international crisis following this event. "As a young man Eliot", he points out, "had witnessed the collapse of the old imperial order and the groundswell of proletarian revolution throughout Europe which followed the Great War. He had worked for Lloyds Bank on the financial implications of the reparations agreements and the post-war redrawing of European boundaries in the Treaty of Versailles" (25). His work for Lloyds Colonial and Foreign Department appears to have given him special insight into the impact of revolution. Smith takes Eliot's apparently deliberate misdating of his essay as evidence of a "hidden agenda" for "Tradition and the Individual Talent":

> If a tardy history delayed its actual writing for another two years, 1917 was in retrospect the necessary symbolic moment for such an essay to be published. Throughout Eliot's life then a deep unconscious association links his slyly subversive text with the momentous events of a Europe in revolutionary ferment. In 1919 the Red Army under Trotsky's command was sweeping unresisted across the frontiers of eastern Europe, as Modernism was advancing on all fronts against an enfeebled cultural orthodoxy. For Eliot the moment of Modernism coincided with the moment of Bolshevism in which traditions and

> frontiers were also overthrown in the creation of a new order. (*Origins of Modernism*, p. 41)

Smith's provocative likening of the (apparently homogeneous and already fully-fledged) artistic forces of "Modernism" – and Eliot in particular (who was not known for his left-wing sympathies) – to the armies of Bolshevism, opens up a number of pressing issues concerning the relation of art and politics, of art and history, and not least the issue of mixing metaphors. This tongue-in-cheek modernist criticism flirts with the unspoken name of the avant-garde, a military term seized by the arts to connote both the revolutionary overthrow of traditional aesthetic orders and the breaking down of barricades between art and life. Having shown him to have held, in 1933, some quirky and unexpected literary "theoretical affinities with Trotsky" (24), it is, nevertheless, refreshingly playful of Smith to figure T. S. Eliot, who famously declared himself, in 1928, in allegiance with classicism, monarchism, and Catholicism, calling himself "classicist in literature, royalist in politics, and anglo-catholic in religion" (Menand: 48), and Ezra Pound, notorious for his fascist sympathies, as "two 'literary Bolsheviks', the Lenin and the Trotsky of Modernism", who, with the publication in 1917 of their volumes of poetry, Eliot's *Prufrock and Other Observations* and Pound's *Homage to Sextus Propertius*, fired "the first shots in the revolution of the word" (*Origins of Modernism*, p. 41). Such humour was not lost on Eliot, who acknowledges, in 1933, "a time when [Pound] and I and our colleagues were mentioned by a writer in *The Morning Post* as 'literary bolsheviks'" (quoted Smith: 29). Smith reads this as a sign "of Eliot's amused if anxious recognition of his role as the father-figure of a Modernist literary revolution now identified in its second generation [W. H. Auden and Stephen Spender] with the political revolution of Marxism" (29). But the absurd analogy of Eliot as Bolshevik depends for its humour, of course, on the elision of significant political and aesthetic differences in the vast spectrum of "Modernist" positions and on the emptying of the term Bolshevism of its particular historical, political – and *aesthetic* – resonances.

How revolutionary, in the Bolshevik sense of the word, is Eliot's work? Revolutionary – or Bolshevik – enough to sustain a reversal of the metaphor, and call Lenin and Trotsky the Eliot and Pound of politics? Does Eliot's vision of a new order in any way resemble that of Lenin or Trotsky? Is the Trotsky of the analogy to be considered as pre-dating the Trotsky expelled from Russia in 1929? These are interesting questions to ponder, and not necessarily straightforward to answer, but we might first acknowledge that a more authentic and less problematic candidate for the title "literary Bolshevik", for example, would presumably be the Russian avant-garde poet Vladimir Mayakovsky, a co-founder of *Lef* ("Left Front of the Arts"), whose manifesto of 1923 announced (in Russian, German and English):

> Comrades! Split leftist art from rightist everywhere!
> With leftist art prepare the European Revolution; in the USSR, strengthen it. . . . Only in conjunction with the Workers' Revolution can we see the dawn of future art.
> We, who have worked for five years in a land of revolution, know:
> That only October has given us new, tremendous ideas that demand new artistic organization.
> Only the October Revolution, which liberated art from bourgeois enslavement, has given freedom to art.
> Down with the boundaries of countries and studios!
> Down with the monks of rightist art!
> Long live the single front of the leftists!
> Long live the art of the Proletarian Revolution!
>
> (Bowlt: 201–2)

This rhetoric powerfully echoes that of earlier Russian futurist manifestos, such as Natan Altman's "'Futurism' and Proletarian Art" (1918), declaring:

> Like the old world, the capitalist world, works of the old art live an individualistic life.
> Only futurist art is constructed on collective bases.
> Only futurist art is right now the art of the proletariat.
>
> (Bowlt: 164)

Eliot's espousal of a radical relationship between individual artist and "Tradition" may well be read with this sort of rhetoric in mind, but only as a refutation, presumably, of such calls for a collective and revolutionary front of artists in the service of a proletarian revolution sweeping away traditional order and hierarchy, marking simultaneous rupture with the artistic and political past. Eliot's manifesto seems framed in the cause of a somewhat different aesthetic and political agenda ("the monks of rightist art", perhaps) – radical-reactionary or counter-revolutionary, that is, rather than revolutionary. "Tradition and the Individual Talent" is not so much a call to unite living contemporaries as "an expression", in Frank Lentricchia's terms, "of Eliot's desire for community-in-history". And community, he explains, perpetuating Eliot's misdating of the essay, "meant for Eliot, in 1917, the literary tradition since, and proceeding from, Homer" (259).

## Orders and contexts: Eliot's essay and the critical discourses of modernism and the avant-garde

It is also worth noting a broader context to Eliot's "amusement" in recollecting, in 1933, his more youthful Bolshevik epithet. Stan Smith points out that at this time, shortly after Hitler's achieving "an absolute majority in the Reichstag" (*Origins of Modernism*, 27), "it was hardly necessary for Eliot . . . to distance himself from his younger contemporaries, that generation of leftists [Auden and Stephen Spender] he had recently begun to publish at Faber and Faber . . . for there is little chance that his audience will identify Eliot's Modernism with theirs" (28–9). But a political context just as salient to Eliot's amusement is the left's growing disaffection with "modernism" itself, emanating from Soviet denunciations of avant-garde practices in favour of socialist realism, and culminating in the 1932 Central Committee of the All-Union Communist Party (Bolsheviks) Decree on the Reconstruction of Literary and Artistic Organisations, which "prepared the ground for the conclusive advocacy of socialist realism at the First All-Union Congress of Soviet Writers in 1934" (Bowlt: 288). Mayakovsky committed suicide in 1930; after which Soviet criticism, forgetting his Futurist credentials and Futurism's claims to revolutionary proletarian status, canonised him, in their own "ideal order", as a Socialist Realist (Jangfeldt: 3). "The attempts to distort Mayakovsky's biography are motivated by a variety of factors", Bengt Jangfeldt has observed of such revisionist tendencies, which seek to "deny his links with the literary milieu of the 1910s and 1920s" and to make of him an exemplary "poet of the revolution" (3–4). But Jangfeldt's service to scholarship in his 1986 edition of the dead poet's love letters, which put the lie to the Soviet distortions he despises, for example, cannot escape the ideological context, on the other side of the Cold War's "iron curtain", in which avant-garde practices rejected by the Soviets in the 1930s, became reinterpreted in the 1950s as libertarian aesthetics, symbol of Western "political freedom", with American Abstract Expressionism its apotheosis. "The alleged separation of art from politics proclaimed throughout the 'free world' with the resurgence of abstraction after World War II was", according to Eva Cockcroft, "part of a general tendency in intellectual circles towards 'objectivity'" (132). She explains how the development of apolitical formalist aesthetics was caught up in Cold War politics:

> By giving their painting an individualist emphasis and eliminating recognizable subject matter, the Abstract Expressionists succeeded in creating an important new art movement. They also contributed, whether they knew it or not, to a purely political phenomenon – the supposed divorce between art and politics which so perfectly served America's needs in the cold war. (132)

Interestingly, the declared politics of individual artists, such as Jackson Pollock (who had been an active leftist in the 1930s), has become irrelevant here, surrendered to the larger ideological order. In fact, "the earlier political activism of some of the Abstract Expressionists" may even be thought of as advantageous: "from a cold warrior's point of view, such linkages to controversial political activities might actually heighten the value of these artists as a propaganda weapon in demonstrating the virtues of 'freedom of expression' in an 'open and free society'" (129).

The formalist critical armature underpinning the new abstractionism not only serves to interpret the work of the individual contemporary artist, but it also places the individual in a newly adjusted and co-opted homogenised formalist-Modernist "tradition", which contains (that is, both includes and limits) political/aesthetic avant-gardism. It is in this murky set of critical and ideological transitions and containments that "Modernism" as a term comes to gain ascendancy over "avant-garde" in Anglophone critical discourse.

> The homogenisation of . . . diverse practices into Modernism as a movement and critical category occurred in the 1950s, by virtue of what Raymond Williams calls "the post-war settlement and its accompanying, complicit academic endorsements". The assumptions underlying this construction were firstly that the initial impetus

> of Modernism was over, and in its selective canonised form was thereafter to be known as "High Modernism"; and secondly that the essence of the Modernist impulse was the spirit of formal experimentation. This second assumption, in fact, was also the key emphasis in Clement Greenberg's influential definition of Modernism in art. According to Greenberg, it was the critical self-reflexive, Kantian spirit that drove Modernist experimentation – the organic development and culmination of which was embodied by American Abstract Expressionism. These ideas came to dominate formulations concerning literary Modernism. (Kolocotroni et al.: xvii–xviii)

Greenberg's influential essay "Towards a Newer Laocoon", first published in *Partisan Review* (1940), traces "the avant-garde's development" towards pure abstractionism, and explains "the present superiority of abstract art" in terms of "its historical justification". His "historical apology for abstract art" (Harrison and Wood: 559) argues:

> The arts, then, have been hunted back to their mediums, and there they have been isolated, concentrated and defined. It is by virtue of its medium that each art is unique and strictly itself. To restore the identity of an art the opacity of its medium must be emphasized. (Harrison and Wood: 559)

Greenberg's use of the term "avant-garde" is semantically restricted by his Kantian framework, to an understanding of how new art breaks from past traditions in art, not how the boundaries between art and the praxis of life might be dissolved. History itself is reduced to art history. By 1961, Greenberg's classic restatement of this thesis, in "Modernist Painting", has replaced the term "avant-garde" with "Modernism": "The essence of Modernism lies, as I see it, in the use of the characteristic methods of a discipline itself – not in order to subvert it, but to entrench it more firmly in its area of competence" (5). The coda to his 1940 essay addresses the present challenge for the contemporary, individual artist:

> The imperative [of abstract art] comes from history, from the age in conjunction with a particular moment reached in a particular tradition of art. This conjunction holds the artist in a vise from which at the present moment he can escape only by surrendering his ambition and returning to a stale past. This is the difficulty for those who are dissatisfied with abstract art. . . . We can only dispose of abstract art

> by assimilating it, by fighting our way through it. Where to? I do not know. (Harrison and Wood: 560)

The tradition of art, in this thesis, has brought about its own aesthetic impasse. It is the historical cause of the present abstractionism but, as "a stale past", it can offer no refuge. Abstract art seems to represent the end (in both senses) of art history. The contemporary artist is trapped in its "vise" unless he wishes to "surrender" (an Eliotic term) back to the dead past. By 1961, Greenberg in "Modernist Painting", is describing Modernism's relationship to the past in less difficult terms:

> And I cannot insist enough that Modernism has never meant anything like a break with the past. It may mean a devolution, an unravelling of anterior tradition, but it also means a continuation. Modernist art develops out of the past without gap or break, and wherever it ends up it will never stop being intelligible in terms of the continuity of art. . . . Nothing could be further from the authentic art of our time than the idea of a rupture of continuity. Art is, among many other things, continuity. Without the past of art, and without the need and compulsion to maintain past standards of excellence, such a thing as Modernist art would be impossible. (Harrison and Wood: 759)

The notion of avant-garde rupture and discontinuity has been displaced by an Eliotic sense of modernism's continuity with the past and past aesthetic traditions. Indeed, Greenberg invokes Eliot in the opening sentence of his 1939 essay "Avant-Garde and Kitsch", where he observes that "one and the same civilization produces simultaneously two such different things as a poem by T. S. Eliot and a Tin Pan Alley song" and goes on, in Eliotic terms, to consider such a "disparity . . . within the frame of a single cultural tradition" by examining "the relationship between aesthetic experience as met by the specific . . . individual, and the social and historical contexts in which that experience takes place" (Harrison and Wood: 530). His new emphasis, in the 1961 essay, on continuity with the past echoes Eliot's famous invocation of "tradition" in "Tradition and the Individual Talent". Greenberg's theories belong, then, to an "ideal order" of formalist criticism that reaches back, through and beyond Eliot, to the aesthetic formalism of Bloomsbury art critics Roger Fry and Clive Bell, first formulated, as we have seen, between 1910 and 1912. It is in the context of this theoretical lineage, from the formalism of Fry and Bell to the formalist Modernism of Greenberg, that Eliot's revolutionary essay has been critically positioned.

## "Tradition and the Individual Talent", Part I

In the first part of "Tradition and the Individual Talent", Eliot sets out the basis of institutionalised literary study: the relation between the individual writer and a past canon of dead colleagues. Yet dialogue and disagreement with the living, the collective forging of poetics, or factionalising among the living, seem to be indicated by his assertion that "No poet, no artist of any art, has his complete meaning alone." But this is no acknowledgement of contemporary, living, poetic movements, or of dialogue with contemporary comrade poets, or of blade-whetting on disagreements with contemporary foes, but rather a longer, retrospective view of the individual's relation to the past:

> His significance, his appreciation is the appreciation of his relation to the dead poets and artists. You cannot value him alone; you must set him, for contrast and comparison, among the dead. I mean this as a principle of aesthetic, not merely historical criticism. (54)

His endorsement of tradition, and of understanding any new, individual artist within the context of tradition, hardly seems radical at all – he seems to sanction continuity with, rather than rupturing of, the past; and his only sense of the collective is in the placing of a solitary living practitioner "among the dead" – until Eliot explains the aesthetic dynamics of this authoritarian creed, opening up complicated concerns about how "the new" work of art may be understood as such:

> The necessity that he shall conform, that he shall cohere, is not onesided; what happens when a new work of art is created is something that happens simultaneously to all works of art which preceded it. The existing monuments form an ideal order among themselves, which is modified by the introduction of the new (the really new) work of art among them. The existing order is complete before the new work arrives; for order to persist after the supervention of novelty, the *whole* existing order must be, if ever so slightly, altered;

> and so the relations, proportions, values of each work of art toward the whole are readjusted; and this is conformity between the old and the new. Whoever has approved this idea of order, of the form of the European, of English literature will not find it preposterous that the past should be altered by the present as much as the present is directed by the past. And the poet who is aware of this will be aware of great difficulties and responsibilities. (54)

Here, Eliot's rhetorical sojourn "among the dead" continues with a graveyard metaphor: "an ideal order" of "existing monuments" adjusts to include a new one. Just as the terrain of a cemetery is altered by the digging of a new grave, and the erection of a new stone, so the literary canon alters with the arrival of a new poet. The choice of "monument" to represent the work of art, suggests that the work in turn is a monument to the poet's identity, whatever else it may represent or elegise. Eliot's vision here might be interpreted as a kind of "Poets' Corner" on a grand scale, the place in Westminster Abbey reserved for the interment of the nation's literary greats. The dead, it seems, are never far from the literary imagination, in the aftermath of the Great War; and while it is possible to understand Eliot's "idea of order" as applying to an ahistorical, abstract aesthetic order, it is difficult, considering 1919, the time of publication, not to think of the material, historical and human sources of art, of the new kinds of art such a cataclysm spawned and of the youthful artistic potential it cruelly cut short.

## Monuments and memorials: Eliot's essay and the commemoration of the war dead

Eliot's choice of lexis indeed reflects the huge public undertaking at the time to commemorate the dead of the Great War by the erection of memorials in every community, village, township and city. In 1918 a pamphlet on war shrines was published by the Civic Arts Association (King: 145); and a specially appointed committee at the Royal Academy, for example, published advice in *The Times* on 6 April 1918, on procedures for commissioning and choosing sites for memorials, recommending that, where the memorial is to be placed in or near existing buildings, "careful regard should be paid to the scale and character of the architecture of the building and to any adjacent monument" (3). Eliot's essay recalls this rhetoric. Indeed, Eliot's essay was published in September and December 1919, a period bridging the first anniversary and commemoration of Armistice Day, on 11 November 1919. Edward Lutyens was first commissioned to design the Cenotaph at Whitehall, in London, the national public monument to the dead of the Great War, as "a temporary structure of wood and plaster, marked to look as if it were made of stone blocks" for the Peace Day military parade on 19 July 1919 celebrating the signing of the Treaty of Versailles (King: 141); and the "permanent stone version which now stands in Whitehall was unveiled by the King as part of the Armistice Day ceremonies in 1920" (King: 143). Its design, when still "a temporary structure in 1919 . . . struck such a chord that the form was reproduced in stone, and was the prototype for war memorials across the nation" (Gardiner and Wenborn: 143). Alex King shows that this proliferating network of memorials both unified individual communities in a larger sense of national identity, and allowed for a sense of individual and local loss:

> Throughout the country, the erection of war memorials and the conduct of Armistice Day ceremonies followed common patterns, suggesting a nationwide uniformity of aims and attitudes, and a desire to conform to national stereotypes. Nonetheless, commemoration focused closely on the part played in the war by local communities, and on the local people who had been killed. (20)

The institution of the tradition of Armistice Day ceremonies, and the erection of monuments of remembrance, is born of a collective of diverse individual, and local, participants and monuments. Each new local monument is joined to the larger order of existing national monuments. Eliot's literary model of tradition and individual talent resembles this.

The design of many memorials, furthermore, while commemorating the loss of named individuals, often emphasised the anonymity of their figures (where they were used), so that the bereaved onlooker "could imagine that the figure specifically depicted the individual they personally mourned" (King: 139). And this anonymity, as King also points out, "was exploited most dramatically in the burial of an Unknown Warrior on 11 November 1920, the same day that the Cenotaph in Whitehall was unveiled" (139). The tomb itself is a slab: "the crucial image was not the tomb itself, but the story of the selection of the body from the cemeteries on the Western front, in circumstances which guaranteed it would remain unidentifiable" (139). The Unknown Warrior, then, is archetypal of war memorials of the period in making the single anonymous, unidentifiable, and therefore, impersonal, individual stand for the larger collective of the war dead. And Eliot's model of individual talent in relation to tradition replicates the dynamics of this model. In the midst of a culture busy with the planning of the memorialising of the dead of the Great War, and with the actual initiation of ceremonies for their memorial, it is little wonder that Eliot's reflections, in the autumn of 1919, on the individual poet and posterity are imbued with the discourse of the graveyard, and of the commemorative monument. And little wonder too that war elegy dominates and suffuses poetry in every quarter, not merely that by "war poets". A year later, for example, Pound cites and adapts Pierre Ronsard in his epigraph to "Hugh Selwyn Mauberley" (1920): "I.E.P. Ode Pour L'Election de son Sépulchre" (an ode on the poet's choice of tomb). But poetry is also formally recruited for the business of official memorialising. Rudyard Kipling, for example, was employed by the Imperial War Graves Commission to "devise almost all [its] verbal formula, from 'Their Name Liveth for Evermore', carved on the large 'Stone of Remembrance' in each cemetery, to the words incised on headstones over the bodies of the unidentified: 'A Soldier of the Great War/Known unto God'" (Fussell, *The Great War and Modern Memory*: 70).

Maud Ellmann (following Peter Middleton) finds Eliot's essay's "attitude to death . . . a reaction to the war just ended" and "an attempt to come to terms with the immolation of the West by disavowing its finality" (40). In Eliot's own poetic (anti-) monument to the war dead, *The Waste Land*, the horror of the sheer number of war dead is communicated in the apt citation from Dante's *Inferno*: "A crowd flowed over London Bridge, so many / I had not thought death had undone so many" (see *Inferno*, 3.55–7). Hell has relocated to the "Unreal City". But the instability of Europe post-war and post-Bolshevik Revolution, as Smith suggests, may well also resonate in Eliot's call for order. His use of "monuments" might also be taken as ironic reference to Lenin's Plan for Monumental Propaganda, which was conceived and launched in April 1918, and which instigated the creation and installation of (an evolving) Socialist Realist statuary commemorating revolutionary heroes. Trotsky, in a speech at the Sixth Congress of the Soviets, Moscow, on 9 November 1918, declared:

> In the squares of Soviet cities we are erecting monuments to our great men, the leaders of socialism. We are sure that these works of art will be dear to the hearts of every worker and the entire mass of the people. Along with this, we must say to every one of them in Moscow, Petrograd and in the most out-of-the-way places: "See, the Soviet power has put up a monument to Lassalle. Lassalle is dear to you but if the bourgeois breaks through the front and comes here, he will sweep away that monument, together with the Soviet power and all the achievements that we have now won. That means all workers, all to whom the Soviet power is dear, must defend it in arms. (Quoted Lodder: 19–20)

Christina Lodder offers the following analysis of the "sixty-six distinguished figures deemed worthy of sculptural attention":

> This list was divided into six groups, the largest of which, the "revolutionaries and social activists", consisted of thirty-one foreign and Russian names, including Marx, Engels, Spartacus, Lassalle, Danton, Robespierre and Robert Owen. The other groups represented writers and poets (twenty named, including Tolstoi, Dostoevski, Uspenski and Shevchenko); philosophers and scholars (three, including Lomonov); artists (seven, including Vrubel and Rublev); composers (three – Musorgski, Skriabin and Chopin); and performers (two). (20)

Lodder comments on the "cultural liberalism" of this list, suggesting it "may have been calculated to present a contrast to the repressive Tsarist regime which had forbidden, for instance, the erection of statues to Shevchenko, Tolstoi and Chopin" (21). Yet, the Bolshevik state was not going to tolerate the continued existence of Tsarist statuary, as the title of Lenin's decree, published in *Izvestiya* and *Pravda* in April 1918, makes clear: "The Removal of Monuments Erected in Honour of the Tsars and their Servants and the Production of Projects for Monuments to the Russian Socialist Revolution". Eliot's monumental plan for poets, in which the "existing monuments form an ideal order among themselves, which is modified by the introduction of the new (the really new) work of art among them", suggests he follows the advice of the British Royal Academicians rather than the example of the Bolsheviks, an analogy erased by his misdating of the essay to 1917. But perhaps his antipathy to Milton and most of the Romantic poets, recorded in other essays, is tantamount to a demolition.

## Critics of Eliot's "ideal order": Philip Hobsbaum, Louis Menand, Maude Ellmann, Terry Eagleton, Tom Leonard

Interestingly, Eliot, an American expatriate, addresses himself to "European" and "English" literature: and we might wonder whether his tremulous model of literary order reflects a peculiarly American ambivalence to past and present European culture. Does this model imply a recognition that a great deal – the shaping of past and present Europe – hangs in the balance? It certainly communicates a sense of urgency in identifying the "great difficulties" and "responsibilities" for the poet "aware" of the interrelations between past and present. But these portents remain vague and abstract enough to apply, presumably, to any moment in culture.

Philip Hobsbaum has argued, in *Tradition and Experiment in English Poetry* (1979), that Eliot's "Tradition", *pace* Eliot, is in fact essentially American, and he offers insightful readings of Eliot's work through Walt Whitman's foundational American poetics, finding many striking "verbal parallels" (268). "Who, long before Eliot," he asks, "worked through evocative vibration, phanopoeia, montage, free verse and the rest? The answer is obvious: Whitman" (266). Hobsbaum demonstrates that Eliot's "Tradition" is not as European as he declares it, and goes so far as to suggest in his critique that the aesthetic "qualities" we have come to term "modernism" are to be more accurately rendered as the "quality" of "Americanness" (288). Hobsbaum's argument on Eliot's "Tradition" is constructed in the context of a broad study of English poetics, in which he seeks to show how the "damaging" influence of American modernists, such as Eliot and Pound, has diverted the course of English poetics from a traditional lyric stream that, after Thomas Hardy, falters at American diversions (294). Hobsbaum rightly teaches us to be suspicious of reading Eliot's thesis on tradition entirely on Eliot's terms. He asks why the "palpable fact" of Eliot's debt to Whitman "was not noted by critics and editors as intelligent as Leavis, Roberts and Empson". He replies: "we can only point to the salient characteristics of Eliot's work: that he, more than any other poet, has succeeded in constructing his own literary history. Unfortunately, it is largely fictional" (266). Eliot's prescribed and declared "ideal order", then, may indeed differ in the case of his actual poetic practice. But his essay is still also significant, nevertheless, in its influential thoughts on how we might posit the relationship of individual to tradition.

While his argument furnishes us with useful insights into developments within streams of English and American poetics, Hobsbaum tends to encourage with his approach a separatist, nation-based model which is ultimately inadequate to the understanding of the international forum of avant-garde poetics in which Eliot may also simultaneously be placed. This continuum, which includes nineteenth-century American poets such as Poe and Whitman, as well as the European, such as Baudelaire, and the later Apollinaire, Mayakovsky and Schwitters, cannot readily be reduced to a national poetics. Identifying Whitman as Eliot's "American" source is helpful for understanding Eliot in the context of American poetics, but it must at the same time be acknowledged that Whitman himself also contributed a strain of democratic, or revolutionary, poetry to avant-garde European poetics. The fact that Whitman's poetry was enormously popular in pre-revolutionary Russia, for example, is not presumably to be taken as a sign of literary American expansionism, but as evidence of poetic transitions along international lines, crossing national boundaries, in which American poetics are remade alongside the European beyond national categorisation.

Menand rightly worries that "Eliot is so automatically associated with the defence of a traditional canon that it has become difficult for some readers to see exactly what he is saying here" (Menand: 32). It is understandable that Eliot's authoritarian lexis here ("conform", "cohere", "conformity", and five iterations of "order") might indeed help "some readers" to think of his thesis as conservative. But Eliot's abstract and flexible model of canonicity is not to be confused with the laying down of a fixed canon:

> The term, "ideal order" is the crux of the misreading: it is clearly intended philosophically, not prescriptively. Our perception of the new work of art depends on our perception of the history of art, which takes a certain shape – is 'idealised' in our minds. But once we have encountered the new work, that idea of tradition is modified in turn. Value – by implication, significance of any sort – is a function of relation. Hence the tradition cannot be monolithic. (Menand: 32)

Eliot's "ideal order" may not be read as "prescriptive" here, but we do not need to read much further in the essay to discover the kind of "ideal order" he has in mind.

> He must be aware that the mind of Europe – the mind of his own country – a mind which he learns in time to be much more important than his own private mind – a mind which changes, and that this change is a development which abandons nothing *en route*, which does not superannuate either Shakespeare, or Homer, or the rock drawing of the Magdalenian draughtsmen.

Eliot frames the relationship of individual talent to tradition first in nationalistic terms: the "private mind" of the individual is to submit to "the mind of his own country", which in turn is a microcosm of "the mind of Europe", in which are suspended Shakespeare, Homer and primitive cave drawings. This list of cultural samples resembles the list Clive Bell assembles as examples of "significant form": "Sta. Sophia and the windows at Chartres, Mexican sculpture, a Persian bowl, Chinese carpets, Giotto's frescoes at Padua, and the masterpieces of Poussin, Piero della Francesca, and Cézanne" (*Art*, pp. 7–8). For Eliot, "the mind of Europe" is an ideal order, then, which admits and contains change. But it is not merely a list to which new items are added; it is continuously recomposing itself to accommodate the new; yet it has direction, a teleology. At the same time as the list confers synchronous status on its items, confirming "that art never improves, but that the material of art is never quite the same" (54), it is also "develop[ing]" chronologically from the visual art of the cavemen to Homeric poetry to the works of Shakespeare and beyond. What is it "*en route*" to? A final item on the list; or a larger transcendent context or continental "mind" frame? America, perhaps? The typically American obsession with lists (as itemised by Emerson and indeed, Whitman, for example) in itself might suggest so. The infinite, perhaps?

Eliot is here using the "rhetoric of organicism", as Maud Ellmann notes: "He speaks as if tradition had emerged according to the laws of nature, rather than through the social, economic and political exclusions which institute the canon by expelling any works that challenge its hegemony" (37–8). She endorses Terry Eagleton's observation that Eliot's "Tradition" is "a labile, self-transformative organism extended in space and time, constantly reorganised by the present; but this radical historical relativism is then endowed with the status of absolute classical authority" (Eagleton: 147). Tom Leonard thinks through some of the consequences of "the dominant literary tradition still 'taught' in educational institutions" where "a dominant value-system has been allowed to marginalize that which does not correspond to it, declaring it deviant and therefore invalid. It has been able to do so by the method of making the mode of expression of these dominant values literally synonymous with 'objectivity'" (36). He focuses on Eliot's "Tradition" as a reaction of privilege to the democratic currents of Romanticism:

> Now you can range through the nineteenth-century literary criticism into the twentieth, from the introduction to the *Lyrical Ballads*, Coleridge via Germany, Arnold, Browning, Ruskin, Carlyle right through until you eventually arrive in the room that Mr Eliot is sorting out his objective correlative in, and had you lived through the period in question, and had had an attentive ear, you would have noticed as time progressed that the voices around you discussing the books you were reading, seemed to sound more and more sort of, ehm, "objective". The trouble was that after Wordsworth had rrolled in Earrth's diurrnial urrn, and education was getting a bit universalised, the chaps hit on this super wheeze, namely how to turn your own voice into an object of social status. Nothing sinister, nothing undemocratic. All you needed to acquire this property yourself, was a fair bit of money. But if your own voice became an object that you shared in common with other fellows who happened also to have a fair bit of money, how could this voice, as object, be other than objective? Now, when you opened your mouth, you had the power to be im-personal. (34–5)

Where Eagleton finds in Eliot's model of tradition a flexible "self-transformative organism . . . constantly reorganised by the present" harnessed to the service of classical authority, Leonard finds the perfect social mechanism for the perpetuation of privilege:

> When one as an outsider attempts dialogue, one addresses not simply a person but a closed system of value, which stands between the two human beings in attempted communication. To speak when addressed, one must attempt first of all to digest all the components of that system of value oneself, in order that one can oneself stand at a tangent, and reply to the person who has addressed you, from within that closed system of value that is given. In so doing, one will of course have enlarged that closed system slightly, by the addition of one's own contribution, while one exists personally unchanged outside it. And all the components of that value-system will have

> been fractionally altered, too, by the addition of one's own contribution. This, of course, is the Theory of the Magic Thing. (37)

Leonard interprets Eliot's tradition as a closed system in ways that might well trouble Menand, but he is picking up on some of Eliot's implicit imagery in the essay, which seems to figure tradition as a rigid electronic circuit, albeit that some points are better connected to the power supply than others. Eliot warns that the poet "must be very conscious of the main current, which does not at all flow invariably through the most distinguished reputations" ("Tradition", p. 55). The living poet begins to resemble Dr Frankenstein in recharging with the energy of continuity his otherwise dead and disparate ancestors. Nor are table-turning and necromancy far from Eliot's rhetorical interest in reviving and communing with the dead. Perhaps different parts of the tradition become charged and illuminated in accordance with each new addition to the circuit. The relation of individual talent to tradition is, of course, performed by Eliot's virtuoso poem *The Waste Land* (1922), which simultaneously revives, embodies and reorganises the poetic canon. But already in print was a poem by his mentor Ezra Pound that provides a near perfect objective correlative for Eliot's thesis: possibly the most famous imagist poem, "In a Station of the Metro", which was published in *The New Freewoman* (August 1913), the magazine which was renamed *The Egoist* (and in which Eliot's essay is published). It conforms to most of Pound's strictures in his manifesto for Imagism (published in "A Retrospect" (1918), and in earlier form as "A Few Don'ts", 1913), in its "direct treatment of the 'thing'", its pared verbal economy, and its phrasal rather than metrical composition (*Literary Essasys,* 3). But Pound's poem also anticipates, or at least serendipitously provides a verbal diagram for, Eliot's model of individual talent and tradition. When it was first published, Pound instructed the printers to insert "spaces between the rhythmic units", which also emphasise the orchestration of units of meaning, in terms of subsections and systems:

> The apparition      of these faces      in the crowd      :
> Petals      on a wet, black      bough      .

Pound's poem succinctly combines mechanistic and organicist imagery to suggest individual elements (stations, faces, petals) in relation to larger structures (metro, crowd, bough), while also betraying a whiff of spiritualism in its startling deployment of its only abstract noun (Pound's own advice, in his manifesto, is to "go in fear of abstractions": 5), "apparition", a ghostly term, perhaps suggesting, in compression, that the descent into the modern urban underground resembles antique accounts of a descent into Hell (by Homer, Virgil, or Dante), where apparitions of the dead are encountered in hordes. At the same time, the poem depersonalises the experience by eliding the presence of the lyric first person, and further objectifies it by eliding all verbs. Each individual element appears simultaneously with its larger structure: station and metro, faces and crowd, petals and bough, just as the individual and the tradition, in Eliot's thesis, are simultaneously made (and remade) manifest. Eliot's thesis is perhaps an implicit reading of this poem.

## The "continual surrender": Eliot's model of poetic subjectivity

At the close of the first part of his essay, Eliot returns his focus from the tradition to the individual mind, but in a language suggestive of a religious, mythical, mental context:

> What happens is a continual surrender of himself as he is at the moment to something which is more valuable. The progress of an artist is a continual self-sacrifice, a continual extinction of personality. (55)

What is Eliot's "something which is more valuable"? The national literary canon, perhaps, and a sense of wider transcendent national subjectivity. But the artist's self is not to be permanently subsumed by this larger system, rather it is to be continuously made and remade in a cycle of messianic self-sacrifice and extinction (which according to its own logic must include birth and rebirth of the self). But the emphasis on self-sacrifice and extinction suggests that the preferred state is that of death and impersonality. The self bobs up like a cork only to be pushed back to oblivion. The dynamics of this cyclical creative struggle are also explored by Woolf, as we have seen, in "Modern Novels" and "Modern Fiction". But whereas Woolf's parody emphasises the state of renewal of sovereignty through momentary obliteration by violent assault, Eliot emphasises the counter-state of self-obliteration. The obliteration of the self also means for Eliot the resurrection of the dead since "not only the best, but the most individual parts of his work may be those in which the dead poets, his ancestors, assert their immortality most vigorously" 54).

The poet here is figured as a spiritual medium, or ventriloquist's dummy, for a past tradition of dead, but not quite dead – or better, undead – poets. The living poet gives voice to the dead, and "surrenders his identity to the demonic repetition of the past, reduced to the amanuensis of the dead", in what Maud Ellmann finds to be the "most unsettling interpretation" (38). But he must suppress his own personality to achieve this, or at the very least he must suppress the poetic subjectivity of Romanticism – for it is clear that Eliot does not expect his poet to revive Wordsworth. His theory of impersonality directly contradicts Wordsworth's definition of transcendent poetic subjectivity, in his Preface to *The Lyrical Ballads*, as "the spontaneous overflow of powerful feelings" (*Poetical Works*: 740). With an arresting couple of objective correlatives for the opposing conditions of classical containment and romantic excess, William Blake, another of Eliot's reviled Romantic refusés (see his essay on Blake), warns: "the cistern contains; the fountain overflows" (151). Eliot of course favours the cistern (and how it delights some of his less reverent readers that T. S. Eliot anagrammatically flushes toilets!). He seems to recognise that to push the fountain back into the cistern is a poetic task that can never be completed: it is a perpetual struggle, "a continual self-sacrifice, a continual extinction of personality". But the poet's self, paradoxically, is in a sense reaffirmed by this cycle of extinction and resurrection. Eliot "implies that the author gains his place with the immortals at the price of the suppression of himself", Ellmann observes. "In this way, the artist universalises his identity at the very moment that he seems to be negated" (38).

A similar paradox is observable in Wordsworth's famous account, in *The Prelude*, of the poetic mind in relation to Nature, where he describes an "auxiliary light" that "Came from my mind, which on the setting sun / Bestowed new splendour . . . and the midnight storm grew darker in the presence of my eye: / Hence my obeisance, my devotion hence,/ And hence my transport" (507). The Romantic poet, paradoxically, serves Nature by subordinating it to himself. Eliot's poet, on the other hand, while not adhering to the notion of "the unified transcendent consciousness that the nineteenth century had understood as 'personality'" (Ellmann: 16), nevertheless serves Tradition by subordinating himself to it in a way that allows his identity, paradoxically, to re-emerge, universalised, within it. For Eliot, as for Pound, Ellmann suggests, "speech and writing also come to signify the battle between self and self-oblivion. As much as they denounce personality, they dread its dissolution even more" (17).

At this point, Eliot resorts to the impartiality of science to support his theory of impersonality.

> There remains to define this process of depersonalisation and its relation to the sense of tradition. It is in this depersonalisation that art may be said to approach the condition of science. I therefore invite you to consider, as a suggestive analogy, the action which takes place when a bit of finely filiated platinum is introduced into a chamber containing oxygen and sulphur dioxide. (Eliot, "Tradition": 55)

Eliot imparts a sense of showmanship, by ending the first part of his essay at this point. Whereas we may now move swiftly on to the second part, Eliot's first readers were left to consider his analogy for all of three months, should they wish, until the December 1919 issue of *The Egoist.*

## Tradition and mourning in *The Egoist* (September 1919): from Eliot's essay to James Joyce's *Ulysses*

But turning the page of the present issue, they would find themselves in Hell, if they but knew it, or at any rate in the middle of the graveyard scene, the "Hades" episode, of James Joyce's *Ulysses.* Extracts of this novel in progress had been appearing in the American *Little Review* since March 1918, and continued despite interventions by the US Postal Authorities until December 1920, after which its editors were convicted of publishing obscenity. *The Egoist,* on the other side of the Atlantic, managed to publish four edited extracts (this was the third) before ceasing in the light of the action against the American magazine. Having followed Eliot's meditations on the living individual talent set "among the dead" of the Tradition, which is to adjust its "ideal order" of "existing monuments" to accommodate the new, the reader of this issue of *The Egoist* now follows Leopold Bloom (from the middle to the end of the "Hades" chapter) around Prospect Cemetery, Dublin, as he follows his companions for the funeral of

Paddy Dignam, an episode that in turn follows Homer's Odysseus on his visit to Hades to consult with the shade of the transsexual prophet Tiresias, in Book XI of *The Odyssey.* In giving new voice to Homer, Joyce's text may well exemplify Eliot's thesis on individual talent and tradition, and in the context of this issue of *The Egoist,* Eliot's essay may be read as an implicit defence of Joyce's controversial work. But it is also productive to consider how the extract from "Hades" both embellishes and differs from Eliot's thesis. Joyce's text may be used to read Eliot's as well as vice versa. And we might also note that Tiresias is the figure, "old man with wrinkled dugs", lurking at the heart of Eliot's own later account of modernity's hell, *The Waste Land.*

This particular sojourn among the dead is rather different from Eliot's. After the latter's eloquent philosophising on death in terms of admission to an ideal order of tradition, Joyce's fiction is refreshingly irreverent in its graphic graveside antics. Communicated in humorous, earthy, at times lugubrious, but also erudite and allusive prose, studded with neologisms, abundant in cultural and literary references, it is playful and poetic, exploring the subjective, internal, observations of Bloom as well as his externalised part in the dialogue and his participation in the funeral proceedings.

> He followed his companions. Mr Kernan and Ned Lambert followed, Hynes walking after them. Corny Kelleher stood by the opened hearse and took out the two wreaths. He handed one to the boy.
>
> Where is that child's funeral disappeared to?
>
> Coffin now. Got here before us, dead as he is. Horse looking round at it with his plume skeowways. Dull eye: collar tight on his neck, pressing on a bloodvessel or something. Do they know what they cart out here every day. Must be twenty or thirty funerals every day? Then Mount Jerome for the protestants. Funerals all over the world every where every minute. Shovelling them under by the thousand double quick. Too many in the world.
>
> Mourners came out through the gates: woman and a girl. Leanjawed harpy, hard woman at a bargain, her bonnet awry. Girl's face stained with dirt and tears, holding the woman's arm looking up at her for a sign to cry. Fish's face, bloodless and livid. ([*The Egoist,* 6: iv] 56)

The comedy of Joyce's exploration of the interminable inevitability, the physical literalism, the mundane materiality, of death, and the sheer numbers of dead to be disposed of, is enhanced by the passage's juxtaposition with Eliot's grander philosophising on individual death and poetic ideal orders. And Eliot's promise of scientific explanation is undercut too by Bloom's own rationalist understanding of death as final, physical decay, and mechanical breakdown, which is comically at odds with religious belief in resurrection:

> Mr Kernan [alluding to the protestant service of the Irish Church] said with solemnity:
>
> – I am the resurrection and the life. That touches a man's inmost heart.
>
> – It does, Mr Bloom said.
>
> Your heart perhaps, but what price the fellow in the six feet by two? No touching that. A pump after all, pumping thousands of gallons of blood every day. One fine day it gets bunged up and there you are. Lots of them lying around here: lungs, hearts, livers. Old rusty pumps: damn the thing else. The resurrection and the life. Once you are dead you are dead. That last day idea. Knocking them all up out of their graves. Get up! Last day! Then every fellow mousing around for his liver and his lights and the rest of his traps. Find damn all of himself in the morning. Pennyweight of powder in a skull. Twelve grammes one pennyweight. (57)

This last imagery of weights and measures overlays materialism with the discourse of capitalism while its alliterative poetry communicates the passing fragility, and slightness of individual mortal remains, which nevertheless perform a kind of natural miracle in eventual dispersal and disappearance, reduction to a "Pennyweight of powder".

Joyce's emphasis on the finality of death clouds Eliot's messianic fantasies of poetic resurrection: "Once you are dead you are dead." But Eliot's notion of the individual's relinquishment of personality to a universal order of tradition that somehow dissolves yet transforms and preserves identity may find comedic objective correlative in Joyce's account of the caretaker's recollection of a joke about two drunks in a graveyard, a joke concerning the memorial and symbolic function for Christianity of the statuary of sepulchres, which he recounts while passing amongst the sepulchres, or "existing monuments" (to literalise Eliot's phrase), of Prospect Cemetery. The repetition of the joke becomes a blasphemous parody of the sacred rites of the graveside; a secular, vernacular tradition in itself, in which the caretaker seems to ritually perform the story as he recounts it:

> One of the drunks spelt out the name: Terence Mulcahy. The other

> drunk was blinking up at a statue of our Saviour the widow had got put up.
>
> The caretaker blinked up at one of the sepulchres they passed. He resumed:
>
> – And after blinking up at it. *Not a bloody bit like the man,* says he. *That's not Mulcahy,* says he, *whoever done it.* (58)

The identity of the dead individual is unrecognisable, displaced and subsumed, in the Christian symbolic order, by that of the transcendent, resurrected, Christ. And this comic critique of Christian iconography, its model of the relation of the individual to the wider scheme of things, also resonates with the concerns of poetic tradition and individual talent. Ultimate authorial responsibility is open to question in both orders. If, in Eliot's model of tradition, the living talent merely gives voice to the dead, we might well ponder with the drunks on "*whoever done it*". And, like Eliot's, Bloom's meditations over the open grave lead to a momentary sense of panic, to a sense of subjective instability, of identity as transitional:

> Pause.
>
> If we were all suddenly somebody else. (59)

Joyce's novel is full of references to resurrection, transubstantiation, metempsychosis, and so on. In this episode, which follows on, in *The Egoist,* from Eliot's thoughts on the messianic return of the poet, transforming and transformed by tradition, it is the possibility of the messianic return of the lost political leader, Parnell, "the chief", that is contemplated and dismissed, as some of the mourners pause at his grave on leaving Dignam's funeral:

> – Some say he is not in that grave at all. That the coffin was filled with stones. That one day he will come again.
>
> Hynes shook his head.
>
> – Parnell will never come again, he said.
>
> Mr Bloom walked unheeded along his grove. Who passed away. Who departed this life. As if they did it of their own accord. Got the shove, all of them. . . . Rusty wreaths hung on knobs, garlands of bronzefoil. Better value that for the money. Still, the flowers are more poetical. The other gets rather tiresome, never withering. Expresses nothing. (59)

Bloom seems here to endorse an aesthetics of decay, preferring the poetry of real, and therefore mortal, flowers, to the eternal, and therefore for him meaningless, bronze effigies. Perhaps the "rusty wreaths hung on knobs, garlands of bronzefoil" represent an atrophied classical tradition in need of new individual talent to revive and reorder it. This verbless juxtaposition of images, noun phrases torn from classical pastoral tradition, shorn of lyric subjectivity, certainly reads, in isolation, like a cruel parody of imagist poetry. Pound's famous "petals on a wet, black bough", incidentally already parodied in an earlier issue of *The Egoist* (January 1914: 36) by Richard Aldington, as "white faces in a black dead faint", have corroded in funereal rain. Bloom, himself nominally, of course, a flower, longs for nature's "withering", despises the false and eternal realm of art and tradition.

# 4 *The Egoist*, War, Hell and Image

## T. S. Eliot, Dora Marsden, John Rodker, Ezra Pound and Richard Aldington

### Introduction

This chapter seeks to explore the contents of two issues of the little magazine *The Egoist*, which constitute the first published context of Eliot's essay "Tradition and the Individual Talent". The editorial powers and philosophies of Harriet Shaw Weaver, Dora Marsden and Eliot are discussed, along with contributions by the poet Evelyn Scott, and avant-garde theatre critic Huntly Carter. Considerable attention is given to the poet and publisher John Rodker, who gives an interesting review of a number of volumes of poetry published by Blackwell. Rodker's column is analysed with close reference to a number of the individual poems and volumes he reviews. This allows us to gauge the impact of Eliotic and Poundian poetics on some of the minor poets of the era; to test Eliot's thesis on tradition and individual talents on his contemporaries. Rodker's review of Aldous Huxley is discussed in some detail, and includes comparisons with the work of Pound, Eliot, Woolf and Yeats. His review of poems by Edith Sitwell, and Osbert Sitwell, receives similar treatment. There follows an excursus into Rodker's own poetry, comparing it with the poetry of Eliot, Pound, Yeats, and the war poet Isaac Rosenberg, and also touching on Harlem poetics. Rodker's treatment of contemporary themes of memorialising the war dead, returns us to the concerns of Eliot's essay.

The books advertised at the back of *The Egoist* are also examined. Close readings are offered of Richard Aldington's volumes of imagist poetry, and Pound's important volume *Quia Pauper Amavi*. A special excursus on the discourse of hell in Pound's "Three Cantos" in that volume again returns us to Eliot's essay and Joyce's "Hades" episode. Then the next issue of *The Egoist* is discussed, and the position of the second instalment of Eliot's essay is considered in relation to Marsden's editorial and to the next episode of Joyce's *Ulysses*, the publication of which work in book form becomes the new project for *The Egoist*, and provides another sense of order and tradition informing Eliot's essay. As well as illuminating Eliot's essay, this exploration of its context in *The Egoist* provides a synchronic exploration of other significant (and sometimes less well known) authors and texts of the period.

## *The Egoist* (September 1919): T. S. Eliot and Dora Marsden

The "Hades" extract from *Ulysses* is not the only piece in the September 1919 issue of *The Egoist* to complement Eliot's meditations on death. We are reminded of the war dead in the regular column immediately preceding Eliot's essay in the magazine: Muriel Ciolkowska's "The French Idea", which reports on the latest French avant-garde journals, books, and art, and includes the following observations on "the graphic historians of war. Those men who may be said to have created a style and founded a school: F. Léger, Taquoy, Marchand, Lhôte, Segonzac, Vallotton, André Mare, Frayé, etc., will convey its features to coming generations." Like Eliot, she approves of objectivity and distance:

> They have uttered its spirit and form with a minimum of subjective comment and have proved that new conditions (the mechanical side of modern warfare, for example) call for, and find in these artists, adequate interpretation. (54)

Death and the question of subjectivity is also the main concern of Dora Marsden's lengthy leading article (one of a very long series), which starts, as always, on the magazine's front page (49). "I wish Dora did not have to have the very front," moaned Eliot in September 1917, "as I should like to do a series of pungent paragraphs (not necessarily all by one hand) instead of my articles, which I feel have been of inferior quality" (*Letters* 1, p. 198). But, alas, Dora always got veteran militant suffragette, Marsden was founder magazine, which began in 1910 as *The Freewoman*, ...minist politics, and was reincarnated in 1913 as *The* ...*ew Freewoman*, when "her interest shifted further towards the 'philosophic individualism' which she saw as underlying all modern movements, including feminism" (Kolocotroni: 331). Encouraged by Pound and Aldington, she renamed it *The Egoist* in 1914, a fitting title and vehicle for Marsden's relentless editorialising on the ego, subjectivity and identity; and a fitting showcase, of course, for Eliot's essay. But a 'strong aura" of "feminism and pacifism", nevertheless was cast in *The Egoist*, an "aura often lost when [modernist] works appear in contemporary editions nowadays, stripped of their original bibliographical codes" (Bornstein, *Material Modernism*: 85–6). Harriet Shaw Weaver succeeded her as editor later in 1914, and Marsden became a contributing editor. When Eliot undertook his own "'contributing editor' job" in 1917 he noted, in a letter to his mother: "it will add to my notoriety. At present it is run mostly by old maids, and I may be a beneficial influence" (*Letters* 1, p. 179). Eliot was to dedicate his *Selected Essays, 1917–32* to Weaver, who is now remembered as the most generous patron and champion of Joyce, and was, according to Eliot, "the only woman connected with publishing whom it is really easy to get on with" (*Letters* 1, p. 348). On the other hand, by July 1919, Eliot confesses to having "only met Miss Marsden once, and then (in strict confidence) frothed at the mouth with antipathy" (315).

Marsden's piece for the issue in which Eliot's "Tradition and the Individual Talent" appears, is a subsection of a long, somewhat opaque and rambling, serialised work, written in quasi-scientific style, "*Philosophy: The Science of Signs* XVII Truth (continued)" and is subtitled: "V How the Theory of the *Ego* requires us to Construe Death". The opening paragraph is representative of Marsden's somewhat turgid prose style, showing little of Eliot's restraint in the deployment of quasi-philosophical and scientific discourse:

> I. A philosophy which has presumed to offer a formula meant to express the facts of life as a whole cannot without affectation show timidity in putting forward a corresponding formula to indicate how that philosophy requires us to construe the phenomenon of death. For in giving the comprehensive formula for life we imply that the universe in its sum and in its parts is intelligible, that we hold something like a clue to its arrangement and that it lies within the power of

> the intellectual means – i.e., *signs* – to construct a conceptual arrangement not only corresponding with every relationship obtaining among spatial things and events but showing also the latter's trend of development and something of what they promise to become. It takes for granted that one has not failed to take cognisance of the great individual facts of life – of which death is one – and to allow place for them. Otherwise one could not make the formulation of their sum. A logic of life must, in short, be ready with a logic of the other great facts of life not excluding even that of death. Hence this chapter. (49)

Like Eliot, she is concerned with death as part of a creative cycle:

> The significance of the event lies with the happening's positive side: what it means as an affair of universal refertilisation and rebirth. The importance of dying lies thus with what it means as an act of life. Of the nature of annihilation it achieves – and can achieve – nothing. (52)

Marsden seeks to outline and logically construe a model of personality that transcends the limits of the physical individual, as her coda to this instalment explains:

> However, if our logic can prove the personalness of the whole world as part of the unity of feeling, it thereby prohibits any identification of personality with the organic body merely. The universe of feeling is always and inevitably personal. It is inconceivable that anything can ever be save as it exists as the personal point of view of things. So everything – the world of external things equally with emotions of our inner world – has to be reckoned as forming the mass of our personality. In short, the latter has to be identified with the *ego* as a whole, not with that impermanent transmuting "limb" of the *ego*, the organic body. (53)

What is at stake for Marsden is the place of the individual personality in the larger scheme of things, and her argument provides an interesting context in which to read Eliot's more eloquent contemplation of the individual talent. Marsden's "universe of feeling" seems to be a network of subjective, "personal", emotion, which subsumes the individual personality while simultaneously, and paradoxically, preserving it:

> Thus identified, the whole matter of the survival as a force of the individualised personality rests upon a different footing. The old paralysing sense of personal insignificance is brought to an end. Personality, weighted with the whole outer world, obviously involves, even for the most materially-minded, treasure too great to be reckoned lost without making a determined speculative effort of the mind to conceive a scheme of salvage. It is just such an effort which, supported by our theory of truth, we make in advancing our conceptional model of the mechanism of the *ego*. (53)

Marsden's model of the ego here does not appear to be gendered, nor does it overtly refer to her feminism. It seems to transcend the political and social struggles of the contemporary material realm in favour of a sense of the individual in relation to a cosmic collective. Eliot's model of the individual in relation to tradition similarly plucks the individual out of any struggle or conflict with contemporaries, or in contemporary politics, into a remote ideal order "among the dead".

## *The Egoist*: Evelyn Scott and Huntly Carter

Flicking through to the back of this issue of *The Egoist*, we find after the extract from *Ulysses* the following diverse contents. There is the second part of "Carl Spitteler" (who was a German-speaking Swiss poet), a review of his satirical verse by Ernest A. Boyd (61–2), in which the "essentially Latin content" of his poetry's Germanic "form" is praised for "a suppleness and plasticity not characteristic of the teutonic genius" (62), and this endorsement of classicism seems in keeping with the line of Eliot's essay. This is followed by a poem by Evelyn Scott, entitled "Women", which somewhat schematically and prosaically puts forward an overtly gendered model of subjectivity (whereas Eliot's model is of course gendered masculine, and makes no reference to the feminine), in its exploration of "mirrors" as a metaphor for women's relation to men:

> Like crystal columns,
> When they bend, they crack;
> Brittle souls,
> Conforming, yet not conforming –
> Mirrors.

Masculine souls
Pass across the mirrors:
Whirling, gliding ecstasies . . . (62)

Scott's poem is a slight, and singular, reminder, perhaps, of the feminist origins of the organ in which it appears, and anticipates Woolf's observation in *A Room of One's Own*, that women "have served all these centuries as looking-glasses possessing the magic and delicious power of reflecting the figure of man at twice its natural size" (53). It is followed by the fourth part of "Towards a Peace Theatre" by Huntly Carter (62–3), in which he argues that conventional theatre is "more or less a War Theatre. It exists to express conflict." He envisages a "peaceful form of drama and technic" whose "spirit and manifestation are as peaceful as those of a true religious observance in which all who take part are re-united unresistingly with reality or the divine world" (*The Egoist*, VI, 4, p. 62). Carter has a vision of dramatic art as a means of quasi-religious transcendence, in opposition to theatre previously conceived "out of a long-continued period of warfare . . . no doubt necessary for the preparation of soldiers" (62). His piece adds to a sense of the seeking of post-war consolation and commemoration that forms a context to Eliot's essay.

## *The Egoist*: John Rodker, reviewer and publisher

The last piece in the magazine is "Blackwelliana" by John Rodker, a review of a number of volumes of poetry published by Blackwells. Rodker, who came from the London East End Jewish milieu that included the poet Isaac Rosenberg and artists Mark Gertler and David Bomberg, was a considerable and well-regarded, avant-garde poet himself – Pound dubbed him a Futurist (see Crozier, "Introduction", p. xvii); he was also an influential translator, an advocator of experimental theatre (see for example, his manifesto for a theatre of pure emotion, "The Theatre", published in *The Egoist*, November 1914), and an important publisher after founding the Imago Press with the writer Mary Butts (to whom he was married). He published Eliot's *Ara Vos Prec* (1919), whose title, "unintelligible to most people" (Eliot, *Letters* 1, p. 338), is from Dante's *Purgatorio*, xxvi.145 ("Now I pray you"); Pound's *Mauberley* (1920); as well as collections of drawings by Wyndham Lewis and Gaudier-Brzeska. He went on to publish Pound's

*Cantos 17–26*, as well as work by Le Corbusier, Valéry, and Freud's works in German. In 1919 he took over from Pound as London editor of the *Little Review*. Like Eliot, he also had connections (although of a different sort, and from an earlier time) with Bloomsbury. As a conscientious objector, along with Lytton Strachey, for example, during the war, he was arrested and jailed (an event noted by Woolf in a letter of April 1917 to her sister). Eliot, who did not meet Virginia and Leonard Woolf until November 1918, in fact, was writing to Rodker, in September and November 1918, of his own "personal difficulties connected with the Military" (*Letters* 1, pp. 242; 252). Rodker wrote reviews for the *Little Review*, and Eliot considered him an "excellent" reviewer, and encouraged his contributions to *The Egoist* (*Letters*, 1, p. 260), although he thought more of Aldington as a writer (erroneously in my view), finding him "more *mature* than Rodker and I expect him to become one of the few to count" (*Letters* 1, p. 324). Rodker's review here, in the September issue of *The Egoist*, is worth considering in some detail, since it gives an instructive and entertaining snapshot of the current state of poetics into which Eliot's pronouncements intervene. It is interesting to try to gauge Rodker's views in comparison with Eliot's. I have also taken the trouble to track down the volumes he reviews, and in the main, concur with his findings.

Rodker opens with imagery reminiscent of that closing Woolf's essay "Modern Novels", published a few months earlier in *The Times Literary Supplement*. Woolf gets her readers to visualise the art of fiction, personified as a masochistic woman, we recall, bidding us to "break her and bully her, honour her and love her, till she yields to our bidding, for so her youth is perpetually renewed and her sovereignty assured" (36). Rodker begins his review with a similar personification of poetry, except that it is the reviewer not the muse who is apparently, at first, the victim:

> Mr. Blackwell is an excellent bully for the muse of present-day Oxford poetry. Not too scrupulous a lady – a little vague as to her person, hardly distinguished and relying mainly on the adage that all cats are grey in the dark of reviewing minds. Only so can the laudatory notices from *The Bookman, The Times, The Literary World* be explained. The modus operandi is that, no doubt, of a certain daily which told a friend that its reviews sought to say all possible good of whatever book. (63)

Rodker's review of Blackwell's latest offerings refreshingly dispenses with such politeness. He continues with metaphors of pimp and prostitute to describe Blackwell's publishing policies:

> Mr. Blackwell is, I believe, not a too exigent bully. I am told he merely mulcts the lady of a fiver for every new client, and will even permit the lady to embark two at a time, or more, as with the "Four Writers" who together send out their venture *The Galleys Laden.*
>
> Whatever the cause, however, the lady is by now somewhat exhausted. The repetition of her labours no longer calls for the same spontaneity of excitement and affection. She may even be bored a little with the apparently unending series of poets who approach her with the same gifts, notably neo-catholic Christs and Maries, love, stars, water in moonlight, &c., the jetsam of a tide which has circumscribed the world for the past five hundred years.
>
> *Galleys Laden* contains nothing significant. (63)

The four poets, Ernest Denny, Nora O'Sullivan, C. Doyle, and Gwen Upcott, indeed offer poetry laden with mawkish clichés, rendered in clumsy mechanical verse. And *Wine and Gall* by "L. and R." is as terrible as Rodker's curt review suggests: it relies, he says, "on cheap antitheses rather mellifluous". His estimation of M. Nightingale's *Verses, Wise and Otherwise* is similarly cutting:

> *Verses, Wise and Otherwise,* are neither. The author uses words like croon, lure of the calling tide, The Dead Thing (with capitals). It is a tragedy of Scholasticism that these people should spend their nights in ecstasy of creation – ecstasy in inverse ratio to the quality of work produced. . . . She is a steady poet, one who will delight that class of reader known to the book trade and advertising world as poetry-lovers. (63)

Nightingale's offending capitalised phrase occurs in the poem "Sea Caves", a sing-song verse slightly reminiscent of Emily Dickinson, but with none of her sharpness or striking imagery:

> I came at the ebb of the calling tide
> Where wandered surges roam
> And a Dead Thing paced with me side by side
> And laughed at the whispering foam
>
> (*Verses, Wise and Otherwise*, p. 41)

We might compare Nightingale's hackneyed sea-imagery with the sparse imagism of H.D.'s poetry in *Sea Garden* (1916), or of "Oread" (1917?), which erotically unhinges its metaphor of sea for wood:

> Whirl up, sea –
> whirl your pointed pines,
> splash your great pines
> on our rocks,
> hurl your green over us,
> cover us with your pools of fir.

We might also compare Eliot's evocation of "the chambers of the sea" that closes his experimental tour-de-force "The Love Song of J. Alfred Prufrock", first published in *Poetry* (1915), and then in his debut volume, *Prufrock and Other Observations* (1917):

> We have lingered in the chambers of the sea
> By sea-girls wreathed with seaweed red and brown
> Till human voices wake us, and we drown.
>
> (lines 129–31)

Eliot's poem explores and rocks the status of lyric poetry, and the lyric self, in a world of urban "yellow fog" (line 15) that swings between mundane urban minutiae rendered surreal ("I have measured out my life with coffee spoons") and vast, cosmic questions ("Do I dare / disturb the universe?"). In a world that contains Eliot's "Prufrock", Nightingale has chosen to launch the sort of poetic observations that such work has all but made redundant.

Nightingale's phrase "Dead Thing", in particular, may well have caught Rodker's eye because he uses it himself, *sans* capitals, in a poem published four years previously, which sweeps away the stale, antiquated poetic lexis and style that Nightingale still favours. "A Slice of Life" is the second poem in Rodker's 1914 volume *Poems.* It is in two brief stanzas, the first of which employs river and seascape – and Dead Thing – imagery, as well as Nightingale's stanza form, but to very different, undercutting, effect:

> The sky broods over the river-
> The waves tumble and flee.
> And down go the dead things ever
> Down to the sea.

Evacuated and celebrated at the same time is the surreal collection of urban refuse and nursery-rhyme imagery itemised in the second stanza:

> A dog, an empty keg,
> An outworn hat.
> And with a broken leg
> A pregnant cat.

This is a judiciously brief collage of images sliced from life, suggesting spent energy or depleted inspiration (the empty keg), discarded poetic form (the outworn hat), and crippled fertility (the maimed and pregnant cat). The title questions the status of these objects, and by extension, the aesthetic object itself, in relation to life: are they part of, or now and forever separated from it? Anticipating the "foul rag-and-bone shop of the heart" of Yeats's 1939 poem "The Circus Animals' Desertion", where he returns to a lost poetic origin, "A mound of refuse or the sweepings of a street, / Old kettles, old bottles, and a broken can" (392), Rodker's brief litany of refuse also anticipates Eliot's own scrap heap of poetic conventions, "fragments . . . shored against my ruins", in the *The Waste Land* (1922). But whereas Rodker here, and Yeats, retain conventional lyric stanzas in which to assemble their refuse, Eliot explodes these conventional containers too.

## *The Egoist*: John Rodker reviews Aldous Huxley

Rodker, in his review, continues to round on academic poetry, for which "*The Herald* and the *Cambridge Magazine* provide all its inspiration," rebuking the writer who "does not call her works poems, and as prose they are pointless". He rebukes A. G. Shirreff for imperialist doggerel: "*Tales of the Sarai* are as witty as a club smoking-room or after-dinner bore. The author wavers between Kipling and W. S. Gilbert. He ruins interesting verses from the Sanskrit by their rendering" (63). Incidentally, Rodker's own poem "The After Dinner Hooter" (1914) magnificently renders the voice of such bores as "Bursting, jarring, bursting . . .", and so on (Rodker, *Poems*: 16). But Rodker does find two volumes in Blackwell's "Initiates: A Series of Poetry by Tried Hands" worthy of some, not unadulterated, praise. The first is Aldous Huxley's *Defeat of Youth and Other Poems*:

> I do not like the sonnet sequence. It seems to me intellectual without conviction – exercises made by every poet in youth and to be scrapped later. The book is less satisfactory than the author's privately printed Christmas booklet *Jonah*, which had a compactness and savour of its own, and which made it one of the books of the year. Certain things are as good, however: "The Reef" – derivations mixed but well imaged – "Crapulous Impression", "Complaint of a Poet Manqué", "Topiary on the Bus". The translations are particularly good, when Mr Huxley is being what is called modern – *i.e.*, using his own senses and not conventionally poetical stuff, he has a definite gift and is to be reckoned with – but rhyme invariably involves him in cliché, inversion, extravagance and redundance. Nevertheless Huxley, thank god! is not of university poetry. (16)

There are twenty-two sonnets in the sequence that Rodker dismisses as an apprentice piece. They describe urban life, set "In the Little Room", with views of "wet and sunlit trees, shops and the stream / Of glittering traffic", for example, or "In the Park", where, somewhat self-consciously, it is reported, "the Park / Has turned the garden of a symbolist"; and draw on an Eliotic imagery ("London unfurls its incense-coloured dusk"), and occasionally incorporate a discourse of imagism – for example, in one interior is glimpsed:

> The silken breastplate of a mandarin,
> Centuries dead, which he had given her.
> Exquisite miracle, when men could spin
> Jay's wing and belly of the kingfisher!
>
> (Huxley: 12)

But Huxley, in conforming to the sonnet form, fails to follow the Imagist fragmentation of metre into musical phrase or free verse. And Rodker notes the similar crime of rhyming in Huxley's translations, which are "L'Après-Midi d'un Faune (From the French of Stéphane Mallarmé)" (44), and "The Louse-Hunters (From the French of Rimbaud)" (48).

Rodker does admire "The Reef", in fifteen quatrains, exploring a psychosexual dreamscape (perhaps under the influence of smoking reefers?), and culminating in a Prufockian question of daring:

> I go to seek that reef, far down, far down
> Below the edge of everyday's desire,

Beyond the magical islands, where of old
I was content, dreaming, to give the lie
To misery. They were all strong and bold
That thither came; and shall I dare to try?

(Huxley: 18–19)

"Crapulous Impression" is in two longer stanzas. The splendid word "crapulous" means hung-over, or ill with drink; so "crapulous impression" suggests, from the poem's content, the speaker's drunken recollection of a conversation at table the night before, but also describes the poem's own compositional procedure, its skewed impressionism, as well as perhaps a rather jaded view of literary impressionism. The sketchiness of the composition and of the speaker's recollection is suggested by stumbling repetition and the use of ellipses. The poem, modern in philosophical attitude and in aesthetics, invokes the still-life genre of visual art and describes a stylised, possibly cubistic pictorialism, with hard delineation and solid colour planes:

Still life, still life . . . the high-lights shine the high-lights shine
Hard and sharp on the bottles: the wine
Stands firmly solid in the glasses,
Smooth yellow ice, through which there passes
The lamp's bright pencil of down-struck light.

(Huxley: 36; ellipses as in original)

This surreal composition of solidifying liquid and light also includes natural objects with industrial finish: "fruits" that "metallically gleam". This is more than *nature morte*, the French for "still-life", this is nature manufactured or cast in bronze. Peripheral human presence is signalled by alienated faces, almost reified by their reflection in the darkened window-glass: "faces against the night / Of the outer room – faces that seem / Part of this still, still life . . . they've lost their soul" (Huxley: 36; his ellipses). The speaker of the poem singles out from the catatonic crowd of "frozen faces" arrayed in this bourgeois setting, the smiling face of the addressee whose voice also seems similarly to thaw from the impassive throng, introducing a metaphysical dialogue, witty and blasphemous, conducted as a game of chess, comedically moving the objects of the still life as its pieces:

And out of the frozen welter of sound
Your voice came quietly, quietly.

> "What about God?" you said. "I have found
> Much to be said for Totality.
> All, I take it, is God: God's all –
> This bottle, for instance . . ." I recall,
> Dimly, that you took God by the neck –
> God-in-the-bottle – and pushed Him across:
> But I, without a moment's loss
> Moved god-in-the-salt in front and shouted: "Check!"
>
> (Huxley: 36; ellipses as in original)

As well as skewing a totalising monotheism with the invocation of the adversarial pagan gods in bottle and salt-cellar, parodying also the planning of military manoeuvres (particularly salient in 1918), Huxley's poem seems to drunkenly skew the imagism of Pound by taking up a face from the crowd, breaking up the glazed composition, inserting dialogue, comedy, and movement into an imagistic "frozen welter of sound". Perhaps Eliot's "A Game of Chess", in *The Waste Land,* which more dramatically, more precariously and more copiously explores a metaphysics of religious doubt, owes something to Huxley's clumsy scrap of a scene, which also seems to anticipate, in compressed form, the significant banquet scene in "The Window", the first part of Woolf's *To the Lighthouse,* where in a room in which the Ramsay family and friends sit around a table, with a "dish of fruit" (150) as centre-piece, and where the play of candlelight on faces against the dark window glass renders a drunken, if not crapulous, impression to the elusive narrator:

> Now all the candles were lit, and the faces on both sides of the table were brought nearer by the candle light, and composed, as they had not been in the twilight, into a party round a table, for the night was now shut off by panes of glass, which, far from giving any accurate view of the outside world, rippled it so strangely that here, inside the room, seemed to be order and dry land; there, outside, a reflection in which things wavered and vanished, waterily. (151)

Like Huxley's interlocutors, Lily Briscoe seems to be playing chess with the accoutrements of the table, which she uses as visual shorthand for her compositional analysis of her painting in progress: "Then her eye caught the salt cellar, which she had placed there to remind her, and she remembered that next morning she would move the tree further towards the middle" (144). Like theirs, her reconfiguration of the objects in a bourgeois table's still life coincides with a recognition of oppositional philosophy: "For at any rate, she said to herself, catching sight of the salt cellar on the pattern, she need not marry, thank Heaven: she need not undergo that degradation. She was saved from that dilution. She would move the tree rather more to the middle" (159).

Huxley's "Complaint of a Poet Manqué", which Rodker also admires, is a humorous account of a poseur who vicariously dresses like a fin-de-siècle, decadent, poet:

> So I grew the hair so long on my head
> That my mother wouldn't know me,
> Till a woman in a night-club said,
> As I was passing by,
> "Hullo, here comes Salome . . . "
>
> (Huxley: 37–8; ellipses as in original)

But this poet confesses "I'm not a poet: but never despair! / I'll madly live the poems I shall never write" (Huxley 38). Rodker also lists as good "Topiary on the Bus". This is in fact a copy error conflating two poems: "Topiary" and "On the Bus". "Topiary" is one long sentence, apparently topiarised of its subject and main verb, which finally do appear ("I sometimes wish") at the end of line 12, preceded by three clauses introduced by "failing", so it is not until line 12 that the reader can identify who is "failing sometimes to understand". The horrific cause of the misunderstanding is inevitably expressed in language that breaches the light, trite, poetic decorum associated with the term "topiary": the topiarist, it transpires, is a sadistic God who is deemed responsible for, and therefore brought into question by, the presence of throngs of mutilated and amputee war veterans visible in urban life.

> Failing sometimes to understand
> Why there are folk whose flesh should seem
> Like carrion puffed with noisome steam,
> Fly-blown to the eye that looks on it,
> Fly-blown to the touch of a hand;
> Why there are men without any legs,
> Whizzing along on little trollies
> With long long arms like apes':

Failing to see why God the Topiarist
Should train and carve and twist
Men's bodies into such fantastic shapes:
Yes, failing to see the point of it all, I sometimes wish
That I were a fabulous thing in a fool's mind,
Or, at the ocean bottom, in a world that is deaf and blind,
Very remote and happy, a great goggling fish.

(Huxley: 38–9)

This uncomfortable, struggling poem is itself perhaps in need of some severe topiary (by Poundian shears). But it has resonances of more honed achievements by poetic betters. Huxley's last two lines parody the desire of Eliot's Prufrock, who "should have been a pair of ragged claws / Scuttling across the floors of silent seas" (lines 73–4). This perhaps alludes to Shakespeare's *Hamlet* ("Prince Hamlet" is cited later in Prufrock) where Hamlet says to Polonius "for you yourself, sir, should be old as I am, if, like a crab, you could go backward" (2.2.205–6). But also compare this with the speaker of Wordsworth's 1807 sonnet, railing against emergent modern capitalism, "The World is Too Much with Us", who declares that "Getting and spending, we lay waste our powers", and would "rather be":

A Pagan suckled in a creed outworn;
So might I, standing on this pleasant lea,
Have glimpses that would make me less forlorn;
Have sight of Proteus rising from the sea;
Or hear old Triton blow his wreathed horn.

(lines 9–14)

Whereas Wordsworth's speaker, looking out to sea, finds some consolation in the defunct sea gods of classical antiquity, Prufrock settles on the figure of the apparently amputated claws of a crab on the sea floor. Huxley's speaker prefers to be there too, "in a world that is deaf and blind", but is "Very remote and happy, a great goggling fish". As well as the amputee veterans, playthings of the gods, is this too the "fabulous thing in a fool's mind"? Is Huxley satirising or finding consolation in the poetic construction of a lyric self in the face of cataclysmic war? In the opening lines of "The Reef" he celebrates "My green aquarium of phantom fish, / Goggling in on me". But the "fabulous thing in a fool's mind" may also refer to the "fools" in Yeats's poem "A Coat" (1914), which marks his casting off, with the help of Pound, his earlier poetry ("a coat / Covered with embroideries / Out of old mythologies"), a poetry still imitated by his followers, themselves rather like Huxley's "Poet Manqué":

> But the fools caught it,
> Wore it in the world's eyes
> As though they wrote it.
> Song, let them take it,
> For there's more enterprise
> In walking naked.
>
> (Yeats: 142)

The ambivalence of Yeats's title (referring to the old poems, but also naming the present one), of course, suggests that even nudity is a form of coat. And while every apprentice poet tries on different styles (see Rodker's dismissal, above, of Huxley's "youthful" attempt at a sonnet sequence), this seems to be an era where dressing-up, masquerade and quick-change in the old, become the subject matter of the new poetry, guises destined for Eliot's *Waste Land* and Yeats's rag-and-bone shop.

"On the Bus" locates the lyric poet in modern urban capitalist transport, showing a self partly-reified to resemble a motor vehicle with an exhaust or factory belching out industrial effluent:

> Sitting on the top of the 'bus,
> I bite my pipe and look at the sky.
> Over my shoulder the smoke streams out
> And my life with it,
> "Conservation of energy," you say.
>
> (Huxley: 39)

William Blake's pastoral piper appears to be gripping a rather different instrument. But the poem does more than conjure up a picture of semi-automaton urban humanity, it also mingles the discourse of lyric poetry (classical and contemporary) with that of contemporary, war-era, urban experience. "Conservation of energy" may refer to political demands for fuel economy as well as to the fashion for poetic economy instigated by Imagism. Huxley's citation of the traditional lyric exclamation of the lover, "I burn", ignites in a pall of industrialism:

But I burn, I tell you, I burn;
And the smoke of me streams out
In a vanishing skein of grey.

(Huxley: 39)

The citation of poetic borrowings is acknowledged in the next lines where, thrown around by the "Crash and bump bump" of the bus, the speaker, exclaiming ". . . my poor bruised body!", also comically declares, in an allusion to well-worn Aeolian allusions, "I am a harp of twittering strings, / An elegant instrument, but infinitely second-hand" (39). This last epithet in turn comprises second-hand Eliotics, in recalling the use of "infinitely" repeated in the following lines from "Preludes", published in *Prufrock* (1917):

I am moved by fancies that are curled
Around these images, and cling:
The notion of some infinitely gentle
Infinitely suffering thing

(Eliot, *Complete Poems*: 23)

But if Eliot's "Infinitely suffering thing" suggests his speaker apprehends intimations of Christian divinity, Huxley's persona apprehends the oncoming of tuberculosis, the word for which makes his penultimate line almost cough: "And if I have not got phthisis it is only an accident." The final line is accordingly, a brief expectoration: "Droll phenomena!" (Huxley: 39).

## *The Egoist*: John Rodker reviews Edith Sitwell, Osbert Sitwell, et al.

Rodker also finds of some merit Edith Sitwell's volume (in the same series as Huxley's), *Clowns' Houses*, although it lacks verbal economy:

> If anything, she is too original and extravagant. Her work nullifies itself by a plethora of mutually exclusive adjectives. It bears, however, the marks of careful working and extreme conscientiousness. She has the same faults as Mr Huxley, but her virtues are different, and at present her work has as much finality as the poems of Wilde which they greatly resemble – namely, nil. An unpleasant habit she has is to use a rather silly anthropomorphic measure for the reduction of the cosmos: –

Eternity and time commence
To merge amid the somnolence
Of winding circles bend on bend
With no beginning and no end

Down which they chase queer tunes that gape
Till they come close – then just escape;
But though Time's barriers are defied
They never are quite satisfied.

> "What the Dean Said" is good in a scholastic, E. M. Forster, way. "Myself on the Merry go-round" is rather an achievement compact (more or less) brilliant too – but doesn't mean much, though an admirable exercise. "Weather Cocks" is charming. At present I find no emotional quality whatever in her work.
>
> (Rodker, *The Egoist:* 63)

Rodker quotes dismissively here from "Minstrels". Incidentally, "What the Dean Said to Silenus" (Sitwell: 10–12) is "Excuse me, Sir, my plums, I think!" The brilliant "Myself on the Merry-Go-Round" (18–19) describes well Sitwell's own cold brilliance ("The giddy sun's kaleidescope / The pivot of a switchback world"), and "Weather Cocks" (14) her straining, bravura showmanship:

A coloured bubble is the world-
A glassy ball that clowns have hurled
Through the rainbow space of laughter.

(Edith Sitwell: 14)

Rodker finds no "emotional quality" in Sitwell, which may of course be a virtue according to Pound or Eliot, but it is difficult to read some of the poems Rodker has chosen not to cite without finding a similar critique actually installed in the poetry itself. For example, "The Dancers" (25), subtitled "(During a great battle, 1916)", seems to be indicting itself in the chilling glissades of its opening stanzas:

The floors are slippery with blood:
The world gyrates too. God is good
That while His wind blows out the light
For those who hourly die for us –
We still can dance, each night.

(Edith Sitwell: 25)

Sitwell's poetry, then, is capable, in places, of making biting comment on the strained relations of poetry while straining itself, and on the grim reality of the Great War, and is more than the "admirable exercise" in formalism that Rodker implies, if not ultimately great poetry.

Rodker closes his review with a swipe at *Songs for Sale*, edited by E. B. C. Jones (the initials mask a woman's identity: Emily Beatrix Coursolles), which is a selection from other volumes in a Blackwells series, Adventurers All:

> I gather that most of those included have at one time or another sat at the feet of Dr. Bridges, but the influence has been dire. W. Blair and E.B.C. Jones seem the only ones in an odd thirty with definite vision, and in Mr Blair's work it is treatment rather than emotion or subject-matter; while Mr. Jones scores once in three with "Jerked Heartstrings in Town". The fault may, however, be the anthologist's, who appears to have chosen particularly badly if the choice was not determined by previous publications of the Adventurers All.
>
> (Rodker, *The Egoist:* 63)

Rodker bemoans the dire influence of Robert Bridges, the current Poet Laureate (1913–30). Wilfred Blair's poems "The Strange Servant" and "Tidings" are stilted fairy songs; and Jones's one success with Rodker is an urbane account of urban unrequited love (27). The selection is on the whole, as Rodker suggests, without much adventure. Edith Sitwell's "Clowns' Houses" (45–6) is included in this volume (though not in fact in the volume of that name). Rodker continues: "T. W. Earp, who has done some good work, is badly represented, as is W. K. Childe." The foolish-sounding T. W. Earp (Tommy – a wealthy aesthete) is in fact represented by a poem, "Departure" (19), that encapsulates in amusing understatement the modern impetus to "make it new":

> I have been reading books
> For about twenty years;
> I have laughed with other men's laughter,
> Wept with their tears.
>
> Life has been a cliché
> All these years.
>
> I would find a gesture of my own.

Earp, of course, merely describes the desire for "a gesture of my own", without recognising, with the avant-garde, that the appropriation, citation and rearrangement of cliché may in itself constitute a radical and new gesture. But the limp gesture of "a gesture of my own" also ironises the idea that any linguistic gesture or utterance may be understood as the property of a solitary individual, rather than socially and collectively born.

Rodker concludes his review, singling out Osbert Sitwell's "Lament of the Mole Catcher" as "surprisingly good", adding: "It has genuine emotion, and might easily be Wordsworth. It has a very real quality and is quite the best thing I have so far seen by him" (63). Rodker's approving identification of Wordsworthian emotion suggests that he holds differing opinions on poetics from Eliot's (soon to be) famous views on "impersonality" expressed in the same issue of *The Egoist*, and his review makes an interesting foil to the classicism of Eliot's essay. Sitwell's poem might indeed almost be set among the portraits of rural workers and vagrants of Wordsworth's *Lyrical Ballads*: his first stanza describes the shambling figure of the mole-catcher, and in the second he "innocently" speaks. But Sitwell sinks further than Wordsworth in mawkish sentimentality. Here, for example, is the gist of the mole-catcher's lament:

> "For forty years I've sought to slay
> The small, the dumb, the blind,
> But now the Lord has made me pay,
> And I am like their kind."
>
> (Osbert Sitwell in Jones, *Songs for Sale*: 44–5)

We might wonder at how "genuine" is an "emotion" which seems so readily to replicate its Wordsworthian model. Sitwell's reworking of lines from Keats's "La Belle Dame", in the first stanza, is more rewarding: "No note he heard from any bird / That sang" recalls Keats's "And no bird sang". But if the form and overt subject matter of Sitwell's pastiched "lyrical ballad" are far from modern, it is perhaps its poignant metaphorical potential to which Rodker responds. The blinded murderer of moles in their tunnels, a router in the underworld, surely resonates with a familiar and more contemporary imagery of leadership in the warfare of the trenches.

## The pacifist poetry of John Rodker (an excursus): readings around T. S. Eliot, Isaac Rosenberg and Ezra Pound

Before leaving Rodker's review, it is worth also briefly considering his own poetic achievement to date. He published his first volume, *Poems*, privately printed with a cover of abstract design by Bomberg, in 1914, and several of these poems had first been published in *The Egoist* in the same year. "Vibro-Massage", for example, appeared in *The Egoist* in September 1914, and shows Rodker's experimentalism with line and ellipses, his taste for a subject matter in a mix of modern urban, erotic and sensuous experiences, his interest in the wavering, elliptical status of the lyric self. It opens with:

> Moist warm towels
> At my face
> Smell queerly . . .
> Chill me. . . .
>
> I am afraid. . . .
>
> . . . Unguents
> smoothed into my face
> like yellow silk
> over my forehead.

The poem achieves a contradictory climax in "Ecstasy / like a kiss . . . / the touch of hated hands", and ends in a similarly oppositional sense of "triste", synaesthetically intimating mortality: "Cold wet towels burn me . . . / their smell of death". Rodker explores bodily and mental experience as coterminous, and this treatment of subjectivity marks out his work as therefore quite differently inflected from that of Pound or Eliot or Lewis, as Andrew Crozier has shown:

> in Rodker we find neither the erasure of the writing subject, nor the ironic objectification of the dramatic subject in its imputed language: both of them modes which constituted the modernity of Pound and Eliot. Furthermore, we find quite the reverse of Lewis's theoretical dissociation of mind and body. Somatic effect is continuous with psychic affect, in a way which removes the new sensations of the mechanical environment from simple astonishment and intellectual fascination. To an extent Pound was right when in 1914 he classified Rodker as a Futurist. Where Rodker differs from Futurism, however, is

> precisely in not objectifying mechanical sensation. His writing is permeated with the affective modes of the self.
>
> (Crozier, "Introduction": xvii)

In connection with these modes of "self", "psychic", "somatic", "industrialised", Rodker also explores the consequent status of the lyric self. For example, in "The Pub" (1914), he gives a jaundiced evocation of the lyric poet in an urban bar, who wearily wonders in the opening lines about his location (in the bar and in the stanza): "How long, how very long have I been sitting here. / Tongue-tied and fixed within this murmuring stability" (16). Lyric automatism nauseates him:

> The automatic piano plays and plays –
> I grow sick, with anguish at the heart.
> The piano thumps, skirls, goes out.
>
> I fumble for a penny –
> More music . . .
> And again I grow sick.
>
> (*Poems*, p. 16)

Mechanical reproduction, delivered on payment, has replaced lyric voice. Repetition of cliché is all. Compare this with Pound's jaded speaker "Hugh Selwyn Mauberley", who finds five years (and the Great War) later, "The pianola 'replaces' / Sappho's barbitos" (1919/20). Pound's quotation marks around "replaces" both replicates and undermines the act of citation – the pianola supplants but can never really replace, and in fact abuts, in the poem, Sappho's "barbitos". Pound's "pianola", furthermore, seems to replicate Rodker's "automatic piano". But his poem's distanced third-person account of Mauberley also puts it some distance from Rodker's lyric "I", a remnant of guttering Romantic subjectivity, which however sick, still functions.

This soiled lyric "I" is tested to the limits somatically, psychically, and linguistically in "The Descent into Hell" (1914), the final poem in Rodker's volume (*Poems*, pp. 21–2). The poem is written in two parallel columns. On the left are occasionally repeated, with slight variations, the statements "A million years pass" and then "Many years pass". These statements are aligned with certain lines, points of departure, in the stanzas arranged in the right-hand column. The reader is instructed in a headnote (in the first edition) as follows: "This poem should be read many times in order that the time-sense may become so essential a part of the poem as not to interfere with the sequence of lines" (184). The visual impact of the poetry on the page suggests the poem as a diagram for an elevator: the stanzas on the right are like a lift shaft, and the statements on the left (printed in smaller point) indicating the passage of time are the levels, or floors, reached by the plummeting narrative on the right. What plummets with the descent is a sense of self. The first stanza is as follows:

A million years has passed.          Woven from many glooms
Out of many glooms
Into many glooms
I was.
I     and yet
Not I.

(*Poems*, p. 21)

The increasingly sparse narrative of the descent of "I" stumbles in the cold and dark, with no foothold on historical reference, blighted by gaps and ellipses, while, on the left, the frequency of the time statements increases with the descent. The poem ends with monosyllabic inflections of the copula, in past tense then present, eliding the pronoun in bleak questions:

Many years pass.          Was?

Many, many years pass.          Am?

(*Poems*, p. 22)

Not long after his review Rodker published his second volume of poems, *Hymns* (1920), some of which had appeared in magazines as early as 1916 and 1918. For example, "Hymn to Death 1914 and On" appeared in *The Egoist* in December 1918. It is a danse-macabre, making fragmented music with fragmented human remains – or with the names for remains, at least:

"Danse-Macabre" Death.
"Dried-guts" death.

They clatter, girn, mow –
femur rattles skull

epiphyses shriek, grate –
Brain    a shrunk pea
quintessential lusts –
rattles
rattles    rattles
rattles.

The onomatopoeic "shriek" of "epiphyses" (which are defined in the dictionary as bones with their own centre of ossification; the pineal gland; or, an ossicle in a sea-urchin) is simultaneously discordant and euphonious, as its polysyllables are played off with relish against the monosyllabic thud of "skull". And just in case the reader is in doubt as to the kind of music played here, Rodker's speaker intervenes with a citation from "race music", and a pointed parenthetical "racial" colloquialism:

O the "bones", the wonderful bones.
[God's the darkey]

Rodker, collaging folksong, "Negro spirituals", with poetic discourse, is playing what Eliot later plays in *The Waste Land*, another danse-macabre: "O O O O that Shakespeherian Rag – ", which marries ragtime to the iambic pentameter (his citation was apparently a hit for the Ziegfield Follies in 1912). The post-Great War period of the "lost generation" was defined by F. Scott Fitzgerald as "the Jazz Age" (9), and the cultural impetus was to come in the 1920s from Harlem, New York. The pioneering anthology *The New Negro: An Interpretation*, edited by Alain Locke, and published in 1925, was the best known forum. Here we find, in a highly stylised and gorgeously illustrated volume (the book decorations and portraits by Winold Reiss), work by Countee Cullen, Jean Toomer, Langston Hughes, Zora Neale Hurston, Claude Mckay, Angelina Grimke, and W. E. B. DuBois, providing a crash course in Black culture, art, music, fiction, poetry and essays, and in education and politics. J. A. Rogers offers, in the essay "Jazz at Home", a wonderful account of the international "contagiousness of jazz" (*New Negro*, p. 216) that should be read alongside Fitzgerald's accounts of the "jazz age" (see Appel). Langston Hughes later recalled that it was "a period (God help us!) when Ethel Barrymore appeared in blackface in *Scarlet Sister Mary*! It was the period when the Negro was in vogue" (*The Big Sea*, p. 172).

But God immediately turns into a drilling sergeant in Rodker's next stanza, bringing the bones to order: "Toes out, click heels, March!" Following this is a reprise of the rattling bones during which dark comedy a voice interjects: "Hi there / take your toes out o' me ribs." After the last "rattle" comes the final cut: a coda in the compressed form of an imagist poem, a citation in translation perhaps, in two juxtaposed, and typically verbless, honed and alliterative lines, mixing courtliness with the sickly stench of mortality:

Her bouquet at this ball
The sweet skull of her lover.

Rodker's experimental virtuosity here with the imagined, and dry, bones of the war dead might be compared with "Dead Man's Dump" (1922), a poem written in 1917 by Rosenberg, who died in action the following year. Rosenberg's poem speaks in a mix of graphic reportage, the odd colloquialism, and classical poetic diction, sometimes in simple sentences, occasionally brushed with antique grammatical inversion:

The air is loud with death,
The dark air spurts with fire,
The explosions ceaseless are.

(lines 39–41, p. 110)

The inverted openness of "ceaseless are" conveys the sense of ceaselessness better than the proposition "are ceaseless", and also communicates a sonic arc in imitation of the explosions it describes. But it still retains an affected archaic clumsiness, nevertheless. Here in Rosenberg's poem the fragmenting body parts have yet to ossify or dry, although they are momentarily caught in a gory imagism, in the first two of these lines:

A man's brains splattered on
A stretcher-bearer's face;
His shook shoulders slipped their load,
But when they bent to look again
The drowning soul was sunk too deep
For human tenderness.

> They left this dead with the older dead,
> Stretched at the crossroads.
>
> (lines 48–55)

As in Rodker's poem, the dead in "Dead Man's Dump" are not formally or fully buried. Where Rodker's coda shows the skull reified as a lover's *memento mori* in a surreal portrayal of the civilian life that continues while the war rages, Rosenberg's poem concludes with a view of remorseful survivors of combat, recording the moment where a fellow-soldier dies, his corpse now part of the object world, the terrain across which they ride:

> We heard his very last sound,
> And our wheels grazed his dead face.
>
> (lines 78–9)

There is no final dumping ground of the dead, as *The Waste Land*, the dumping ground for dead poetry, among other things, seems to teach: " 'That corpse you planted last year in your garden, / Has it begun to sprout?' " (*Complete Poems*, p. 62). The viscera of the war dead return, bottled, in Rodker's later poem, "War Museum – Royal College of Surgeons" (first published in *Collected Poems, 1912–1925* (1930)), where various preserved organs of the dead are on show:

> This is the airman's heart.
> he fell five hundred feet
> and the impetus snapped the hurtling heart
> from its two frail tubes.
>
> And this is W.O. bottle ooo – a liver
> with a large gash.
> In spirit reposes!
>
> And another bottle.
> Six feet of small bowel
> shot into pieces.
> But he died of pneumonia.

Here the first line seems also a riposte to Yeats's poem "An Irish Airman Foresees his Death" (1919), on an airman killed in action (in "this tumult in the clouds").

Rodker's poem, a distillation perhaps of the dried bones of his earlier danse-macabre "Hymn to Death, 1914 and On" and the visceral immediacy available in Rosenberg's "Dead Man's Dump", is born out of the entrails of the war dead. Each stanza, each bottle, each preserved bodily part tells a story of war, and in the process these fragmented, reified remains are partially reanimated. The litany of disembodied parts continues:

And wax masks.
The speechless agony of shotaway faces
And pulpy tongues

These grotesque suspensions perhaps make "one think of", to paraphrase the man himself (in "Preludes", line 21), all Eliot's allusions to disembodied body parts in the *Prufrock* volume of 1917, of the "time / To prepare a face to meet the faces that you meet" ("Prufrock", line 27), as well as "all the hands / that are raising dingy shades / in a thousand furnished rooms" ("Preludes", lines 21–3). The urban, and industrial, office worker's experience of virtual somatic fragmentation and reification cruelly returns, in Rodker's poem, as literally manufactured by war, by-products, bottled parts on display in the medical "war museum"; faces "prepared" in laboratories. Eliot's "Preludes" gives glimpses of salvation in a suggestion of a Christ worn down by urban grotesques, themselves reduced to a collective of semi-automated body parts, with "His soul stretched tight across the skies / That fade behind a city block, / Or trampled by insistent feet / . . . And short square fingers stuffing pipes, / . . . and eyes / Assured of certain certainties, / The conscience of a blackened street" (lines 39–48). Rodker's poem, following its litany of pickled and ruptured body parts, satirically invokes in the final stanza the focus of national post-war conscience, the memorial Tomb of the Unknown Warrior, for whom a new Christ must be manufactured. It is a vicious parody of the still very current public discourse on the aesthetics of war monuments:

Therefore for the unknown warrior
let us make a Christ
sweating blood but speechless.
With the open chest
the snapped heart
the gashed liver

and cutaway bowels,
the pale stomach that died of gas
and an obliterated face
that dribbles a tear from an eye corner.

(Rodker: 125)

Rodker's poem in effect rips the lid off the Tomb of the Unknown Warrior, allowing its grotesquely (and necessarily) unidentifiable, disparate, human remains to speak, not merely with their "pulpy tongues", a message that graphically belies, of course, the kind of unifying, nationalistic sentiment projected, in the official undertaking to memorialise the war dead, onto the smooth and slippery surface of its marble slab. The tradition of memorialising war dead by the veneration of unidentifiable remains continues, but the status of anonymity becomes more difficult to achieve considering the enormous advances in forensic science, as Paul Erickson has noted in connection with Ronald Reagan's more recent ceremonial commemoration of the American dead of the Vietnam War; and his observations are still pertinent to the cultural significance of the earlier Unknown Warrior evoked by Rodker:

> To be so utterly beyond identification it had to lack not only a face and hand or foot prints but all the other miniscule anatomical details which give clues to experts. The reality of the corpse is hideous to contemplate, as terrible as the Vietnam War was and as armed conflict in general remains for many Americans. Stripped of its horrific actuality though, and hidden ceremoniously away in a flag-bedecked casket, the charred and rotted body could act as the perfect vehicle for a message quite different from that which its actuality would convey. Had the ceremony featured an open casket, the image of the Vietnam War would hardly have fit Reagan's communicative strategy. What mattered was not the real body, not the true once-named soldier who fought and died, but the metaphoric cipher that lay in the Capitol rotunda as the President spoke. (Erickson: 56–7; quoted Abel: 58)

Paul Fussell comments on the "inhibition on truth" evident in the typical "heroic grandiosity" of the British choice of term, "The Unknown Warrior", which elevates the Americans' "The Unknown Soldier". But both terms are euphemisms, he suggests, and constitute a continuation of the censorship practised during the war itself:

> Actually, the war was much worse than any description of it possible in the twenties or thirties could suggest. Or, of course, while it was going on. Lloyd George knew this at the time. "The thing is horrible," he said, "and beyond human nature to bear, and I feel I can't go on any longer with the bloody business." He was convinced that if the war could once be described in accurate language, people would insist that it be stopped. "But of course they don't – and can't know. The correspondents don't write and the censorship wouldn't pass the truth." (Fussell, *The Great War and Modern Memory*: 174)

We might also consider how our culture continues with euphemisms and elisions in the ways we define, collect and preserve our "war poetry". "War Museum – Royal College of Surgeons", written in the immediate aftermath, by the conscientious objector Rodker, surely stands as "war poetry" alongside that of Rosenberg, who was killed in action. The poem reads the same anti-war messages, for example, in the viscera of the war dead as Yossarian does in Joseph Heller's later anti-war novel *Catch-22* (1961), a satire born of Heller's experience as a combatant in World War II, but coming to considerable cultural significance during the Vietnam War:

> Yossarian . . . gazed down despondently at the grim secret Snowden had spilled all over the messy floor. It was easy to read the message in his entrails. Man was matter, that was Snowden's secret. Drop him out a window and he'll fall. Set fir to him and he'll burn. Bury him and he'll rot, like other kinds of garbage. That was Snowden's secret. Ripeness was all. (429–30)

"Ripeness was all" refers Heller's readers to *King Lear,* but the message in Snowden's entrails recalls too the "Hades" episode in Joyce's *Ulysses*: "Lots of them lying around here: lungs, hearts, livers. Old rusty pumps: damn the thing else. The resurrection and the life. Once you are dead you are dead." But words, of course, live on. For Eliot, in "Tradition and the Individual Talent", once the poet is dead he continues to speak through the living. And in reciprocation, the living poet is to be "set among the dead" for our measure of him. He transfers, in a rapture of impersonality, to an ideal order of the dead – tradition.

## *The Egoist*: Richard Aldington and Ezra Pound

This issue of *The Egoist* carries other information on contemporary poetry for its readers, in the form of advertisements on the last page (64) for The Egoist Ltd Press. Among them, advertisements appear for a special limited edition of Ezra Pound's *Quia Pauper Amavi*, and for Aldington's *Images*, and for volumes from the Poet's Translation Series: Aldington's translations of *Greek Songs in the Manner of Anacreon*, and Edward Storer's translation of Sappho. Here we see in the heavy spattering of Latin and Greek references, contemporary individual talents, embracing and voicing classical tradition. The translations of Greek fragments are of course classical models for imagist poetry; and their subject matter often seems surprisingly modern. Contemporary resonance is felt in a refrain in Aldington's Anacreontic translations, for example, which voices weariness with war: "Give me the lyre of Homer, far from the note of war; bring me, ah, bring me the sacred drinking cup" (5). In the "Wine-Cup", the libation is to "Hephaistos, graver of silver", who is asked: "make me no panoply of war – what have I to do with battle? – but carve me a hollow wine-cup" (6). There is modern resonance too in "The Painter", who is commanded "Paint the cities for us" (6). But let us now briefly look at Aldington's and then Pound's volume.

*Images*, published in 1919 by The Egoist Ltd, is an enlarged edition of Aldington's earlier *Images*, published in 1915 by the Poetry Bookshop (and by 1919 out of print). Aldington records in his note to the edition the recent falling off of other Imagist publications. Imagist poets such as Pound have moved on with the war. Aldington, on the other hand, continues to bring out more Imagism, including also *Images of War*, and *Images of Desire*, both published in 1919 (by Allen and Unwin), and whose titles, appending "war" and "desire", suggest that pure, unadorned Imagism can no longer do poetic service to the times. But there are some striking images, in *Images*, of modern urban life, such as "Cinema Exit" and "In the Tube", both of which were in the 1915 volume too. "Cinema Exit" describes the moments of exodus "after the click and whirr / Of the glimmering pictures". The films purvey "banal sentimentality" to a "hushed concentration of the people". And at the moment of exit, "Suddenly / A vast-avalanche of greenish-yellow light / Pours over the threshold" in which the audience sweeps along, a flurry of "Swift figures, legs, skirts, white cheeks, hats". This exit from the cinema is beginning to resemble the final movements in some industrial process, confirmed in the last five lines where the crowd has become:

Millions of human vermin
Swarm sweating
Along the night-arched cavernous roads.

(Happily rapid chemical processes
Will disintegrate them all.)

Aldington seems to collapse the gas attacks of trench warfare to combine with cinematic propaganda, poisoning the urban citizen. A similarly sinister industrial process is occurring in "In the Tube", where, as "The electric car jerks", the speaker looks up to see a series of regimented images:

A row of advertisements,
A row of windows,
Set in brown woodwork pitted with brass nails,
A row of hard faces,
Immobile,
In the swaying train.

This is a grim counter to Pound's beautifully economical, lyric ecstasy of "faces in a crowd" caught in "In a Station of the Metro". Aldington's poem blusters with a superfluity of adjectival contempt. His somewhat differently reified "faces" have "eyes of greed, of pitiful blankness, of plethoric complacency", and, forced through the "fluted dingy tunnel", they all conform to "the same thought" betrayed in "brasslike eyes", and shared also by the speaker: "*What right have you to live?*", a question that overturns the traditional lyric boast of the poet's gift of immortality to be bestowed upon the addressee.

Pound's volume is by far the most significant among those advertised in *The Egoist*, a landmark in avant-garde technique and an exemplary exploration of individual talent and tradition. *Quia Pauper Amavi* contains several important poems already published in little magazines such as the *Little Review, Poetry* (Chicago), and *The New Age*: "Langue d'Oc", "Moeurs Contemporaines", Three Cantos, and "Homage to Sextus Propertius". Pound infuses his diverse and learned citations from the "tradition" with breezy Americanese, by turns comical and contemptuous. "Mr Hecatomb Styrax", for example, in the opening poem of "Moeurs Contemporaines" (14), is both "the owner of a large estate / and large muscles", and "A 'blue' and a climber of mountains, [who] has married at the age of 28 / he being at that age a virgin". The poem continues with a sneering lesson exposing the brute ignorance of Styrax, the impervious beneficiary of his imperial and cultural entitlement, a university education, at which he (as a "blue") presumably only excels in sport:

> The term "virgo" being made male in mediaeval Latinity;
>     His ineptitudes
> Have driven his wife from one religious excess to another.
> She has abandoned the vicar
> For he was lacking in vehemence;
> She is now the high-priestess
> Of a modern and ethical cult

Styrax, whose name in Latin is a tree, as well as the resinous gum of the tree, is a blockhead who despite the evidence of his wife's behaviour, "even now . . . / Does not believe in aesthetics". In the second part of the poem we learn of Styrax's brother-in-law who "has taken to the gypsies": "But the son-in-law of Mr. H. Styrax / Objects to perfumed cigarettes". This observation prompts a cutting citation from a Renaissance arch-political theorist and an indictment of the imperial infrastructure:

> In the parlance of Niccolo Machiavelli
>     "Thus things proceed in their circle"
> And thus empire is maintained.

The mediocrity and belles-lettreism of an affected British élite is refreshingly satirised in "Soirée", the third poem in "Moeurs Contemporaines", where a family, or hornets' nest, of vanity publishers is uncovered. Here the incredulous American guest learns that "the mother wrote verses", and "the father wrote verses", and "the youngest son was in a publisher's office", and most devastating and hilarious, "the friend of the second daughter was undergoing a novel". The easy freedom of the poem's American line is complemented by the American colloquialism of the visitor's response:

The young American pilgrim
Exclaimed
"This is a darn'd clever bunch!"

"The young American pilgrim" has reversed the direction of the early pilgrims from England to the New World. He comes back to worship at the shrine of European culture, perhaps, but also to resuscitate it, make it new. Eliot too, we should not forget when reading his pronouncements on the European "tradition", was also a "young American pilgrim". And it takes young arriviste Americans with a dubious and affected nostalgia for a lost courtly aesthetics to carve this new tradition: "They will come no more / The old men with beautiful manners" (Pound, *Quia Pauper Amavi*, p. 17).

## Excursus in Hell: Ezra Pound's "Three Cantos"

The first of the "Three Cantos" (an early version of what became the second of *The Cantos*) is itself a manifesto of the new, modernist manners, and a manifesto for the *Cantos* to come. The "Three Cantos" were first published in *Poetry* in 1917, and went through considerable transformation before surfacing in the first (of nine volumes) of *The Cantos*, published in 1925 (the new Canto I deriving from the earlier Canto III, for example). They are the "so-called Ur-cantos from which the epic that occupied the rest of his poetic career would derive" (Bornstein: 31). Whereas the first of the later *Cantos* opens with Homer's epic hero Odysseus, on his voyage home from the Trojan War, making blood sacrifice to consult with the transsexual prophet Tiresias in the underworld, and encountering his dead friend and fellow-in-arms, Elpenor, "unburied, cast on the wide earth"; the first Ur-canto opens by buttonholing the nineteenth-century poet Robert Browning, as author of *Sordello* (1840), a long and an ill-received, misunderstood and arcane work in pentameter and rhyming couplets, on "the development of a soul" as Browning put it (1). It is a difficult and densely allusive poem. Pound's poem is also simultaneously, of course, addressing Browning's eponymous poet-hero, the elusive troubadour poet (of the twelfth to thirteenth centuries), Sordello himself, a shadowy figure known to the modern world mainly through disparate allusions and fragments of other poets, and his forty extant poems:

> Hang it all, there can be but one "Sordello",
> But say I want to, say I take your whole bag of tricks.

Sordello's and Browning's "bag of tricks" is certainly tricky, if not actually dizzying in Pound's hands. Pound's "Three Cantos" in fact caused Harriet Monroe, the editor of *Poetry*, to take sick: "Since then, I haven't had brains enough to tackle it." (A reaction prompted in many readers of Pound since.) She was not pleased by Pound's "hint from Browning at his most recondite, and erudition in seventeen languages" (quoted Nadel: 5). But even Pound's opening proposition, in relatively plain English, is itself tricky. To begin with, Browning's composition of his *Sordello* famously faltered on discovery of another poem entitled "Sordello" published by Mrs Busk in 1837 ("a romantic narrative in six cantos of predominantly tetrameter lines" in the manner of Sir Walter Scott, and a much inferior effort – Jack and Smith in Browning: 159); so perhaps Pound's ironic statement is hailing Browning's as the superior. But Sordello himself, known to us by glimpses through the accounts of others, is also far from "one". Browning's editors show that Browning first met Sordello, obscurely enough, in a footnote to Hell, or at least to Cary's translation of Dante's *Divina Commedia.* Sordello is encountered by Dante and Virgil, whom he watches pass "a guisa di leon quando si posa" (like a couching lion), and approached by Virgil declares: "'O Mantovano, io son Sordello/ della tua terra!'; e l'un laltro abbracchiava" ('O Mantuan I am Sordello of your city!'; and they embraced) (*Purgatorio,* vi.66, 75–6). Cary's note to *Purgatorio,* vi.75 begins: "The history of Sordello's life is wrapt in the obscurity of romance. That he distinguished himself by his skill in Provençal poetry is certain; and many feats of military prowess have been attributed to him." Cary also points out Dante's "honourable mention" of Sordello – elsewhere that: "remarkable as he was for eloquence, he deserted the vernacular language of his own country, not only in his poems, but in every other kind of writing" (Browning: 164–5). Sordello, a polyglot poet *and* a man of action, is "single[d] out" by Browning's narrator as "Sordello, compassed murkily about / With ravage of six long sad hundred years"; and from his murky obscurity Browning's "Sordello" is singled out by Pound, whose Canto replicates, in format (though not of course in metre), Browning's later editions of his poem, in the use of elucidatory headings in the right margin. "A Quixotic attempt", for example, glosses Browning's opening lines. Pound elucidates his own Quixotic attempt with direction to Browning.

As well as his annotations, Browning further left to posterity a parchment containing "a number of cryptic references to the composition of *Sordello*" (Browning: 160). They are mainly fragments in ancient Greek (including one from Sappho); and one or two seem made for Pound and Eliot, rather than for the Victorian Browning. In particular, there is a citation from the *Elegies* of Theognis: "Dead, yet speaking with a living tongue" (529). The bag of tricks is full of footnotes to hell, then, stuffed with revenant dead poets ventriloquising through the living, just as Eliot prescribes. Pound recognises the incongruent and premature modernity of Browning's "Sordello". His speaker wants to

> Let in your quirks and tweeks, and say the thing's an art-form,
> Your "Sordello," and that the "modern world"
> Needs such a rag-bag to stuff all its thoughts in.
>
> (Pound, *Quia Pauper Amavi*, p. 19)

"Sordello" is a "rag-bag" of citations and allusions, meditations on a fragmentary and obscure poetic identity; and Pound in turn reduces the rag-bag to new rags in which to "stuff" more fragments and tatters. This is to be collage of collage in effect. Elsewhere, in a dialogue of 1918, Pound has a character declare: "I myself am a rag-bag, a mass of sights and citations, but I will not beat down life for the sake of a model." Of his other poetic personae, Propertius, the Seafarer, and Mauberley, Pound declared "all are 'me' in one sense; my personality is certainly a great slag heap of stuff which has to be excluded from each of th[ese] crystallisations" (quoted Albright 64). And of Pound's paradoxical need for a unifying model for his fragmentary and non-unified poetic persona, Daniel Albright observes "no single persona was inclusive enough to be the Sordello of the modernist age; but to present the whole 'slag heap' was simply to present something bulging and ugly, the detritus of self instead of the informing force. The road of the Three Cantos leads to self-insistence, gigantism, Wagnerian opera, and general uffishness and whiffling – not the goals that Pound sought" (64). But while the first Ur-canto is, in some senses, a false start, an erased beginning (Albright: 59), it is hardly totally suppressed, and its opening lines erupt in those of the second of the *Cantos*:

> Hang it all, Robert Browning,
> there can be but the one "Sordello."

> But Sordello, and my Sordello?
> Lo Sordels si fo di Mantovana.

Pound's interjected manifesto on the "bag of tricks" has gone, and Browning is explicitly named rather than glossed in the marginalia (also gone). These lines in a sense themselves follow on from the final line of the first, Homeric, Canto, with Odysseus in Hades, which ends in "so that:". While indicating an abrupt breaking off from Homer's "so that:", this ending may also mark the point of cut and paste, where the opening lines of the second Canto are in fact its sequitur. Remember that Browning first met Sordello in Dante's *Purgatorio*, and Pound's leap from Homer's Odysseus in Hell to buttonholing Browning on Sordello is not such a large one. Browning's "bag of tricks" is not later erased by Pound but tucked up into itself, and seamed onto Homer. Pound's Provencal, in line four, echoes Sordello's greeting of Virgil in the *Purgatorio*.

This digression into Pound's revisitation of Browning's "Sordello" in Homer's underworld, contained in the volume advertised on the back page of *The Egoist*, will serve to return us to Eliot's "Tradition and the Individual Talent", itself tucked up in *The Egoist* with Bloom's visit to the cemetery in Joyce's rendering of Homer's "Hades" episode. But before reading the remaining two sections of Eliot's essay, let us turn to the next issue of *The Egoist* to discover what precedes it.

## *The Egoist* (December 1919): T. S. Eliot, Dora Marsden and James Joyce

The second part of "Tradition and the Individual Talent" appears in *The Egoist* of December 1919. First, Dora Marsden's "*Philosophy: The Science of Signs*" finally, after three and a half years of serialisation, reaches its conclusion with "Part XVIII. The Egoistic Interpretation of Future Time" (65–70). Here, Marsden envisages the coming of "a species of super-men whose life is that of gods-immortal" (67), and she looks forward to:

> A new order from which the hustle of time – which makes man the species existing in a hurry stampeded by its own construction of a future – a new order from which this hustle is absent shall arise and shall supersede the time-order as surely as the time-order itself has

> superseded the spatial. The synthetic meaning of our science, our religion and our philosophy is that this order is here and now in the throes of making. (67)

Her proto-fascist, sub-Nietzschean babble culminates in an account of death: "*death* must be, not the negation of life, but some variation of it" (68). Rather as Eliot's ideal order of the dead is immanent in the living poet, so Marsden describes the transformation of the individual at death into a wider, but immanent and enhanced state of being:

> The forces of the *ego* have not been dissipated by living. They have been transferred from one part of the *ego* to another, where, at death, they are available for purposes of refertilisation in a measure higher than, but proportionate to, what they themselves are. There, they conceive the potentiality of a new and stronger *time* and a new and stronger *ego*; perceiving body, world and space. Not a different universe therefore awaits us, but a renewed and further developed one. (69)

The fate of Marsden's "*ego*" might almost describe the fate of *The Egoist*, whose publication as a magazine ceases with this very issue, only to be reincarnated in the higher order of book form, as the "Notice to Readers" explains:

> *There will be no issue of* THE EGOIST *in journalistic form in* 1920. In place of such issues the matter now running serially in the periodical will be published in book form. This temporary change has been decided upon mainly on account of its greater suitability at this particular stage to the matter itself. For instance, and in the first place, the Science of Signs series . . . requires considerable remodelling to fit it for permanent statement in book form. (70)

Eliot in fact considered Marsden's serialised work a major handicap to the success of The *Egoist*: "The fact that the paper was primarily a means for getting her philosophical articles into print, and that its appearance was at irregular intervals owing to the length of time it took her to write them, I think militated against the success of the paper with many people who did not want to read them" (*Letters* 1, p. 315). But while the diversion of Marsden's editorial energies from the magazine toward preparation of her book is one reason for the halt in publication, the more significant cause for this change of strategy was the débâcle over *The Egoist*'s other serial publication, Joyce's *Ulysses*:

> Moreover, we have had to contend against what has proved a very serious handicap to the adequate serial publication of Mr Joyce's novel Ulysses. . . . As we have at last found a printer willing to make an unmutilated copy of the text, we have decided to abandon its further serial publication and to publish instead the entire work in book form as soon as it is itself completed. The high importance which Mr Joyce's work has already assumed for our generation, both as to literary matter and form, makes the prospect of a new and complete book by him an event which of itself would justify deviation from the convention of a regular issue. (70)

The disparate fragments of Joyce's work so far published in mutilated parts in magazines, and still in progress, are to be salvaged, restored and unified into book form. The first edition, first impression, of *Ulysses* was published by Sylvia Beach's Shakespeare and Co., in February 1922; and it is the second impression, of October 1922, that was issued with the imprint "Published for Egoist Press, London by John Rodker, Paris" (Johnson: 741). Weaver had been trying to get *Ulysses* published as a book for some time; and in April 1918 approached Leonard and Virginia Woolf at the Hogarth Press, but the Press was unable to cope with such a lengthy work at the time. Virginia Woolf's diary account of Weaver's visit is instructive and amusing:

> I did my best to make her reveal herself, in spite of her appearance, all that the Editress of the Egoist ought to be, but she remained inalterably modest judicious & decorous. Her neat mauve suit fitted both soul & body; her grey gloves laid straight by her plate symbolised domestic rectitude; her table manners were those of a well bred hen. We could get no talk to go. Possibly the poor woman was impeded by her sense that what she had in the brownpaper parcel was quite out of keeping with her own contents. But then how did she ever come in contact with Joyce & the rest? Why does their filth seek exit from her mouth? Heaven knows. She is incompetent from the business point of view & was uncertain what arrangements to make. We both looked at the MS. Which seems to be an attempt to push the bounds of expression further on, but still all in the same direction. And so she went. (*Diary* 1, p. 140)

Woolf's sense of the "brilliancy" and "sordidity" of Joyce's work, its innovation and its limitations, seems to have been forged here. Woolf's graphic description of Weaver's ventriloquising or spouting of Joyce's "filth" also points up the peculiar function of publishing handmaiden to male authors played by so many women of the period, a gender politics that later feminist criticism has explored, with particular attention to Joyce's debt to Beach and Weaver.

The "Notice to Readers" continues with a lengthy discussion of censorship, the importance of Joyce's work, the achievements of *The Egoist* magazine and the recent and forthcoming publications of the Egoist Press. Wyndham Lewis's *The Caliph's Design*, in particular, is pushed for its "explanation of the 'vorticist' standpoint, a brilliant criticism of contemporary and recent art movements in Paris and elsewhere, and a forcible indictment of dilettantism in painting and of pretentiousness and insincerity in modern art and architecture" (71). It is also announced that the press is "now able to promise for the early spring *The Art of Poetry*, by Mr T. S. Eliot" (71). This last word to Eliot in the notice may explain the fact that it is the second part of his "Tradition and the Individual Talent" that follows the notice, and not, as one might expect after its rallying support of Joyce's *Ulysses*, the next extract from the very work that is the main concern of the notice, and the cause of *The Egoist*'s cessation as a journal and transformation fully into book publisher. An effect of positioning "Tradition and the Individual Talent II" after the notice, then, is to read Eliot's pronouncements with particular application to the matter that precedes it, and to the business of Joyce's position as an individual talent in relation to tradition, which we might understand, as the notice says, in relation to both "literary matter and form". Not only does Eliot's thesis apply to the living Joyce's voicing of Homer in his transposition of the *Odyssey* onto modern-day Dublin, but it also resonates in the role of the magazine as it transfers from the publication of separate instalments to the project to unify the work in the larger order of the book.

# 5 "Tradition" and "Mrs Brown"
## T. S. Eliot and Virginia Woolf

### Introduction

This chapter moves to a comparative reading of Eliot's essay on tradition and Woolf's essay on 1910, modernity and change, "Mr Bennett and Mrs Brown". It explores the emerging gender divide in these manifestos. This leads us to the gender-based arguments of Part II. The chapter begins, however, with a reading of Eliot's scientific discourse, in "Tradition and the Individual Talent" and elsewhere, as understood and recorded by Woolf. Eliot's allusions to Dante's hell are explored, as is a range of his imagery in comparison with Woolf's, in "Modern Novels", the earlier version of Woolf's "Modern Fiction". His essay's engagement with classical myth and allusions to the Trojan War lead to consideration of Joyce's *Ulysses* and modernist narratives of hell. Eliot's debt to Keats and his engagement with the poetics of Romanticism he reviles leads to comparison of his formalism with that of his Bloomsbury colleague, Clive Bell. "Tradition and the Individual Talent" is then considered in the significant context of the massive undertaking to publish Joyce's *Ulysses.*

The chapter shifts its focus to Woolf by exploring her feminist prospectus for "Shakespeare's sister", in *A Room of One's Own,* as a gendered reading of Eliot's essay on tradition. Woolf's earlier feminist or gendered correctives to Eliot are then explored in her other great manifesto of modernism, "Mr Bennett and Mrs Brown". This discussion returns us to Woolf's famous statement on 1910 with which Part I of this book opens. A distinctively feminist reading of the political contexts of 1910 and of the Post-Impressionist exhibition is put forward. And emerging from this comes a gendered comparison of modernist uses of myth, in particular of Trojan war narratives, in Eliot and Woolf. This chapter, and Part I, conclude with the identification in Woolf's and Eliot's canonical "modernist essays", of a gender divide opening up in modernist and avant-garde writing. This divide becomes the focus of Part II.

## "Tradition and the Individual Talent" II: Virginia Woolf reads T. S. Eliot, the "scientist"

But let us return now to Eliot's essay, the first part of which invited the reader of the September issue of *The Egoist* "to consider, as a suggestive analogy" (for his theory of impersonality), "the action which takes place when a bit of finely filiated platinum is introduced into a chamber containing oxygen and sulphur dioxide". In the second part of the essay, in the December issue, he explains:

> The analogy was that of the catalyst. When the two gases previously mentioned are mixed in the presence of a filament of platinum, they form sulphurous acid. This combination takes place only if the platinum is present; nevertheless the newly formed acid contains no trace of platinum, and the platinum itself is apparently unaffected: has remained inert, neutral, and unchanged. The mind of the poet is the shred of platinum. It may partly or exclusively operate upon the experience of the man himself; but, the more perfect the artist, the more completely separate in him will be the man who suffers and the mind which creates; the more perfectly will the mind digest and transmute into passions which are its material. (72)

Just as there is no trace of the platinum that was catalyst to the sulphuric acid, so the "mind of the poet" is absent from that which he creates; and that which he creates is the equivalent to oil of vitriol, the product achieved by platinum's being catalyst to the two gases. Sulphur dioxide, the gas mixed with oxygen, is "a suffocating gas discharged in waste from industrial processes, used in manufacture of sulphuric acid, and in bleaching, preserving etc." (Chambers Dictionary). Eliot's scientific, industrial metaphor is further exploited by him when he offers the following metaphorical elucidation of the gases as emotions and feelings:

> The experience, you will notice, the elements which enter the presence of the transforming catalyst, are of two kinds: emotions and feel-

> ings. The effect of a work of art upon the person who enjoys it is an experience different in kind from any experience not in art. It may be formed out of one emotion, or may be a combination of several; and various feelings, inhering for the great writer in particular words or phrases or images, may be added to compose the final result. Or great poetry may be made without the direct use of any emotion whatever: composed out of feelings solely. (72)

Eliot, the impresario critic, adopts the rhetoric and persona of a scientific demonstrator ("you will notice"); and, interestingly, in June 1919 he is actually portrayed in print as a "scientist" (Woolf, *Essays* 3, p. 56) by Leonard and Virginia Woolf, who jointly and anonymously (and somewhat reluctantly) reviewed their own Hogarth Press publication of Eliot's *Poems* for the *Athenaeum*, under the heading "Is This Poetry?" Virginia Woolf confesses that she "broke down" (*Letters* 2, p. 373) while attempting this review, and later told Eliot that it was Leonard, not herself, who reviewed his poems in the *Athenaeum* (*Letters* 2, p. 437), but she clearly seems to have been party to the following observations, which anticipate Eliot's main tenets in "Tradition and the Individual Talent" published only a few months afterwards:

> Mr Eliot is always quite consciously "trying for" something, and something which has grown out of and developed beyond all the poems of all the dead poets. Poetry to him seems to be not so much an art as a science, a vast and noble and amusing body of communal feeling upon which the contemporary poet must take a firm stand and then launch himself into the unknown in search of new discoveries. This is the attitude not of the conventional poet, but of the scientist who with the help of working hypotheses hopes to add something, a theory perhaps or a new microbe, to the corpus of human knowledge. (*Essays* 3, pp. 55–6)

Woolf's use of "trying for" implies perhaps failure. Her language here also suggests that Eliot's mantle of scientist precedes his essay. And in logging her first meeting with Eliot, furthermore, in November 1918, Woolf records a similar account of her impressions of Eliot's "poetic creed", this time emphasising the ventriloquism of the ancients through the new:

> I became more or less conscious of a very intricate & highly organised framework of poetic belief; owing to his caution, & his excessive care in

> the use of language, we did not discover much about it. I think he believes in "living phrases" & their difference from dead ones; in writing with extreme care, in observing all syntax & grammar; & so making this new poetry flower on the stem of the oldest. (*Diary* 1, p. 219)

Woolf's choice of floral imagery reinforces an organicist interpretation of Eliot's evolving ideas on tradition. And interestingly, many years later when Woolf sets out her own "philosophy" in "A Sketch of the Past" (1939), she employs a similar floral metaphor to describe the revelation to her of a dualistic, organicist, model of perception: "that was the real flower; part earth; part flower" (*Moments of Being*, p. 71). Any individual object is in fact the sum of itself and its context, just as for Eliot each individual is also constituted by and through the tradition.

## "Tradition" II: Dante's Hell and Virginia Woolf's "particles"

The whiff of sulphur in Eliot's scientific experiment may also emanate from mythic, literary sources, as his choice of a concrete literary example, taken from "Canto XV of the *Inferno* (Brunetto Latini)", suggests. This passage from "the floor of hell" (XVI.33), Eliot claims,

> is a working up of the emotion evident in the situation; but the effect, though single as that of any work of art, is obtained by considerable complexity of detail. The last quatrain gives an image, a feeling attaching to an image, which 'came', which did not develop simply out of what precedes, but which was probably in suspension in the poet's mind until the proper combination arrived for it to add itself to. (72)

Brunetto Latini (1220–1294), a Florentine intellectual and a notary, who lived in exile for some time, and may have taught Dante himself, was author of the encyclopedic work on history, ethics, philosophy, rhetoric, and politics, "The Treasure", which, Dante declares to Latini's soul, on meeting him in the *Inferno*, "instructed me how man may be eternal" (XV.85). Latini's last words to him are: "I recommend you to read my work, *The Treasure*, / In which I still live" (XV.118–19), which seems in keeping with Eliot's thesis. The last quatrain of the canto, which Eliot singles out for its precipitant imagery, offers the following simile for Latini as he turns away:

> [He] seemed to be one of those
> Who, at Verona, run for the green cloth,
> Through the open country; and he seemed to be the one
> Who wins the race, and not the one who loses.
>
> (XV.121–4)

David Higgins suggests that "the image of the cross-country runners of Verona may . . . point up his attack on presumptuous intellectuals . . . who perversely chase after the corruptible crown of worldly honours and an ephemeral immortality in this life", and he interprets it also in the context of the canto's earlier image of naked runners, a critique of sexual deviants (534). But whatever our interpretation, it is the mechanism of the image's sudden appearance that Eliot draws attention to. It is not, according to him, a development of earlier imagery. Is Eliot himself anxious to disassociate the two images? At any rate, the example allows him to put forward the following model of the poet's mind:

> The poet's mind is in fact a receptacle for seizing and storing up numberless feelings, phrases, images, which remain there until all the particles which can unite to form a new compound are present together. (72)

This model of the mind receiving and processing unrelated and juxtaposed "particles" seems close to that put forward by Woolf in her famous "Look within" passage describing Joyce's method in "Modern Fiction" (1925), which responds in particular to the "Hades" episode published in the *Little Review* (September 1918). The earlier version of Woolf's essay, published in *The Times Literary Supplement* of April 1919, as "Modern Novels", gives the following draft of this passage:

> but as often as not we may suspect some moment of hesitation in which the question suggests itself whether life is like this after all? . . . The mind, exposed to the ordinary course of life, receives upon its surface a myriad impressions – trivial, fantastic, evanescent, or engraved with the sharpness of steel. From all sides they come, an incessant shower of innumerable atoms, composing in their sum what we might venture to call life itself; and to figure further as the semi-transparent envelope, or luminous halo, surrounding us from the beginning of consciousness to the end. Is it not perhaps the chief task of the novelist to convey this incessantly varying spirit with

> whatever stress or sudden deviation it may display, and as little admixture of the alien and external as possible? (*Essays* 3, p. 33)

Eliot's "receptacle" mind of the poet is similar to Woolf's model for the novelist's mind. They both employ alchemical imagery to describe the processing of the atoms or particles that fall. Eliot's example from Dante, furthermore, also illustrates Woolf's sense of "sudden deviation". Eliot emphasises the process rather than the content when he explains: "For it is not the 'greatness', the intensity, of the emotions, the components, but the intensity of the artistic process, the pressure, so to speak, under which the fusion takes place, that counts" (*The Egoist*, VI, 5, p. 72). He uses examples from classical Greek tragedy (Aeschylus) and epic (Homer), from Shakespearean tragedy, and from Keats's poetry to illustrate the "Great variety . . . possible in the process of transmutation of emotion".

> the murder of Agamemnon, or the agony of Othello, gives an artistic effect apparently closer to a possible original than the scenes from Dante. In the *Agamemnon*, the artistic emotion approximates to the emotion of an actual spectator; in *Othello* to the emotion of the protagonist himself. But the difference between art and the event is always absolute; the combination which is the murder of Agamemnon is probably as complex as that which is the voyage of Ulysses. In either case there has been a fusion of elements. The ode of Keats contains a number of feelings which have nothing particular to do with the nightingale, but which the nightingale, partly perhaps because of its attractive name, and partly because of its reputation, served to bring together. (*The Egoist*, VI, 5, p. 72)

Eliot seems to be emphasising the aesthetic mechanism, "the fusion of elements", that presents the "murder of Agamemnon, or the agony of Othello", rather than the murder and the agony *per se*, in the same way as Keats's "nightingale" is an objective correlative for something already in his ode, partly by bringing cultural significance by its name, partly its "reputation" (mythical associations, past citations in poetry, and so on). But it is worth noting that the examples he chooses are in some ways significant and interrelated. The murder of Agamemnon by his unfaithful and monstrous wife, Clytemnestra, on his return from the Trojan War, is not only the subject of Aeschylus's play the *Agamemnon*, it is also recounted by Homer. In the *Odyssey*, in the

Hades episode of Book XI, most significantly, Homer's protagonist, Odysseus (or Ulysses), takes counsel from the shade of Agamemnon who tells him of Clytemnestra's unwifely treachery, saying "she, with her heart set on utter wickedness, has shed shame on herself and on women yet to be, even upon her that doeth uprightly" (417). And Odysseus, concurring with this universally extended condemnation of women, replies: "Ah verily has Zeus . . . visited wondrous hatred on the race of Atreus from the first because of the counsels of women. For Helen's sake many of us perished, and against thee Clytemnestra spread a snare whilst thou was afar." No woman, however virtuous seeming, is to be trusted. Agamemnon, the victim of his monstrous wife Clytemnestra, further advises Odysseus on how he should manage his return to his own wife, Penelope, whom he nevertheless acknowledges as faithful and "wise". Even so, he tells Odysseus: "in secret and not openly . . . bring thy ship to the shore of thy dear native land; for no longer is there faith in women" (419). This advice Odysseus heeds on his return to Ithaca. When Eliot observes that "the combination which is the murder of Agamemnon is probably as complex as that which is the voyage of Ulysses", he is alerting us not only to the poetic process he is describing in both events, but also, incidentally, to the way Homer has himself "fused" in his epic these particular elements or components, the story of Agamemnon and the story of Odysseus, themselves "combinations" of other "elements" – Agamemnon's story is part of Odysseus's story.

## "Tradition" II: T. S. Eliot's "Ulysses" and James Joyce's "Hades"

Eliot's preference for the protagonist's name, "Ulysses", also, of course, further serves to remind the reader of Joyce's novel, *Ulysses*, the focal point of this, the last issue of *The Egoist* in magazine form. So, Eliot's vocabulary in describing the artistic process here echoes Woolf's in her account of Joyce's aesthetic, as exemplified for her in his "Hades" episode; and his argument also has pertinence for the context in which it appears, the issues of *The Egoist*, which are the vehicle for Joyce's work, and for "Hades" (in the previous issue). Significantly, Eliot's essay is interrupted by the "Hades" episode, then, which immediately follows Part I of "Tradition and the Individual Talent". And conversely, Part II of the essay this time precedes the next episode from Joyce ("Wandering Rocks") in the next issue of *The*

*Egoist,* but follows on immediately from the editorial defending Joyce's novel. In Joyce's "Hades", furthermore, there are intimations of uxorial infidelity and monstrousness when, for example, Bloom reflects on Martin Cunningham who has an "awful drunkard of a wife . . . Leading him the life of the damned" (Joyce, *Ulysses,* ed. Johnson: 93) and the fidelity of his own wife is implicitly questioned in an exchange between Menton and Lambert at the graveside:

> – In God's name, John Henry Menton said, what did she marry a coon like that for? She had plenty of game in her then.
> – Has still, Ned Lambert said. (*Ulysses*: 102)

Shakespeare's tragic protagonist Othello, who suffers excruciating jealousy, and mistakenly believes his wife unfaithful, may also have significance for Joyce's protagonist Bloom, whose return to his own Penelope has yet (at the time of Eliot's essay) to be written by Joyce, and was not in fact published until the novel appeared in 1922.

## "Tradition" II: romanticism, revenge and the theory of impersonality

The "inviolable voice" of Keats's nightingale, on the other hand, surfaces in Eliot's *The Waste Land* of the same year ("'Jug jug' to dirty ears"). Keats's own theory of poetic impersonality may also be prompting Eliot's. In a letter of 1818 Keats declared:

> A Poet is the most unpoetical thing of any thing in existence; because he has no Identity – he is continually in for – and filling some other Body – the Sun, the Moon, the Sea and Men and Women who are creatures of impulse are poetical and have about them an unchangeable attribute – the poet has none. (Keats, *Letters,* p. 227)

When Eliot talks of the "continual surrender" of the poet's self, and of the "progress of an artist [a]s a continual self-sacrifice, a continual extinction of personality" he is almost surrendering himself to the voicing of Keats, who finds that a poet "has no nature", and extinguishes his own identity:

> When I am in a room with People if ever I am free from speculating on creations of my own brain, then not myself goes home to myself:

> but the identity of every one in the room begins to press upon me that, I am in a very little time annihilated. (Keats, *Letters*, p. 227)

Eliot continues, in "Tradition and the Individual Talent", to press his theory of impersonality, which refutes the Romantic notion of a unified and transcendent poetic subjectivity, and which figures the poet and poem as medium:

> The point of view which I am struggling to attack is perhaps related to the metaphysical theory of the substantial unity of the soul: for my meaning is, that the poet has, not a 'personality' to express, but a particular medium, which is only a medium and not a personality, in which impressions and experiences combine in peculiar and unexpected ways. Impressions and experiences which are important in the man may take no place in poetry, and those which become important in the poetry may play quite a negligible part in the man, the personality. (72)

It is the medium onto which the atoms fall and become fused into the new. The poet's mind is the catalyst. The "numberless feelings, phrases, images" and "emotions", cited earlier in the essay, have become "impressions and experiences", and constitute the elements that combine and fuse in the poet's mind. Perhaps "emotions" and "feelings" are too close to the transcendent subjectivity of the Wordsworthian "spontaneous overflow of powerful feelings" and "emotion recollected in tranquillity". Eliot's poet and poem are the medium for feelings and emotions from diverse sources, not merely from the individual "man, the personality". Eliot now offers up an obscure passage "unfamiliar enough to be regarded with fresh attention in the light – or darkness – of these observations" (72). His facetious reference to the darkness of his observations suggests he relishes obscurantism rather than enlightenment, but perhaps it is also in keeping with the dark, infernal subtexts in his essay. The passage is from Act 3 of Cyril Tourneur's *The Revenger's Tragedy* (1607):

> And now me thinks I could e'en chide myself
> For doting on her beauty, though her death
> Shall be revenged after no common action.
> Does the silkworm expend her yellow labours
> For thee? For thee does she undo herself?
> Are lordships sold to maintain ladyships

> For the poor benefit of a bewildering minute?
> Why does yon fellow falsify highways,
> And put his life between the judge's lips,
> To refine such a thing – keeps horse and men
> To beat their valours for her? . . .
>
> [Act 3, Scene 4]

Eliot's analysis of this avenging speech allows him to arrive at a new understanding of emotion as "art emotion":

> In this passage . . . there is a combination of positive and negative emotions . . . This balance of contrasted emotion is in the dramatic situation to which the speech is pertinent, but that situation alone is inadequate to it. This is, so to speak, the structural emotion, provided by the drama. But the whole effect, the dominant tone, is due to the fact that a number of floating feelings, having an affinity to this emotion by no means superficially evident, have combined with it to give us a new art emotion. (*The Egoist*, VI, 5: 72)

With the term "art emotion", Eliot moves closer to Clive Bell's notion of aesthetic emotion, which, we recall, he ascribed first to Post-Impressionist art, and then to all great art. Bell recognises a quality uniting "all objects that provoke our aesthetic emotions", a quality "common to Sta. Sophia and the windows at Chartres, Mexican sculpture, a Persian bowl, Chinese carpets, Giotto's frescoes at Padua, and the masterpieces of Poussin, Piero della Francesca, and Cézanne" (*Art*, pp. 7–8). The quality Bell names as common to all the components in his ideal order is "significant form", and Eliot goes on in his short coda, Part III of his essay, to discuss "*significant* emotion". At the close of Part II, he comes close to Wordsworth's recommendation to poets to use "the language really spoken by men" when he declares: "The business of the poet is not to find new emotions, but to use ordinary ones." But these are transformed in the art; and the poet's business is also

> in working them up into poetry, to express feelings which are not in actual emotions at all. And emotions he has never experienced will serve his turn as well as those familiar to him. Consequently we must believe that "emotion recollected in tranquillity" is an inexact formula. (73)

Eliot voices Wordsworth only to correct him for failing to give that which he does not set out to supply – a scientific "formula": "For it is neither emotion, nor recollection, nor, without distortion of meaning, tranquillity." Eliot reiterates his somewhat Bergsonian theory of poetic fusion: "It is a concentration, and a new thing resulting from the concentration, of a very great number of experiences which to the practical and active person would not seem to be experiences at all; it is a concentration which does not happen consciously or of deliberation." If this seems to repeat Worsdworth's paradoxical view of the poet as both ordinary and as singled out for his special powers, Eliot again distances himself by denouncing Wordsworth's key terms: "These experiences are not 'recollected' and they finally unite in an atmosphere which is 'tranquil' only in that it is a passive attending upon the event" (73). He concedes that poetry does also involve the "conscious and deliberate". But it is Wordsworth's definition of poetry as the "spontaneous overflow of powerful feeling" that Eliot is countering in one of the most quoted sentences of his essay: "Poetry is not a turning loose of emotion, but an escape from emotion; it is not the expression of personality, but an escape from personality" (73).

## "Tradition and the Individual Talent" III: Order, Myth, *Ulysses*

The brief, third part of "Tradition and the Individual Talent" opens with an epigraph in Greek from Aristotle's *De Anima* ("On the Soul", 1.4), which translates as: "The mind is doubtless something more divine and unimpressionable", and picks up on Eliot's earlier qualification at the close of Part II of the essay that "Of course, this is not the whole story". But rather than disappear into the realms of mysticism, Eliot prefers to keep his essay as pragmatic, as commonsensical, and as scientific as possible, to "confine" it to "such practical conclusions as can be applied by the responsible person interested in poetry". Romanticism is implicitly therefore *ir*responsible in this argument. In savaging biographical and subjective readings of poetry and recommending attention to its formalist procedures, Eliot repeats his thesis of impersonality as the self-immolation of the living poet in the process of giving voice to the dead poets of the past tradition:

> To divert interest from the poet to the poetry is a laudable aim: for it would conduce to a juster estimation of actual poetry, good and bad.

> There are many people who appreciate the expression of sincere emotion in verse, and there is a smaller number of people who can appreciate technical excellence. But very few know when there is an expression of *significant* emotion, emotion which has its life in the poem and not in the history of the poet. The emotion of art is impersonal. And the poet cannot reach this impersonality without surrendering himself wholly to the work to be done. And he is not likely to know what is to be done unless he lives in what is not merely the present, but the present moment of the past, unless he is conscious, not of what is dead, but of what is already living. (73)

That final phrase of the essay, "what is already living", is ominous. Eliot's "present moment of the past", perhaps comparable with Bergson's durée, is also a somewhat eerie, haunted, gothic place where the dead still walk; and the dead still talk – through the orifices of the living. And these propositions about the past in the present are particularly appropriate in the context of *The Egoist*, where Joyce's *Ulysses* is lurching towards Paris to be born, "the new (the really new) work of art" that simultaneously communicates and rearranges Homer's *Odyssey* and the "ideal order" which somehow always and already contains them both. To be new is not to be revolutionary but to "conform" and "cohere" to, and thereby to renew, the past. Here in "Tradition and the Individual Talent" hangs immanent Eliot's later defence of *Ulysses*, in the essay "*Ulysses*, Order and Myth" (1923), where Joyce's "mythical method" is also understood to be his own, in *The Waste Land* published, like the novel, the year before. Myth has become the trans- and a-historical glue of tradition, the means by which the work of art is unified, and by which the past is "already living". Eagleton has scornfully encapsulated the ideological implications of Eliot's recourse to myth: "The crisis of European society – global war, severe class-conflict, failing capitalist economies – might be resolved by turning one's back on history altogether and putting mythology in its place" (*Literary Theory*, p. 41).

## Virginia Woolf and T. S. Eliot: "Shakespeare's sister" and "Tradition"

If some of Woolf's imagery in "Modern Fiction", her "luminous halo", her alchemical metaphors, and her personification of fiction as renewed through violent annihilation, seem to be picked up in Eliot's essay, so Woolf seems to take up, and subvert, Eliot's imagery in her later work. Her portrait of Judith Shakespeare, for example, that forms the coda to *A Room of One's Own* (1929), seems to reverberate with Eliot's model of a collective dead speaking through the living. This is Woolf's prophesy of a woman poet to equal or rival Shakespeare – "Shakespeare's sister" – and her urging for the collective preparation for her appearance. But in reviving a Judith Shakespeare who never lived, Woolf is regendering male tradition, inventing a woman's tradition, before voicing it for women, and as a woman. Whereas Eliot addresses an existing, living, and implicitly male poet or individual talent who acts as medium to the collective dead past, Woolf, on the other hand, seems to defer the arrival of Shakespeare's sister in a celebration of women's past, present, and future collective literary achievement "– I am talking of the common life which is the real life and not of the little separate lives which we live as individuals" (148–9). Like Eliot's, Woolf's "individual talent" must sacrifice herself to the larger tradition. But unlike Eliot's "individual talent", who is the host to a vampiric past, Shakespeare's sister is a messianic, vampiric figure who "lives in you and in me" (148) and who feeds off the dead (and the yet to die): she will draw "her life from the lives of the unknown who were her forerunners" (149), but she has yet to appear. She may be the common writer to Woolf's "common reader" (a term she borrows, or "voices" in her skewed Eliotic fashion, from Samuel Johnson), but she has yet to "put on the body which she has so often laid down" (149). Just as Eliot's theory of the individual talent's giving voice to the dead has been the guide to his multivocal anti-elegy *The Waste Land*, so Woolf's somewhat different sense of a collective authorial voice, here (along with the multivocal narrative of *A Room of One's Own*, itself) has been seen to explain and anticipate Woolf's more formally stylised and poetic, multivocal novel-elegy, *The Waves* (1931). Eliot's present is confined to sojourning with the dead, giving voice to the literary corpses of the past, whereas Woolf's present, while in some ways preoccupied with picking over the corpses of the past male tradition and synthesising a female one, is formulated as the anterior to an ever deferring, yet already present, feminist future.

It is tempting to linger even longer in the pages of *The Egoist*, and consider the contents that follow Eliot's essay in the December issue. There is a poem by William Carlos Williams ("Chicago"), for example, and further thoughts on "The French Idea" by Madame Muriel

Ciolkowska, and another extract from Joyce's *Ulysses* – "Wandering Rocks", as well as an advertisement for the new review entitled *Action*. But we must get back to 1910, and to Woolf. Much earlier than *A Room of One's Own*, we can see how Woolf is offering feminist correctives to Eliot's theories; and this occurs in the essay "Mr Bennett and Mrs Brown" (1924), published the year before her final version of "Modern Fiction", and very much taking up its argument.

## "Mr Bennett and Mrs Brown" (1924): formalist or feminist?

"Mr Bennett and Mrs Brown" was published in the *Criterion* of July 1924, as "Character in Fiction", and like many of Woolf's essays, evolved from a speech (in this instance to the Cambridge Heretics Society). Many of its rhetorical features survive into the published text. Here Woolf continues her assault on the Edwardians, Wells, Galsworthy and Bennett, for their materialist conventions, and her uneven defence of the Georgians, Joyce, Eliot, Forster, Lytton Strachey, and D. H. Lawrence, whose work, she declares, must make us "reconcile ourselves to a season of failures and fragments" (*Essays* 3, p. 435). The essay's title is derived from its central, virtuoso, conceit whereby Woolf illustrates the inadequacies of the Edwardian novelists as she makes a number of attempts, using their materialist "tools", to construct a fictional narrative about the character of "Mrs Brown", a stranger encountered on a train. The essay also contains the famous assertion that: "on or about December 1910 human character changed" (421). As we have seen, this has come to represent for many cultural commentators the cataclysmic moment of modernity, the inception of the avant-garde, the shock of the new. In the context of the essay, it marks the shift from the Edwardian to the Georgian era, when "all human relations have shifted – those between masters and servants, husbands and wives, parents and children. And when human relations change there is at the same time a change in religion, conduct, politics, and literature" (422). Before examining her statement in more detail, we might note that, in general, Woolf is not arguing that literature merely changes in terms of subject matter to *reflect* new, modern experience, but that literary form itself undergoes radical, and turbulent, transformation: "And so the smashing and the crashing began. . . . Grammar is violated; syntax disintegrated" (434). The work of Joyce, Eliot and Strachey illustrate the point that modern literature has necessarily become caught up in the business of finding new form. And by this time *Ulysses* has been published as a book, and in the same year as Eliot's *The Waste Land.* Readers must "tolerate the spasmodic, the obscure, the fragmentary, the failure" (436). The self-reflexive, fragmentary, subjective and momentary qualities of modernist writing are here acknowledged and celebrated.

Like "Modern Fiction", this essay has been read as if it is untainted by Woolf's feminism, despite the fact that there "are spots of it all over her work", as her distressed friend E. M. Forster observed, "and it was constantly in her mind" (22); and this probably helped to keep Woolf's work in an otherwise male modernist canon in the mid-twentieth century. But as soon as "Mrs Brown" comes into focus in the essay, a feminist subtext becomes apparent. I have argued elsewhere that Woolf's manifesto on 1910 seems to resonate both with the formalism of Fry's and Bell's formulations on modern European art and with the formulations and practices of British suffragist artists, and that these very different theoretical and aesthetic factors are caught up in the staging and reception of the Post-Impressionist exhibition of 1910. We have already looked at these formalist theories and at the climate of political unrest as an important context to the exhibition, but it is worth noting also the particularly feminist element to that unrest.

## Post-Impressionism in feminist contexts: gendered readings of Virginia Woolf's "1910"

Contemporary critical reception of Post-Impressionism and Woolf's literary engagement with it, I have suggested, is influenced by the suffragette activism occurring at the time of the 1910 exhibition, culminating in "Black Friday", when a demonstration ended in violent assault upon most of its participants at the hands of the police. On 18 November 1910 (the Post-Impressionist Exhibition opened ten days earlier on 8 November), Suffragettes massed to demonstrate at Westminster against the loss of the Conciliation Bill (proposing the enfranchisement of a narrow category of women) due to the crisis in Parliament and the imminent fall of the Asquith government. Mass assault and arrest followed. Woolf did not participate in the demonstration, but she did attend the huge rally at the Albert Hall in preparation for it, a few days earlier (Woolf, *Letters* 1, p. 438). What is of interest in this discussion is a wider critical argument over the significance of text and context: 1910 is a critical moment in the interpenetration of these spheres when the art on gallery walls was brought into dialogue with the political events on the streets outside. And we can see their interpenetrating discourse at work in Woolf's discussion of 1910. And I now want to consider how this argument may be understood to be mobilised against Eliot's reading of tradition and myth.

"On or about" *September* 1910, then, the suffrage artist Mary Lowndes published a manifesto-style essay, "On Banners and Banner Making". Her language may be discerned in Woolf's later feminist and aesthetic manifestos. For example, Lowndes' declaration that the feminist colours will "illumine woman's own adventure" seems to anticipate some of Woolf's phrasing in *A Room of One's Own* (1929): Mary Beton instructs Mary Carmichael, the aspiring novelist, "above all, you must illumine your own soul"; and *Life's Adventure* is the title of Mary Carmichael's novel (Woolf, 1929: 135, 142). In 1910, Lowndes, as I have shown elsewhere, describes the art of suffrage banner-making in terms uncannily similar to those of later Post-Impressionist theories: "A banner is not a literary affair, it is not a placard: leave such to boards and sandwichmen" (174). Anticipating the flavour of Clive Bell's 1912 observations on "the makers of Christmas-cards and diagrams", she identifies the non-verbal political significance of feminist colourism, while at the same time drawing on a discourse of aestheticism: "A banner is a thing to float in the wind, to flicker in the breeze, to flirt its colours for your pleasure . . . you do not want to read it, you want to worship it" (174, 178). Like Bell's (Post-Impressionist) art, these political banners are not to be decoded so much as worshipped, a point Lowndes interestingly emphasises with allusion to classical myth. "Troy Town" is Lowndes's fictional example of a patriarchal town in need of suffragist banners: "Imagine to yourself, my reader, Miss Blank, the active Secretary of the newly-formed Branch Society of Troy Town" (173). This allusion suggests the set of (patriarchal) myths associated with the Trojan War; and is in keeping with suffragist tastes for the reappropriation and refiguring of imagery from the powerful cultural sources of classical myth. Suffragist demonstrators not only employed mythic emblems but often dressed for parades and pageants as (in)famous heroines and goddesses from history and mythology (Tickner, 1987: 125–6). This feminist appropriation of classical myth for political, avant-garde activism in the public sphere is diametrically opposite to the cultural function that Eliot seeks for myth. For him myth is a refuge from history, not a resource for revolutionary change.

Woolf's elaboration on her choice of 1910 as a significant date, then, is worth careful consideration in the light of suffragist as well as Post-Impressionist aesthetics, but she is also pitching this argument in the context of a continuing critical dialogue with Eliot; 1910's shift in human relations, represented in the work of Samuel Butler and Bernard Shaw, Woolf sees symbolised in the figure of "one's cook": "The Victorian cook lived like a leviathan in the lower depths, formidable, silent, obscure, inscrutable; the Georgian cook is a creature of sunshine and fresh air; in and out of the drawing room, now to borrow the *Daily Herald*, now to ask advice about a hat" (*Essays* 3, p. 422). The imagery of a woman servant emerging leviathan-like from the dark depths of the kitchen into sunlight and may suggest a shift from women's dark, subliminal, creaturely existence to luminous, colourful liberation. Woolf's vocabulary is similar to that of Mary Lowndes's 1910 essay on suffrage colourist banner-making: "now into public life comes trooping the feminine; and with the feminine creature come the banners of past times" (Lowndes: 173).

December 1910 may mean for Woolf, then, material improvement for women workers, and the emergence of women from intellectual darkness into prismatic enlightenment, from obscurity into public life. This emergence from the dark also reverberates with the classical narratives of heroic re-emergence from Hell, or Hades. It is not Odysseus, or Aeneas, or Dante who emerges from a sojourn among the dead, but a mere woman. After the creaturely cook, Woolf gives a "more solemn instance . . . of the power of the human race to change": a revised reading of the *Agamemnon*, in which "sympathies" (usually reserved for the patriarchal order sanctioned by Athena) may now be "almost entirely with Clytemnestra", who avenged her daughter's death by murdering her husband Agamemnon on his return from the Trojan War. This classical allusion becomes more potently feminist when considered in relation to suffragist use of such imagery and Lowndes's references to "Troy Town" in 1910. And it is also worth comparing Eliot's pronouncements on the *Agamemnon* in "Tradition and the Individual Talent", where in observing "the murder of Agamemnon" sympathies appear to remain entirely with Agamemnon. Trojan War mythology is hardly a settled, unifying order, but a site of conflicting and gendered narratives of power. To sympathise with Clytemnestra is to overturn the epic and tragic, patriarchal literary and cultural traditions that have sprung from Homer and Aeschylus. Agamemnon's advice to Odysseus in Hades is only one side of the story.

In asking us to "consider the married life of the Carlyles", Woolf returns to the theme of women's servitude, perhaps mindful of the suffragette scorn for Thomas Carlyle (resulting in a cleaver attack on his portrait in the National Gallery) (Atkinson: 163). For Woolf, he personifies "the horrible domestic tradition which made it seemly for a woman of genius to spend her time chasing beetles, scouring saucepans, instead of writing books". Woolf spells out this tradition's hierarchised, gendered, relations as she announces its demise: "All human relations have shifted – those between masters and servants, husbands and wives, parents and children. And when human relations change there is at the same time a change in religion, conduct, politics and literature. Let us agree to place one of these changes about the year 1910" (*Essays*, 3: 422). The shocking suffrage events of 1910 surrounding the Post-Impressionist exhibition inform Woolf's compelling identification of this revolutionary date (Goldman, *Feminist Aesthetics*, pp. 111–12).

For Eliot, on the other hand, 1910 meant, if anything and as far as we can gather, the philosophical apotheosis of Bergsonism, as he outlines in the syllabus for his lectures on French Literature for Oxford University Extension Lectures of 1916. His final lecture examines "the philosophy of 1910", noting that "Bergson was then the most noticed figure in Paris", and identifying three important qualities in his philosophy (in common with Maeterlink): "The use of science against science"; "Mysticism"; and "Optimism" (Moody, *Thomas Stern Eliot Poet*: 49), all traits he explores in "Tradition and the Individual Talent". But Woolf's interest in pinpointing December 1910 as an historical moment of cultural and political change is in direct opposition to Eliot's notions of tradition and myth, which insist on an eternal, unifying order beyond and outside history. In Woolf's and Eliot's canonical "modernist essays", there is a gender divide opening up, a divide that becomes a chasm when we examine their canonical "modernist" works. Part II will examine the gender wars of modernism, the conflicts of which, we might say, are staged in Hell.

# Part II

# Image, Gender, Apocalypse

The primary pigment of poetry is the IMAGE

(Pound, "Vortex", 1914, *Blast*, 1: 154)

So saying the spirit of the prince, Teiresias, went back into the house of Hades

(Homer, *Odyssey* XI: 150–1)

# 6 Rude Mouths
## Wyndham Lewis, Gertrude Stein, H.D., Virginia Woolf, Nathanael West and Ezra Pound

### Introduction to Part II and Chapter 6

Part II: "Image, Gender, Apocalypse", our corridor in which "time passes", looks at the currency of the image in a selection of texts from the Imagist movement onwards, and opens up questions of gender, class, race and war as points of transition, opposition, and crisis, and of montage and collage of the image as the dominant avant-garde aesthetic mode. The springboard "image" is the vortex, as outlined in the springboard magazine, *Blast.* "Blast", of course, is a curse condemning its targets to eternal damnation, and the arena for "Image, Gender, Apocalypse" is Hell. We are not going to linger over the pages of *Blast,* as we did over *The Egoist,* but will use Pound's declaration on the image there, as the catapult (such is the energy of the vortex) out to the gender war located with the transsexual Tiresias, somewhere in the "house of Hades". The gender struggle over the mythopoesis of Hell, which began to emerge in our discussions in Part I, contributes to the major transition that marks the period 1910–45: the rise of women and the working classes, the creation and establishment, along with that of the infernal military–industrial complex, of a welfare state; and broadening the public sphere, the opening up of professions to women and men previously excluded on grounds of class, race and/or gender. Both support and opposition to these transitions are conducted in the literary gender wars of the era, staged in Hell.

This chapter begins with readings of gender politics in *Blast,* looking at the work of Henri Gaudier-Brzeska, Ezra Pound, Wyndham

Lewis, T. S. Eliot and Jessie Dismorr. This leads to a discussion of gendered figures of automation in Eliot's *The Waste Land* and Woolf's *To the Lighthouse.* There follows a discussion of reactionary cultural models of motherhood in the work of Oswald Spengler and D. H. Lawrence, and a reading of gender in Yeats's apocalyptic poem "The Second Coming", followed by a nod to Pound's response to Eliot's *The Waste Land,* couched in terms of rivalling spermatic poetics. A reading of gender politics and myth in some crucial passages in Woolf's "Time Passes", the middle section of *To the Lighthouse,* opens up to a wider discussion of modernist discourses of hell, myth, gender, lesbian poetics and androgyny in the work of Stein, Woolf, Eliot, H.D., Nathanael West, Pound and others. Comparative close readings emerge of Pound's "Hell Cantos" and Stein's poem *Before the Flowers of Friendship Faded Friendship Faded,* and of Eliot's *The Waste Land* and Richard Wright's poem "Between the World and Me".

## *Blast* and the phallic vortex: Henri Gaudier-Brzeska, Ezra Pound, Wyndham Lewis, T. S. Eliot and Jessie Dismorr

Wyndham Lewis's vorticist little magazine, *Blast,* short-lived in only two issues, *Blast* 1 (June 1914), and *Blast* War Number (July 1915), has, since republication in facsimile form (see Lewis, *Blast* and *Blast,* 2), become a set text on many undergraduate courses on the era. And it is a wonderful resource, particularly as it constitutes probably the most avant-garde publication produced in Britain for the whole period. In huge, energetic, experimental typography *Blast* 1 fires off several pages of manifestos and declarations, positioning itself in the spectrum of avant-gardes somewhere between Italian Futurism ("the latest form of Impressionism") and Picasso's Cubism, and celebrating individualism (the vortex is "nothing to do with 'the People'"), the ego and an intensely priapic masculine poetics. It celebrates the fusion of body and machine, equating Picasso's cubist constructions, for example, with "a sort of machinery": "These mysterious machines of modern art are what they are TO BE ALIVE" (140). Rebecca West is the only woman contributor in an otherwise male panoply that includes Pound, Lewis, Ford Madox Hueffer (later Ford), and the sculptor Gaudier Brzeska (although Pound does reproduce as exemplary, a poem by H.D.). Pound's, now legendary, anti-Semitism is overtly on show too, in his poem "Salutation the Third": "Let us be done with

Jews and Jobbery, / Let us SPIT upon those who fawn on the JEWS for their money" (Lewis, *Blast* 1: 45). And Paul Peppis helpfully explores Vorticist nationalism in his recent book *Literature, Politics, and the English Avant-Garde: Nation and Empire, 1901–1918* (2000). *Blast* is also a showcase for visual as well as verbal art, and work by Gaudier Brzeska, Lewis, Wadsworth, Epstein, and other avant-garde visual artists is reproduced in its pages. The Vortex is a gendered image, then, and it is masculine. But there is only a slight whiff of misogyny, in *Blast*'s "word of advice" (1: 151–2) to the Suffragettes. Their feminist activism is applauded:

> WE ADMIRE YOUR ENERGY. YOU AND ARTISTS ARE THE ONLY THINGS (YOU DON'T MIND BEING CALLED THINGS?) LEFT IN ENGLAND WITH A LITTLE LIFE IN THEM. (151)

But *Blast* does not approve of the Suffragette campaign's vandalising works of art:

> ONLY LEAVE WORKS OF ART ALONE.
> YOU MIGHT SOME DAY DESTROY A GOOD PICTURE BY ACCIDENT.
> . . . IF YOU DESTROY A GREAT WORK OF ART you are destroying a greater soul than if you annihilated a whole district of London.
> LEAVE ART ALONE, BRAVE COMRADES! (151–2)

The most notorious act of suffragette vandalism against art is probably Mary Richardson's attack on Velázquez's *Toilet of Venus*, or *The Rokeby Venus*, as it was known, which hung in the National Gallery guarded by detectives. In her memoir, *Laugh of Defiance* (1953), she recalls making five blows with her axe before being hauled off: "Two Baedeker guide books, truly aimed by German tourists, came cracking against the back of my neck. By this time, too, the detective . . . sprang on me and dragged the axe from my hand. As if out of the very walls angry people seemed to appear round me" (169). Such acts might readily be understood as truly avant-garde performance art, but the suffragist movements were also capable of constructive as well destructive performances, and they should also be recalled for their massive organised pageant-like rallies, resplendent in glorious colourful banners and floats and costumes (see Tickner).

The "phallic direction" of *Blast* 2 is perhaps symbolised by Gaudier-

Brzeska's phallic sculpture of Ezra Pound's head reproduced in its pages. Gaudier-Brzeska's "Vortex Gaudier-Brzeska", which was "Written from the Trenches", with its chilling declaration that "THIS WAR IS A GREAT REMEDY" (echoing Marinetti's "war is the total hygiene of the world"), is all the more powerful and frightening for the notice of his death "in charge at Neuville St. Vaast, on June 5th, 1915" (Lewis, *Blast* 2: 34) that follows it. His defiance in championing the vortex is all the more poignant and heroic:

> MY VIEWS ON SCULPTURE REMAIN ABSOLUTELY THE SAME,
> IT IS THE VORTEX OF WILL, OF DECISION, THAT BEGINS.
> I SHALL DERIVE MY EMOTIONS SOLELY FROM THE ARRANGEMENT OF SURFACES, I shall present my emotions by the ARRANGEMENT OF MY SURFACES, THE PLANES AND LINES BY WHICH THEY ARE DEFINED.

He applies his formalist credo to the context of trench warfare in which he finds himself:

> Just as this hill where the Germans are solidly entrenched, gives me a nasty feeling, solely because its gentle slopes are broken by earthworks, which throw long shadows at sunset. Just so I get feeling, of whatsoever definition, from a statue ACCORDING TO ITS SLOPES, varied to infinity.

This is Clive Bell's "Significant Form" taken to Hell. And although Lewis and the Vorticists fell out with Bloomsbury, interestingly enough over the Ideal Home Exhibition, such declarations show common ground with the hard-line formalist wing of Bloomsbury, and illuminates these theories in a more overtly masculinist light. In "The European War and Great Communities", it is prophesied by Lewis: "Everything will be arranged for the best convenience of War. Murder and destruction is man's fundamental occupation." And "Women's function" is to be "the manufacturing of children (even more important than cartridges and khaki suits) . . . and they evidently realize this thoroughly." Lewis's black satirical humour continues:

> It takes the deft women we employ anything from twelve to sixteen years to fill and polish these little human cartridges, and they of

> course get fond of them in the process. However, all this is not our fault, and is absolutely necessary. We only begin decaying like goods kept too long, if we are not killed or otherwise disposed of. Is this not proof of our function? (16)

We might compare the imagery of humanity as machinery or industrial process in the poems by Jessie Dismorr and Eliot reproduced in this issue of *Blast.* Dismorr seems to be describing the kind of birth pangs Lewis's war prophesy has in mind in her surreal "Monologue", where "I squeezed out with intact body" and "Details of equipment delight me. / I admire my arrogant spiked tresses, the disposition of my perpetually foreshortened limbs, / Also the new machinery that wields the chains of muscles fitted beneath my close coat of skin" (65). Whereas Dismorr's speaker utters her paeon to a machine body as if from the interior, subject position of a vorticist portrait, the "I" of Eliot's "Rhapsody on a Windy Night", on the other hand, observes an exterior, object world populated by semi-automata: "So the hand of a child, automatic, / Slipped out and pocketed a toy that was running along the quai. / I could see nothing behind that child's eye" (51). The lamp speaks to him of "female smells in shuttered rooms, / And cigarettes in corridors / And cocktail smells in bars" (51), as if all were equally by-products of industrial manufacture.

## Gender and the "automatic hand": T. S. Eliot's *The Waste Land* and Virginia Woolf's *To the Lighthouse*

Eliot later raises another "automatic hand", in *The Waste Land,* where after the desultory, infernal, urban sex scene between the "young man carbuncular" and "the typist home at teatime", watched over by the subterranean Tiresias, the girl, now alone, "smoothes her hair with automatic hand, / And puts a record on the gramophone" (lines 255–6). Perhaps this misogynistic emblem of semi-automated, reified womanhood is taken up and countered by Woolf, in *To the Lighthouse,* where there is an occasional disembodied, raised hand, most notably where Mrs Ramsay feels her husband's "mind like a raised hand shadowing her mind" (189). And in the darkness of "Time Passes", a disembodied and countering hand is raised against implicit violence: "Sometimes a hand was raised as if to clutch something or ward off something" (196); Eliot and Woolf fist-fight in Hell!

The impact of gendered readings of "modernism" has been to show how certain male modernists (re)produced an "Unreal City", reviled as infernal and populated by semi-automated and monstrously disfigured humanity. This male modernist view perpetuates a misogynist French symbolist tradition that transferred Romantic visions of a feminised Nature to equally disturbing Decadent visions of the City as a woman, following Baudelaire who can, for example, trade metaphors between a woman's cunt and the street's gutter. This imagery appears in a poem where the female addressee is "blind and deaf machine" and also has "eyes lit up like shops' (Baudelaire: 38–9; translated by Katharine Swarbrick). The later Eliotic figuring of urban geography, and technological commodity, as feminine is splendidly burlesqued in a classic exchange between Rufus T. Firefly, President of Freedonia, and a statuesque society hostess and benefactress, Mrs Teasdale, aka Groucho Marx and Margaret Dumont, in the Marx brothers' film *Duck Soup* (1933):

> *Mrs T.* I've sponsored your appointment because I feel you are the most able statesman in all Freedonia.
>
> *Firefly* Well, that covers a lot of ground. Say, you cover a lot of ground yourself. You better beat it. I hear they're going to tear you down and put up an office building where you're standing. You can leave in a taxi. If you can't get a taxi you can leave in a huff. If that's too soon, you can leave in a minute and a huff. You know you haven't stopped talking since I came here? You must have been vaccinated with a phonograph needle.
>
> (Anobile: 143)

Mrs Teasdale's arm seems to have an Eliotic "automatic hand".

## The monstrous mothers and modern women of Oswald Spengler and D. H. Lawrence: gendering the beast in W. B. Yeats's "The Second Coming"

Certain female "modernists", on the other hand, are more inclined to celebrate urban space as representative of the public and civic spheres that are opening up to women, and negotiated by them, throughout the period. (Compare, for example, "Prufrock" with *Mrs*

*Dalloway.*) Reactionary male modernism gets its standard of ideal womanhood from a vision made popular by the likes of Max Nordau, in *Degeneration*, and later by Oswald Spengler, in *The Decline of the West.* They link the decline of civilisation to the rise in women's liberation, the use of contraceptives, and women's neglect of familial and domestic duties. Spengler celebrates "The primary woman, the peasant woman, [who] is mother", and for him, modern, urban women who scorn fertility and their maternal function are responsible for the collapse of the "whole pyramid of cultural man", which "crumbles from the summit, first the world-cities, then the provincial forms, and finally the land itself, whose best blood has incontinently poured into the towns, merely to bolster them awhile. At last, only the primitive blood remains, alive, but robbed of its strongest and most promising elements" (*Decline* 2, p. 105). It is for this primary motherhood that the protagonist of D. H. Lawrence's *Sons and Lovers* "whimper[s]" at its close. Elsewhere, in an essay anthologised in Scott's *The Gender of Modernism*, Lawrence describes "the tragedy of the modern woman" in the following terms:

> She becomes cocksure, she puts all her passion and energy and years of her life into some effort or assertion, without ever listening to the denial which she ought to take into count. She is cocksure, but she is a hen all the time. Frightened of her own henny self, she rushes to mad lengths about votes, or welfare, or sports, or business: she is marvellous, out-manning the man. But alas, it is all fundamentally disconnected. (Scott: 229)

Lawrence suggests that "the eggs she has laid, votes, or miles of typewriting, years of business efficiency" are no substitute for the real eggs of authentic motherhood:

> The lovely henny surety, the hensureness which is the real bliss of every female, has been denied her: she had never had it. Having lived her life with such utmost strenuousness and cocksureness, she has missed her life altogether. Nothingness! (229)

We might also compare with this, Yeats's Spenglerian prophesy of modernity's monstrous, yet paradoxically elided, figure of motherhood, in the messianic poem "The Second Coming" (1919; 1920):

> but now I know
> That twenty centuries of stony sleep
> Were vexed to nightmare by a rocking cradle,
> And what rough beast, its hour come round at last,
> Slouches towards Bethlehem to be born?

Whose hand rocks the cradle? How is the yet to be born "rough beast" able to slouch towards Bethlehem? The self-rocking cradle perhaps suggests an automated, even industrialised, maternity; whereas the collapsing of maternal and foetal identities into the self-mobilising unborn beast suggests this anti-Christ to be a monstrous self-replicating matriarchy, rendering masculinity redundant. The chilling sense of reduplication, sans nuptials, is reduplicated in the poem's own verbal repetitions where several words and phrases perform a "second coming", starting with the opening line's "Turning and turning"; then the following are also repeated: "falcon", "loosed", "surely", "at hand", and "the Second Coming" itself. The botched nature of this reproductive process is also communicated in the many half- or near-repetitions of syllables.

## Sperm wars: T. S. Eliot and Ezra Pound

The phallic detonations of *Blast*, it seems, are merely early rounds fired in a gender war that is fought right across the period. It is difficult to apply the term "transition" to such turbulent, internecine warfare. The "transition" of the subterranean, maternal mother into the new woman of the public sphere was far from smooth. If women writers seem to be easing and celebrating her birth, the men often appear to be supplying the cultural prophylactics; or speaking their own "phallic direction", as here Pound does in a letter to Eliot; praising the latest draft of *The Waste Land*, and "wracked by the seven jealousies", he portrays himself in verse as "E.P. hopeless and helpless", following Yeats:

> Balls and balls and balls again
> Can not touch his fellow men.
> His foaming and abundant cream
> Has coated his world. The coat of a dream;
> Or say that the upjut of his sperm
> Has rendered his senses pachyderm.

> Grudge not the oyster his stiff saliva
> Envy not the diligent diver. Et in aeternitate.

After this celebratory critique of encrusting spermatics and autoeroticism (for he has been flagellating himself in the letter for "exuding my deformative secretions . . . I go into nacre and objets d'art"), Pound signs off: "It is after all a grrrreat littttterary period / Thanks for the Agamemnon" (Eliot, *Letters* 1, p. 499). Agamemnon, and the Trojan War, of course, are the very stuff of this gender war.

## Gender and Hell in "Time Passes": Virginia Woolf's *To the Lighthouse*

> So with the lamps all put out, the moon sunk, and a thin rain drumming on the roof a down-pouring of immense darkness began. Nothing, it seemed, could survive the flood, the profusion of darkness which, creeping in at keyholes and crevices, stole round window blinds, came into bedrooms, swallowed up here a jug and basin, there a bowl of red and yellow dahlias, there the sharp edges and firm bulk of a chest of drawers. Not only was furniture confounded; there was scarcely anything left of body or mind by which one could say "This is he" or "This is she." Sometimes a hand was raised as if to clutch something or ward off something, or somebody groaned, or somebody laughed aloud as if sharing a joke with nothingness.
>
> (*To the Lighthouse*, p. 195)

This is the second section of "Time Passes", the corridor running between two blocks, the central part of *To the Lighthouse*'s "triadic" (Moore: 62) movement, and a work that in draft form was also published separately, and in French translation (see Haule). Part One, "The Window", suggesting a means of natural illumination and its reception, gives an account of one day and a candle-lit and moon-lit evening in the period before the Great War, sometime around 1910. "Time Passes" is characterised mainly by darkness, and covers the war years, and describes the interior of the house, now empty, as an allegory for the passage of time. Part Three, "The Lighthouse", again suggestive of illumination, this time artificially generated rather than passively received, describes one, post-war, day in the 1920s, leading to vision, enlightenment, lyric consolation. There is a transformation, then, from window to lighthouse. The "down-pouring of immense darkness" (195) in "Time Passes" marks the occlusion of one way of life, or one sense of subjectivity, and leads to the emergence of another. It is a descent into darkness, into Hell, even. The Ramsays' holiday home becomes "the house of Hades". And while it is important to take seriously Woolf's claim that *To the Lighthouse* is an elegy, we might also acknowledge its allusions to epic, a poetic tradition from Homer and Virgil to Milton, that locates some of its action, at least, in Hell. The epic hero is able to descend there and re-emerge, earning in Odysseus's case the epithet of "twice dying", and suggestive of a moment of rebirth and renewal.

This essentially elegiac, transitional, movement in "Time Passes" may be considered in terms of gendered and contested subjectivity. In a reversal of the divisions in Genesis emanating from the moment God declares "Let there be light", here darkness falls so deeply that "there was scarcely anything left of body or mind by which one could say 'This is he' or 'This is she.'" In "Time Passes", then, a gender-based transition is effected: it begins with the extinguishing of lights in the pre-war house, which act echoes Sir Edward Grey's famous remark in the pre-war dusk of August 1914: "The lamps are going out all over Europe; we shall not see them lit again in our lifetime" (Buchan: 98). The last light to go belongs to the poet Mr Carmichael "who liked to lie awake a little reading Virgil, [and who] kept his candle burning rather longer than the rest" (*To the Lighthouse*, p. 195); and it ends with Lily Briscoe's waking in a new dawn light. Emphasis transfers from masculine experience to feminine. For this to occur, the relationship and gendering of traditional subject–object oppositions undergo considerable change ("Not only was furniture confounded; there was scarcely anything left of body or mind by which one could say 'This is he' or 'This is she'"(196)). So, if the first part of the novel presents a study of old order, pre-war values (the promotion of marriage and children as the social norm, careers and intellectual pursuits as the public domain of men, and domestic duties as the private realm of women), then the final part shows their considerable erosion: Lily Briscoe the artist (along with others) dissents from the pre-war marital prospectus pushed by Mrs Ramsay, the housewife, whose death in the intervening years comes to stand for the passing of those values. And the turning point is in the notorious parenthetical sentence where her death is related:

> [Mr. Ramsay stumbling along a passage stretched his arms out one dark morning, but Mrs. Ramsay having died rather suddenly the night before he stretched his arms out. They remained empty.] (200)

This is the infernal low point of "Time Passes", the sojourn among the dead of *To the Lighthouse*, for there are other deaths recorded here, each in parenthesis – the fall of a son in the Great War, the loss of a daughter in the pain of giving birth. But it is the death of the novel's central character, Mrs Ramsay, so casually reported, that most shocks. The notorious stumbling sentence in which the patriarch, Mr Ramsay, reaches out for his faithful wife only to clasp thin air, has given editors considerable trouble (especially as the first American edition gives a substantive variant). Hermione Lee urges readers to find an allusion here to De Quincey, *Suspira de Profundis*: "for the temptation of suicide when 'we stretch out our arms in darkness' " (De Quincey: 120; Lee: 252), and she puts forward a biographical reading of the novel in also noting that the "Ramsay deaths reflect the shocks of bereavement in Woolf's childhood and early adulthood: her mother died in 1895, her half-sister, Stella, in 1897, and her brother, Thoby, in 1906" (Lee: 252). And what this biographical gloss on the family deaths also implicitly provides is a biographical gloss on the allusion to suicide, as if Woolf's suicide in 1941 has bearing on her novel of 1927. But suicide seems a red-herring here. There is no indication that Ramsay is tempted to suicide because his wife has been lost, nor that she herself committed suicide.

But the passage may well allude to, and in fact be citing, the far more appropriate account, in Ovid's *Metamorphoses*, of a husband losing his wife at the gates of Hell – the story of Orpheus and Eurydice. Ovid describes the moment of the husband's realisation of the loss of his wife as follows: "bracchiaque intendens prendique et prendere certans / nil nisi cedentes infelix arripit auras" (Book X, lines 58–9). The Loeb translation of 1916, by Frank Justus Miller (printed in Britain and America), gives this as "He stretched out his arms, eager to catch her or to feel her clasp; but, unhappy one, he clasped nothing but the yielding air" (Ovid: 68–9). The literal translation would be "and stretching out his arms", but standard translation practice, in such a syntactic context communicating a sequence of actions, might well render the participle of the verb as the past imperfect or even perfect tense, "stretched" (a continued or finite action). It is difficult to express the moment where the expectant outreached arms realise disappointment, and clasp nothing. Both Ovid and Woolf show a subtle, and searching, syntactic awareness of the impossibility of the husband's attempts to take hold of an absence. And "those fumbling airs" (*To the Lighthouse*, p. 196), then, that eerily roam around the Ramsays' house in "Time Passes", may well be blowing with the "yielding airs" that are the object of Orpheus's unhappy embrace. Mrs Ramsay, like Eurydice, dies twice (Book X, line 64; Ovid: 68–9), and becomes a reified absence. Ovid plays off the adjectival present participles "certans" and "cedentes" ("eager" or "striving (for)" and "yielding") against the finality of "arripit". The verb *arripio* means "to seize", but also "to take possession of". So Orpheus seizes yielding air, a metaphor, standing in the place of the disappeared woman, and a construction in the accusative that still objectifies her in her dramatic absence.

The objectification of the absent, dead woman is not, however, communicated by Woolf's syntax in the crucial parenthetical sentence. Woolf uses the English equivalent of the Latin construction, the ablative absolute (which is not used by Ovid in his sentence): "Mrs. Ramsay having died rather suddenly the night before", which is used where the action described is not performed by anything present in the main sentence. Presumably, it would in fact be syntactically possible to use the past participle where, in Latin, the *absent*, dead Mrs Ramsay would be in the accusative, and would be the object of the verb, that is to say that "the out-stretching arms clasped the missing-and-having-died-the-night-before Mrs Ramsay", but this would suggest her presence nevertheless. Woolf's ablative absolute construction trips and shocks the reader, just as Mr Ramsay himself goes through the motion of reaching out for his already absent wife. She is not in the sentence. The ablative absolute furthermore gives her a strong sense of agency, even in communicating her death. In Latin either construction (past participle or ablative absolute) depends on the particular inflections of noun and verb, and its impact to some extent depends on its position in the line, but punctuation is in any case redundant. Woolf's ablative absolute similarly needs no commas (which were supplied by a later printer); and their absence enhances the semantic slippage between clauses in "the night before" and "he stretched". (The dead Mrs Ramsay is her husband's absent and prior feminine origin.) But it also reminds us that the collagistic juxtaposition of phrases in experimental, avant-garde texts (and *To the Lighthouse* is a mosaic of juxtaposed sections and parentheses) may sometimes be grounded in the syntax of the classical sources they spring from.

Mr Ramsay also seems to have learned the lesson of Andrew Marvell's *carpe diem* of "To his Coy Mistress": "The grave's a fine and private place, / But none, I think, do there embrace" (22). In the following account of image and gender wars, the gaping mouth of the grave, of Hell, is never far.

## Gender, modernism, myth: Gertrude Stein, H.D., Mina Loy, Virginia Woolf, Nathanael West and Ezra Pound

I want to look at some aspects of the aftermath of the "first heave", or initial fragmentation, of "Modernism" in terms of gender and subjectivity, and in relation to modernist engagements with classical, mythical sources. Their vigorous engagement with classical texts marks, for modernist and avant-garde writers, a vexed relationship with the past, and signals their equally vexed concerns to place modernity in relation to tradition. Do modern texts break entirely from ancient ones, or merely remake them anew? I will be focusing on examples from Ezra Pound, H.D. and Gertrude Stein, and briefly referring to Virginia Woolf. The change in the critical approach to modernism, which has enabled such readings, is succinctly illustrated by a glance at two or three book titles. The influence of such books as Shari Benstock's study *Women of the Left Bank: Paris, 1900–1940* (1986), and Bonnie Kime Scott's anthology *The Gender of Modernism* (1990), illustrates how much Modernist studies have changed since Hugh Kenner's *The Pound Era: The Age of Ezra Pound, T. S. Eliot, James Joyce and Wyndham Lewis* (1972) topped reading lists in the 1970s.

During this period we were encouraged to think of the measure of modernism as a man. The American satirist Nathanael West, who visited modernism's epicentre, Paris, in the 1920s as a young aesthete and aspiring avant-garde writer (he met the French Surrealists and was befriended by Phillippe Soupault), wrote an entertaining short story that illustrates, for me, this masculine mythology. "The Impostor" gives an account of Paris in the 1920s, and of Beano, a young man who has no artistic talent except for his fantastic ability to *masquerade* as a brilliant avant-garde sculptor: "Here was a man who could talk a whole gallery full of art works and looked like a genius yet couldn't draw worth a damn" (414). The desperate Beano has a moment of revelation when he realises, or decides, "that all the anatomy books were wrong because they used a man only five feet ten inches tall for their charts. Some used a man even shorter. They should have used a man six feet tall because the perfect, modern man is six feet tall. . . . A new anatomy book had to be written, and not until he had written it could he even think of drawing or sculpture" (416). Later Beano joins the expatriate Americans drinking at the *Dome*. He has acquired from the morgue the corpse of a six-foot sailor "fished from the Seine", which is sitting wrapped in paper in the back of his taxi, and the story relates the Dadaist events that follow. Beano's dead man, reminiscent of the dead Phlebas in Part IV ("Death by Water") of Eliot's *The Waste Land*, may be seen as the masculinist measure of modernism – modernism as a dead man (and we only have to think of all the dead of the Great War to understand why). But it is also a red-herring. The corpse over which Modernist poetics arise and Modernist critics swarm may well be female (see Bronfen). Or is it both? We might begin to wonder what *is* the gender status of a corpse anyway.

Unlike Pound and H.D., Stein was never an Imagist. Her collection of poems *Tender Buttons* (1914) is highly experimental: in it she tests poetry almost into prose; experiments in rhythm, repetition, and grammar. Although perhaps some of her poetry appears imagistic on the page, Stein's disruptive organisation of language makes for a dynamism very much at odds with the *haiku*-like stasis of Imagism. Stein's most famous poem is the circular and repetitive "A rose is a rose is a rose". This has been interpreted as exemplifying modernism's self-reflexive aestheticism: the caressing of the noun, as Stein herself calls it in her lecture "Poetry and Grammar":

> Poetry is concerned with using with abusing, with losing with wanting, with denying with avoiding with adoring with replacing the noun. It is doing that always doing that, doing that and doing nothing but that. Poetry is doing nothing but using losing refusing and pleasing and betraying and caressing nouns. That is what poetry does, that is what poetry has to do no matter what kind of poetry it is. And there are a great many kinds of poetry.
>
> When I said.
>
> A rose is a rose is a rose is a rose.
>
> And then later made that into a ring I made poetry and what did I do I caressed completely caressed and addressed a noun.

Mina Loy's poem "Gertrude Stein" celebrates Stein as:

> Curie
> of the laboratory
> of vocabulary
>   she crushed
> the tonnage
> of consciousness
> congealed to phrases
>   to extract
> a radium of the word
>
> (Loy: 94)

Stein's "radium of the word", like Pound's imagist "radiant node or cluster", is not some sort of Eliotic impersonal technique, but one vitally concerned with gender. Stein is, we might say, more emphatically a *woman* technician. Loy's poem perhaps points up a parallel between radium and language as material that may prove lethal to the woman investigating it. Woolf offers a feminised version of the scientific laboratory in *A Room of One's Own*, where she describes the new subject matter that women's writing will broach: "Chloe liked Olivia. They shared a laboratory together. . . ." (125). Woolf's refrain here, "Chloe likes Olivia", has become a critical slogan for lesbian writing. The narrator explains: "For if Chloe likes Olivia and Mary Carmichael knows how to express it she will light a torch in that vast chamber where nobody has yet been" (126). And of their sharing the laboratory, she further elucidates that it "will make their friendship more varied and lasting because it will be less personal" (126). Eliot's scientific theory of "impersonality" is surely being undermined here by Sapphic humour.

## Gender, modernism, myth: androgyny in Virginia Woolf's *A Room of One's Own* and T. S. Eliot's *The Waste Land*

Woolf, of course, has been credited with her own theory of impersonality, in her vexing discussion, in *A Room of One's Own*, of androgyny (a theory she derives from Samuel Taylor Coleridge's work):

> It is fatal to be a man or woman pure and simple; one must be woman-manly or man-womanly. It is fatal for a woman to lay the

> least stress on any grievance; to plead even with justice any cause; in any way to speak consciously as a woman. And fatal is no figure of speech; for anything written with that conscious bias is doomed to death. It ceases to be fertilized. . . . Some collaboration has to take place in the mind between the woman and the man before the art of creation can be accomplished. Some marriage of opposites has to be accomplished. (*A Room of One's Own*: 136)

Woolf's theory of androgyny has been interpreted as positioning her argument beyond feminist concerns, yet it is conceived in the context of her analysis of women and fiction, and is proposed as a goal not yet attained by most of her contemporaries because of inequalities between men and women. Shakespeare, the poet playwright, is Woolf's ideal androgynous writer. She lists others – all men – who have also achieved androgyny (Keats, Sterne, Cowper, Lamb, and Proust – the only contemporary). Carolyn G. Heilbrun and Nancy Topping Bazin were the first critics to explore Woolf's theory of androgyny. Showalter's attack on it, in her famous chapter "Virginia Woolf and the Flight into Androgyny", marks the start of continuing ferocious theoretical debate on the subject (see also DiBattista; Moi). For critics like Moi, Woolf's theory of androgyny anticipates the French feminist concept of "différance". Androgyny may not be impersonal then so much as dually gendered. Woolf's narrator is inspired to her theory by the sight of a girl and a young man getting into a taxi:

> The sight was ordinary enough; what was strange was the rhythmical order with which my imagination had invested it; and the fact that the ordinary sight of two people getting into a cab had the power to communicate something of their own seeming satisfaction. The sight of two people coming down the street and meeting at the corner seems to ease the mind of some strain, I thought, watching the taxi turn and make off." (144)

This act of urban voyeurism distinctly echoes that of the voyeuristic Tiresias, in Eliot's *The Waste Land*, who also watches the traffic on the street:

> At the violet hour, when the eyes and back
> Turn upward from the desk, when the human engine waits
> Like a taxi throbbing waiting,
> I Tiresias, though blind, throbbing between two lives,

> Old man with wrinkled female breasts . . .
> Perceived the scene, and foretold the rest . . .
>
> (*Complete Poems*: 68)

Woolf's taxi surely throbs with Eliotic cargo. Eliot, furthermore, directs us to Ovid's account of Tiresias in the *Metamorphoses* and to Sappho in his note on Tiresias's account of "the evening hour that strives / Homeward, and brings sailor home from sea" (68), but we might also think, ignoring his lead, of Odysseus's return to Penelope, foretold by Agamemnon in Hades, and following the hero's consultation with Tiresias who also foretells of his journey home. Tiresias, in *The Waste Land*, spies on the urban couple as they make love, "nuptials" that Woolf perhaps alludes to, in her account of writerly androgyny, as a post-coital moment when "The curtains must be close drawn. The writer, I thought, once his experience is over, must lie back and let his mind celebrate its nuptials in darkness" (*A Room of One's Own*, p. 156). How does this model of androgyny sit with Chloe and Olivia in their laboratory? Woolf's appraisal of the achievements of women writers suggests that before stepping into the throbbing taxi with a young man, women still need time to catch up together in their laboratory. And Stein's lesbian poetics surely locate her in the laboratory with Chloe and Olivia, rather than in the Tiresian taxi.

## Rude mouths and Sapphics: Gertrude Stein, H.D. and Ezra Pound

Stein's circular rose poem may also be inscribing the feminine: and this may be understood, in more recent feminist literary theoretical terms, as *écriture feminine.* It is an erotic celebration of a recovered origin of feminine poetics: a "rude mouth". Whereas women modernist poets like Stein and H.D. are interested in recovering this rude mouth, poets such as the patriarchal Ezra Pound, I would argue, want to reify its loss. Ezra Pound's intensely masculinist poetry is underwritten by his statement that "POETRY SPEAKS PHALLIC DIRECTION". Pound, we recall, is the man who instigated Marsden's turning of the magazine *The New Freewoman* into *The Egoist*, and who turned his back on Imagism when it became too feminine: what he derogatorily (and paradoxically) termed "Amygism" (referring to Amy Lowell). And it is argued now that modernist poetry is concerned not with impersonality and androgyny, but with opposing, gendered poetics.

One of the partially lost origins of feminine poetics is the ancient Greek poet Sappho, whose work survives only in fragments, often extant only in quotations as examples for later, mainly male, poets to study for metrical or grammatical interest. Sappho was an important source for both Pound and H.D. but they approach her work very differently. Pound, although he conjures, at times, these lost Sapphic feminine origins, ultimately produces an intensely masculine poetry. He talks, like Emerson before him, of poetry as "spermatics". In "Hugh Selwyn Mauberley", we learn that "Christ follows Dionysus, / Phallic and ambrosial". That is, Christian asceticism has, as Maud Ellmann puts it, "supplanted the erotic mysteries of Dionysus": "The cult of Eleusis, 'phallic and ambrosial', surrenders to the tyranny of eunuchs" (Maud Ellmann: 153, 154). This is Pound's condemnation of contemporary poetry. In "Hugh Selwyn Mauberley" (Pound's transitional poem towards the *Cantos*), it is "Bright Apollo", Phoebus, who ultimately stands as the lost measure of masculine poetics. I will be looking in what follows at examples of how these three poets (Pound, H.D. and Stein) differently engage Apollonian poetics. I'm arguing that, rather than look at modernist poetry in terms of impersonality and androgyny, or in terms of the Tiresian sexually transgressive, liberated from stable gender codes (as perhaps it is possible to read Eliot's *The Waste Land*), we might discover a *war* of the sexes, and attempts at entrenched, gendered poetics. Breaking (blasting) open the pentameter and caressing the noun may be seen in terms of opposing, gendered poetics.

I want now to compare two poems, by Pound and H.D., which engage with Sappho: Pound's Imagist poem "Papyrus", which mimics and in a sense reifies a Sapphic fragment, with H.D.'s "FRAGMENT 113", which in fact fleshes out and augments the Sapphic fragment 113, "Neither honey nor the bee for me", into an overflowing lyrical catalogue of sensual lesbian erotics. I will then look at one of Pound's "Hell Cantos", before returning to Gertrude Stein.

## The Sapphics of Ezra Pound's "Papyrus"

Spring . . . . . . .
Too long . . . . . .
Gongula . . . . . .

(*Personae*: 122)

Written at a time when (papyrus and literary) fragments were being recovered and collated for publication, Pound's "fragment", smartly entitled "Papyrus", presents itself as the remains of ancient writing, and is in fact, as Gongula signals, derived from a real Sappho fragment (in which the word "Gongula" appears), a "scrap of a parchment copy made thirteen centuries later" on which at "an upper left-hand corner learning assisted by chemicals makes out a few letters" (Kenner: 5). We have only the residue, only the first, largely conjectured, word of each line. And this Pound turns into a "witticism", according to Kenner (6). Pound's "Papyrus" is in effect a synthetic version of lost, fragmented writing, perhaps communicating a sense of lost plenitude, and it has been interpreted as standing for the nature of all language; and as a poem of longing, of wishing to return the lost whole, lost plenitude. Lacanian and Kristevan theories may be of use here. But in another sense, rather than opening up a poetics of lost origins, the poem may also actually *reify* the loss. Note how the ellipses have become hardened, stylised features of the poem, frozen, almost turned to stone perhaps. The image, then, exemplifies the hard, dry, pebble-like, classical perfection of the "impersonal" poetry that Pound and T. E. Hulme sought to restore in the wake of "the emotional slither" they found in moribund nineteenth-century poetry. Is this poem a patriarchal palimpsest; an act of masculine inscription (reifying the loss of the feminine)? H.D.'s first novel, incidentally, was entitled *Palimpsest* (1926). The perverse, typographical solidity of "Papyrus", I am suggesting, makes this not a poem of longing, so much as a poem enforcing, and reifying, loss by means of an encrusting, spermatic poetics. I would argue that it is indeed an act of masculine inscription, reifying the loss of the feminine. This becomes clearer when we compare it with H.D.'s "FRAGMENT 113", which is also derived from a fragment by Sappho (and I will later refer it to Pound's "Hell Canto", Canto XV).

## The Sapphics of H.D.'s "FRAGMENT 113"

Not honey,
not the plunder of the bee
from meadow or sand-flower
or mountainbush;
from winter-flower or shoot

born of the later heat:
not honey, not the sweet
stain on the lips and teeth:
not honey, not the deep
plunge of soft belly
and the clinging of the gold-edged
pollen-dusted feet;
. . .

(*Collected Poems*: 131)

To understand what H.D. is doing with the fragment here, let us consider first how Sappho was treated in the nineteenth century. As we've been discussing, Sappho is considered the lost origin of classical lyric poetry and is the most famous – if not the first – woman poet. There is a wonderful nineteenth-century volume of Sappho that brings together the various attempts to imitate her work in English. All by men, of course: from Herbert to Swinburne. (Swinburne, incidentally, whom Pound admired, and who is the sort of nineteenth-century poet Pound is scrutinising in "Hugh Selwyn Mauberley", is one of Sappho's best translators.) This is how Henry Thornton Wharton, the book's editor, glosses "FRAGMENT 113":

> Neither honey nor the bee for me" [in Greek it is alliterative: meli melissa]: A proverb quoted by many late authors, referring to those who wish for good unmixed with evil. They seem to be the words of the bride. This, and the second line of fr. 62, and many other verses, show Sappho's fondness for alliteration; frs. 4 and 5, among several others, show that she did not ignore the charm of assonance. (146–7)

Wharton is typically most interested in technique – alliteration and assonance. And Pound himself thought highly of Sappho's technical achievements too. How does H.D's treatment of a Sappho fragment compare with Pound's? Does her poem read like a fragment? No. It is more like a fleshing out of the original. It is a sensual augmentation, protesting too much. The accumulation of "Nots" far from enforcing the negative, the absence of these things like honey and lips and belly and mouth – actually piles them up sumptuously; and this form of negation is a device of classical rhetoric. Does H.D.'s poem constitute an answer to Sappho's line – or is it a continuation of the line? Whatever, it is in a woman's voice cataloguing the sensuous delights of female sexuality: a pleasure that the speaker, or the woman she addresses is turning away from. Look at the chiastic movement in "Not iris – old desire": this is the sweetness perhaps. Is the sting of the bee rejection? The poem turns a few lines later at "but if you turn again". Is this an invitation to return to these delights – or is the speaker addressing a lover who has turned from her? (Compare this with Sappho's "Hymn to Aphrodite").

What does she mean by "neglect the lyre note"? Instead of its trembling string what is she offering: a different feminine poetics in "arm and throat", and in "heat, more passionate / of bone and white shell / and fiery tempered steel" (131). What does she mean by rejecting the figure of the iris and its destructive relation to "the fleck of the sun's fire"? Is this a rejection of the sun Apollo (a rejection of masculine, heterosexist poetics)?. I find these lines troubling. On the one hand, they suggest that the addressee should drop her instrument and pay attention to her lover; turn from art to real live pleasure. But on the other hand, why is H.D., in a poem about Sappho, talking about the neglect of the lyre, the symbol and origin of lyric poetry?

## Gendered poetics and mythical methods

Let us think about these origins; the foundational stories of masculine poetics: the myths of Orpheus and Apollo. Orpheus, with his lyre, was a poet so talented he could charm wild animals to sleep. But he offended the God Dionysus by neglecting him in favour of devotion to Apollo. As a punishment Orpheus was pursued and torn to pieces by the Thracian women (Maenads or Bacchantes), and his singing head floated out to Lesbos. (There is a very gory account of all this in Ovid's *Metamorphoses* XI). Apollo, God of music, and by extension poetry, on the other hand, is associated with the sun-Phoebus, "the bright one", who founded his shrine at Delphi by slaying a monstrous python. The story of Apollo and the Python has many permutations: from Perseus and Andromeda to St George and the Dragon. But significantly, the python slain by Apollo at Delphi is, in the earliest accounts of this conflict, female. One of the acclaimed sources of Western lyric poetry is founded on the destruction of this she-dragon, who, in her association with Hera's opposition to Athena, represents a monstrous autonomous femininity, alien to that approved by and approving of patriarchy:

> She was a monstrous creature, huge and savage, guilty of terrible violence against the people and the flocks of the land. To meet her meant death to any man. She had, moreover, been nurse to Typhaon, Hera's monstrous child, whom the queen of the gods had borne in anger at Zeus, because he had brought forth Athena from his head, and had had no need of her, his wedded wife. Deciding to equal Zeus's feat by producing a child without male help, Hera succeeded, but the child she bore was the monstrous Typhaon, like neither to gods nor to mortal men. She turned him over to the Delphinian drakaina, an evil to evil. (Fontenrose, *Python: A Study of Delphic Myth and its Origins*: 14)

Hera and the she-dragon represent a reviled and redundant femininity in the new patriarchal economy. Athena, we remember, made the crucial judgement in favour of patrilineal primacy when she sanctioned Orestes' vengeance on his mother, Clytemnestra, for the murder of his father, her husband Agamemnon. Athena puts this above Clytemnestra's avenging the sacrifice by Agamemnon of their daughter Iphigenia. Athena, who wears on her girdle the head of the snake-haired Gorgon Medusa, was herself born from Zeus's head. She has no loyalty to feminine bonds, no sympathy with women. The she-dragon, Python, may be seen as the matriarchal or feminine tradition against which stands Athena – the man's woman, or patriarchal woman.

Consider these myths of "monstrous women", then, such as Medusa the Gorgon, Medea, and Clytemnestra (who attracts new sympathy, according to Woolf, in 1910). Apollo's slaughter of the female Python may be seen as his sacking of an earlier female oracular shrine. The previously feminine associations of Apollo's shrine are erased so that Apollo appears to be founding a shrine for the first time, not displacing one he opposes. One of Apollo's first acts on founding his shrine was to try to rape Daphne who was transformed into the laurel tree – his poetic emblem. If the dominant tradition of poetry is constructed on the grave of the feminine, and involves the (attempted) rape and reification of the feminine, women writers may find problems negotiating a form founded on their own displacement and destruction. The act of inscription, of illumination, may be simultaneously an act of (self-)erasure and occlusion. One solution is to resurrect the drakaina as a positive source for women's writing. Virginia Woolf may playfully be making modified allusion to this in

*Mrs Dalloway* where she describes "the voice of no age or sex, the voice of an ancient spring spouting from the earth" which is yet the voice of "the battered woman", issuing from "so rude a mouth, a mere hole in the earth". What she sings sounds and looks like Schwitters' "Ur Sonata": "ee um fah um so / foo swee too eem oo— ". But is this sound poem gendered? This "rude mouth" may connote the pre-Apollonian Pythian spring or shrine, a source of feminine inspiration. Is Gertrude Stein's and H.D.'s poetry suggesting this alternative, feminine poetic tradition?

## Gender and oblivion: Ezra Pound's "Hell Cantos"

If a rejection of such "masculine poetics" is happening in H.D.'s and Stein's poetry, it suggests that this search for a revival of a feminine tradition in poetry is at odds with the agenda of male modernist poets like Pound and Eliot. It does not appear that H.D. is looking for a Fisher King! How does this fit with theories of modernist poetry and impersonality, aestheticism and self-reflexiveness? Whereas H.D. fleshes out and revives a lost feminine poetics, is it that Pound enshrines and reifies that loss, in order to assert and inscribe over it a masculine poetics? Maud Ellmann describes the poetics of Pound's self-inscription as "the battle between self and self-oblivion". But self-oblivion is in this context associated with dissolution into the feminine (object). Self-assertion comes by being tested against, then dominating, the feminine. This is nowhere more apparent than in Pound's "Hell Cantos". In my following discussion of Canto XV, I follow Ellmann's observations on Pound's self-inscription in the Cantos, where his engagement with financial and poetic economies turns on the pun on his own name: Pound.

> [The "compulsion of the name"] informs Pound's theory too, for it is in his economics that he literally *makes his name*. . . . Pound shows that the author is a function of his signature, produced within a certain moment, medium, milieu. In the end, his work insinuates that "personality" is nothing but the mystified effect of the demonic insistence of the name. (Maud Ellman: 16–17)

Pound's Cantos, like Dante's *Divine Comedy*, which he follows, perform a journey out of darkness into light, a passage enacted in the

Hell Canto (XV). In Canto XCVIII, the voice of an ancient philosopher, Ocellus, tells us that it is "our job to build light". This is not a journey towards a transcendent source of light, but the light Pound moves towards is made new, self-erected, self-made. Dante's Hell, according to Pound, "is the state of man dominated by his passions, who has lost 'the good of the intelligence'" (*The Spirit of Romance*, p. 118). Intelligence is marked by light:

> Dante or Dante's intelligence may come to mean "Everyman" or "Manhood", whereat his journey becomes a symbol of mankind's struggle upward out of ignorance into the clear light of philosophy. (Pound, *The Spirit of Romance*, p. 116)

Canto XV is the second of Pound's "Hell Cantos". These Cantos are set in London of 1919 and 1920, and show this Hell to be inhabited by everything that Pound despises about post-war England. Eliot summarises:

> It consists (I may have overlooked one or two species) of politicians, profiteers, financiers, newspaper proprietors and their hired men, *agents provocateurs*, Calvin, St Clement of Alexandria, the English, vice-crusaders, liars, the stupid, pedants, preachers, those who do not believe in Social Credit, bishops, lady golfers, fabians, conservatives and imperialists; and all "those who have set money-lust before the pleasures of the senses." (Eliot, *After Strange Gods*, p. 42–3)

Lloyd George, President Wilson and Winston Churchill are among the names behind the ellipses. Eliot thought Pound's Hell trivial because, unlike Dante's, there are no sympathetic or ambiguous descriptions: the inhabitants are clearly not redeemable to the author.

The first Hell Canto (XIV) opens with the Italian's line: "I came to a place mute of all light"; and the second closes with the speaker emerging to faint in the sun: "Helion t' Helion" – that is Helios, the sun, Phoebus, Apollo. Whereas Virgil is Dante's guide, Pound takes Plotinus the Neoplatonic philosopher of light as his guide out of the hell of London. At the close of Canto XV, Plotinus leaves the speaker "blind with the sunlight, / Swollen-eyed, rested, / lids sinking, darkness unconscious". This cycle of self-assertion and oblivion has strengthened the ego, who is "swollen-eyed" by the experience. But how does he escape and arrive blinking and fainting into the sun?

Plotinus gets him to pray to the Medusa. Perseus-like, using the petrifying gaze of the gorgon to solidify a pathway over the heaving mess of hell's oblivion, they make their escape. By turning the reviled feminine against itself, solidifying, reifying it, they can walk over it and out to the sun.

> Keep your eyes on the mirror!
> Prayed we to the Medusa,
> petrifying the soil to the shield,
> Holding it downward
> he hardened the track
> Inch before us, by inch,
> the matter resisting,
> The heads rose from the shield,
> hissing, held downwards.
> Devouring maggots,
> the face only half potent,
> The serpents' tongues
> grazing the swill top,
> Hammering the souse into hardness,
> the narrow rast,
> Half the width of a sword's edge.
>
> (*Cantos*: 70)

This is an act of phallic spermatic inscription, if ever there was one – phallogocentric: if we acknowledge the "word" in the "sword" here. The gorgon face is only 'half potent' because it is turned in on Hell, on the feminine itself perhaps. But now let us leave Pound in Hell and turn to that "mama of Dada", Gertrude Stein.

## Sapphics and gender erasures: Gertrude Stein's *Before the Flowers of Friendship Faded Friendship Faded*

This patriarchal tradition of erasure of the feminine, then, as Rachel Blau DuPlessis has also identified it (86), is the framework I will be using to read Stein's "Flowers of Friendship". Stein saw *Before the Flowers of Friendship Faded Friendship Faded* as constituting a breakthrough in her poetic technique. It marks a departure from her technique in *Tender Buttons,* where "I was making poetry but and it seriously troubled me, dimly I knew that nouns made poetry but in prose I no longer needed the help of nouns and in poetry did I need the help of nouns. Was there not a way of naming things that would not invent names, but mean names without naming them." In *Tender Buttons* Stein had sought to evade a "naming" which we might consider patriarchal inscription (for to name, from Genesis on, is to claim dominion over, to own): "Think of all that early poetry" she reminds us, "think of Homer, think of Chaucer, think of the Bible and you will see what I mean you will really realize that they were drunk with nouns, to name to know how to name earth sea and sky and all that was in them was enough to make them live and love in names, and that is what poetry is." In *Tender Buttons* Stein seeks to name without naming. *Tender Buttons* is divided into three parts: "Objects", "Rooms" and "Food". It is now argued by feminist criticism that these are references to the feminine; and that Stein's project is to rescue the feminine from reification; from being the object, *named and owned.* This interpretation is assisted by recognising that the very title, *Tender Buttons,* refers to the clitoris – the site of autonomous feminine pleasure. So is Stein offering an alternative poetics to Pound's? If for him "Poetry speaks phallic direction", does it for her speak "clitoral direction"?

The poem *Before the Flowers of Friendship Faded Friendship Faded* came about not from Stein's direct observation of things, objects, people, etc.; not from trying to give noun status to what has been suppressed (the feminine), we might gather, but from the attempt to translate a poem by a man. The débâcle with Hugnet is recounted in *The Autobiography of Alice B. Toklas,* where Stein, ventriloquising through the narrative persona of her lover and amanuensis, Alice B. Toklas, tells us:

> Georges Hugnet wrote a poem called Enfance [sic]. Gertrude Stein offered to translate it for him but instead she wrote a poem about it. This at first pleased Georges Hugnet too much and then did not please him at all. Gertrude Stein then called the poem Before the Flowers of Friendship Faded Friendship Faded [sic]. Everybody mixed themselves up in all of this. The group broke up. (247)

The flower then is the poem that Georges gave to Gertrude to translate – but before this poem faded into her poem, his friendship – and several other people's – also faded! What is left from this sequence of erasures is Gertrude Stein's poem. After the quarrel with Hugnet, she continues in *The Autobiography,* Gertrude Stein "consoled herself by telling all about it in a delightful short story called From Left to Right and which was printed in the London Harper's Bazaar". The story is in fact called "Left to Right: A Study in the New Manner, by Gertrude Stein", and sports a 2-line epigraph: "Everybody / Knows all about this Thing . . . " Georges Hugnet appears in it as "Arthur William"; Stein is presumably the first-person narrator. The title, "Left to Right", which may refer to the parallel layout of Hugnet's original poem and Stein's translation in (which appeared in the magazine *Pagany*), also seems to describe Stein's precautions, after the row, against meeting with the Hugnet camp in the street: "And now before I go out I always look up and down to see that none of them are coming."

In her portrait, *Henry James*, Stein gives a rather cryptic account of the great significance for her of her attempt to translate Hugnet's poem:

> An accident is when a thing happens. A coincidence is when a thing is going to happen and does.
>
> DUET
>
> And so it is not an accident but a coincidence that there is a difference between Shakespeare's sonnets and Shakespeare's plays. The coincidence is with *Before the Flowers of Friendship Faded Friendship Faded.* (*Writings, 1932–1946*, p. 149).

The significance of Shakespeare is more clearly explained by Stein in a "Transatlantic Interview" in 1946:

> A young French poet had begun to write, and I was asked to translate his poems, and there I made a rather startling discovery that other people's words are quite different from one's own, and that they can not be the result of your internal troubles as a writer. They have a totally different sense than when they are your own words. This solved for me the problem of Shakespeare's sonnets, which are so unlike any of his other work. These may have been his own idea, undoubtedly they were, but the words have none of the violence that exists in any of the poems, in any of the plays. They have a roughness and a violence in their juxtaposition which the sonnets do not have, and this brought me to a great deal of illumination of narrative, because most narrative is based not about your opinions but upon someone else's. (*A Primer*, p. 19)

And the technical, narratorial consequences of this discovery coming out of her attempts to "translate" Hugnet are further explored in her essay *Narration*:

> Hitherto I had always been writing, with a concentration of recognition of the thing that was to be existing as my writing as it was being written. And now, the recognition was prepared beforehand there it was already recognition a thing I could recognize because it had been recognized before I began my writing, and a very queer thing was happening. . . . The words as they came out had a different relation than any words I had hitherto been writing. . . . I realized that words came out differently if there is no recognition as the words are forming because recognition had already taken place. (51–2)

Stein is in the act of translating – not objects, or experience, into words – but words into other words. She seems to have had a Saussurean moment: language, she recognises, refers not to the object world, but to itself. We might also consider classical models of imitation. Traditionally, most (male) poets would try their hand at imitating Homer, Virgil, Horace, Ovid and Catullus – as well as paying some homage to the fragmented and elided Sappho. But Stein, translating a contemporary male poet, writes her own poem *on* his – as her subtitle tells us, "*Written on a poem by Georges Hugnet*". Is this a reversal of the classical Delphic tradition? A reversal of the erasure of feminine sources? A supplementing of lost Sapphics? Does her account of this in the context of her writing on grammar and narration subvert the patriarchal tradition of grammatical commentary on Sapphic fragments?

In the title, subtitle, and opening lines of the poem there seems to be a war going on between grammatical sense, verbal sensuality, free association, rhythm and repetition. Is there perhaps the remains of the persona in George Hugnet's poem fading, drowning in Stein's? In the many sections that follow there seems to be a struggle between masculine and feminine discourses and sexualities. There are references to bizarre arrangements and positions: "So he says. It is easy to put heads together really. Head to head it is easily done and easily said head to head." The rhythm builds up into moments of unison which in context suggest the interrogation of sexual relations: the questioning of joining two into one in cadences suggestive of merging and splitting. Yet during all this the male seems to be on his way out:

"He went and came and had to go. No one has had to say he had to go come here to go go there to go go go to come to come to go to go and come and go." Is this the masculine ebbing out of a poem about feminine experience? Is this the obliteration of a masculine discourse and the celebration *on top of it* of lesbian sexuality? What do you make of the last stanza?

> There are a few here now and the rest can follow a cow,
> the rest can follow now there are a few here now,
> They are all here now the rest can follow a cow
> . . .
> Who can be made to think and die
> And any one can come and cry and sing.
> Which made butter look yellow
> And a hope be relieved
> By all of it in case
> Of my name.
> What is my name.
> That is the game
> Georges Hugnet
> By Gertrude Stein.

"Cow" in Gertrude Stein's circles, we now understand, was lesbian slang for orgasm. In the last lines Stein disrupts the business of naming. Who is the "I" in the poem? Is it gendered? Unlike Pound's renewing and self-obliterating, resurrecting subject which ultimately tests and asserts itself over a reified, reviled feminine, Stein's subject here seems to be pulling itself free of a masculine subjectivity, to reinscribe and celebrate the feminine over – *and on top of* – the masculine. But, in this feminist/postmodernist reading of Stein's text, am I constructing or projecting, in the absence of Hugnet's poem (in French or in translation), a phantom "heterosexist" and patriarchal version of "Enfances"? Interestingly, Juliana Spahr who has read both, in introducing a recent reprinting of the *Pagany* edition of the poems in parallel, in Carcanet's *Exact Change Yearbook* (1995), agrees with this reading, and finds Hugnet's poem heterosexist:

> Stein actively opposes translation's normative impulse to make another culture discernible and digestible; while Hugnet's poems are often concerned with heterosexual sex, male genitalia, and onanism, these are all absent in Stein's poems. . . . Moments like these, in

> which the writer/translator is also reader, are radical ones. Such moments, for example, allow Stein to pursue her own political, cultural agenda and to abandon the poems' heterosexism and replace it with her relationship with Toklas. As she writes, "I love my love with an a / Because she is a queen." (Spahr: 41)

Stein's poem, by virtue of its apparent violent displacement of Hugnet's, may be read as an awesome and in places authoritarian lesbian text, but, restored to dialogue with Hugnet's poem, perhaps – *pace* Spahr – it may be read differently: as part of a "duet", as she hints in *Henry James*. I have recently been enjoying a critical "duet" with the French scholar, Katharine Swarbrick, who has been translating Hugnet's *Enfances* and considering how Stein's and his poems are in some kind of polymorphously perverse dialogue.

## Modernism and gender: Angelina Grimke's "The Black Finger" and Nathanael West's *The Day of the Locust*

We might wonder about the viability of approaches that divide men and women "modernists" along a strict line of gender apartheid (as Sandra Gilbert and Susan Gubar tend to do in *No Man's Land*). H.D.'s poem "Oread", for example, seems to be celebrating the phallic with its imperative "Whirl your pointed pines", perhaps the attraction for Pound in citing it in *Blast* (*Blast* 1: 154). And what do we make of Angelina Grimke's "The Black Finger" (Locke: 148), an erotic, phallic, imagist poem, published in *The New Negro* (1925)? It is set out in the shape of a column, the letter "I", a finger. The first line, introducing the image, is a departure from Pound's Imagism where the reader receives no entry into or preparation for the image: "I have just seen a most beautiful thing", is rather like the more democratic (lower case) entry into an image by William Carlos Williams at the opening of his famous poem "The Red Wheelbarrow": "everything depends upon". Grimke lists the qualities of the finger as "Slim and still", "Sensitive, / Exquisite", a flurry of unPoundian adjectives caressing the noun. But in keeping with Imagism, and reminiscent of H.D. in its eroticism, it closes with two erotically charged questions addressed to the image: "Why, beautiful finger, are you black? / And why are you pointing upwards?" Questions of race traverse issues of sexuality and subjectivity inscribed here; and the description of the finger "Against a gold,

gold sky, / A straight black cypress" suggests an eroticism "glazed" (to borrow from Williams' poem) in rich aestheticism (gold inlay on ebony perhaps), but the tree metaphor also suggests a more sinister, and melancholy reading – the associations of the cypress with mourning, and the grotesque associations, in America, of the tree as an instrument for lynching. Compare the song made famous by Billie Holiday, "Strange Fruit".

Consider, too, for example, West's brilliantly subversive accounts of cross-dressers, homosexuals and androgynes, encapsulated for many critics by the textual masquerade of the man known only as "Miss Lonelyhearts", but which have met with the far-reaching disapproval of Gilbert and Gubar, who place West in the company of T. S. Eliot, D. H. Lawrence, Ernest Hemingway and William Faulkner – literary men "who record their horror at a battle men are losing" (*No Man's Land* 1, p. 40). West and the other male modernists are for Gilbert and Gubar misogynist and homophobic. Whereas "literary women generally persisted in seeking an ontological 'wild free thing', a third sex beyond gender", these men "continued for the most part to express anxieties about . . . sex change in texts focusing on transvestism and transsexualism". Enforcing their gender-based apartheid, Gilbert and Gubar simplistically place West's work amongst male-authored texts of Spenglerian vision that "in various ways express a nausea associated with the blurring of gender boundaries" (*No Man's Land* 2, pp. 365–6). But there is no nausea expressed when West undermines such gender boundaries in, for example, his moving depiction of a transvestite in *The Day of the Locust.* Here, "a young man in a tight evening gown of red silk sing[s] a lullaby" in a seedy nightclub:

> He had a soft, throbbing voice and his gestures were matronly, tender and aborted, a series of unconscious caresses. What he was doing was in no sense parody; it was too simple and too restrained. It wasn't even theatrical. This dark young man with his thin, hairless arms and soft, rounded shoulders, who rocked an imaginary cradle as he crooned, was really a woman.
>
> When he had finished, there was a great deal of applause. The young man shook himself and became an actor again. He tripped on his train, as though he weren't used to it, lifted his skirts to show he was wearing Paris garters, then strode off swinging his shoulders. His imitation of a man was awkward and obscene. (370–1)

We might also wonder whether this young man's "performance" of two genders points in fact to a third gender position which cannot readily be categorised as masculine or feminine (see Garber); or do transvestites obey a strict gender divide too?

## Modernism and gender: the transgressive politics of feminine inscription

But now, let us turn from West's lyrical celebration of transvestism, and acknowledgement of the complexities of subversive inscription of gender, to consider Stein's "Flowers of Friendship" poem as an apparent attempt at a strictly *feminine* poetic language. Is it like Cixous's *écriture féminine*? Is it constructive? Or does it maintain a stereotype of women's language as "psychobabble" – beyond rational discourse? And we might also ask these questions in our following discussion of Molly Bloom's soliloquy, in Joyce's *Ulysses*, which has attracted positive and negative feminist readings (note that Cixous, herself, is a Joyce scholar). It should be noted that there is considerable debate among feminist critics and theorists about the claims made for the kind of "subversive" feminist avant-garde aesthetic practices we have started to explore. Rita Felski's book *The Gender of Modernity* (1995) is an important intervention in this debate:

> Writers such as Gertrude Stein are often singled out for attention by feminist critics because of their defiance of linguistic and social conventions and their transgressive questioning of femininity. Such a reclamation of a female avant-garde tradition undoubtedly forms an important part of the feminist rewriting of literary history through its creation of a pantheon of major, inspiratory women artists. Yet it also often perpetuates an unfortunate dichotomy of literary and political value which identifies formal experimentation as the most authentically resistive practice, with a consequent stigma attached both to representational art forms and to the regressive, sentimental texts of mass culture. . . . To equate modernity with modernism, to assume that experimental art is necessarily the privileged cultural vehicle of gender politics, is surely to ignore the implications of the feminist critique not just for methods but for objects of analysis. . . . Recent feminist work in the area of popular culture and cultural studies has paved the way for a rethinking of women's modernity that can include a consideration of the politics of experimental art but that

> can go beyond the isolated hypostatization of the modernist text. (Felski, *The Gender of Modernity*, pp. 28, 29)

Felski warns against the simplistic privileging of avant-garde experimentalism as the site of transgressive gender politics and rightly alerts us to the gender politics at work in realist, main-stream texts and popular culture. But what is needed, in fact, is closer attention to specific experimental and avant-garde texts, and the careful elucidation of their allusions, inflections and nuances. This closer scrutiny moves us beyond the basic and flawed assumptions and recognitions of experimentalism as inherently transgressive, and allows for more precise consideration of the particular qualities of, and transitions in, new and emergent, avant-garde languages.

## Myth and dissolution: gender and race in T. S. Eliot's *The Waste Land* and Richard Wright's "Between the World and Me"

Such gender-based readings that perpetuate the "hypostatization of the modernist text" are not of course restricted to women-authored texts. The gender-transgressive, deconstructive, modes of the work of Pound and Eliot have been thoroughly explored and have served some critics to exonerate them from the more condemnatory accounts of how these men's reactionary, and patriarchal, politics may inform their poems. We might therefore read against the grain of the reactionary politics that Eagleton has found in *The Waste Land*'s "mythical method":

> Deep below finance capitalism lay the Fisher King, potent images of birth, death and resurrection in which human beings might discover a common identity. Eliot accordingly published . . . a poem which intimates that fertility cults hold the clue to the salvation of the west. His scandalous avant-garde techniques were deployed for the most arriere-garde ends: they wrenched apart routine consciousness so as to revive in the reader a sense of common identity in the blood and guts. (*Literary Theory*, p. 41 )

Perhaps Eagleton's account of *The Waste Land* holds, as far as authorial intention can be ascertained from such essays as "*Ulysses*, Order and Myth", but it is less easily applicable to actual readings of the poem. Whatever Eliot's mythical posturing, surely the poem fails to bring unity. Do the closing words "Shantih shantih shantih" deliver the "Peace which passeth understanding" that Eliot's note on his citation from an Upanishad directs us to? Does the reader transcend history in a unifying mystical and mythical reverie that recruits us as proto-fascist, blood and soil, patriots? It has been argued that readers of *The Waste Land* may also be interpellated as authoritarian ideologues by virtue of the readerly impetus (that the poem itself creates) to set the poem in order. Its collaged, fragmented contents, on the other hand, may always and already be undoing the authoritarian gestures the poem inspires. In this way conventional (gender) politics are radically subverted.

*The Waste Land* is endlessly fascinating, and I am often convinced by such deconstructive readings. On the other hand, it is also tempting, or perhaps possible after all, to read the poem as adhering to a patriarchal ideology of myth. There is a tradition, common in the visual arts, of selecting for depiction, a particular moment in the telling of a myth. Titian's *Diana and Actaeon*, for example, which hangs in the Scottish National Gallery, shows Actaeon at the moment he surprises the chaste goddess of hunting at her bath. But also, just visible on the horizon, is a stag, which signals Actaeon's awful fate – his transformation by the outraged Diana into the quarry for his own hounds, a fate that links him with Orpheus, who was torn apart by the wild Bacchantean women. These narratives describing the obliteration of the masculine (poetic) subject are part of a traditional discourse of patriarchal myth, whereby the subject is all the more affirmed and confirmed by its violent annihilation and loss of self, a pre-messianic myth that Frazer famously explores in *The Golden Bough* (see Goldman, *Feminist Aesthetics*). And we can see how the monstrous women in classical mythology, such as Medea, Clytemnestra, and the gorgon, function as the reviled "other", in this cyclical economy of patriarchal subjectivity. So how might a modern artist depict the moment of obliteration of the masculine subject? I would suggest that *The Waste Land* is the literary equivalent: the subject at the moment of annihilation, surrounded on all sides by misogynist depictions of feminine sexuality, has glimpses of the affirmed and unified patriarchal identity at its borders and horizons. This is Donne's "Batter my heart" rewritten for the twentieth century ("Batter my heart with automatic hand", perhaps). We might also read Stein's "Flowers of Friendship" as exploring but overturning the same cycle of testing. In her poem we might observe that patriarchal "things fall apart" and that "the centre cannot hold" (to steal from Yeats) its central masculine subject. Eliot's poem, however, revolves around its smallest, most coherent, fourth part, "Death by Water", a medallion piece, a kind of *memento mori,* the simple elegy to Phlebas the Phoenician. It offers a decentred moment of potential resurrection. But perhaps the forces of monstrous femininity overcome the central subject, and affirmation of the masculine self is permanently lost in the wastes (and *waists*) of *The Waste Land.*

We must also consider the apparently racial otherness of this monstrous femininity, signalled perhaps in the rhythm of ragtime that breaks up Shakespearean iambics, as we noted earlier, and the elliptical references to Conrad's *Heart of Darkness* excised by Pound. This fragmenting, schismatic model of the white, masculine, subject torn apart and tested by a frenzied dark feminine other is completely overturned in an early poem by Richard Wright, "Between the World and Me", published in a popular anthology of the late 1930s, *Proletarian Literature of the United States: An Anthology* (1939), where a psuedo-Romantic lyric "I" narrates in Whitmanesque lines the events of "one morning while in the woods", following his discovery of "the thing". Here he lists (in true American vein) the Eliotic components of an avant-garde assemblage: "A vacant shoe, an empty tie, a ripped shirt, a lonely hat, and a pair of trousers stiff with black blood" (Hicks, Gold *et al.*: 203). Wright locates the aftermath of a lynching on one of Eliot's "vacant lots" (see "Preludes"), and grounds his metaphysical fretting over the status of modern, urban subjectivity in a materialist, sexual and racial politics. The contents of Yeats's "foul rag-and-bone shop", his deserting poetical abstractions, those "circus animals", seem to have landed in a nasty, literalist universe: "And upon the trampled grass were buttons, dead matches, butt-ends of cigars and cigarettes, peanut shells, a drained gin-flask, and a whore's lipstick" (Hicks, Gold *et al.*: 203). And in an inverse of Eliotic ressurection through violence, the subject of Wright's poem is transformed at the same location "cooled by a baptism of gasoline" (Hicks, Gold *et al.*: 203). Not quite your "Death by Water". But like Phlebas he has become his own *memento mori,* monument to his own lynching: "Now I am dry bones and my face a stony skull staring in yellow surprise at the sun . . ." And we might "consider" somewhat differently Eliot's "Phlebas, who was once handsome and tall as you". (Personally, these lines always make me think of my childhood terror at the display, in the church gate of a neighbouring village in Yorkshire, of three human skulls, on show since mediaeval times. Beneath them is the legend (in Latin and English): "Today Me, Tomorrow Thee". They were hung for stealing sheep.) But it is time to return home to Penelope, the mother of modernist man's homecoming.

# 7 Gender Wars in Hell
## James Joyce, Kurt Schwitters, Gertrude Stein and Virginia Woolf

### Introduction

Readings of modernist gender wars in Hell continue in this chapter with a discussion of the treatment of the Penelope myth in Joyce's *Ulysses* and Woolf's *To the Lighthouse*, examining images of monstrous femininity and affirmative wives in the figures of Molly Bloom and Mrs Ramsay. Joyce's collage technique and his creation Molly Bloom are then compared with the collage technique and the heroine of Schwitters' famous (failed) avant-garde poem "An Anna Blume". Further exploration of gender wars and hell, in brief samplings from Stein, William Carlos Williams and Woolf, bring to a close the chapter and Part II, the middle passage of this book. Apocalypse follows.

### James Joyce and Virginia Woolf place Penelope: Molly Bloom and Mrs Ramsay

> It is the epic of two races (Israel–Ireland) and at the same time the cycle of the human body as well as a little story of a day (life). The character of Ulysses has fascinated me ever since boyhood. . . . My intention is not only to render the myth *sub specie temporis nostri* but also to allow each adventure (that is, every hour, every organ, every art being interconnected and interrelated in the somatic scheme of the whole) to condition and even to create its own technique. Each adventure is so to speak one person although it is composed of persons – as Aquinas relates of the heavenly hosts. (Joyce, *Selected Letters*: 271)

In his much cited letter of 1920, explaining the blue print of *Ulysses,* Joyce shows how his writing fuses his Homeric model, overlaid as it is with Old and New Testaments, Jewish and Catholic cultures, not only with a map of Dublin (presumably his "*sub specie temporis nostri*"), but also with a map of the body. Whereas Eliot, in "*Ulysses,* Order and Myth", wants Homeric myth to stand as Joyce's "way of controlling, of ordering, of giving a shape and a significance to the immense panorama of futility and anarchy which is contemporary history" (Kolocotroni et al.: 373), Joyce himself during its composition understands his text somatically, with time, art, and bodily parts (organs) suspended in it. And it is the bodily parts and functions he so gloriously inscribes that incur the wrath of the censors. Pound, in his "Paris Letter" to *The Dial* (1922), defends the work against American hypocrisy here, in the light of its sleazy media coverage of the film star Fatty Arbuckle's trial, which was over a sordid affair allegedly concerning the fatal insertion of a bottle into a young girl's vagina:

> All men should "Unite to give praise to *Ulysses*"; those who will not, may content themselves with a place in the lower intellectual orders. . . . And the book is banned in America, where every child of seven has ample opportunity to drink in the details of the Arbuckle case. (Pound/Joyce: 194)

And in a line in keeping with Eliot's "Tradition and the Individual Talent", he locates *Ulysses* in a tradition of progressive novels, in which Flaubert stands as the new Homer: "Joyce has taken up the art of writing where Flaubert left it. . . . *Ulysses* has more form than any novel of Flaubert's" (194). But as well as acknowledging these wider literary orders and contexts, let us note Joyce, in a letter to Budgen of 1921, giving sacrilegious emphasis to the organic, somatic ordering of the text, which occurs with the final addition of the Penelope episode, Molly Bloom's stream-of-consciousness soliloquy, written in eight very long, seamless sentences:

> Penelope is the clou of the book. The first sentence contains 2500 words. There are eight sentences in the episode. It begins and ends with the female word yes. It turns like the huge earth ball slowly surely and evenly round and round spinning, its four cardinal points being the female breasts, arse, womb and cunt expressed by the words *because, bottom* (in all senses bottom button, bottom of the

> class, bottom of the sea, bottom of his heart), *woman, yes.* Though probably more obscene than any preceding episode it seems to me to be perfectly sane full amoral fertilisable untrustworthy engaging shrewd limited prudent indifferent *Weß. Ich bin der Fleisch der stets bejaht.* (Joyce, *Selected Letters*: 285)

"Clou" means, according to the dictionary, "chief point of interest: dominant idea", and in French it means "nail". And "Penelope" may really be considered to nail the rest of the book together, given that Joyce was correcting and revising the earlier chapters in proof while simultaneously composing this last chapter. For example, in mid-August 1921, he was, according to Jeri Johnson, "making final corrections to the placards of 'Telemachus', 'Nestor', 'Proteus', 'Calypso', and 'Lotus Eaters'; making initial revisions and additions to the placards of 'Hades', 'Lestrygonians', 'Scylla and Charybdis', and 'Wandering Rocks'; writing 'Ithaca' with his right hand and 'Penelope' with his left" (xliv). "Clou" is rather a phallic term to use of such a cunt-centred episode as "Penelope", yet this perverse or paradoxical analogy is in keeping with Joyce's other logical and figurative perversions and paradoxes in the letter. The German is a skewed citation from Goethe's *Faust* 1, where Mephistopheles, agent of Hell, declares "I am the spirit that always denies." Joyce gives this statement in antithesis: "I am the flesh that is constantly yessed" ("bejaht", being the adjectival participle of the verb meaning "to affirm") (see Scott, *Joyce and Feminism*, p. 156).

But Joyce is not merely overturning the infernal propositions of Mephistopheles, he is also blasphemously inscribing the Christian gesture of the sign of the cross with the cardinal points of the female body: "breasts, arse, womb and cunt", which he signals with the words "*because, bottom . . . , woman, yes*". This double signification of the sign of the cross as the sign of the female body is confusing: is it ultimately a Christian or an anti-Christian gesture? The South African, anti-apartheid activist Albie Sachs records how an old Jewish joke came to him when he came round after surviving a car bomb which blew off one of his arms. With the remaining arm he made the sign of the cross. But the shock of the attack had not in fact converted him to religion: he was merely making a thoroughly materialist check of "spectacles, testicles, wallet and watch" (12). Harry Blamires, in his indispensable guide to *Ulysses*, does not find Joyce's somatic sign of the cross at all contradictory or confusing:

> Molly is the Mystical Body, born on the Rock, and before the end of the episode blood as well as water flows from her, reminding us of our double inheritance, as natural men born into the order of nature and as Christians saved by the redeeming Blood. (225)

I presume I am not alone among readers of *Ulysses* and of Blamires in not feeling, or even wanting to feel, included in Blamires's "us". His naïve, patriarchal and patronising explication continues with the observation that "To enter the mind of Molly Bloom is also to be lifted bodily on to a great revolving sphere, swinging about its axis and about its centre with a sure system and symmetry yet to be fully explored. That the sphere has its macrocosmic significance in terms of the female body we know from Joyce himself" (225), and he quotes from the letter cited above. Richard Ellmann, on the other hand, succinctly points out that Molly's menstrual flow "is human blood, not divine. Menstruation is Promethean"; and in "allowing Molly" (his "Gea-Tellus") "to menstruate at the end Joyce consecrates the blood in the chamberpot rather than the blood in the chalice. . . . For this blood is substance, not more or less than substance. The great human potentiality is substantiation, not transubstantiation, or subsubstantiation" (*Ulysses on the Liffey*: 158, 171)

And how do we interpret Molly's affirmative and climactic refrain, the "yes" that corresponds to "cunt" in Joyce's schema? An affirmation of material, physical life; or a confirmation of masculine subjectivity (the womanly "yes" symbolically embedded in the Anglophonic reading of the syllables in "Ulysses")? If our sympathies are now, since December 1910, "almost entirely with Clytemnestra", as Woolf argues, then what are we to make of her polar opposite, the loyal wife Penelope? The energy of Joyce's text, of course, plays on the paranoia of Bloom, and of Odysseus before him, concerning Molly's and Penelope's fidelity. And Joyce acknowledges Molly's indiscretions, just as the many suitors of Penelope slaughtered by Odysseus, on his return point to her perhaps politically expedient (in the absence of her husband) extra-marital dalliances. By refusing to marry any of the suitors, Penelope in effect stands in for Ulysses until his return. But, unlike the unfaithful Clytemnestra, who has taken up with her suitor, and who murders her husband on his return, Penelope says "yes" to her returning husband, and so too does Molly Bloom. Whatever the exact terms or technicalities of their fidelity, both Penelope and Molly ultimately embrace and yield to their husbands.

Perhaps Woolf is countering Molly's yeses in her deployment of this very affirmative at the opening and closing of *To the Lighthouse.* The first word of the novel is "Yes", and it is uttered by the patriarchal wife, Mrs Ramsay, to mollify (excuse the pun) her son: "'YES, of course, if it's fine to-morrow,' said Mrs Ramsay. 'But you'll have to be up with the lark,' she added. To her son these words conveyed an extraordinary joy" (11). And Mrs Ramsay is a woman who likes to say "Yes" to her husband, too: "Her husband was so sensible, so just. And so she said, 'Yes; all children go through stages'" (105); "He would like a little solitude. Yes, she said. It annoyed him that she did not protest" (110). The closing words of Part One, "The Window", are hers unspoken, in victorious self-subordination, to her husband: "'Yes, you were right. It's going to be wet to-morrow.' She had not said it, but he knew it. And she looked at him smiling. For she had triumphed again" (191). Mrs Ramsay's "Yes" is deployed as an affirmation of patriarchal matrimony at every turn. Section 15 of "The Window", for example, comprises only one sentence, spoken by the patriarchal daughter Prue (who will die in childbirth in the parentheses of "Time Passes"): "'Yes,' said Prue, in her considering way, answering her mother's question, 'I think Nancy did go with them' (124; see also 113, 142, 163). And it is interesting to watch how "yes" is deployed in the mouths of the surviving characters after Mrs Ramsay's death (see 228, 230). Woolf is surely satirising Molly Bloom's affirmative, orgasmic recollection of her marriage acceptance, when she has Lily imagine Mrs Ramsay's own acceptance of Mr Ramsay's hand:

> Letting herself be helped by him, Mrs. Ramsay had thought (Lily supposed) the time has come now; Yes, she would say it now. Yes, she would marry him. And she stepped slowly, quietly on shore. Probably she said one word only, letting her hand rest still in his. I will marry you, she might have said, with her hand in his; but no more. (304)

In *To the Lighthouse,* "yes" is also sometimes followed by "but" (see 11, 106); and after Lily Briscoe implicitly refuses the widowed Mr Ramsay's mournful advances, she finally says yes, not to a man, but to her own art, in the closing paragraph of the novel, which is rhythmically punctuated by two yeses:

> Quickly, as if she were recalled by something over there, she turned to her canvas. There it was – her picture. Yes, with all its green and

> blues, its lines running up and across, its attempt at something. It would be hung in the attics, she thought; it would be destroyed. But what did that matter? she asked herself, taking up her brush again. She looked at the steps; they were empty; she looked at her canvas; it was blurred. With a sudden intensity, as if she saw it clear for a second, she drew a line there, in the centre. It was done; it was finished. Yes, she thought, laying down her brush in extreme fatigue, I have had my vision. (319)

A major transition in *To the Lighthouse* has been a transition in the gendered performance of "yes" – from its utterance by the subordinate patriarchal wife, to its declaration by the self-affirming woman artist.

The last words of the novel are in fact "THE END"; whereas the last words of *Ulysses* are not in fact Molly's yeses but the signature of exiled time and place: "*Trieste-Zurich-Paris*, / 1914–1921". Civil war in Ireland and the Great War in Europe are embraced by those dates; and territorial war is also located with Molly, in her epic associations, as Lamb, mediating Homer, in *The Adventures of Ulysses* (1808) (a crib Joyce himself recommends), identified in his summary of the significance of the Penelope episode:

> So from that time the land had rest from the suitors. And the happy Ithacans with songs and solemn sacrifices of praise to the gods celebrated the return of Ulysses: for he that had been so long absent was returned to wreak the evil upon the heads of the doers; in the place where they had done the evil, there wreaked he his vengeance upon them. (202–3)

Homer's gory account of Odysseus's bloodthirsty slaughter of his wife's suitors on returning home is distilled into the cuckolded Bloom's rivalry with Boylan for Molly's affection. Ellmann explains in a note that "Molly's menstruation also establishes that she is not with child by Boylan" (194); Bloom, following Odysseus, can reclaim his territory.

### The dissident collage of James Joyce and Kurt Schwitters: Molly Bloom and Anna Blume

Joyce's choice of the name "Molly Bloom" for his Penelope pre-dates the famous and widely circulated avant-garde poem "An Anna

Blume" (1919) by Schwitters, but it is instructive to compare the two. Joyce's Blooms were in print by 1918 (when the "Calypso" episode appeared in the *Little Review*), but, as we have noted, Molly Bloom's soliloquy (the final, eighteenth episode) was composed in 1921 while "the first six episodes" of the book were already set in print. "From this point on, Joyce corrected, and added to, all of the previously published episodes and 'completed', then continually enlarged, the remaining four" (Johnson xliii).

Schwitters's poem opens with the romantic declaration: "O Thou, beloved of my twenty seven senses, / I love thine" (I am quoting from Schwitters's own 1943 English translation "Anna Blossom Has Wheels"), and is in fact an assemblage of romantic clichés and "banalities" collected from diverse sources, including conversations, newspaper clippings, "often overtly political lines", too (Nill: 17), and so on. At one point Anna seems to have become a speeding car, caught up in the canvassing of collective politics or popular marketeering:

> Anna Blume, rote, Anna Blume, wie sagen die Leute?
> *Preisfrage*:
> 1. Anna Blume hat ein Vogel,
> 2. Anna Blume ist rot.
> 3. Welche Farbe hat der Vogel (15)

> [Red Blossom, red Anna Blossom, how say the people?
> *Price question*:
> 1. Anna Blossom has wheels
> 2. Anna Blossom is red.
> 3. What colours are the wheels? (16)]

In this collaged discourse, reminiscent of Stein's syntactic playfulness in *Tender Buttons* (1914), the fast changing Anna speeds so quickly through the fragments arranged by Schwitters that her colours are unfixed: "Blue is the colour of thy yellow hair. / Red is the whirl of thy green wheels" (16). But not quickly enough: despite Schwitters' declared satiric intent, the poem actually became very popular as a sentimental love poem, so earning the scorn of the German Dadaists. For them, Schwitters's had failed to turn romantic discourse against itself and instead had merely reinscribed it. (But it is not only because of this that Schwitters may be considered less radical than some Dadaists. Compared with the later, overtly anti-Nazi photomontages of the communist Dadaist John Heartfield, for example, Schwitters's collage work may well appear tame.)

As well as the collagistic soliloquy by Molly Bloom, Joyce's "Nausicaa" episode (the thirteenth) in particular, seems in keeping with the structural logic of Schwitters's "An Anna Blume". In "Nausicaa" the free indirect discourse presenting, indeed producing, Gerty Macdowell is in "a lexicon provided courtesy of Madame Vera Verity, Miss Cummins, the litany of Our Lady of Loreto, the *Lady's Pictorial,* with a passing glance at Walker's dictionary. Here popular discourses vie with one another for air time" (Jeri Johnson: 899–900).

> Heart of mine! She would follow her dream of love, the dictates of her heart that told her he was her all in all, the only man in all the world for her for love was the master guide. Nothing else mattered. Come what might she would be wild, untrammelled, free. (*Ulysses,* p. 348)

Does Joyce satirise or celebrate the construction of feminine identity in the discourse of cheap romance, piety, and journalese? There exists a marvellous publicity shot of the Hollywood pin-up Marilyn Monroe posing over a copy of *Ulysses,* ostentatiously open at the last pages of Molly Bloom's soliloquy, which perhaps symbolises the way the novel, like Schwitters's "An Anna Blume" before it, has come, in some quarters, to be culturally accepted. These questions extend to the synthetic linguistic assemblage of "Anna Livia Plurabelle" in *Finnegans Wake* (1939), another narrative located in Homer's Hades and Dante's Hell. The status of Molly Bloom's soliloquy in the larger body, or system, of *Ulysses,* may be similar to that of the medallion piece, "Death By Water", in *The Waste Land.* It is both the measure and the making of the entire text. It is also simultaneously both a liberating discourse of the feminine, and a trophy of feminine subordination, the atrophied, and contained, feminine flow, an appendage to the patriarchal epic, hanging from the main body rather as the Gorgon's head, reified by her own reflected stare, hangs at the girdle of the patriarchal Goddess Athena.

## Gender wars in Hell and Hellenism: Gertrude Stein, William Carlos Williams and Virginia Woolf

How different was the reception of Stein's attempt to write in the voice of the feminine "other"! Her *Autobiography of Alice B. Toklas* (1933) is a tour-de-force in modernist ventriloquism. Written in the voice of Stein's lover and amanuensis (to whom Stein would dictate her work), it is of course an act of narcissistic inscription, whereby Stein has Toklas declare:

> I may say that only three times in my life have I met a genius and each time a bell within me rang and I was not mistaken, and I may say in each case it was before there was any general recognition of the quality of genius in them. The three geniuses of whom I wish to speak are Gertrude Stein, Pablo Picasso and Alfred Whitehead. (3)

Compare Toklas's trio with the commonly invoked, legendary, triad of Jewish geniuses, in "conspiracy" to revolutionise the mind, spanning science, sculpture and poetry: Einstein, Epstein, and Gertrude Stein. Like the artist and model Nina Hamnett's autobiography, *Laughing Torso* (1932), Stein's novel gives a splendid, gossiping account of avant-garde life in Paris in the first decades of the twentieth century. But her refracting self-portrait did not please many of her contemporaries also portrayed in her rendition of Alice's undulating and hypnotic prose. In February 1935, *transition* published the infamous "Testimony Against Gertrude Stein", attacking *Autobiography of Alice B. Toklas* for the inaccurate portrayal of the many members of the Parisian avant-garde, including Braque, Salmon, Tzara and Matisse, who signed it (McMillan: 176). Jolas, quoting Madame Matisse, saw Stein's crime as presenting "the epoch 'without taste and without relation to reality'" (176).

"Hellenism, especially the modern sort, is too staid, too chilly, too little fecundative to impregnate my world," declares William Carlos Williams, in his "Prologue" to *Kora in Hell: Improvisations* (1918) (*Imaginations*, p. 12). It is impregnation by the "phallic direction" of H.D.'s Hellenism that Williams is seeking to avoid. He finds Eliot "a subtle conformist" (24), and credits Pound, "the best enemy United States verse has", with "a middle-aging blight of the imagination" (26–7), consigning the impersonality and objectivity of the expatriates in London to the Inferno: "But confine them in hell for their paretic assumption that there is no alternative but their own groove" (27). But Williams, like Pound, is heading out of Imagism into his own Hellenic Hell, as his title *Kora in Hell* suggests. He was, in fact, "indebted to Pound for the title. We had talked about Kora, the Greek parallel of Persephone, the legend of Springtime captured and taken to Hades. I thought of myself as Springtime and I felt I was on my way to Hell (but

I didn't go very far). That was what the Improvisations were trying to say . . . " (3–4). Williams goes far enough into Hell in his *Improvisations* to show us his own snatches of infernal gender wars. The text is a collage of dissonant discourses, and includes, for example, an image of Homer in "a butcher's shop . . . no more than any other beggar" (61–2); or, following a section with the proposition that "history is an attempt to make the past seem stable and of course it's all a lie", the question of "whether 'twas Pope Clement raped Persephone or – did the devil wear a mitre in that year?" (41); or a scene between the "haggard husband pirouett[ing] in tights" and the "wolf-lean wife . . . rolling butter pats": "Oh call me a lady and think you've caged me. Hell's loose every minute, you hear?" (39).

Gender has proved a useful study entry into the schisms in the avant-garde and a welcome intervention in a field previously dominated by an unselfconscious patriarchal criticism, but traversed also, as it must be, by issues of race, class and war, it can only assist in, rather than totally account for, the literature of this or any other period. Yet gender, as Claire Colebrook explains, in fact provides the metaphorical staging and basis for so many of the wider, and apparently unconnected, concerns of modernist literature and culture. By the time of the Second World War, furthermore, the avant-garde is still poised for a gender war in Hell; but it is also simultaneously looking beyond such conflicts. Woolf's *Between the Acts* (1941), for example, an indictment of the brute masculinity and patriarchy of fascism if ever there was one, ends with the opening of dialogue (diatribe or duet, we do not know) between a previously antagonistic husband and wife, at a particularly poignant and exposed moment of deep and infernal cultural darkness:

> Alone, enmity was bared; also love. Before they slept, they must fight, as the dog fights with the vixen, in the heart of darkness, in the fields of the night. . . . The house had lost its shelter. It was night before roads were made, or houses. It was the night that dwellers in caves had watched from some high place rocks.
>
> Then the curtain rose. They spoke. (197)

Do we follow language out of the darkness?

# Part III

# Apocalypse 1945

Oh! Blessed rage for order, pale Ramon,
The maker's rage to order words of the sea,
Words of the fragrant portals, dimly-starred,
And of ourselves and of our origins,
In ghostlier demarcations, keener sounds.
(Wallace Stevens, "The Idea of Order at Key West", 1935)

# 8 Order, Night, Rage
## Wallace Stevens, Gertrude Stein, Eugene Jolas, James Joyce, W. H. Auden and Nathanael West

### Introduction

"Part III: Apocalypse 1945", our second block, and final part, looks at avant-garde regroupings during the 1930s and 1940s to 1945, in the face of resurgent realism, the nemesis apparent of modernism and avant-gardism. It aims to show that, nevertheless, modernist and avant-garde practices continue to flourish. The springboard "image" is Picasso's *Guernica*; and the little magazine in focus is *transition*. There is discussion too of the Apocalypse movement, and of work by David Gascoyne and Dylan Thomas and W. S. Graham. I have chosen to emphasise such authors, along with the work of canonical "modernist" writers in the later phase (Joyce, Stein, Woolf, Pound, Stevens and Williams) and of mavericks such as Schwitters and West, more than work by canonical "thirties" and "forties" writers such as W. H. Auden, Christopher Isherwood, Graham Greene. The important, and my preferred, literary landmarks in this period of the 1930s and 1940s are Wallace Stevens's "The Idea of Order at Key West" (1935), Gertrude Stein's *Dr Faustus Lights the Lights* (1938; 1949), Nathanael West's *The Day of the Locust* (1939), Virginia Woolf's "Thoughts on Peace in an Air Raid" (1940), William Carlos Williams's "Paterson: The Falls" (1944), Pound's *Pisan Cantos* (1945) and Schwitters's PIN (1946). I choose this route, hardly a "road less traveled by", in the happily biased opinion that what counts here is to mark the indomitable persistence of, and sometimes precarious transitions of, avant-garde and modernist practices, in the teeth of the socialist realist backlash and of the rise of fascism, a persistence that Joyce, Gascoyne, Stein, West, Schwitters et al. represent, whether their careers are ending or beginning, more or less, with the dropping of the atomic bomb.

This chapter begins with a reading of Wallace Stevens's poem of the mid-1930s, "The Idea of Order at Key West", and turns to the wars on avant-garde and modernist aesthetics conducted by Stalinists and Nazis in the same decade. In this context, the achievements of the little magazine *transition* are brought into focus with a discussion of Eugene Jolas's influential survey on "night mindedness" among avant-garde writers, in the "Night, Myth, Language" issue of 1938. And it is here we find coming to an end the serialisation of Joyce's great "Work in Progress", soon to be published in book form as *Finnegans Wake* in the same year. A reading follows of gender, hell, and apocalypse in Gertrude Stein's stunning play *Dr Faustus Lights the Lights,* also written in 1938. A comparative discussion of Picasso's famous painting *Guernica,* conceived in protest at the fascist coup in Spain, and W. H. Auden's poem "Spain", leads to the chapter's main focus, Nathanael West's apocalyptic Hollywood novel *The Day of the Locust,* which is read through Schwitters's avant-garde play *Revolution in Revon,* a text West first encountered in the pages of *transition* magazine.

## Rage for order: sound and semantics in the poetry of Wallace Stevens

Stevens always maintained that the "pale Ramon" of his poem "The Idea of Order at Key West", earlier addressed as Ramon Fernandez, "was not intended to be anyone at all" and that there is no conscious reference to the real literary critic of the same name. The speaker of his poem is not buttonholing this literary critic when demanding, in an earlier line, "Ramon Fernandez, tell me, if you know," but his name is there purely for euphonious reasons because it arrived, and is in keeping, with the order of the poem's "keener sounds", themselves "ghostlier demarcations" of the "melancholy strain" of sounds not recorded, but heard and eulogised by the speaker in a poem by Wordsworth, and issued in the "voice so thrilling" of his eponymous "Solitary Reaper", which informs Stevens's poem. When Wordsworth's speaker says "I saw her singing", we are implicitly reminded of the visual dimension of the written word, while simultaneously being informed of the act of hearing the oral tradition of

Gaelic song of the "Highland Lass" whose (audible but incomprehensible) voice is "breaking the silence of the seas" (although it may well be the cuckoo's voice, to which hers is compared, that achieves this, Wordsworth's lines are ambiguous). Wordsworth's source for the poem was not, by the way, a personal recollection of hearing this sublime sound, but a written account he read in someone else's journal of a Hebridean tour. Not having the Gaelic, Wordsworth's speaker asks "Will no one tell me what she sings?", and in so doing opens up as his object the creative dimensions, the compositional tensions of poetry – the pull and push of sound against semantics.

The Solitary Reaper is herself an exotic spectacle, just as fetishised as her song in its incomprehensibility to the observer, but her song comes to stand for a kind of pure poetry, or artifice, which has its border with the sounds encountered in nature. And Wordsworth's poem about the pull and push of sound against semantics is a source for the sublimely poised exploration of the pull and push of sound against semantics in Stevens's poem. "The Idea of Order at Key West" has its own geographical bearings too, of course, and temporal ones, but it is nevertheless possible to follow a thread out of this poem, down an arcade of art, through Wordsworth's poem, his friend's journal, back – but to what? A nothingness, or an originating, feminine, sound, perhaps like the melancholy euphonious syllable "O", itself a foundational zero, that Poe claims as the font of his poem "The Raven". We are thus returned to the introduction of this book, to "this primary emphasis on the poem's performance of sound in nineteenth-century American poetics [that] finds strong resonance in the European avant-garde performance of (primal) sound poetry of the early twentieth century"; and we are returned to Balso's "O" at the arsehole of the Trojan Horse. Rude mouths, indeed.

The reader's and critic's impetus to hunt down a living "pale Ramon" is of course symptomatic of a "blessed rage for order" afflicting all parties with an interest in the production and reception of art. Poet, reader, and critic of course may reside, and do, in one body, but are also dispersed as roles among many. The primary rage is the God-like poet's, "The maker's rage to order words of the sea" – the rage to somehow order semantics and sound. But the reader's and critic's rage to semantic order is nevertheless a noble one, and inevitable. The alternative is silence, broken only by the reverent and pure recitation of the poem, celebrating the pleasures of the order of sound. There are larger social and political orders in which poet, reader, and critic find themselves and the poem, located perhaps in "a room of one's own", library, classroom, bar, or stadium, larger abstract, philosophical and ideological orders. And there are subjective orders available in the poem that shape, for us, our senses of identity.

The singer in Stevens's poem "was the single artificer of the world / In which she sang", and in "Tea at the Palaz of Hoon", we read that "I was myself the compass of that sea." The self is the measure of, and orders, the sea, and the self is its arena: "I was the world in which I walked." This is beginning to get suffocatingly solipsistic, and isolate. "I" finds itself looking at the world of the self and finds that "what I saw / Or heard came not but from myself; / And there I found myself more truly and more strange." But why try to chase this "I" disappearing up its own Cartesian fundament, insanely following the fault-lines in the subjectivity that can only partially know itself as object? What is magnificent about the poem is not its dancing along the cracks in Cartesian subjectivity, if that is what is happening, but the sensuous pleasure, the euphony, of its alliterating, rhythmical sounds rising in the throat. Who cares who "pale Ramon" is, anyway? "Pale Ramon" is sound. He delights, he does not mean, he does not instruct.

## Apocalypse of the avant-garde: Andrei Zhdanov, Adolf Hitler and the birth of Cold War aesthetics

But it is not only the arcane literary specialist, locked up in an archive or a department of English or American or cultural studies, who might care. In the 1930s, a decade of economic depression and extremist political action, the world was already full of the most unlikely, and even more frightening people with a rage to order art and poetics, a rage for order far exceeding (even) Eliot's:

> Comrades, in the name of the Central Committee of the All-Union Communist Party of Bolsheviks and the Soviet People's Commissars of the Union of Soviet Socialist Republics, allow me to present our warmest greetings to the first congress of Soviet writers and thereby to all the writers of our Soviet Union – headed by the great proletarian writer Aleksei Maksimovich Gorky [*Loud applause*]. (Bowlt: 292)

The throat clearing belongs to Andrei Zhdanov, in his speech at the First All-Union Congress of Soviet Writers, in 1934 (following the

Soviet Reformation of Literary–Artistic Organisations in 1932). These are his instructions:

> *Soviet literature must be able to show our heroes, must be able to catch a glimpse of our tomorrow. This will not be a utopia, because our tomorrow is being prepared today by our systematic and conscious work....*
>
> Create works with a high level of craftsmanship, with high ideological and artistic content!
>
> *Be as active as you can in organizing the transformation of the human consciousness in the spirit of Socialism!*
>
> *Be in the vanguard of the fighters for a classless Socialist society!* [*Loud applause*]. (Bowlt: 294)

Thus joyful, experimental, avant-garde, "modernist" aesthetics became outlawed on the Left, and thus began, some say, the Cold War. For an illustration of the kind of impact this ideology had on aesthetics, let us briefly think back to Walter Lippmann's portrait of John Reed in *The New Republic* (1914):

> He assumed that all capitalists were fat, bald, and unctuous, that reformers were cowardly or scheming, that all newspapers are corrupt . . . and that the trade unions are a fraud on labor. He made an effort to believe that the working class is not composed of miners, plumbers and working men generally, but is a fine, statuesque giant who stands on a high hill facing the sun. He wrote stories about the night court and plays about ladies in Kimonos. He talked with tolerable intelligence about dynamite, and thought he saw the intimate connection between the cubists and the IWW. He even read a few pages of Bergson. (quoted Aaron: 38)

Reed (immortalised by Warren Beatty in his blockbuster film *Reds*) was the star reporter for the radical paper, *The Masses.* He was to surpass his 1914 book on the Mexican revolution with his avant-garde, montage-style, account of the Russian Revolution, in *Ten Days that Shook the World* (1919), an international best-seller, sporting reproductions of Russian placards and posters, with a preface by Lenin, that ran to twelve Soviet editions before it was suspended in 1930. By the 1930s, of course, writers on the Left were certainly not encouraged to make such "intimate connections" between Cubist aesthetics and left-wing politics: modernist aesthetics were off the menu. The Left, as the common caricature has it, were supposed to write about happy tractor drivers! Not all Left aesthetics, of course, identified with this realist stance, as is clear from the work of Bertolt Brecht, for example, or of Walter Benjamin and the Frankfurt School. But the impact of the Soviet state-sanctioned drive for realism was enormous, and had repercussions through the entire spectrum of left-wing politics.

The aesthetics of realism appealed also to the leaders of the extreme Right. Adolf Hitler opened his infamous exhibition of *Entartete Kunst* ("Degenerate Art"), in Munich in July 1937 (see Dunlop: 224ff.), with a menacing speech vilifying the work on show – these were avant-garde works of art considered to exemplify the plague of corruption, insanity, degeneration and cultural bolshevism that he wished to purge Germany of:

> Cubism, Dadaism, Futurism, Impressionism, etc., have nothing to do with our German people. . . . Works of art which cannot be understood in themselves but, for the justification of their existence, need those bombastic instructions for their use, finally reaching that intimidated soul, who is patiently willing to accept such stupid or impertinent nonsense – these works of art from now on will not find their way to the German people. . . . Many of our young artists will now recognize in what is being offered them which road they should take; but perhaps they will also gain a new impetus from the greatness of the times in which we live, and from which we take courage and, above all, retain the courage to produce a really diligent and, thus, in the final run, competent work. . . . I HEREWITH DECLARE THE GREAT EXHIBITION OF GERMAN ART IN MUNICH OPENED! (Chipp: 482–3)

Darkness indeed descends.

## "Night, Myth, Language": *transition* (1938), Eugene Jolas and James Joyce's "Work in Progress"

But what, in these great times, constitutes enlightenment? In the Spring issue of 1938, *transition* celebrates its tenth anniversary publishing the "degenerate" material of Hitler's nightmares. The editorial heading, "Frontierless Decade", proclaims an avant-garde ethos of internationalism. The editor, Eugene Jolas, recalls the "basic aim" of the magazine in 1927, when it was founded, to be that "of opposing to the then prevailing photographic naturalism a more imaginative concept of prose and poetry. It encouraged a new style by postulating the metamorphosis of reality" (Jolas: 7). Avant-garde styles, emergent in the 1920s, have been taken up in the 1930s, then, as a means for change in an international arena. And translation of avant-garde texts, enabling dialogue between different national languages, is one of *transition*'s most important achievements:

> As a documentary organ, *Transition* began by bringing to the attention of Anglo-Saxon readers translated stories and poems from various camps, including expressionism, post-expressionism, dadaism, surréalism. It also introduced original work by most of the unorthodox writers of the British Isles and America, as well as countless continental independents who had heretofore been ignored by both the conservative and the radical magazines.

*Transition*'s work of translation and cultural exchange also enabled avant-garde projects to construct *new* international languages: "*Transition* is in search of the Euramerican language of the future" (9). But there are no strictures as to the form of such languages, or to content for that matter, or indeed that such projects are compulsory. Recalling *transition*'s "Revolution of the Word", Jolas reminds his readers that "It did not imply that every writer should invent a language of his own, but simply that the writer should have more liberty than he had possessed heretofore in subjugating syntax and vocabulary to his individual ends" (8).

Just as the issues of *The Egoist* we examined in Part II championed Joyce's *Ulysses* at the point of its transition from publication in the magazine to publication as a book, so this Tenth Anniversary issue of *transition* champions Joyce's new "*Work in Progress*", whose publication in book form is imminent, and from which the magazine has, from the first issue, "published seriatim eighteen fragments", and for which "difficult and new work" many of its writers have "also served as interpreters". These explications were collected and published in 1929 as *Our Exagmination round his Factification for Incamination of Work in Progress.* Jolas's closing remarks distance *transition* from the political dogma of those on the Left who chose to follow the new Marxist orthodoxy of Soviet socialist realism and sociologically-based critique, and challenge the Hitlerian zeal for a nationalist aesthetic:

> Throughout its ten years of existence, *Transition* has faithfully adhered to a belief in the primacy of the creative spirit. Nor did it climb on the band-wagon, when a split occurred in the ranks of writers everywhere simultaneously with the world depression in 1930, but took its stand on the side of a metaphysical, as opposed to a materialist-economic interpretation of life. In 1932 it announced: "Poetry is vertical". The bankruptcy of sociological literature and art should now be fairly obvious even to the most zealous activist of the arts.
>
> *Transition* will continue to seek a pan-symbolic, panlinguistic synthesis in the conception of a four-dimensional universe. (9)

Jolas's "now" is November 1937, the date at the foot of his editorial.

This issue of *transition* runs to nearly four hundred pages, and has enough material to sustain an undergraduate course in modernism and the avant-garde. I am going to briefly discuss just one section of it, "Night, Myth, Language", which occupies pages 153 to 245, but before doing so will glance down the list of contents. In the first part, after Jolas's editorial, is an impressive collection of writing (prose, drama and poetry in a number of languages) and images, by some of the most important avant-gardistes of the period, by some who were soon to become the giants of the post-war period, and by some whose names have not yet attained, to the present day at least, the "household" status of their colleagues:

*Xavier Abril:* Asesinado en el Alba
*Hans Arp:* Deux Poèmes
*Jacques Baron:* Pour la Paix
*Barzun:* Fragment de l'Universal Poème [a simultanist composition across ten page lengths in concertina]
*Samuel Beckett:* Ooftish
*Kay Boyle:* A Complaint for M and M
*André Breton:* Letter from "Mad Love"
*Hoelderlin:* The Titans
*Eugene Jolas:* Night of Greunewald
*James Joyce:* Fragment from "Work in Progress"
*Franz Kafka:* Metamorphosis (Conclusion)
*Wassilij Kandinsky:* Blick and Blitz
*Niall Montgomery:* Swing Tides of March This Time Darling
*Anaïs Nin:* The House of Incest (Fragment)
*Georges Pelorson:* Le vrai Visage (II)
*George Reavey:* Dismissing Progress and its Progenitors

*William Saroyan:* The Slot-Machine (Fragment)
*Camille Schuwer:* Coréâme
*Phillippe Soupault:* Manhattan: Poème
*James Johnson Sweeney:* Lemon Tree; Oranges and Lemons
*Dorothy Van Ghent:* The Rose and the Skull
*Le Corbusier:* Reproductions (3)

After the section of contents headed "NIGHT, MYTH, LANGUAGE", there follows, under the heading "THE EAR", one item: Chester K. MacKee's "Confiteor", a musical score. The next section, "THE EYE", lists the names of sixteen visual artists whose work is reproduced (in black and white), including Hans Arp, Paul Klee, Sophie Tauber, Max Ernst, and Kandinsky who is also responsible for the magnificent abstract design on the cover. Under "COMMENTARIES" are the following four items: Samuel Beckett on Denis Devlin's *Intercessions*; Max Brod on "Franz Kafka's Letter to his Father"; Gabrielle Buffet-Picabia on "Arthur Cravan and American Dada"; and Henry Miller's "The Cosmological Eye", a meditation on the visual art of his friend Hans Reichel. The last section is headed "INTER-RACIAL" (which would possibly now be, in today's euphemistic terms, "multicultural"), and has the following five items: an essay on "Prehistoric Stones" located in various countries, with several photographic illustrations; Martha Champion Huot's introduction, transcription, and translation of some "Musquakie Indian 'Love' Songs"; the black and white reproduction of an "Australian Bark Drawing"; and Michel Leiris's "Oraison Funèbre d'un Chasseur", an account in French of Sudanese ritual. Quite why these ethnic pieces are segregated at the back of a journal claiming to be "frontierless" is not really explained.

But the "heart of darkness" of this issue of *transition* is the section "NIGHT, MYTH, LANGUAGE", which celebrates the "nightmindedness" that is Joyce's special gift to avant-garde, courtesy of "his protean book of the night" (169), the novel soon to be formally known as *Work in Progress*, in which Jolas and his readers "have already followed most of the purgatorial, multiple characters, blundering through their larval and anthropological transmigrations", and traced the conflicts waged on this "nocturnal stage", awed by his "lowly puns, irrational junctions, cross-currents from more than forty languages" (174). Purgatorial darkness is here transformed, a cause of celebration, a new life-affirming trope, remote from the infernal, Spenglerian horrors delineated by Eliot and Pound. Joyce's apparent heresy is countered by a theological argument, citing "felix culpa", the doctrine of the "happy fall" (172). *Transition*'s most interesting testament to this nocturnal joy, in "NIGHT, MYTH, LANGUAGE", is the "Inquiry into the Spirit and Language of the Night", which is answered in twelve pages by fourteen writers, including Sherwood Anderson, Kenneth Burke, Malcom Cowley, T. S. Eliot, Michael Gold, Ernest Hemingway and Archibald Macleish. Jolas asked them to answer the following questions:

> 1. *What was your most recent characteristic dream (or day-dream, waking-sleeping hallucination, phantasma)?*
> 2. *Have you observed any ancestral myths or symbols in your collective unconscious?*
> 3. *Have you ever felt the need for a new language to express the experiences of your night mind?* (233)

The answers, all fascinating, range from the fulsome and enthusiastic to the dry and cynical, but I am restricting myself to quoting the most hilarious reply only, which is by the author of *The Waste Land*, whose return is the very model of poetic impersonality:

> I am afraid I cannot be of much use to you with your questionnaire. Questions number 1 and 2 are really matters I prefer to keep to myself. The answer to number 3 is definitely *no*. I am not, as a matter of fact, particularly interested in my "night mind". This is not a general assertion about night-minds, nor does it carry any suggestions about other people's interest in their night-minds. It is only that I find my own quite uninteresting. (236)

## Gender apocalypse in hell: Gertrude Stein's *Dr Faustus Lights the Lights*

Meanwhile, *transition*'s own fallen angel, expelled from Jolas's Joycean nocturnal revels, is herself, in 1938, exploring the inferno. Stein's stunning play *Dr Faustus Lights the Lights* was written in 1938 (but published posthumously in 1949). The cast includes Doctor Faustus, Mephisto, a dog who says "thank you" and who performs a duet with Faustus, a boy, and a viper who bites the mysterious doubled female presence whose "name is Marguerite Ida and Helena Annabel", and who fears going to hell (582). The action is illuminated by "electric" lights. Faustus is repeatedly urged by a country woman, a "woman at the window", to cure Marguerite Ida and Helena Annabel (perhaps a more euphonious vision of the sinisterly redoubling "rough beast" prophesied by Yeats), most of which matter is compressed in the following passage:

> The country woman with the sickle looks in at the window and sings Well well this is the Doctor Faustus and he has not gone to hell he has pretty lights and they light so very well and there is a dog and he says thank you and there is a little boy oh yes little boy there you are you just are there yes little boy you are and there is Marguerite Ida and Helena Annabel and a viper did bite her, oh cure her Doctor Faustus cure her Doctor Faustus cure her what is the use of your having been to hell if Marguerite Ida and Helena Annabel is not to be all well.

At the close of the play, when Mephisto "strides up" to usher Faustus to hell, Faustus

> sinks into darkness and it is all dark and the little boy and little girl sing
>
> Please Mr. Viper listen to me he is he and she is she and we are we please Mr Viper listen to me.
>
> CURTAIN
>
> (Stein, *Writings, 1932–1946*, p. 607)

Compare Woolf's infernal "down-pouring of immense darkness", inverting Genesis, in "Time Passes" where "there was scarcely anything left of body or mind by which one could say 'This is he' or 'This is she.'" Stein's vision of hell at the final curtain appears to be one where a gender apartheid enforces "he is he and she is she", reinscribing the primary division in Genesis. But this rage to order may nevertheless be simultaneously (always and already) overturned by Stein's fantastically fluid syntax, the repetitious, redoubling alliterative euphony of her poetry.

## Images of Apocalypse: Pablo Picasso's *Guernica* and W. H. Auden's Spain

Pablo Picasso's monumental mural painting *Guernica* (1937), painted in late Cubist style and "entirely in black, white, and grey", was exhibited as the centre-piece of the Spanish pavilion at the Paris World Exhibition in 1937, and constitutes "the last great history painting", according to Robert Hughes, for whom it "was also the last modern painting of major importance that took its subject from politics with the intention of changing the way large numbers of people thought and felt about power" (111). Picasso himself made contradictory statements on the relationship between art and politics (text and context). On the one hand, Picasso declares in an interview in 1945, the artist is "a political being, constantly alive to heartrending, fiery, or happy events, to which he responds in every way" – "No, painting is not done to decorate apartments" he expands: "It is an instrument of war for attack and defense against the enemy" (Chipp: 487). But on the other hand he insists, in another interview, also in 1945, that there is "no deliberate sense of propaganda in my painting". Picasso's exception to this rule is *Guernica*: "In that there is a deliberate appeal to people, a deliberate sense of propaganda" (Chipp: 489). Picasso was moved to paint it in response to the bombing, by the German Luftwaffe, of the Basque town Guernica, during the Spanish Civil War. This monstrous act was the first aerial mass bombardment of civilians in history, since when ordinary citizens, and not only trained armed forces, all over the world have come to be counted as quasi-legitimate targets of war, whatever the actual laws of combat. The razing of Guernica, as Hughes points out, "was taken up by the world press, beginning with *The Times* in London, as the arch-symbol of Fascist barbarity" (110). Picasso's *Guernica* on display in Paris constituted "a virtually official utterance by the Republican government of Spain" (110), but it has come to represent a more universal protest against the brutality of war.

Auden's poem *Spain*, first published in 1937 to raise proceeds for Medical Aid to Spain, may perhaps be considered a literary companion piece to Picasso's great painting. Auden revised his poem in 1940, and this version is the one usually anthologised. Auden chose to omit the first version from his *Collected Poems* of 1965. One source of his discomfort and regret is in the following two lines of stanza 21:

> Today the inevitable increase in the chances of death;
> The conscious acceptance of necessary murder.

He later changed this latter line to "The conscious acceptance of guilt in the fact of murder" (Fuller: 259). Stan Smith offers the most instructive analysis of how Auden's turn from this stark moment of "acceptance of guilt in the fact of murder", certainly not communicated in Picasso's work, has been culturally received since, and how the historical body of Auden criticism, accounting for the trajectory of his poetic career, bifurcates and fissures along Cold War fault-lines, fault-lines the poet himself, nevertheless, uncomfortably straddles. According to one fable of Auden, outlined by Smith:

> there was a good little boy from a solid middle-class background, who went to public school and Oxford, fell into bad company, and became a Marxist and a Freudian. Then he went to Spain during a civil war and saw that Marxists were a bad thing because they closed down all the churches. So he ran away to America and became a Christian. After this he was a lot happier and became a grand old man of letters. Then in his old age he came home to Europe and Oxford, and died peacefully in his bed. He lived happily ever after in his poems. (Smith, *ReReading Literature*, p. 1)

The crux of the inverse fable is as follows: "During his brief flirtation with Marxism he wrote some powerful political poems, most of which he subsequently disowned. Thereafter he wrote much insipid verse which was lauded for the wrong reasons. Though this poetry proclaimed his reconciliation with the status quo it could not conceal the great unhappiness of his wasted talent" (2). In his illuminating rereading of Auden, Smith happily does not travel either of these divergent roads, nor does he pave a compromised middle way, preferring instead a more rewarding, complicated and subtle, and admirably less linear, set of inroads into questions of power, gender, sexuality and order. But with this warm injunction to make Smith your guide to Auden's inferno, I vote to jump West.

## Images of Apocalypse: Pablo Picasso's *Guernica* and Nathanael West's Hollywood

Out of the frying pan into the fire. Picasso's *Guernica* has been cited as the model for the painting envisioned by Tod Hackett at the apocalyptic close of *The Day of the Locust* (1939) by Nathanael West, who was the object, incidentally of a cold war demolition job by Auden in his diagnostic essay "Interlude: West's Disease" (1963). West, who was possibly regarded retrospectively, in that later Cold War climate, as "prematurely anti-fascist", was in fact "one of the sponsors for the Hollywood fund-raising exhibition of . . . *Guernica*", and was certainly familiar with Picasso's painting (Martin: 350). But I dispute George V. Griffith's view of a simple parallel between *Guernica* and Tod Hackett's painting "The Burning of Los Angeles". Finding remarkable similarity between the imagery of *Guernica* and West's final mob scene in which Tod's painting is envisaged, Griffith concludes that "both depict a terrified crowd on whom and in whom the forces of an irrational violence and brutality have been unleashed. Images of flight and of terror predominate." Griffith's alignment of West's rampaging mob with the figures in *Guernica* who "flee from the onslaught of the German bombers" leads him to read West's figure of the "Hollywood stage child", Adore Loomis, who actually provokes the mob violence, as "similarly in flight" (Griffith). Allusions to *Guernica* are discernible: for example, Picasso's gaping-jawed horse "centrally lifted above the crowd" (Griffith) seems to be quoted in West's description of a figure "shoved against the sky, his jaw hanging as though he wanted to scream but couldn't" (415). But the view of West's mob scene as straightforwardly in the tradition of "representations of the Massacre of the Innocents and the Apocalypse" (Griffith) is to some extent mistaken, I suggest. To cast this monstrous child ("a most unpleasant small boy", as Alvin B. Kernan recognises) and/or mob as innocent victims of fascism, on a par with the citizens of Guernica who suffered the first mass aerial bombardment of civilians, is to miss the satiric power of West's collage. His juxtaposing of imagery of the violent excesses of Hollywood consumerism and allusions to Picasso's highly publicised propaganda against fascist interventions in Spain may invite different interpretations. *The Day of the Locust*, as West's Anti-Nazi League colleagues and fellow campaigners for Spanish Refuge Relief unhappily recognised, in fact seems relentlessly to focus on emergent Hollywood fascism – not its opponents. "Whereas the Marxists emphasized the revolution," it was noted, "West emphasized its betrayal" (John Bright; quoted Martin: 353). (That the vectors of fascism may also be read as its victims, of course, is another argument.)

West's text not only cites *Guernica* as a way of discerning in an American context the opposing forces of the Spanish Civil War, as Griffith suggests, but it also engages, as I have argued elsewhere (see Goldman, 1996), an earlier phase of historical fascism through its collagistic citation of a work by Kurt Schwitters, itself belonging and speaking to an earlier collagistic phase of avant-garde art. Significantly, Schwitters' work is made available to West through the good offices of *transition* magazine. The final, apocalyptic chapter of *The Day of the Locust* is my focus. It is another sojourn in Hell, and another homage to Homer. For these reasons, West's final chapter is the centre-piece of this, the third part of my book.

## Images of Apocalypse: the burning city in Nathanael West's *The Day of the Locust*

Originally entitled *The Cheated,* this novel is a savage indictment of Hollywood, focusing on the losers at its fringes rather than the success stories at its centre. Here, we have a panorama of grotesques. Displaced, marginalised, politically illiterate characters vie for life in a seedy world of prostitution, violence and sleazy corruption (it's wonderful!). This is the California where people "come to die" (411). The artist Tod Hackett (whose first name is German for death) seems a harbinger of this Californian brand of death; and his imagined completion of the never actually executed painting, "The Burning of Los Angeles", apocalyptically coincides, in the final chapter, with the mindless and bloody riot by a savagely debased and bored celebrity-seeking movie crowd. As in Woolf's *To the Lighthouse,* the painting, co-terminous with the novel in which it appears, may be seen as an analogue for the novel itself as well as for Art more generally. But these inviting parallels may also be confusing.

Hackett finds himself outside "Kahn's Persian Palace Theatre" where the world-premiere of a movie is about to happen (408). The intertext with Coleridge is difficult to miss given West's reference to a huge electric sign reading "MR. KAHN A PLEASURE DOME DECREED" (note the omission of "stately"), beneath which the gathering and restless crowd is goaded to hysteria by a young man with a microphone, and "hustled and shoved" by the police (409, 410). Rita Barnard, drawing on Walter Benjamin, investigates this intertext to contrast Coleridge's poem with West's palace. She finds "Kubla Khan" "a perfect encapsulation of all that Benjamin associates with the auratic", that is, she ventures "a true wish . . . born of a sense of loss, that would find fulfilment in a life devoted to the achievement of poetic craft". On the other hand, "the utopian fantasy embodied in Mr. Kahn's Persian Palace Theater", she observes, "is perfectly accessible, offering luxury and an exotic ‘experience’ to all comers at a small price. . . . But the taste of luxury the ‘pleasure dome’ offers is short-lived and the experience vicarious.” It is difficult to disagree with her conclusion that

> All the spectacular assertions of the presence of utopia – the electric sign, the searchlight, the lavishness of the building, the impending arrival of the stars – finally amount to the artificial repackaging of “aura”: they are the present signs of the absence of magic, or religious awe. (181)

But as we shall see, the sign, by virtue of its formal positioning rather than its signified literary allusion, also points to the presence of a Schwitters text, itself collaged – or repackaged – by West. This allows for a less melancholic reading than Barnard’s. Like many readers of West, Barnard lapses into reading literary allusions and references to the Hollywood culture industry in a way that ignores the complex constructedness of West’s disruptive textual surface. “It is difficult to find”, according to Matthew Roberts, “a work of American fiction more plainly resonant with Adorno’s culture industry thesis than *The Day of the Locust*” (61); and this, I suggest, may account for the critical foregrounding of West’s negative critique of consumerism in the light of Frankfurt School theories, at the expense of more precise, textually based investigations into his engagement of historic avant-garde practices.

The crowd, we read, “tolerated the police, just as a bull elephant does when he allows a small boy to drive him with a light stick” (410). We may hear in this the distant thunder of the “elephantine close-ups” of literary positions West earlier links with Schwitters (see Chapter 1), a connection I will strengthen later. The crowd, of course, is soon to turn *rogue* elephant. But a point not always properly acknowledged by West critics is that this is a crowd made up of middle-class pleasure-seekers who, having made it to California, “discover sunshine isn’t enough”:

> They don’t know what to do with their time. They haven’t the mental equipment for leisure, the money nor the physical equipment for pleasure. . . . If only a plane would crash once in a while . . . Oranges can’t titillate their jaded palates. Nothing can be violent enough to make taut their slack minds and bodies. They have been cheated and betrayed. They have slaved and saved for nothing. (411–12)

These are the members of the gathering mob watched by Tod: the disaffected middle classes. It is in the context of this mob that Homer Simpson comes to the attention of Tod. Belying the grand epical associations of his first name, Homer Simpson is a pathetic character who is described, like many of West's characters, as "a badly made automaton" whose "features were set in a rigid mechanical grin. He had his trousers on over his nightgown and part of it hung out of his open fly. In both hands were suitcases" (412). The allusion to epic and his partially reified condition suggest Homer Simpson may be read as a Brechtian figure. As if to reinforce his poetic antecedents, Homer moves "blindly" through traffic and crowds. Oblivious to the police grabbing and hustling him, he is left by Tod "sitting quietly on a bench, minding his own business" (413). It is at this moment of Homeric bewilderment that Adore Loomis, the hideous child with a "nasty temper", begins his provocation. It is his tormenting of Homer that seems to precipitate the mob into violence. At first, however, Homer completely ignores Adore's agitational antics (the child dances a pocketbook on the end of a string and "runs through a series of insulting gestures"). The name Adore Loomis suggests we read this stage child as a cross between Ezra Pound and Adolf Hitler: a personification of emergent Hollywood right-wing aestheticising politics. Homer's passivity only infuriates Adore further.

> If Tod had known that the boy held a stone in his hand, he would have interfered. But he felt sure that Homer wouldn't hurt the child and was waiting to see if he wouldn't move because of his pestering. When Adore raised his arm, it was too late. The stone hit Homer in the face. The boy turned to flee, but tripped and fell. Before he could scramble away, Homer landed on his back with both feet, then jumped again. (415)

Unable to prevent Adore's crushing beneath the immovable "stone column" Homer has become (415), Tod is carried off by the crowd and crushed and ground by its motions. Overhearing talk of lynching Homer as a pervert, he witnesses the molestation of a young girl caught in the "spasm" of the mob; and in the midst of all this carnage he has a vision of his painting, "The Burning of Los Angeles". West inserts Tod's painting into the narrative as if it were part of the action.

> As he stood on his good leg, clinging desperately to the iron rail, he could see all the rough charcoal strokes with which he had blocked it

> out on the big canvas. Across the top, parallel with the frame, he had drawn the burning city, a great bonfire of architectural styles, ranging from Egyptian to Cape Cod colonial. Through the center, winding from left to right, was a long hill street and down it, spilling into middle foreground, came the mob carrying baseball bats and torches. For the faces of its members, he was using the innumerable sketches he had made of the people who come to California to die; the cultists of all sorts, economic as well as religious, the wave, airplane, funeral and preview watchers – all those poor devils who can only be stirred by the promise of miracles and then only to violence. (419–20)

Here art and life seem to interpenetrate: it is difficult to place Tod's frame. His "block[ing] out" of the iron rail on his canvas is ambiguously signalled: is his painting a refuge from or a depiction of the scene? Perhaps it is more of an intervention: whatever his intentions, Tod Hackett is implicated in the mob action as he both struggles in it and mentally depicts it. Perhaps signalling this crisis in aesthetics, the novel ends with Tod's removal by the police, the noise of whose siren he at first "thought he was making . . . himself". The last lines of the novel explore this confusion over voicing and authority:

> He felt his lips with his hands. They were clamped tight. He knew then it was the siren. For some reason this made him laugh and he began to imitate the siren as loud as he could. (421)

If Tod's version of "do[ing] the police in many voices" seems to gesture towards the despair traditionally read in the grim collagistic posturing of *The Waste Land* (compare Wisker: 100), his laughter, I suggest, transports us to more joyful avant-garde antecedents. But the standard critical response to this last chapter – and to the novel – is to find in it confirmation of West's "bleak and absurd vision" and dark irony; to see the crowd as representative of all humanity; and to show how this mindless mob violence is both a product of and a reaction against "the vacuity of life" in contrast to Hollywood's "manufactured fantasies" (Wisker: 112). It is for many a study in nihilism. West's "great strength" is for many "his pessimism, his nastiness" (Hyman: 39).

Yet we know that in *The Day of the Locust*, and in its final mob scene, West offers not a vision of *all* humanity, but a depiction of a certain social sector. The novel tells us so, as we have seen. West himself acknowledges this as a deliberate satiric strategy: his target is the proto-fascist middle-class mob. In a letter to Malcolm Cowley, he confesses that he "found it impossible to include" in his new novel the activities of Hollywood's left-wing "progressive movement", with which he sympathised: "I tried to describe a meeting of the Anti-Nazi League, but it didn't fit and I had to substitute a whore-house and a dirty film. The terribly sincere struggle of the League came out comic when I touched it and even libelous" (Wisker: 96). West here alerts us both to his glorious refusal of the techniques of socialist realism, by then *de rigueur* on the Left, as we have seen, and to his own selective method of satire. "If I put into 'Day of the Locust' any of the sincere, honest people who work here and are making such a great, progressive fight," he wrote to a friend, "those chapters couldn't be written satirically and the whole fabric of the peculiar half world which I attempted to create would be badly torn by them" (Martin: 336).

The critical view of West's satire as universal rather than selective has contributed to further confusion over the intertextual links between Tod's painting, "The Burning of Los Angeles", a vision of (envisioned in) a middle-class mob, and West's poem, "Burn the Cities" (1933), a strange celebration of the ascendancy of Marxism over Christianity. The first sixteen lines of this poem were published in *Contempo* (1933); the rest appeared for the first time in Jay Martin's biography (329–31). Given the epic significance of Homer Simpson's first name, we might well be encouraged to find parallels between the burning city in Tod's painting and West's novel, and the fate of the ancient city of Troy, which was sacked and burned many times. And this cyclical sacking of Troy may also resonate in West's poem. But there are crucial differences between this poem and Tod's painting. These two works have, nevertheless, been judged as making equivalent statements, and by extension West's poem is read as a kind of blueprint for the close of the novel itself. "Burn the Cities", for Barnard, "presents an image that forecasts the ending of *The Day of the Locust*": "the image of the destructive flames of social revolution" (212).

But "Burn the Cities", only partially published in West's life-time, addresses a very different constituency of disaffected people than the one in *The Day of the Locust.* This bizarre poem does not address a mob of jaded Californian pleasure-seekers, but "Workers of the World": French, English, Indian and African. These workers are invited, in the final posthumously published stanza, to "Burn the cities", burn Paris ("Twice burned city / Warehouse of the arts") and London:

Slow cold city
Do not despair
London will burn
It will burn
In the heat of tired eyes
In the grease of fish and chips
The English worker will burn it
With coal from Wales
With oil from Persia
The Indian will give him fire
Africa is the land of fire
London is cold
It will nurse the flame
London is tired
It will welcome the flame
London is lecherous
It will embrace the flame
London will burn.

(Martin: 329)

The imagery here of London's nursing the flame set by "Workers of the World" may suggest refrains from the songbook of the Industrial Workers of the World which "fans the flames of discontent". West's poem may be read as a forlorn version of a similar lyric project – again, figurative, not literal. Tod's painting, "The Burning of Los Angeles", however, in its depiction of a proto-Fascist middle class mob, seems to be more powerfully resonant of the actual burning of the Reichstag in February 1933, than of the fictive conflagration in West's poem.

These resonances suggest a complicated intertextual surface to West's work which requires more careful critical attention than the orthodox view, succinctly expressed by Alistair Wisker, allows: "In *The Day of the Locust* as in 'Burn the Cities' the present is carried unceremoniously to the mortuary. A violent throwing over of what exists seems to be the only way to reach what will be" (137). Wisker's apocalyptic invocation of West's and Grosz's *Americana* editorial ignores the vital question of who precisely is portrayed in these works as the "morticians of the present": in neither case do they appear to be "laughing morticians", and in neither case can we make an easy identification with West himself. But it is evident that the middle-class proto-fascists in Tod's painting are not the "Workers of the World" of West's poem.

Roberts, in one of the most interesting discussions of West's relation to the European avant-garde, does not consider West's poem, but, declaring "Tod's status as a textual representative for both the author and the reader", he reads "The Burning of Los Angeles" itself as "an allegory for *The Day of the Locust*". This strategy is dangerous, in my view, not only because it ignores West's complicated intertextual play with his own poem, but also because it ignores the collagistic surface of the text which does not allow for the easy identification of Tod Hackett with author or reader. My exploration of West's collaging of a Schwitters work further undermines Roberts's case. *The Day of the Locust*, I suggest, is not a bleak, absurdist, ironical, nihilist vision, but a bleak – outrageously funny – and richly textured dissident, anti-fascist satire.

## Apocalypse in *transition*: Kurt Schwitters's *Revolution in Revon* and Nathanael West's *The Day of the Locust*

The key to my proposed reading lies with West's artistic debt to Schwitters, who, like West, has been characterised, as we have discussed, in comparison with his contemporaries, as "a-political" in both his art and his life. But the fact that neither man was in the Communist Party should not preclude readings of their work as politically engaged. After all, Schwitters, like his more overtly politicised Dadaist rival Grosz, was forced to flee Nazi Germany (bravely smuggling out anti-fascist microfilm) (Richter: 153–4). He is famous, too, for his spontaneous (and daring) public remark when forced into jurying a German art exhibition to which had been submitted several portraits of Nazi leaders: "Shall we hang them or stand them up against a wall?" (Elderfield: 198)

The writer Josephine Herbst, in her memoir of West, recalls a "delirious autumn" (1932) when for three days she and West barely slept (Herbst, we might note, is German for autumn):

> We walked through fields of tall grass, plucked the antlered horns of red sumac, talked of Pushkin for whom autumn had been the creative season. We drank Pennsylvania bootleg rye and homemade red wine; read aloud Carl Sternheim's *A Pair of Underdrawers*, recited poems by Hans Arp, "the tap drummer", and Schwitters' *Revolution in Revon*. (Herbst: 22)

The works by Sternheim, Arp and Schwitters, cited by Herbst, all appear in the late 1920s issues of the magazine *transition,* and this is presumably what Herbst and West read. *Revolution in Revon,* translated by Jolas himself, appeared in the 1927 *transition.* It was written shortly after the German Revolution (1918/19), and first published in *Der Sturm* in 1922. Schwitters also gave many live performances of this work. He was, he claims, still a Dadaist when he wrote it.

"Revon" is a reversal of the last letters of Hanover, Schwitters's home until he fled. "Revon", he tells us in a cumbersome footnote, means "Law". It is the name of the newspaper edited by the ignorant art critic with the incredibly long (and ever expanding) name, "Dr Friedrich August Leopold Kasimir Amadeus Gneomar Luictius Obadja Jona Micha Nahum Habakuk Zephanja Haggai Sacharja Malcachi Pothook" (*Revolution,* p. 60), a source of much trouble in what follows.

*Revolution in Revon,* to summarise, is mainly in prose, and contains snappy dialogue interspersed with apparently unrelated lyrics and nonsense elements (about elephants, mostly). It moves in repetitive, declarative, cycles. The plot, such as it is, turns around a persistently agitative child who denounces a passive, silent, standing man. It opens thus:

> They must be curious trees indeed, where the big elephants go walking, without bumping each other!
> The child was playing.
> And saw a man standing.
> "Mama," said the child – the Mother: "Yes."
> "Mama," – "Yes!"
> "Mama," – "Yes!"
> "Mama, a man is standing there!" – "Yes!"
> "Mama, a man is standing there!" – "Yes!"
> "Mama, a man is standing there!" – "Where?"
>
> (60)

The child's agitation triggers a series of events leading to the gathering of an angry crowd (including art critics, academics, the press and the law) who break into a riot. The police try to quell the riot and arrest all the wrong people. The mob riots again:

> A child was crushed between two stout women. Am I not a sweet lad? They threw the crushed remains of the child heedlessly under their

> feet. The eye sees the heaven open. A few of the smaller persons took possession of the dead child, and stood on it, because they wanted to see something, too. (74)

After the revolution parliament is restored to the sound of "an electric bell" (76).

West borrows, adapts and collages elements from *Revolution in Revon* for his riot scene: the silent, passive man, the child provocateur, the mindless mob. Even his references to elephants take on new significance. West's interspersal of lyrics and other art works into the narrative of *The Day of the Locust* finds precedence in Schwitters's work. The positioning of Mr Kahn's huge electric sign above West's mob echoes the appearance, or textual intervention, above the crowd in *Revolution in Revon* of gigantic letters spelling "PRA" (the reversal of "Arp", the name of another Dadaist; a linguistic play on such letters is also taken up by Joyce in the *Wake*) (*Revolution*, p. 74). So the "comic–serious entry of art into life" that Wisker sees in Kahn's sign is doing more than "ironically immortalizing Coleridge" (124). West's intertext with Coleridge, and the gesture towards a lost romantic dream of aesthetic compensation understood by Barnard, is complicated by its collaging with a text born out of the Dadaist avant-garde's assault on (amongst other things) Romantic transcendental aesthetics. West's final police siren echoes Schwitters's final electric bell, signalling the restoration of order. But we must consider the possible kinds of order both texts allude to at their borders.

West's collagistic incorporation of Schwitters's collagistic text also echoes Schwitters's own collagistic debt to an earlier Dadaist performance. The standing man may well have an ancestor in Hugo Ball's automaton masquerade at the Cabaret Voltaire in Zurich in 1916. Remaining motionless, encased in rigid cylindrical garb, and chanting sound poetry, Ball caused a riot amongst "serious representatives of the middle class". Accounts of the event include elephants and a curious child:

> For one fleeting moment, I thought I glimpsed, beneath my Cubist mask, an adolescent's pallid, distressed face, the half-scared, half-curious face of a trembling ten-year-old eagerly hanging upon a priest's each and every word during the mass for the dead or some other important mass in his native parish. Just at that moment, the electric light was switched off, as I had requested it be beforehand;

> and, dripping with sweat, I was carried off the podium to the exit. (Quoted Richter: 38–9)

The child agitator, Adore Loomis, may also have another, less timid, ancestor supplied by *transition*. In the 1930 edition we find a satiric portrait of Hitler by George Grosz, entitled "The Little Agitator".

Like Homer Simpson, Schwitters's standing man seems to be an automaton: "His suit was rather curious, really rather very curious. It was not plugged nor mended, but nailed with planks and surrounded with wire. A perambulating *Merzplastik*" (*Revolution*, p. 74) Like West's much harried Homer and Tod himself, Schwitters's standing man, berated by journalists, critics, the public and the law, may be understood as a reflection on the social and political role of the artist in turbulent times. As the reference to "Merz" invites, he has been interpreted as a portrait of Schwitters himself – but as allegedly retreating from politics into a haven of art. But *Revolution in Revon*, on the contrary, may be interpreted as offering a model of aesthetic reproduction and reading in which even stasis (saying nothing) has political consequences – a fairer reflection, perhaps, on the context in which it was written. This notion of art as always and already an intervention in the world is borne out by accounts of Schwitters's actual performances of the work: apparently his readings of *Revolution in Revon*, like Ball's earlier performances, caused riots to which the police had to be called.

As importantly, *Revolution in Revon* may also be read as a satire of the failed German Revolution in the aftermath of which emerged the Fascist counter-movement leading to Hitler's chancellorship. This would explain why Hanover, already reversed to "Revon" in Schwitters's title, is seen to undergo a "great and glorious revolution" which will presumably return it to Hanover again! In his footnote Schwitters explains that his Dada work, like Dada, "holds the mirror up to the world. Here is mirrored the Revon of 1919" (*Revolution*, p. 60). His spectacular, non-mimetic, feat of reversed writing, then, "mirrors" the political upheavals and reversals of this period. The presence of repressive law and order in and at the margins of the piece, and the resumption of parliament at the end, may well suggest the uneasy Weimar climate, in which the new democracy entrusted its defence to the profoundly anti-democratic militia of the old regime, stamping out communism at the cost of revitalising German Militarism. Nathanael West's use of Kurt Schwitters's work nearly twenty years later, on the eve of the Second World War, suggests a timely exploration of such matters. Tod Hackett's desperate imitation of a police siren at the close of *The Day of the Locust,* then, becomes more than merely an instance of the absurd: it is an alarm signal – all the way from Weimar.

West's last chapter conceals its own revolutions and reversals too. Closing with an argument, West's earlier draft makes explicit reference to oppositional factors excluded from the final version, in Tod's angry response to the accusation that his painting exaggerates "the importance of Southern California's screwballs" who "might be desperate enough to burn a few houses in Hollywood, but . . . were the pick of America's madmen and not at all typical of the country as a whole":

> This made Tod still more angry. He changed the image Claude had used from "pick" to "cream of America's madmen" and shouted that the milk from which it was skimmed was just as rich in violence. The Angelenos would be first, but their brothers all over the country would follow. Only the working classes would resist. There would be civil war.
>
> He raved on until the doctor came and put him to sleep.
>
> ("The Original Final Chapter of *The Day of the Locust*", Wisker: 171)

This glimmer of a reference to class struggle in the draft might have been more palatable to critics on the Left (although John Keyes (Bloom: 173) calls the novel itself "successful proletarian literature"), but, in keeping with his understanding of the selective focus of satire, West's literary anti-fascism remains implicit in the final version. It is implicit in his very technique – immanent, perhaps, in his work's collagistic and rich textual surface. Barnard dangerously retorts at West's closing mob scene: "why grieve as the flames lick . . . ?" For her, *The Day of the Locust* can only echo Adorno's "gloomy vision of revolution"; for her, "a dark hint at a kind of revolutionary nihilism is all we get from West". Yet the half-hidden pleasures of West's collagistic debt to Schwitters, recalling both his own celebratory re-reading of Schwitters's text in that "delirious autumn" with Herbst and *Revon*'s own re-readings of revolution, offer a less dystopic dialectical reading of an undeniably gloomy moment between Guernica/*Guernica* and the holocaust to come. For West, reflecting on his omissions in *The Day of the Locust,* and conscious of his shortcomings in the eyes of his more orthodox contemporaries on the Left, “there is a place for the fellow who yells fire and indicates where some of the smoke is coming from without actually dragging the hose to the spot” (Martin: 336). Yet, I would add, somehow, simultaneously, he may also be fanning other flames.

# 9 Apocalypse, Auschwitz, the Bomb and After
## Virginia Woolf, David Gascoyne, Paul Celan, Ezra Pound, William Carlos Williams, Gertrude Stein and Kurt Schwitters

### Introduction

This chapter begins on the brink of world war, with ominous warnings on gender, race and war, in Woolf's "Thoughts on Peace in an Air Raid" (1940), and Richard Wright's preface to his ground-breaking novel of the same year, *Native Son* (1940), invoking the horror of Poe. It looks at the more hopeful apocalyptic visions of the surrealist-influenced writers associated with, and at the fringes of, the British Apocalypse movement, Dylan Thomas, W. S. Graham, David Gascoyne. The horrific realisation of the inferno in Hitler's death factories is addressed through the Holocaust writing of Paul Celan, Rudolf Vrba and Cynthia Ozick. And a different sort of poetics of hell is glimpsed in the fascist collaborator Pound's *Pisan Cantos*, written from his post-war internment by the Americans for treason. Also explored is the optimism of William Carlos Williams's apocalyptic vision in *The Wedge* and *Paterson*. The chapter, and the book's final part, close with readings of the poetics of Gertrude Stein, Raoul Hausmann and Kurt Schwitters in the mid-1940s. Their words serve as this book's conclusion, marking a post-war place of Apocalypse from which modernism's and the avant-garde's new ladders start. Transitions continue.

## Apocalypse: war, gender, race

Three years on from Guernica/*Guernica*, Woolf, who had considered including photographs of victims of the Spanish atrocities in *Three Guineas*, meditates in "Thoughts on Peace in an Air Raid" (1940), while German bombs drop on English civilian targets, on the "queer experience, lying in the dark and listening to the zoom of a hornet which may at any moment sting you to death". She warns:

> Unless we can think peace into existence we – not this one body in its one bed but millions of bodies yet to be born – will lie in the same darkness and hear the same death rattle overhead. Let us think what we can do to create the only efficient air-raid shelter while the guns on the hill go pop pop pop and the searchlights finger the clouds and now and then, sometimes close at hand, sometimes far away, a bomb drops. (*Death of the Moth*, p. 154)

Hell here is staged as a gender apartheid, it is men at war in the sky ("the defenders are men, the attackers are men"), while women "must lie weaponless to-night" listening for the bombs. But women must "fight with the mind", free the men "from the machine", and "compensate the man for the loss of his gun".

Meanwhile, in the same year, Richard Wright, who incidentally was in the habit of reading Stein's experimental prose (the early story "Melanctha", for example, which is a study in black women's stream-of-consciousness) to black, industrial workers, terrorised white America with his chilling novel *Native Son* (1940), in which a story of Black America unfolds in an avant-garde narrative that shifts between collage, montage, reportage and stream-of-consciousness. It is the story of Bigger, a black man who finds himself on trial for the sexual murder of a white, liberal woman he has accidentally killed, and whose deliberate murder of a black woman goes unnoticed. Wright concludes his preface, "How Bigger was Born", with a reflection on the state of American letters, ominously noting, in the light of Black American experience, that "if Poe were alive, he would not have to invent horror; horror would invent him" (Kolocotroni et al.: 618).

## Night readings: Dylan Thomas, W. S. Graham, David Gascoyne and the poetics of the New Apocalypse

> There are signs that the great movement of liberation begun by Surrealism, or privately achieved by such poets as George Barker and Dylan Thomas, is now being continued and systematized by some of the younger writers, who are trying to give it a more positive direction. These younger writers have formed into a group known as "The Apocalypse". They have already published two collective books, "The New Apocalypse" (Fortune Press, 1939) and "The White Horseman" (Routledge, 1941), as well as being particularly active in America, where they have published most of their work and founded a group called "the International Workshop", which they later left in almost entirely American hands. (Scarfe: 155)

So Francis Scarfe opens his chapter, "Apocalypse", in his popular stock-taking of poetry at the turn of a new decade, *Auden and After: The Liberation of Poetry, 1930–1941* (1942). The leaders are given as Nicholas Moore, Henry Treece, J. F. Hendry and G. S. Fraser, and their agreed "aims" and "points" are summarised by Scarfe as follows:

> (1) That Man was in need of greater freedom, economic no less than aesthetic, from machines and mechanistic thinking.
> (2) That no existent political system, Left or Right; no artistic ideology, Surrealism or the political school of Auden, was able to provide this freedom.
> (3) That the Machine Age had exerted too strong an influence on art, and had prevented the individual development of Man.
> (4) That myth, as a personal means of reintegrating the personality, had been neglected and despised. (156)

But if this is beginning to sound somewhat Eliotic in its Spenglerian dread and its interest in myth as unifying agency, then, note that the Apocalyptic movement, according to Scarfe, shuns objectivism, if not exactly Eliot impersonality, and the Apocalyptic movement

> is to mean liberation from a purely objective world, a reaction against the objective world, a reaction against the objective reporting of the 'thirties, against mass-observation and the parochial conception of "observing" which was evolved by the followers of Auden and

> Grigson. Its literary ancestors are said to be Revelations, Shakespeare, Webster, Blake, Donne, Hopkins and Kafka. (157)

Eliot's ideal order of "Tradition" has been reorganised so that Classicism embraces Romanticism, Donne ("a prejudice unquestionably taken up from the Eliot generation") is side by side with Blake. Anarchism, organicism, and a customised surrealism are the key qualities: "Apocalypse is, then, a de-mechanizing, or a de-materializing, of Surrealism."

Dylan Thomas, one of the fathers of Apocalypse, was converted to the avant-garde partly through the offices of *transition*, in 1933 or 1934, when according to his friend J. H. Martin, he "turned to the extreme avant-garde, to Joyce and the Paris magazine *transition*" (quoted McMillan: 159). Thomas's work also appeared in the magazine. McMillan identifies the centrality of the image in Thomas's poetic credo, and cites his letter to Treece defending his use of complex imagery:

> it consciously is not my method to move concentrically round a central image. . . . A poem by myself needs a host of images. I make one image – though 'make' is not the word, I let, perhaps, an image be "made" emotionally in me and then apply to it what intellectual and critical forces I possess – let it breed of the other two together, a fourth contradictory image, and let them all, within my imposed formal limits, conflict. (Thomas, *Letters*, p. 190)

Thomas's revelation of the word, in his poem "In the Beginning", is in keeping with *transition*'s "revolution of the word", and begins with the darkness fissured by light in Genesis: "In the beginning was the word, the word / That from the solid bases of the light / Abstracted all the letters of the void" (Thomas, *Collected Poems*, p. 23). McMillan comments: "With Thomas, as with his contemporaries who were more closely allied with *transition*, the word has regained a place of respect" (165).

"The poets associated with the 'New Apocalypse'", Crozier reminds us, are "the poets most typically associated with the vices of forties" ("Thrills" p. 228), noting also that they "tend to deny Thomas's influence" (228). But the reach of Apocalypse he shows goes well beyond this decade, extending to *The Nightfishing* (1955), the superb work of W. S. Graham (1918–86), a fringe member of Apocalypse, and quotes the following lines from the third section: "See how, like an early self, it's loathe to leave . . . This wedge driven in / To the twisting water, we rode. The bow shores / the long rollers." Crozier marks the "moral as well as formal issues here: the personification of the natural world; the vigorous, energized language; the release of individual words ('shores' . . . ) into equivalent syntactic and semantic relations, which are consequences of the way the poem's discourse marginalizes the self" ("Thrills", p. 229). Tony Lopez points to the Homeric and Christian antecedents of the poem, and compares its first section to "the Telemachus chapters of Joyce's *Ulysses,* in that both have instances of calling to a voyage and static images left behind" (67).

> I bent to the lamp. I cupped
> My hand to the glass chimney.
> Yet it was a stranger's breath
> From out my mouth that
> Shed the light.
>
> (Graham, *Collected Poems,* p. 92)

Lopez finds "the stranger's breath" to be "just the same kind of self-consciousness" that Joyce renders as Stephen's, adding, "and that Joyce's book is in some part a late Homeric voyage-text, is very much to the point" (67). But "the stranger's breath" may also be Eliot's, or at least the enactment of his thesis of "Tradition and the Individual Talent": the dead speaking through the living. The "shores" of Section 3 recall the fragments shored in *The Waste Land,* and Lopez points to other Eliotic intertexts. Graham's fretting shores of sea and self, like the torrents of Williams's river-self in "Paterson: The Falls" (1944), itself a fragment of the greater *Paterson* to come (1946–58) that flows through the mid-decades of the twentieth century, bursting through the order of orthodox, epochal demarcations, also return us to the fretting, liminal poetics of subjectivity of Stevens's "Idea of Order at Key West". At the close of Graham's poem, the nightmindedness of "The Nightfishing", the living legacy in 1955 of an unstoppable avant-gardism reaching back decades, speaks its own life-affirming resurrection of the word:

> So I spoke and died.
> So within the dead
> Of night and the dead

Of all my life those
Words died and awoke. (107)

Returning to the Apocalypse of the 1940s, we might gather that just as the apocalypse poet inflects differently, speaks differently, and enlarges and stretches the poetic language that is the legacy of earlier avant-garde works, poetic apocalyptic vision is differently inflected, differently revealing, in the work of each apocalypse poet, as is implied in Henry Treece's book title, *How I See Apocalypse.*

David Gascoyne (1916–2001) is another poet of the Apocalypse whose career extends well beyond the chronological limits of this book. His volume *Poems 1937–1942,* published by Poetry London in 1943, was illustrated by the artist Graham Sutherland, and was, he tells us in his prefatory note, "originally planned as two separate ensembles: 'The Open Tomb' (1937), and 'The Conquest of Defeat' (1939–42), but it has now seemed more expedient to combine the two under the present title, and to re-arrange the whole order of the poems" (p. iv). The second poem in the second of his five sections, which is a group of "metaphysical (or 'metapsychological') poems" (and in which appears "The Open Tomb"), is "Inferno", which itself follows the poem "World Without End". It is a first-person narrative of revelation that has elided its lyric "I", so that the crucial inscription of revelation, "Was shown", appears without a directly stated subject except as "my self", who is "My searcher and destroyer". This Eliotic subject, in its continual cycle of extinction and resurrection, is "wandering", like the speaker of Blake's "London", and, like a Wordsworthian subject, is "One evening . . . led". What leads is a subjective emotional condition, signalled by the metaphor of an ensign (the sign of a sign), "the scarlet and black flag / Of anger and despondency", and the speaker is led through a mental landscape whose urban metaphors, turning the Eliotic consciousness of the street inside out, are the "unnamed streets of a great nameless town", to a revelation of "the Void that undermines the world:" The colon following the "world" takes us to the brink, the precipice, of the void. We must turn the page of the first edition (from page 9 to 10), to read what follows, in all its shocking proximity, and go with the poem "over the edge:" as follows:

For all that eye can claim is impotent –
Sky, solid brick of buildings, masks of flesh –

Against the splintering of that screen which shields
Man's puny consciousness from hell: over the edge
Of a thin inch's fraction lie in wait for him
  Bottomless depths of roaring emptiness.

The last line is not, does not constitute, of course, a void. It is language making and celebrating presence, survival at the existential brink of "Bottomless depths of roaring emptiness".

For all the poem's urban bomb-site imagery, the Hell of Gascoyne's poem is metaphysical or psychological, but it is placed in a collection that closes with a section of "poems of time and place" (p. iv), and whose final poem is "Rain and the Tyrants", describing the perpetual ineffectual baptism since "Homer's time" of rain, which is "without the power to make less hard / The wooden heads of tyrants". The poem drizzles from its opening "I" who must "stand and watch", to its first, and closing full stop at the last line with "A shower of drizzling rain / Making the flags hang wet." There is a melancholy euphony here and in the figuring of the rain "which falls / Across all Europe's map / Wrapping all men alive in the same moist envelope". The enveloping, womb-like, "luminous halo" that Woolf finds in Joyce's aesthetic at the close of the Great War is given here, during the Second World War, more material (less transcendental) viscous, flesh-like qualities, its feminine associations perhaps pushed further. It performs a similar ceremony to that of the snow at the close of Joyce's "The Dead"; but, like the rain, the poem seems to know it too is ineffectual against the tyrants. Yet, like the rain's damp comfort, "Despite the soldiers loading arms, / Despite the newspapers' alarms", it persists.

## Auschwitz and the Inferno: the Holocaust writing of Paul Celan, Rudolf Vrba and Cynthia Ozick

Schwarze Milch der Frühe wir trinken sie abends
wir trinken sie mittags und morgens wir trinken sie nachts

Black milk of daybreak we drink it at evening
we drink it at midday and morning we drink it at night
  (Paul Celan, "Todesfugue" ("Death Fugue", translated by Felstiner), 1944)

The metaphysical, metaphorical "hell" of Gascoyne's moving poem "Inferno" becomes an aesthetic luxury, denied to the occupants and to the surviving, recording witnesses, of the literal inferno built by the Third Reich. Paul Celan, who changed his name from Antschel when his first poems were published in 1947, is clearly aware of the politics of choosing to continue to write in German. And for him (a survivor of the camps), language was the only thing that remained intact after the war (Hamburger, in Celan). But, let us also consider, what is the metaphorical status and politics of the poem's later refrain, "der Tod ist ein Meister aus Deutschland" ("Death is a master from Deutschland")? What the tenor, what the vehicle in "Black milk of daybreak we drink you at night?" "The act of metaphor then", according to a character in Thomas Pynchon's novel *The Crying of Lot 49* (1966), "was a thrust at truth and a lie, depending where you were: inside, safe, or outside, lost. Oedipa did not know where she was" (89). Inside metaphor, its "tenor", is that ultimately unknowable signified – available, in postmodernist logic, as merely another signifier. But to be "outside" metaphor is to somehow read (or not) only its vehicular qualities, trapped in a physical, material realm of signifiers, without access to the signified, the tenor. Or it may be, that to be outside is to *constitute* in some sense metaphor's own outside, its vehicle or signifier. What might it mean to be outside, embodying, the metaphors of race, physiognomy?

And metaphor depends on difference, alienation, to function. The gender politics of metaphor identify the signifier's otherness as always and already feminine (the aesthetic is a woman). The "true" feminine becomes knowable, inscribable, only as an absence. The larger political consequences, beyond gender (but staged through gender), of these aesthetic questions, are evident in Benjamin's pronouncement, in his epilogue to "The Work of Art in the Age of Mechanical Reproduction" (1936), on the extent to which self-alienation, and reification, have enabled modern humanity to "experience its own destruction as an aesthetic pleasure of the first order. This is the situation of politics which Fascism is rendering aesthetic. Communism responds by politicising art" (242). We have considered some of the aesthetic consequences of the Communist response; now for some consequences of the aestheticising jackboot. In Celan's poem, the refrain, "dein goldenes haar Margarete / dein aschenes haar Sulamith" ("Your golden hair Margarete / your ashen hair Shulamith"), juxtaposes one woman as the emblem of Aryan beauty, carrier and vehicle for the German race; the other, emblem of Jewishness, denied humanity, already industrially processed by the furnaces of the death camp. This is the crisis of metaphor enacted in Celan's poem. In a syntax that is not so much ruptured as sinisterly seamless, unstoppable process, Death's allegory is shockingly literal: "he whistles his hounds to come close / he whistles his Jews into rows has them shovel a grave in the ground / he commands us play up for the dance". These activities are metonymic (the vehicle/signifier is a quality or aspect of the tenor/signified) – the "Holocaust" is signified in these sample acts of brutality. But this poem is not merely reportage (or following the reflective–aesthetic line of "modernism is realism"), though the bearing of witness is significant. This poem is opening up to account the role of writing and language, German language and "literary" language too, in the cultural and ideological construction of Nazism and Fascism: "A man lives in the house he plays with his vipers he writes / he writes when it grows dark to Deutschland your golden hair Margareta / Your ashen hair Shulamith".

The post-war body of testimony to the literalisms here is huge. I will confine my brief discussion to one of the most powerful accounts of Auschwitz, one that in my view should be made as widely available today as Anne Frank's Diary. Rudolf Vrba, one of the few successful escapees from Auschwitz, appends in his book, *I Cannot Forgive* (1964), his deposition "for submission at the trial of Adolf Eichmann in Tel Aviv" (1961), which testifies on the "exact" numbers of people exterminated there. He explains how he was "well in a position" to make such calculations, because he worked for two years "as a member of the so-called *Sonderkommando* in the Property department" (Vrba and Bestic: 269). This infernal place was called by the inmates "Canada" (a kind of promised land). In Chapter 9, Vrba describes how he was transferred from the Buna Plant, where he was certain to have very swiftly met his death as one of the slaves who helped build the factories for I. G. Farben, and marched

> into Canada, the commercial heart of Auschwitz, warehouse of the bodysnatchers where hundreds of prisoners worked frantically to sort, segregate and classify the clothes and the food and the valuables of those whose bodies were still burning, whose ashes would soon be used as fertiliser. (127)

And what Vrba lists is the contents of the foulest rag-and-bone shop of the heartless. He describes two huge mountains of belongings, "twin peaks": one of "trunks, cases, rucksacks, kit bags and parcels", the other of 50,000 blankets; then he spies another of prams, another of "pots and pans from a thousand kitchens in a dozen countries" (128). In his "Epilogue", Vrba explains one rationale for the genocide at Auschwitz as the means to aid the German war effort: "Artificial teeth and limbs, spectacles, prams . . . they all flowed back to Germany. Nothing was wasted, not even the victims' hair which was used to caulk the warheads of torpedoes, or the bones and ashes which became fine fertiliser" (266; Vrba's ellipses). This grim gloss on the "ashen hair" in Celan's poem, also resonates back to absurdly literalise and ground, for a moment, the dumping-ground discourse of *The Waste Land*, or of "The Circus Animals' Desertion", the reified, fragmented body-parts, rags and detritus of the verbal collagist's trousseau, suspended between two world wars. But one visual image in Vrba's book speaks volumes on the horrific literalness of the inferno at Auschwitz. The name of the man pictured with Heinrich Himmler, in Illustration V, demonstrates an uncanny poetic justice: "Dr Engineer Faust (of I. G. Farben) shows Heinrich Himmler round the Buna Plant where the author worked and thousands died."

The question of writing, after Auschwitz, is bound up with the black irony in the three words written over its entrance, *Arbeit Macht Frei* ("Work Makes Free"). But it is not merely our reading and understanding of *these* words, metonymically standing, as they do, for the more long-winded and larger body of rhetoric of the Nazi leadership, that undergoes transition with the knowledge of the crimes committed beyond them. The linguistic anxieties of postmodernism are triggered too. Readings of the reactionaries of earlier phases of "modernist" literature are also complicated by this later historical context, bringing Eliot's theories of authoritarianism, for example, his poetry's anti-Semitic allusions, and Pound's more explicitly fascist incantations and anti-Semitic invective, under sharper scrutiny. The ensuing crisis in critical interpretation of politics and poetry, which has sometimes resulted in a marked reluctance among undergraduates these days to study work by male "modernists", has contributed to the bankruptcy of the term "Modernism". It is time to return to the term "Avant-garde", which for all its confused previous usage, at least is equipped to address and open up the questions of art and politics that "Modernism" has served to close down.

Manifestos on the ethics and aesthetics of "holocaust" writing have also been emerging since the 1940s. And there are powerful debates concerning issues of historiography, testimony, reportage, and fictional accounts, and even the appropriateness of humour (of which there is a rich vein in Holocaust literature: see, for example, Romain Gary's hilarious and savage novel *The Dance of Genghis Cohn*, 1968). The heat and scope of these debates are not that remote from the clashes of the 1930s over realism and avant-gardism. The American writer Cynthia Ozick, for example, has declared in interview (1993):

> I believe with all my heart and soul that [the Holocaust] ought to remain exclusively attached to document and history. But it won't. Already Steven Spielberg is looking to build a make-believe gas chamber at Auschwitz, to accommodate the plot of a movie. Already the furnaces have escaped utterly into mythopoesis, and the Holocaust as "idea" is used both malevolently and benevolently, as Alvin Rosenfeld shows us in his book, *Imagining Hitler*. If the Holocaust becomes commensurate with the literary imagination, then what of those recrudescent Nazis, the so-called revisionists, who claim the events themselves are nothing but imaginings? (Kauvar: 390)

Ozick, however, is the author of "The Shawl" (1980), a short story: set in Auschwitz, to which she later added "Rosa" (1983), an account of the experiences of the surviving protagonists' life in America, and both were published in book form as *The Shawl* (1991), the epigraph to which is a citation from Celan's poem: "dein goldenes Haar Margarete / dein aschenes Haar Sulamith". Elaine Kauvar has pointed out that in also "invoking the Roman poet's hell in her novella [Ozick's], the storyteller becomes a kind of 'Virgil of the German hell,' a guide into the subterranean world of a survivor". Ozick's invocation of Dante's poetic guide to the Inferno, in a work of fiction, seems to contradict her earlier declaration. And Kauvar also points out that she puts forward an opposing, scientific analogy to apply to the testimony of survivors: "In 1988, five years after the publication of 'Rosa', Ozick wrote of Primo Levi, 'He has been a Darwin of the death camps: not the Virgil of the German hell but its scientific investigator'"(*Cynthia Ozick's Fiction*, p. 201). The analogy for Levi of Darwin, whose theory of natural selection became grist to the Nazi mills, is a troubling one.

## Ezra Pound's Apocalypse: approaching the *Pisan Cantos*

But to return to matters of fiction. The cultural significance of an invocation of Virgil and Dante, of the classical poetic discourses of the inferno, in a fictional or poetic exploration of Nazi and Fascist atrocities, is not readily intelligible, in and after the twentieth century, without some consideration of the work of those who have so recently descended to that place, invoking Mussolini and Hitler. Post-holocaust readers do not need him for a guide exactly (of Virgil's stature), but they will at least encounter Pound, nevertheless – "a man on whom the sun has gone down" – just as Dante encountered Sinon, on the brink somewhere of the tenth trench. The *Pisan Cantos* were written from his confinement in 1945, literally caged, in the US Army Detention Training Centre, near Pisa ("from the death cells in sight of Mt Taishan @ Pisa", Pound, *Cantos*, p. 453), in "physical conditions both humiliating and cruel, if not, in 1945, unique", as Michael Alexander observes (192), and before his committal to St Elizabeth's Hospital for the Criminally Insane, in Washington, on being declared medically unfit to stand trial. These poems are as daunting for most readers as Pound's own earlier chosen "bag of tricks" for the *Cantos*, the *Sordello* of Browning. Indeed, Alexander has likened the critic "confronting the *Pisan Cantos*" to "Satan facing Chaos in *Paradise* Lost":

> Into this wild abyss the wary Fiend
> Stood on the brink of hell and looked a while,
> Pondering his voyage; for no narrow frith
> He had to cross.
>
> (II, 917–20; Alexander: 196)

Pound's droll retort for his friend Eliot, in the first Pisan Canto, LXXIV, "yet say this to the Possum: a bang, not a whimper" (451), is a darkly funny corrective, and a timely deflation of Eliot's posturing finale, two decades earlier, to "The Hollow Men" (1925): "*This is the way the world ends/ This is the way the world ends / This is the way the world ends / Not with a bang but a whimper.*" Pound's stunning metaphors for the surprising lightness of touch of the iron fist's call to order are by turns alchemical, poetically allusive, lyrically melancholic, and seductive in their euphonious deployment; and they have something to teach us even as we resist and abhor the politics that Pound embraced:

Hast 'ou seen the rose in the steel dust
(or swansdown ever?)
so light is the urging, so ordered the dark petals of iron
we who have passed over Lethe.

The "rose in the steel dust" refers to the response of iron-filings to the field of a magnet, imagery that Pound also explores in his essay "Medievalism"; while the juxtaposed parenthetical reference to "swansdown" is a citation from Ben Jonson's lyric "Her Triumph" (1624). Lethe is classical Hell's river. It flows through Hades and its waters "induce forgetfulness of this life and reincarnation" (Brooker, *Student's Guide*, p. 321). But who in Pound's poem are the "we who have passed over Lethe" (and, reading the line in isolation, we might be forgiven for momentarily thinking them the inmates of Auschwitz)? Amnesiac Fascists? We need to respond to these questions in the context of the issues raised by Wendy Flory in her discussion of "Pound and anti-Semitism": "Pound as 'designated fascist intellectual' has served since 1945 as stand-in for all those individuals of the silent majority in Germany, in occupied France and Belgium, in Britain and the United States who, by quietly aiding or standing quietly by, made the Holocaust possible" (300). And we might ponder that line, "so light is the urging, so ordered the dark petals of iron".

## Apocalypse and silence: poetics after Adorno

The much bandied axiom, plucked from the writing of Theodor Adorno, suggesting the barbarity of writing lyric poetry after Auschwitz, or more broadly, making art after the Shoah, is monumentally belied by those who, whether publicly or privately, did continue (and still continue) to create, and were (and still are) moved to create, to bear witness, to commemorate, to protest, to mourn, to elegise, to celebrate those lost in, and those surviving, that almost unspeakable loss. Silence, if chosen, if interval, contributes to the function, the decorum of speech; enforced, permanent, is the void. In "The Problem of Suffering" (1963), Adorno reflects further on, but does not retract, his famous dictum: "I have no wish to soften the saying that to write lyric poetry after Auschwitz is barbaric; it expresses in negative form the impulse which inspires committed literature" (Harrison and Wood: 761). In a sophisticated argument, he explains that he now re-

reads it, as Harrison and Wood summarise, "not as a total prohibition on art but as a prohibition on committed art. For its very commitment required . . . *entente* with the world which was to be affected." (Whenever I hear the word "prohibition" I reach for the "Ur Sonata"). Adorno worries that "when genocide becomes part of the cultural heritage in the themes of committed literature, it becomes easier to continue to play along with the culture which gave birth to murder" (761). And he fears that "the distinction between executioners and victims becomes blurred; both, after all, are equally suspended above the possibility of nothingness, which of course is generally not quite so uncomfortable for the executioners" (762). I can see how these observations might be applied to Spielberg's film, a film that also worries Ozick, but can it be meaningfully applied to the "committed" work of Claude Lanszman, in *Shoah*? Here, the distinction between executioners and victims is quite clear by their actions. But where any cultural analysis of the heritage of genocide must start is surely with the acknowledgement that both executioners and victims are human, perhaps not so comfortable an acknowledgement in considering the executioner.

dein goldenes Haar Margarete
dein aschenes Haar Sulamith

## William Carlos Williams's Apocalypse: art, war and *The Wedge*

> The war is the first and only thing in the world today.
>
> The arts generally are not, nor is this writing a diversion from that relief, a turning away. It is the war or part of it, merely a different sector in the field. (*Collected Later Poems*, p. 3)

So William Carlos Williams introduces his poems in *The Wedge* (1944). Art is war, not relief from it. He finds fault with the critics on the Left who anticipate a silencing of poetry for optimistic reasons, predicting that "after socialism has been achieved it's likely there will be no further use for poetry, that it will disappear" (*Collected Later Poems*, p. 3). Williams demolishes psychoanalytical and Marxist accounts of poetry as compensation, or escape, and employs the machine rhetoric of earlier avant-gardistes in advancing his materialist model of poetry: "To make two bald statements: There's nothing sentimental about a machine, and: A poem is a small (or large) machine made of words" (4). He recalls early Imagist demands for economy in declaring: "When I say there's nothing sentimental about a poem I mean that there can be no part, as in any other machine, that is redundant" (4). He concludes with a celebration of formalism as a mode of revelation:

> When a man makes a poem, makes it, mind you, he takes words as he finds them interrelated about and composes them – without distortion which would mar their exact significances – into an intense expression of his perceptions and ardors that they may constitute a revelation in the speech that he uses. It isn't what he says that counts as a work of art, it's what he makes, with such intensity of perception that it lives with an intrinsic movement of its own to verify its own authenticity. . . . To me all sonnets say the same thing of no importance. What does it matter what the line "says"? (5)

This dismissal of content may also constitute a declaration of the political significance of material form. Williams's title, *The Wedge*, if we do consider semantic content, suggests the collection of poems as a material object of intervention. And the first poem, "A Sort of Song" (7), presents, in its first stanza, the act of writing as a snake striking. The second begins by interposing the broken proposition " – through metaphor to reconcile / the people and the stones", suggesting the political work of the word, already in action, between people and objects. It ends with two injunctions: "Compose.", followed by his, formally appropriate parenthetical slogan "(No ideas but in things)"; and "Invent!", followed by the declaration: "Saxifrage is my flower that splits / the rocks." The dividing, gender politics of original sin are compressed in this pastoral of snake, flower, and rock. And again, the penetrating wedge of Williams's volume title is read in the rock-splitting saxifrage, Williams's writing metaphor.

But, *The Wedge,* as a *title,* also recalls the famous avant-garde abstraction by the Russian Suprematist artist El Lissitsky, for the Bolshivik propaganda poster *Beat the Whites with the Red Wedge* (1919). Robert Hughes describes this image as "quite decipherable, given the length of time one might normally accord it in a museum: the sharp red triangle, symbolizing the power of the Bolsheviks, thrust into the scattered units of White Russians" (93). Lissitsky understood his avant-garde abstractions as material, revolutionary, interventions. But Hughes questions their effectiveness for his contemporaries: "The same motif was proposed as a public sculpture by the artist Nikolai Kolli. . . . But what could it have meant when glimpsed in a Russian street – let alone a country village – in 1919? Not much; the language was too new" (93). Such avant-garde language was no longer new in 1944, although it had undergone many transitions and suffered huge political opposition by Left and Right alike. Yet it survives.

Among the poems in *The Wedge* is "Paterson: The Falls" (*Collected Later Poems*, pp. 10–11), a seed of Williams's great, collagistic epic of prose and poetry, *Paterson*, which was published in five books between 1946 and 1958. "Paterson: The Falls" begins with a question: "What common language to unravel?" This is to be an unmaking and remaking of avant-garde language. Perhaps following Wordsworth's famous apocalypse in *The Prelude* (VI), Williams's revelation is in the river Paterson's Falls "combed into straight lines / from that rafter of a rock's / lip". How perfectly balanced is the edge of this orifice. And the plan for *Paterson* erupts like saxifrage: "Strike in! the middle of / some trenchant phrase, some / well packed clause. Then . . . / This is my plan." And *Paterson* springs and floods for over a decade after, remaking language. This project marks a continuing and splendid tradition in transformations of, and transitions in avant-garde poetics.

## Apocalypse and the bomb: Gertrude Stein's "Reflection on the Atomic Bomb" and Raoul Hausmann's and Kurt Schwitters's manifesto of "PIN"

The first atomic bomb was dropped on Hiroshima by the US Air Force on 6 August 1945. A second was dropped on Nagasaki on 9 August 1945. In its stark light, Gertrude Stein, having survived the war under Vichy rule, in the French countryside, goes on (to paraphrase Beckett), before she dies of stomach cancer in October 1946, to finish her feminist libretto *The Mother of Us All* (1946); to have her play *Yes Is For A Very Young Man* produced in Pasadena; to publish her last prose work, *Brewsie and Willie* (1946); and to reflect on the atomic bomb, in her "Reflection on the Atomic Bomb" (published posthumously in 1947). Her reflection on the atomic bomb is in three paragraphs, the first of which is as follows: "They asked me what I thought of the atomic bomb. I said I had not been able to take any interest in it" (*Writings, 1932–1946*, p. 823). The third paragraph is only slightly longer, and no less a studied piece of banality: "Everybody gets so much information all day long that they lose their common sense. They listen so much that they forget to be natural. This is a nice story" (823). These simple detonations enclose a much larger paragraph comprising eight sentences of varying length, and accumulating, repetitious chains of syllogism. This larger paragraph mushrooms between its slender escorts a little like the sadly now familiar, legendary cloud formation that is the signature of the atomic bomb. In the heart of the paragraph is a very long sentence, and in the heart of that very long sentence is one word, in parenthesis, "(bomb)", which becomes the focal point of the page. This is the sentence:

> If they are not as destructive as all that then they are just a little more or less destructive than other things and that means that in spite of all destruction there are always lots left on this earth to be interested or to be interesting and the thing that destroys is just one of the things that concerns the people inventing it or the people shooting it off, but really nobody else can do anything about it so you have to just live along like always, so you see the atomic (bomb) is not at all interesting, not any more interesting than any other machine, and machines are only interesting in being invented or in what they do, so why be interested. (823)

In its stark light, Kurt Schwitters, having fled Nazi Germany via Oslo, and having spent seventeen months between 1940 and 1941 in British internment camps (as a German alien), followed by four productive years making visual and (increasingly Anglophone) verbal art in London, and despite learning of the destruction of his "Merzbau" (assemblage) in the bombardment of Hanover, and despite suffering a stroke in 1944, goes on, before he dies in January 1948, to begin his third "Merzbau", this time on Cylinders Farm, Little Langdale, in the English Lake District (and which barn wall "Merzbau" you can now visit at the collection of modern art of the University of Newcastle), and to produce with Raoul Hausmann the manifesto of PIN, entitled "Present Inter Noumenal" (1946), which begins with the proposition: "Poetry does not serve any more for needs", and which consists of eighteen propositions set out in justified margins, each proposition beginning on a new line, the final three of which are centred, balancing all that precedes on the monosyllabic acronym for the title: PIN. And no, this serene arrangement does not sprawl the sprawl of Prufrock's "formulated, sprawling on a pin". But it neatly shows how this book, *Modernism, 1910–1945: Image to Apocalypse*, has charted the vast and numerous transitions between two miniature manifestos: between Ezra Pound's injunction "Make It New" and Raoul Hausmann's and Kurt Schwitters's celebration, "Poetry Intervenes Now"; from "MIN" to "PIN".

This is how "PIN" ends or begins, depending on where your eye starts from:

> PRESENT Poetry is neither FOR nor AGAINST, neither classic, nor romantic, nor surrealistic
> It integrates BEING and it IS
> Poetry Intervenes Now
> Presence Is New
> PIN

Hausmann's and Schwitters's names and the date (27.xii.1946) flank the pivotal "PIN". A similar visual arrangement occurs with the companion poem "PIN" (1946), which under the title, "PIN", begins at the top with:

> A fancy
> A thing of fan
> The right thing of phan

As "fancy" unfurls to "fan" and then "phan", so too the discourse of Poundian Imagism unfurls well beyond its original rigid confines. It may recall, first, Pound's borrowed "fan of white silk", the addressee of "FAN-PIECE, FOR HER IMPERIAL LORD" (*Lustra*, 1916), not any longer a thing "also . . . laid aside", but instead a thing laid open and vitally transformed in an expanding sequence, which in turn includes "The right thing of phan", recalling, but again also *redirecting*, Pound's homage to "PHANOPOEIA . . . a casting of images upon the visual imagination" (see Chapter 1). It is clear that from the earlier phanopoeic origins with which this book started, whether in Imagism, or in Apollinaire's calligrammes, or in Dada and Merz assemblages, Schwitters and Hausmann (and many others) danced off down very different roads from the one taken by Pound. But these roads meet and cross, nevertheless, in the wars of the image, the struggles to make new revelations.

The lines of Schwitters's and Hausmann's "PIN" extend further and further, but in ragged variegation, towards the other margin, in a Steinian threat of prose. This is how "PIN" ends or begins, depending on where your eye starts from:

> You prefer the language, when you understand by it things,
> which everybody knows by heart already. We prefer the
> language, which provides you a new feeling for new whiskers to
> come
> Give up your human feelings and please go through our fan
> pin and you will know, that it was worth while.
>
> PIN
>
> The thing of phan-fan

# Chronology

| Dates | | Literary events | Cultural events | Historical events |
|---|---|---|---|---|
| **1910** | Mark Twain d. (b. 1835)<br>William James d. (b. 1842)<br>Tolstoy d. (b. 1828) | W. B. Yeats, *The Green Helmet*<br>Ezra Pound, *Gaudier-Brzeska*<br>E. M. Forster, *Howards End*<br>Ford Madox Ford, *A Call*<br>Henri Matisse, *The Dance*<br>Arnold Schoenberg, *The Red Gaze*<br>H. G. Wells, *The History of Mr Polly*<br>Arnold Bennett, *Clayhanger* | First Post-Impressionist exhibition, London<br>*Dreadnought* Hoax<br>Igor Stravinsky, *Firebird* (ballet)<br>Manifesto of Russian Acmeism<br>W. E. B. DuBois (ed.), *The Crisis* | Edward VII dies<br>George V accedes<br>Asquith government in crisis due to widespread political unrest in Britain: miners' strike, Suffragette agitation and campaign for Irish Home Rule<br>Union of South Africa |
| **1911** | Tennessee Williams b. (d. 1983)<br>Gustav Mahler d. (b. 1860)<br>Elizabeth Bishop b. (d. 1973) | Pound, *Canzoni*<br>Katherine Mansfield, *In a German Pension*<br>J. G. Frazer, *The Golden Bough*, Part Three: *The Dying God*<br>D. H. Lawrence, *The White Peacock*<br>Joseph Conrad, *Under Western Eyes*<br>T. E. Hulme, "Romanticism and Classicism"<br>Charlotte Gilman Perkins, *The Man-Made World* | *Rhythm*<br>Rutherford's nuclear theory of the atom<br>Der Blau Reiter (The Blue Rider) group founded, Munich | Revolution in Mexico<br>Amundsen to South Pole |

| Dates | | Literary events | Cultural events | Historical events |
|---|---|---|---|---|
| **1912** | Strindberg d. (b. 1849) | Pound, *Ripostes*<br><br>Marcel Duchamp, *Nude Descending a Staircase*<br><br>Jane Harrison, *Themis: A Study in the Social Origins of Greek Religion*<br><br>Jung, *Psychology of the Unconscious*<br><br>Pablo Picasso, *Still Life with Chair Caning* | Second Post-Impressionist exhibition, London<br><br>Futurist exhibition, Paris<br><br>The first Simultaneist verbal/visual art work: Blaise Cendrars' poem combines with Sonia Delaunay's abstract in *The Trans-Siberian*<br><br>The first acclaimed fully abstract painting, *Amorpha, Fugue in Two Colours* by Frantisek Kupka, shown at the Salon d'Automne, Paris, and featured in Gaumont news reel released across Europe | Sinking of *Titanic*<br><br>Balkans Wars (1912–13) |
| **1913** | Muriel Rukeyser b. (d. 1980) | Pound, *Personae* (1909; 1913; 1926)<br><br>Guillaume Apollinaire, *Cubist Painters*, and *Alcools*<br><br>Harrison, *Ancient Art and Ritual*<br><br>Sigmund Freud, *Totem and Taboo*<br><br>D. H. Lawrence, *Sons and Lovers*, and *Love Poems*<br><br>Robert Frost, *A Boy's Will*<br><br>Marcel Proust, *Swann's Way*<br><br>Blaise Cendrars, *Tower* | The Armory Show, New York<br><br>Filippo Marinetti, "Manifesto of Futurism"<br><br>Russian Futurist Manifesto<br><br>Einstein's General Theory of Relativity<br><br>Bohr discovers atomic structure<br><br>Roger Fry founds Omega Workshops, London<br><br>Ideal Home "rumpus": Wyndham Lewis falls out with Roger Fry | Woodrow Wilson (Democrat) elected in America (succeeding Republican William H. Taft 1909–12) |

| *Dates* | | *Literary events* | *Cultural events* | *Historical events* |
|---|---|---|---|---|
| **1913** | | Thomas Mann, *Death in Venice*<br>William Carlos Williams, *The Tempers*<br>Jacob Epstein, *The Rock Drill* (1913–14)<br>Stravinsky, *The Rite of Spring* | | |
| **1914** | Dylan Thomas b. (d. 1953)<br>Ralph Ellison b. (d. 1994)<br>Bernard Malamud b. | Pound (ed.), *Des Imagistes*<br>James Joyce, *Dubliners*<br>Gertrude Stein, *Tender Buttons*<br>Frost, *North of Boston*<br>Yeats, *Responsibilities*<br>Karl Kraus, "In These Great Times"<br>John Rodker, *Poems*<br>Giorgio de Chirico, *Melancholy and Mystery of the Street*<br>Robert Delaunay, *Homage to Blériot* | *Blast*<br>*Egoist*<br>Eliot meets Pound, London<br>*The Little Review* | Great War begins<br>Ludlow Massacre, Colorado, in which National Guard shot dead 36 and injured over 100 striking miners |
| **1915** | Henri Gaudier-Brzeska d. (b. 1891)<br>Rupert Brooke d. (b. 1887)<br>Saul Bellow b.<br>Flannery O' Connor b. (d. 1964)<br>John Cornford b. (d. 1936)<br>Booker T. Washington d. (b. 1856) | Rupert Brooke, *1914 and other Poems*<br>Virginia Woolf, *The Voyage Out*<br>Ezra Pound, *Cathay*<br>Dorothy Richardson, *Pilgrimage* (1915–38)<br>Lawrence, *The Rainbow*<br>*Some Imagist Poets* | | Sinking of *Lusitania*<br>Joe Hill is executed, Utah<br>Ku Klux Klan reformed |

| Dates | | Literary events | Cultural events | Historical events |
|---|---|---|---|---|
| **1915** | | Ford, *The Good Soldier*<br>Marcel Duchamp, *The Bride Stripped Bare by Her Bachelors, Even (Large Glass)* (1915–23) | | |
| **1916** | Henry James d. (b. 1843) | Joyce, *A Portrait of the Artist as a Young Man*<br>H.D., *Sea Garden*<br>Pound, *Lustra*<br>Apollinaire, *Le Poète Assassiné*<br>Henri Barbusse, *Le Feu*<br>Picabia, *La Fille Née Sans Mère* | Dada and Cabaret Voltaire, Zürich | The Easter Rising, Dublin, followed by execution of the Irish Nationalist leaders |
| **1917** | Edward Thomas d. (b. 1878)<br>T. E. Hulme d. (b. 1883)<br>Robert Lowell b. (d. 1977) | T. S. Eliot, *Prufrock and Other Observations*<br>Pound, "Three Cantos"<br>Duchamp, *Fountain*<br>Apollinaire, *Les Mamelles des Tirésias*<br>H. L. Mencken, *A Book of Prefaces* | | America joins War<br>Russian Bolshevik Revolution<br>Balfour Declaration (pledge for establishment of national home for Jews in Palestine) |
| **1918** | Guillaume Apollinaire d. (b. 1880)<br>Isaac Rosenberg d. (b. 1890)<br>Wilfred Owen d. (b. 1893)<br>Henry Adams d. (b. 1838) | Apollinaire, *Calligrammes*<br>Joyce, *Exiles*<br>Lewis, *Tarr*<br>Mansfield, *Prelude*<br>May Sinclair, "The Novels of Dorothy Richardson" | Posthumous publication of *Poems* by Gerard Manley Hopkins (1844–89)<br>Berlin Dada launched<br>Tristan Tzara, "Dada Manifesto, 1918" | Women over 30 get vote, and vote made universal for men in Britain<br>Russian Tsar executed<br>Spartakus Uprising, Berlin |

| *Dates* | | *Literary events* | *Cultural events* | *Historical events* |
|---|---|---|---|---|
| **1918** | Muriel Spark b. | Lytton Strachey, *Eminent Victorians*<br>Woolf, *Night and Day*<br>Willa Cather, *My Antonia*<br>Rebecca West, *The Return of the Soldier*<br>Oswald Spengler, *The Decline of the West* (1918–22) | Lenin's Plan for Monumental Propaganda launched | |
| **1919** | Doris Lessing b. | Kurt Schwitters, "An Anna Blume"<br>Ezra Pound, *Hugh Selwyn Mauberley*<br>W. B. Yeats, *The Wild Swans at Coole*<br>John Reed, *Ten Days That Shook the World*<br>Claude McKay, "If We Must Die"<br>Karl Kraus, *The Last Days of Mankind*<br>Woolf, "Modern Novels"<br>Eliot, "Tradition and the Individual Talent"<br>Pound, *Quia Pauper Amavi*<br>Sinclair, *Mary Olivier: A Life*<br>Thomas Hardy, *Collected Poems*<br>El Lissitsky, *Beat the Whites with the Red Wedge* | Bahaus is founded, Weimar<br>"Manifesto of the Bahaus"<br>Armistice Day Celebrations<br>First Atlantic flight | Treaty of Versailles<br>Break-up of Austrian Empire<br>"Red Scare", America<br>Rosa Luxemburg and Karl Liebknecht murdered by German Freikorps<br>Weimar Republic established |

| Dates | | Literary events | Cultural events | Historical events |
|---|---|---|---|---|
| **1920** | John Reed d. (b. 1887) | Wilfred Owen, *Poems*<br><br>Freud, *Beyond the Pleasure Principle*<br><br>Roger Fry, *Vision and Design*<br><br>F. Scott Fitzgerald, *This Side of Paradise*<br><br>Jessie Weston, *From Ritual to Romance*<br><br>Eliot, *The Sacred Wood*<br><br>Richard Huelsenbeck, *En Avant Dada: A History of Dada*<br><br>Yeats, *Michael Robartes and the Dancer*<br><br>Lawrence, *Women in Love*<br><br>Katherine Mansfield, *Bliss and Other Stories*<br><br>Williams, *Kora in Hell*<br><br>Picabia, *Sainte Vierge*<br><br>Rodker, *Hymns* | Edward Lutyens's (permanent) Cenotaph erected<br><br>Burial of Unknown Warrior<br><br>Dada festival, Paris<br><br>First International Convention of (Marcus Garvey's) United Negro Improvement Association, Harlem<br><br>*Contact* | League of Nations<br><br>Prohibition, America<br><br>2nd Congress of Comintern, Petrograd and Moscow |
| 1921 | | John Dos Passos, *Three Soldiers*<br><br>Mencken, *Prejudices*<br><br>Aldous Huxley, *Crome Yellow* | | Warren Harding (Republican) elected, America<br><br>First Quota Laws restricting immi-grants to America<br><br>Irish Independence<br><br>New Economic Policy in USSR |

| Dates | | Literary events | Cultural events | Historical events |
|---|---|---|---|---|
| 1922 | Marcel Proust d. (b. 1871)<br><br>Philip Larkin b. (d. 1985) | Eliot, *The Waste Land*<br><br>Joyce, *Ulysses*<br><br>Woolf, *Jacob's Room*<br><br>Edith Sitwell, *Façade*<br><br>Schwitters, "Ur Sonata" (1922–32), and *Revolution in Revon*<br><br>e. e. cummings, *The Enormous Room* | *Criterion*<br><br>British Broadcasting Corporation is founded | Mussolini's March on Rome<br><br>Irish Free State established<br><br>Bonar Law British Conservative leader of government |
| 1923 | Katherine Mansfield d. (b. 1888)<br><br>Nadine Gordimer b. | Freud, *Ego and Id*<br><br>Stevens, *Harmonium*<br><br>Williams, *Spring and All*<br><br>e. e. cummings, *Tulips and Chimneys*<br><br>Mina Loy, *Lunar Baedecke*<br><br>Mary Butts, *Speed the Plough*<br><br>Leon Trotsky, *Literature and Revolution* | Schwitters' first "Merzbau" built, Hanover<br><br>*Merz* founded<br><br>*Lef* ("Left Front of the Arts") manifesto<br><br>Bessie Smith's first record, "Downhearted Blues", sells record-breaking 780,000 copies | Calvin Coolidge (Republican) elected, America<br><br>Union of Soviet Socialist Republics founded<br><br>German inflation<br><br>Stanley Baldwin becomes prime minister of Britain |
| 1924 | Joseph Conrad d. (b. 1857)<br><br>Joseph Kafka d. (b. 1883)<br><br>James Baldwin b. (d. 1987) | Woolf, "Mr Bennett and Mrs Brown"<br><br>Hulme, *Speculations*<br><br>Marianne Moore, *Observations*<br><br>Forster, *A Passage to India*<br><br>Mann, *The Magic Mountain*<br><br>Harrison, *Mythology* | First Surrealist Manifesto<br><br>*Transatlantic Review* | Ramsay MacDonald forms Britain's first, and short lived, Labour government<br><br>"Zinoviev Letter" brings down government<br><br>Stanley Baldwin leads Conservatives back to power<br><br>Italian Fascist State inaugurated<br><br>Lenin dies |

| Dates | | Literary events | Cultural events | Historical events |
|---|---|---|---|---|
| **1925** | Erik Satie d. (b. 1866)<br><br>Gore Vidal b. | Woolf, *Mrs Dalloway* and *The Common Reader*<br><br>Stein, *The Making of Americans*<br><br>F. Scott Fitzgerald, *The Great Gatsby*<br><br>Alain Locke (ed.), *The New Negro*<br><br>Yeats, *A Vision*<br><br>Franz Kafka, *The Trial*<br><br>Adolf Hitler, *Mein Kampf*<br><br>Ernest Hemingway, *In Our Time*<br><br>Williams, *In the American Grain*<br><br>John Dos Passos, *Manhattan Transfer*<br><br>Theodor Dreiser, *An American Tragedy*<br><br>Hugh MacDiarmid, *Sangschaw*<br><br>Edwin Muir, *First Poems* | Neue Sachlichkeit exhibition, Berlin<br><br>Emily Dickinson, *Complete Poems*, posthumously published<br><br>Josephine Baker, *La Revue Nègre*, Paris<br><br>Bessie Smith buys her own Pullman railroad car, and records "St. Louis Blues" with Louis Armstrong | Stalin begins rise to dictatorship<br><br>Teapot Dome scandal, America |
| **1926** | Allen Ginsberg b. (d. 2000) | Langston Hughes, *The Weary Blues*<br><br>H.D., *Palimpsest*<br><br>Stein, "Composition as Explanation"<br><br>Hughes, "The Negro Artist and the Racial Mountain"<br><br>Hemingway, *The Sun Also Rises*<br><br>Graves and Laura [Riding] Jackson, *Modernist Poetry* | | General Strike, Britain |

| Dates | | Literary events | Cultural events | Historical events |
|---|---|---|---|---|
| **1926** | | Sean O'Casey, *The Plough and the Stars*<br>MacDiarmid, *A Drunk Man Looks at the Thistle*<br>Fritz Lang, *Metropolis* | | |
| **1927** | Isadora Duncan d. (b. 1877)<br>John Ashbery b. | Woolf, *To the Lighthouse*<br>Stein, *Four Saints in Three Acts*<br>Alfred Döblin, *Berlin Alexanderplatz*<br>Joyce, *Pomes Penyeach*<br>Kafka, *Amerika*<br>Lewis, *The Wild Body*<br>Hemingway, *Men Without Women*<br>Hughes, *Fine Clothes to the Jew*<br>Eliot, *Journey of the Magi*<br>Jean Rhys, *The Left Bank* | *transition*<br>Lindbergh flies Atlantic solo | Trotsky expelled by Stalin |
| **1928** | Thomas Hardy d. (b. 1840)<br>Jane Harrison d. (b. 1850) | Yeats, *The Tower*<br>Lawrence, *Lady Chatterley's Lover* and *Collected Poems*<br>Woolf, *Orlando*<br>Sergei Eisenstein, *October* (film)<br>Joyce, *Anna Livia Plurabelle*<br>Claude McKay, *Home to Harlem* | Radclyffe Hall's *The Well of Loneliness* banned for obscenity<br>George Gershwin, *An American in Paris* | Sixth World Congress of International Communist Party adopts policy advocating self-determination of American Negroes |

| Dates | | Literary events | Cultural events | Historical events |
|---|---|---|---|---|
| **1928** | | Djuna Barnes, *Ladies' Almanack*<br>René Magritte, *The Treason of Images* (1928–9) | | |
| **1929** | Adrienne Rich b. | Bertolt Brecht, *The Threepenny Opera*<br>Robert Graves, *Goodbye to All That*<br>Woolf, *A Room of One's Own*<br>Hemingway, *A Farewell to Arms*<br>Lawrence, *Pansies*<br>William Faulkner, *The Sound and the Fury*<br>Jean Cocteau, *Les Enfants Terribles*<br>J. B. Priestley, *The Good Companions*<br>C. Day Lewis, *Transitional Poem* | Second Surrealist Manifesto<br>Museum of Modern Art opens in New York<br>Luis Buñuel and Salvador Dali, *Un Chien Andalou* (surrealist film) | Wall Street crash<br>Herbert Hoover (Republican) elected, America<br>Stalin's autocratic dictatorship begins<br>Ramsay MacDonald's second Cabinet, Britain (1929–31) |
| **1930** | D.H. Lawrence d. (b.1885)<br>Mayakovsky d. (b.1893)<br>Derek Walcott b.<br>Ted Hughes b. (d. 1998)<br>Harold Pinter b.<br>Chinua Achebe b. | Lewis, *The Apes of God*<br>Eliot, *Ash Wednesday*<br>Hart Crane, *The Bridge*<br>Dos Passos, *U.S.A.* (1930–6)<br>Michael Gold, *Jews without Money*<br>Faulkner, *As I Lay Dying*<br>Rhys, *After Leaving Mr MacKenzie*<br>Auden, *Poems*<br>William Empson, *Seven Types of Ambiguity* | | Black Muslim movement founded, Detroit |

| Dates | | Literary events | Cultural events | Historical events |
|---|---|---|---|---|
| **1930** | | F. R. Leavis, *Mass Civilisation and Minority Culture* | | |
| **1931** | Alice Munro b.<br>Toni Morrison b. | Woolf, *The Waves*, and *The Second Common Reader*<br>Eugene O'Neill, *Mourning Becomes Electra*<br>Nathanael West, *The Dream Life of Balso Snell* | | Resignation of British government and formation of a "National Government" MacDonald Cabinet (1931–4)<br>Gold standard abandoned |
| **1932** | Geoffrey Hill b.<br>V. S. Naipaul b.<br>Sylvia Plath b. (d. 1963)<br>Lytton Strachey d. (b. 1880) | W.H. Auden, *The Orators*<br>Aldous Huxley, *Brave New World*<br>Nathanael West, *Miss Lonelyhearts*<br>Lewis Grassic Gibbon, *A Scots Quair* (1932–4)<br>Kay Boyle, *Plagued by a Nightingale*<br>Nina Hamnet, *Laughing Torso*<br>John Heartfield, *Adolf the Superman: Swallows Gold and Spouts Junk* | Soviet Reformation of Literary–Artistic Organisations | |
| **1933** | | Stein, *The Autobiography of Alice B. Toklas*<br>Eliot, *The Use of Poetry and the Use of Criticism*<br>Max Ernst, *Une Semaine de Bonté* (collage novel)<br>Yeats, *The Winding Stair* | | Hitler becomes Chancellor of Germany<br>The burning of the Reichstag<br>F. D. Roosevelt (Democrat) elected (1933–45), America, and ushers in The New Deal |

| Dates | | Literary events | Cultural events | Historical events |
|---|---|---|---|---|
| **1933** | | Woolf, *Flush*<br>Walter Greenwood, *Love on the Dole*<br>George Orwell, *Down and Out in Paris and London* | | |
| **1934** | Imamu Amiri Baraka b. | Nathanael West, *A Cool Million*<br>Pound, *The A.B.C. of Reading*<br>Zora Neale Hurston, *Jonah's Gourd Vine*<br>Nancy Cunard (ed.), *Negro: An Anthology*<br>Wyndham Lewis, *Men without Art*<br>Fitzgerald, *Tender is the Night*<br>Rhys, *Voyage in the Dark*<br>Graves, *I, Claudius*<br>Orwell, *Burmese Days* | Congress of Soviet Writers<br>Federal Writers' Project, America | |
| **1935** | Charlotte Gilman Perkins d. (b. 1860) | Stevens, *Ideas of Order*<br>Hurston, *Mules and Men*<br>Muriel Rukeyser, *Theory of Flight*<br>Eliot, *Murder in the Cathedral*, and *Four Quartets* (1935–42)<br>W. H. Auden and Christopher Isherwood, *The Dog Beneath the Skin*<br>Auden (ed.), *The Poet's Tongue* | | Italian invasion of Abyssinia<br>Baldwin Government's policy of appeasement (1935–7) |

| Dates | | Literary events | Cultural events | Historical events |
|---|---|---|---|---|
| **1935** | | Isherwood, *Mr Norris Changes Trains*<br>Patrick Hamilton, *Twenty Thousand Streets under the Sky: A London Trilogy*<br>George Dangerfield, *The Strange Death of Liberal England* | | |
| **1936** | A. E. Housman d. (b.1859)<br>Karl Kraus d. (b. 1874)<br>John Cornford d. (b. 1915) | Dylan Thomas, *Twenty-five Poems*<br>Michael Roberts (ed.), *The Faber Book of Modern Verse*<br>Yeats (ed.), *The Oxford Book of Modern Verse 1892–1935*<br>Stevie Smith, *Novel on Yellow Paper*<br>Alain Locke (ed.), *Negro Art Past and Present*<br>Walter Benjamin, *The Work of Art in the Age of Mechanical Reproduction*<br>Margaret Mitchell, *Gone with the Wind* | Charles Chaplin, *Modern Times* (film) | Abdication crisis<br>Spanish Civil War<br>Stalin's "Great Purge" (1936–8) eliminating "Old Bolsheviks", by arrest, detention, execution on monumental scale |
| **1937** | Bessie Smith d. (b. 1894)<br>Edith Wharton d. (b. 1862)<br>Antonio Gramsci d. (b. 1891) | Stevens, *The Man with the Blue Guitar*<br>Woolf, *The Years*<br>Barnes, *Nightwood*<br>David Jones, *In Parenthesis* | Entartete Kunst (Degenerate Art) Exhibition, Munich<br>New Bauhaus, Chicago<br>Picasso, *Guernica* | Policy of appeasement continued by Neville Chamberlain's government (1937–40) |

| Dates | | Literary events | Cultural events | Historical events |
|---|---|---|---|---|
| **1937** | Mary Butts d. (b. 1890)<br>Tony Harrison b. | Lewis, *Blasting and Bombardiering: Autobiography (1914–1926)*<br>Isherwood, *Sally Bowles*<br>Orwell, *The Road to Wigan Pier* | | |
| **1938** | Les Murray b. | Stein, *Dr Faustus Lights the Lights* (1938; 1949)<br>Woolf, *Three Guineas*<br>Samuel Beckett, *Murphy*<br>Louis MacNeice, *The Agamemnon of Aeschylus*<br>Robert McAlmon, *Being Geniuses Together, 1920–1930*<br>Richard Wright, *Uncle Tom's Children*<br>Pat Sloan (ed.), *John Cornford: A Memoir*<br>Orwell, *Homage to Catalonia* | International Surrealist Exhibition, Paris<br>Breton, Trotsky, Rivera, Manifesto: "Towards a Free Revolutionary Art" | "Crystal Night", organised pogroms against Jews throughout Germany |
| **1939** | W. B. Yeats d. (b. 1865)<br>Sigmund Freud d. (b. 1856)<br>Ford Madox Ford d. (b. 1873)<br>Seamus Heaney b. | Joyce, *Finnegans Wake*<br>Nathanael West, *The Day of the Locust*<br>Isherwood, *Goodbye to Berlin*<br>Eliot, *Old Possum's Book of Practical Cats*<br>Rhys, *Good Morning Midnight* | | German–Soviet non-aggression pact<br>German–Italian "Pact of Steel"<br>World War II begins |

| Dates | | Literary events | Cultural events | Historical events |
|---|---|---|---|---|
| **1939** | | John Steinbeck, *The Grapes of Wrath* | | |
| **1940** | F. Scott Fitzgerald d. (b. 1896)<br>Nathanael West d. (b. 1903)<br>Eric Gill d. (b. 1882)<br>Walter Benjamin d. (b. 1892) | Wright, *Native Son*<br>Hemingway, *For Whom the Bell Tolls*<br>Eliot, *East Coker*<br>Christina Stead, *The Man Who Loved Children*<br>Carson McCullers, *The Heart is a Lonely Hunter*<br>Orwell, *Inside the Whale* | | Winston Churchill forms Coalition Government, Britain<br>Paris falls to Germans |
| **1941** | James Joyce d. (b. 1882)<br>Virginia Woolf d. (b. 1882)<br>Sherwood Anderson d. (b. 1876) | Fitzgerald, *The Last Tycoon*<br>Hamilton, *Hangover Square*<br>James Agee, *Let Us Now Praise Famous Men*<br>Rebecca West, *Black Lamb and Grey Falcon* | | Trotsky assassinated, Mexico<br>Pearl Harbor<br>America joins war |
| **1942** | | Stevens, *Notes Toward a Supreme Fiction*<br>Faulkner, *Go Down, Moses*<br>Eliot, *Little Gidding*<br>Albert Camus, *The Outsider* | Ralph Ellison (ed.), *Negro Quarterly* | |
| **1943** | | | Jackson Pollock, *Guardians of the Secret* | Race riots, Detroit and Harlem<br>Dissolution of the Comintern |

| Dates | | Literary events | Cultural events | Historical events |
| --- | --- | --- | --- | --- |
| **1944** | Wassily Kandinsky d. (b. 1866)<br>Eavan Boland b. | William Carlos Williams, *The Wedge*<br>H.D., *The Walls Do Not Fall*<br>Tennessee Williams, *The Glass Menagerie*<br>Saul Bellow, *Dangling Man* | | |
| **1945** | Paul Valéry d. (b. 1871)<br>Arthur Symons d. (b. 1865)<br>Theodor Dreiser d. (b. 1871) | Pound, *Pisan Cantos*<br>Dylan Thomas, *Fern Hill*<br>Wright, *Black Boy*<br>Hughes, *The Big Sea*<br>Evelyn Waugh, *Brideshead Revisited*<br>Orwell, *Animal Farm* | | Dresden bombing<br>Atomic bombs dropped on Hiroshima and Nagasaki<br>End of World War II<br>Partition of Germany<br>Nuremberg Trials (1945–6) |

# Annotated Bibliography

Schwitters, Kurt, *Ursonate (1922–32): Original Performance by Kurt Schwitters*, CD (Germany: WERGO, 1994).

Listen, read, think.

Lewis, Wyndham, *Blast* 1(1914), and *Blast* 2 (1915), ed. Bradford Morrow (Santa Rosa: Black Sparrow Press, 1993, 1997).

Look, read, think.

Shattuck, Roger, *The Banquet Years: The Arts in France, 1885 to World War I*, rev. edn (London: Jonathan Cape, 1969).

Wonderful introduction to the first phase of Parisian avant-garde life – literature, art and music. Shattuck focuses on Alfred Jarry, Henri Rousseau, Erik Satie and Guillaume Apollinaire.

Richter, Hans, *Dada: Art and Anti-Art* (London: Thames and Hudson, 1965)

Remains a standard and entertaining entry into an understanding of the main activists in the historical avant-garde.

*Modernism/Modernity* journal (available on-line at http://muse.jhu.edu/journals/mod/).

Excellent resource; stimulating forum for current debates in criticism on modernism and avant-garde literature (extending to the present day).

Scott, Bonnie Kime, *The Gender of Modernism* (Bloomington: Indiana University Press, 1990).

First-rate source book that played major role in transforming critical and pedagogical approaches to the field.

Kolocotroni, Vassiliki, Jane Goldman and Olga Taxidou (eds), *Modernism:*

*An Anthology of Sources and Documents* (Edinburgh and Chicago: Edinburgh University Press and the University of Chicago Press, 1998).

A labour of love, making available a huge range of material (literary, political, cultural) from Karl Marx to Richard Wright.

Bürger, Peter, *Theory of the Avant-Garde* (1974), trans. Michael Shaw (Minneapolis: University of Minnesota Press, 1984).

Indispensable, foundational work on theorising avant-garde and modernism.

Murphy, Richard, *Theorizing the Avant-Garde: Modernism, Expressionism, and the Problems of Postmodernity* (Cambridge: Cambridge University Press, 1999).

Fascinating and challenging response to theoretical issues raised by Bürger. Opens up avant-garde theory to embrace German expressionism, previously considered outwith the borders of the historical avant-garde.

Scheunemann, Dietrich (ed.), *European Avant-Garde: New Perspectives* (Amsterdam: Rodopi, 2000).

The first publication from a sustained and systematic, international and interdisciplinary, critical project to interrogate, revise, and open up avant-garde theory both in terms of broadening historical readings, and in terms of reassessing the neo-avant-garde and contemporary.

Kenner, Hugh, *The Pound Era: The Age of T. S. Eliot, James Joyce and Wyndham Lewis* (1972).

Classic canonical account of the era. Excellent, sensitive and informative readings (in its own patriarchal bounds).

Fussell, Paul, *The Great War and Modern Memory* (Oxford: Oxford University Press, 1975).

This classic is an excellent introduction to the era and offers a stimulating account of the cultural functions of literature in the period of the Great War and after. Fascinating reading.

Van Wienen, Mark W., *Partisans and Poets: The Political Work of American Poetry in the Great War* (Cambridge: Cambridge University Press, 1997).

Wienen's ground-breaking work is not only a fascinating introduction to the critically neglected field of partisan literature of the period; it also puts forward a challenging thesis on the relationship between radical politics and poetics.

Nicholls, Peter, *Modernisms: A Literary Guide* (Basingstoke: Palgrave Macmillan, 1995).

An excellent overview of the period, situating Anglophone modernism in broader European contexts.

Smith, Stan, *The Origins of Modernism* (Hemel Hempstead: Harvester, 1987).

An excellent analysis of canonical male modernists with incisive close readings of major works put in productive dialogue with cultural and political contexts.

Berman, Jessica, *Modernist Fiction, Cosmopolitanism, and the Politics of Community* (Cambridge: Cambridge University Press, 2001).

Berman breaks new ground in this engaging and sensitive examination of concepts of collectivity, commonality, shared voice and exchange of experience, in the work of Henry James, Marcel Proust, Virginia Woolf and Gertrude Stein.

Julius, Anthony, *T. S. Eliot, Anti-Semitism, and Literary Form* (Cambridge: Cambridge University Press, 1995).

At the political sharp end of recent projects to historicise modernism, this is the book that forced into central focus the issue of reactionary politics and modernist aesthetics.

Alexander, Michael, *The Poetic Achievement of Ezra Pound* (1979; Edinburgh: Edinburgh University Press, 1998).

Remains the best guide to Pound's work, both as an introduction and as a critical touchstone to be frequently revisited.

Ellmann, Maud, *The Poetics of Impersonality: T. S. Eliot and Ezra Pound* (Brighton: Harvester, 1987).

Excellent, lucid and engaging investigation of subjectivity and language in canonical modernism

Meisel, Perry, *The Absent Father: Virginia Woolf and Walter Pater* (New

Haven: Yale University Press, 1980).

Wonderful book that examines Woolf's (unacknowledged) debt to Pater's aesthetic. Illuminating on both Pater and Woolf, and on wider questions of nineteenth-century aesthetics and modernism.

Minow-Pinkney, Makiko, *Virginia Woolf and the Question of the Subject* (Brighton: Harvester, 1987).

The first sustained Kristevan reading of a major modernist author, which transcends its specific study of Woolf and opens up deconstructive and Lacanian readings in modernism.

Goldman, Jane, *The Feminist Aesthetics of Virginia Woolf: Modernism, Post-Impressionism and the Politics of the Visual* (Cambridge: Cambridge University Press, 1998).

A revisionary reading of Bloomsbury aesthetics, connecting the suffragist aesthetics of the public sphere with the formalism of high modernism.

Humm, Maggie, *Modernist Women and Visual Cultures: Virginia Woolf, Vanessa Bell, Photography and Cinema* (Edinburgh: Edinburgh University Press, 2002).

Stimulating discussion of photography and cinema in the work of Woolf, Stein, H.D., Dorothy Richardson and Colette.

# Bibliography and References


Aaron, Daniel, *Writers on the Left: Episodes in American Literary Communism* (New York: Harcourt, 1961).

Abel, Daniel, "Television, Politics, and the Body in Thomas Pynchon's *Vineland*", *Imprimatur*, II, 2/3 (Autumn 1996): 58–69.

Adamowicz, Elza, *Surrealist Collage in Text and Image: Dissecting the Exquisite Corpse* (Cambridge: Cambridge University Press, 1998).

Adams, Henry, *The Education of Henry Adams* (1907).

Ades, Dawn, *Dada and Surrealism* (London: Thames and Hudson, 1974).

Adorno, Theodor, "The Problem of Suffering" (1963), *Art in Theory, 1900–1990: An Anthology of Changing Ideas*, ed. Charles Harrison and Paul Wood (Oxford: Blackwell, 1992).

Albright, Daniel, "Early Cantos I–XLI", *The Cambridge Companion to Ezra Pound*, ed. Ira B. Nadel (Cambridge: Cambridge University Press, 1999).

Aldington, Richard, *The Complete Poems* (London: Allan Wingate, 1948).

Alexander, Michael, *The Poetic Achievement of Ezra Pound* (1979; Edinburgh: Edinburgh University Press, 1998).

Anobile, Richard J. (ed.), *Why a Duck? Visual and Verbal Gems from the Marx Brothers Movies* (London: Studio Vistas, 1971).

Antliff, Mark, *Inventing Bergson: Cultural Politics and the Parisian Avant-Garde* (Princeton, NJ: Princeton University Press, 1993).

Appel Jr, Alfred, *Jazz Modernism: From Ellington and Armstrong to Matisse and Joyce* (New York: Knopf, 2002).

Atkinson, Diane, *The Suffragettes in Pictures* (London: Sutton, 1996).

Auden, W. H., *Collected Poems* (London: Faber, 1976).

——, "Interlude: West's Disease", *The Dyer's Hand and Other Essays* (1963).

Auerbach, Erich, *Mimesis: The Representation of Reality in Western Literature* (1946), trans. Willard R. Trask (Princeton, NJ: Princeton University Press, 1953).

Banfield, Ann, *The Phantom Table: Woolf, Fry, Russell and the Epistemology of Modernism* (Cambridge: Cambridge University Press, 2000).

Barnard, Rita, *The Great Depression and the Culture of Abundance: Kenneth Fearing, Nathanael West, and Mass Culture in the 1930s* (Cambridge: Cambridge University Press, 1995.

Baudelaire, Charles, *Les Fleurs du Mal*, ed. Yves Florenne (Montrouge, France: Brodard et Taupin, 1972).

Bazin, Nancy Topping, *Virginia Woolf and the Androgynous Vision* (New Brunswick: Rutgers University Press, 1973).

Beckett, Samuel, et al., *Our Exagmination Round his Factification for Incamination of Work in Progress* (1929).

Bell, Clive, *Art* (London: Chatto & Windus, 1914).

——, "The English Group", *Second Post-Impressionist Exhibition*, Grafton Galleries, Exhibition Catalogue (London: 1912).

Bell, Quentin, *Virginia Woolf: A Biography* (London, 1972).

Bell, Vanessa, *Selected Letters of Vanessa Bell*, ed. Regina Marler (London: Bloomsbury, 1993).

Benjamin, Walter, *Charles Baudelaire: A Lyric Poet in the Era of High Capitalism*, trans. Harry Zohn (London and New York: Verso, 1983).

——, "On Language as Such and on the Language of Man" (1916), *Selected Writings, 1913–1926*, ed. Marcus Bullock and Michael W. Jennings (Cambridge, MA and London: The Belknap Press of Harvard University Press, 1996).

Benjamin, Walter, "The Work of Art in the Age of Mechanical Reproduction" (1936), *Illuminations: Essays and Reflections*, trans. Harry Zohn, ed. Hannah Arendt (New York: Schocken Books, 1988).

Bennett, Arnold, [as "Jacob Tonson"], "Neo-Impressionism and Literature" (1910), *Books and Persons. Being Comments on a Past Epoch, 1908–1911* (London, 1917).

Benstock, Shari, *Women of the Left Bank: Paris, 1900–1940* (London: Virago, 1986).

Bergson, Henri, *Time and Free Will: An Essay on the Immediate Data of Consciousness* (1889), trans F. L. Pogson (London, 1971).

Berman, Jessica, *Modernist Fiction, Cosmopolitanism, and the Politics of Community* (Cambridge: Cambridge University Press, 2001).

Blake, William, *Complete Writings*, ed. Geoffrey Keynes (Oxford: Oxford University Press, 1971).

Blamires, Harry, *The New Bloomsday Book: A Guide to Ulysses*, rev. edn (London: Routledge, 1989).

Bloom, Harold (ed.), *Modern Critical Views: Nathanael West* (New York, 1986).

Bornstein, George, "Pound and the Making of Modernism", *The Cambridge Companion to Ezra Pound*, ed. Ira B. Nadel (Cambridge: Cambridge University Press, 1999).

——, *Material Modernism: The Politics of the Page* (Cambridge: Cambridge University Press, 2001).

Bowlt, John E. (ed.), *Russian Art of the Avant-Garde: Theory and Criticism, 1902–1934*, rev. and enlarged edn (London: Thames and Hudson, 1988).

Bowness, Alan, "Introduction", *Post-Impressionism: Cross-Currents in European Painting*, ed. John House and Mary Anne Stevens (London: Royal Academy of Arts in association with Weidenfeld and Nicolson, 1979).

Boyd, William, *Any Human Heart: The Intimate Journals of Logan MountStuart* (London: Penguin, 2002).

Bradbury, Malcolm and James McFarlane, *Modernism, 1890–1930* (Harmondsworth: Penguin, 1976).

Bronfen, Elizabeth, *Over Her Dead Body* (Manchester: Manchester University Press, 1991).

Brooker, Peter (ed.), *Modernism/Postmodernism* (London: Longmans, 1992).

—— (ed.), *A Student's Guide to the Selected Poems of Ezra Pound* (London: Faber, 1979).

Brown, Jane, *Lutyens and the Edwardians: An English Architect and His Clients* (London: Viking, 1996).

Brown, Milton W., *The Story of the Armory Show*, 2nd edn (New York: Abbeville Press, 1988).

Browning, Robert, *The Poetical Works of Robert Browning*, vol. II: *Strafford, Sordello*, ed. Ian Jack and Margaret Smith (Oxford: Clarendon, 1984).

Buchan, John, *The People's King, George V: A Narrative of Twenty-Five Years* (Boston, 1935).

Budgen, Frank, *James Joyce and the Making of "Ulysses" and Other Writings* (Oxford: Oxford University Press, 1972).

Bullen, J. B. (ed.), *Post-Impressionists in England* (London and New York, 1988).

Bürger, Peter, *Theory of the Avant-Garde* (1974), trans. Michael Shaw (Minneapolis: University of Minnesota Press, 1984) .

Butler, Christopher, *Early Modernism: Literature, Music and Painting in Europe, 1900–1916* (Oxford: Clarendon Press, 1994).

Calinescu, Matei, *Five Faces of Modernity: Modernism, Avant-Garde, Decadence, Kitsch, Postmodernism* (Durham, NC: Duke University Press, 1987).

Carter, Huntly, "Towards a Peace Theatre', *The Egoist*, VI:4 (September 1919), 62–3.

Caws, Mary Ann and Sarah Bird Wright, *Bloomsbury and France: Art and Friends* (Oxford: Oxford University Press, 2000).

Celan, Paul, *The Poems of Paul Celan*, trans. Michael Hamburger (London: Anvil Press, 1988).

Childs, Peter, *Modernism* (London and New York: Routledge, 2000).

Chipp, Herschel B. (ed.), *Theories of Modern Art* (1968).

Cockcroft, Eva, "Abstract Expressionism: Weapon of the Cold War", *Art Forum*, 12: 10 (June 1974).

Colebrook, Claire, forthcoming *Transitions* volume on Gender.

Conrad, Joseph, *Heart of Darkness* (1902; New York: Dover, 1990).

Cook, Ebenezer, "The Post-Impressionists", *Post-Impressionists in England*, ed. J. B. Bullen (London and New York: Routledge, 1988).

Crozier, Andrew, "Introduction", *Poems and Adolphe, 1920*, by John Rodker, ed. Andrew Crozier (Manchester: Carcanet, 1996).

——, "Thrills and Frills: Poetry as Figures of Empirical Lyricism", *Society and Literature, 1945–1970*, ed. Alan Sinfield (London: Methuen, 1983).

H.D. [Hilda Dolittle], *Collected Poems, 1912–1944* (Manchester: Carcanet, 1984).

Dangerfield, George, *The Strange Death of Liberal England* (London: Constable, 1936).

Dante, *The Divine Comedy*, trans. C. H. Sisson (Oxford: Oxford University Press, 1993).

Denny, Ernest, Nora O' Sullivan, C. Doyle and Gwen Upshot, *Galleys Laden: Poems by Four Writers* (Oxford: Blackwell, 1918).

De Quincey, Thomas, *Suspiria de Profundis* (1845), in *Confessions of an English Opium Eater and Other Writings* (Oxford: Oxford University Press, 1985).

de Saint-Simon, Henri, *Opinions littéraires, philosophiques et industrielles* (1825).

DiBattista, Maria, *Virginia Woolf's Major Novels: The Fables of Anon* (New Haven, CT: Yale University Press, 1980).

Donne, John, *The Complete English Poems of John Donne*, ed. C. A. Patrides (London: Dent, 1985).

Dunlop, Ian, *The Shock of the New: Seven Historic Exhibitions of Modern Art* (London: Weidenfeld & Nicolson, 1972).

Du Plessis, Rachel Blau, *The Pink Guitar: Writing as Feminist Practice* (London: Routledge, 1990).

Eagleton, Terry, *Literary Theory: An Introduction* (Oxford: Blackwell, 1983).

Edwards, Steve (ed.), *Art and Its Histories: A Reader* (New Haven, CT, and London: Yale University Press, 1999) .

*The Egoist*, VI:4 (September 1919).

*The Egoist*, VI:5 (December 1919).

Elderfield, John, *Kurt Schwitters* (London: Thames and Hudson, 1985).

Eliot, T. S., *The Letters of T. S. Eliot*, vol. 1: *1898–1922*, ed. Valerie Eliot (San Diego, New York, London: Harcourt, 1998).

——, *The Complete Poems and Plays of T. S. Eliot* (London: Faber, 1969).

——, *After Strange Gods: A Primer of Modern Heresy* (London: Faber, 1934).

——, "Tradition and the Individual Talent", *The Egoist*, VI:4 (September 1919), 54–5, and VI:5 (December 1919), 72–3.

——, "*Ulysses*, Order and Myth" (1923), *Modernism: An Anthology*, ed. Kolocotroni et al.

——, "William Blake" (1920), *Selected Essays* (London: Faber, 1932).

Ellmann, Maud, *The Poetics of Impersonality: T. S. Eliot and Ezra Pound* (Brighton: Harvester, 1987).

Ellman, Richard, *James Joyce* (Oxford: Oxford University Press, 1959).

——, *Ulysses on the Liffey* (London: Faber, 1984).

Ellmann, Richard and Charles Feidelson (eds), *The Modern Tradition* (Oxford: Oxford University Press, 1965).

Erickson, Paul, *Reagan Speaks: The Making of an American Myth* (New York, 1985).

Eysteinnson, Astradur, *The Concept of Modernism* (1990).

Fargnoli, A. Nicholas and Michael Patrick Gillespie, *James Joyce A to Z* (London: Bloomsbury, 1997).

Faulkner, Peter (ed.), *A Modernist Reader: Modernism in England, 1910–1930* (London: Batsford, 1986).

——, *Modernism* (London: Methuen, 1977).

Felski, Rita, *Beyond Feminist Aesthetics: Feminist Literature and Social Change* (Cambridge, MA, and London: Harvard University Press, 1989).

——, *The Gender of Modernity* (Cambridge, MA, and London: Harvard University Press, 1995).

Fitch, Noel Riley (ed.), *In Transition: A Paris Anthology: Writing and Art from* transition *Magazine, 1927–1930* (London: Secker & Warburg, 1990).

Fitzgerald, F. Scott, "Echoes of the Jazz Age" (1931), *The Crack-up with Other Pieces and Stories* (Harmondsworth: Penguin, 1974).

Flory, Wendy, "Pound and Anti-semitism", *The Cambridge Companion to Ezra Pound*, ed. Ira B. Nadel (Cambridge: Cambridge University Press, 1999).

Foner, Philip S., *History of the Labor Movement in the United States*, vol. 4: *The Industrial Workers of the World, 1905–1917* (New York, 1965).

Fontenrose, Joseph, *Python: A Study of Delphic Myth and its Origins* (1959).

Forster, E. M., "Virginia Woolf" (1941), *Virginia Woolf: A Collection of Critical Essays*, ed. Claire Sprague (Englewood Cliffs, NJ: Prentice-Hall, 1971).

Frascina, Francis (ed.), *Pollock and After: The Critical Debate* (London: Harper and Row, 1985).

Frascina, Francis and Charles Harrison (eds), *Modernist Art and Modernism: A Critical Anthology* (London: Harper and Row, 1982).

Frazer, James George, *The Golden Bough*, Part Three: *The Dying God*, vol. 4 (London, 1911).

Friedman, Susan Stanford, "Definitional Excursions: The Meanings of Modern/Modernity/Modernism", *Modernism/Modernity*, 8, 3 (2001): 493–513.

Frisby, David, *Fragments of Modernity: Theories of Modernity in the Work of Simmel, Kraceur and Benjamin* (Cambridge: Polity Press, 1985).

Fry, Roger, "Introduction", *Second Post-Impressionist Exhibition,* Grafton Galleries, Exhibition Catalogue (London, 1912).

——, *Vision and Design* (London: Chatto & Windus, 1920).

Fuller, John, *A Reader's Guide to W. H. Auden* (London: Thames & Hudson, 1970).

Fussell, Paul, *The Great War and Modern Memory* (Oxford: Oxford University Press, 1975).

——, "Can Graham Greene Write English?", *The Boy Scout Handbook and Other Observations* (Oxford: Oxford University Press, 1982).

Gambrell, Alice, *Women Intellectuals, Modernism, and Difference: Transatlantic Culture, 1919–1945* (Cambridge: Cambridge University Press, 1997).

Garber, Marjorie, *Vested Interest: Cross-Dressing and Cultural Anxiety* (New York: Routledge, 1992).

Gardiner, Juliet and Neil Wenborn (eds), *The History Today Companion to British History* (London: Collins, 1995).

Gary, Romain, *The Dance of Genghis Cohn* (London: Jonathan Cape, 1968).

Gascoyne, David, *Poems, 1937–1942* (London: P. L. Editions, 1943).

——, *Selected Prose, 1934–1966,* ed. Roger Scott (London: Enitharmon, 1988).

Gilbert, Sandra and Susan Gubar, *No Man's Land: The Place of the Woman Writer in the Twentieth Century,* 3 vols (New Haven, CT: Yale University Press, 1988–95).

Goldberg, RoseLee, *Performance: Live Art, 1909 to the Present* (London: Thames and Hudson, 1979).

Jane Goldman, "'Miss Lonelyhearts and the Party Dress': Cross-dressing and Collage in the Satires of Nathanael West", *The Glasgow Review,* 2 (Autumn 1993): 40–54.

——, "Dada Goes West: Re-Reading Revolution in *The Day of the Locust*", *Imprimatur,* II, 1/2 (Autumn 1996): 20–36.

——, *The Feminist Aesthetics of Virginia Woolf: Modernism, Post-Impressionism and the Politics of the Visual* (Cambridge, 1998).

——, "Virginia Woolf and Post-Impressionism: French Art, English Theory, and Feminist Practice", *Miscelánea: A Journal of English and American Studies,* 20 (1999): 173–92.

—— (ed.), *The Icon Critical Guide to Virginia Woolf* (Cambridge, 1997).

Graham, W. S., *Collected Poems, 1942–1977* (London and Boston: Faber & Faber, 1979).

Green, Barbara, *Spectacular Confessions: Autobiography, Performative Activism, and the Sites of Suffrage, 1905–1938* (Basingstoke: Macmillan, 1997).

Greenberg, Clement, "Towards a Newer Laocoon" (1940), *Art in Theory, 1900–1990,* ed. Charles Harrison and Paul Wood (Oxford: Blackwell, 1992).

——, "Modernist Painting" (1961), *Art in Theory, 1900–1990*, ed. Charles Harrison and Paul Wood (Oxford: Blackwell, 1992).

——, "Avant-Garde and Kitsch", *Art in Theory, 1900–1990*, ed. Charles Harrison and Paul Wood (Oxford: Blackwell, 1992).

——, *Art and Culture* (London: Thames & Hudson, 1973).

Griffith, George V., "Guernica in Hollywood: A Picasso Allusion in *The Day of the Locust*", *Notes on Modern American Literature*, 6:3 (1982), item 22.

Guiguet, Jean, *Virginia Woolf and Her Works* (New York: Harcourt Brace Jovanovich, 1965).

Haftmann, Walter, *Painting in the Twentieth Century*, trans. Ralph Manheim (London, 1965).

Hamnett, Nina, *Laughing Torso* (London: Constable, 1932).

Hanscome, Gillian and Virginia Smyers, *Writing for their Lives* (London: Women's Press, 1987).

Harrison, Charles and Paul Wood (eds), *Art in Theory, 1900–1990: An Anthology of Changing Ideas* (Oxford: Blackwell, 1992).

Harrison, Thomas, *1910: The Emancipation of Dissonance* (Berkeley, CA: University of California Press, 1996).

Haule, James M., "'Temps passe' and the Original Typescript: an Early Version of the 'Time Passes' Section of *To the Lighthouse*", *Twentieth-Century Literature*, 29:3 (Fall 1983), 267–77.

Heilbrun, Carolyn G., *Toward a Recognition of Androgyny* (New York: Knopf, 1973).

Heller, Joseph, *Catch-22* (1961; London Jonathan Cape, 1962).

Herbst, Josephine, "Nathanael West" (1961), *Nathanael West: A Collection of Critical Essays*, ed. Jay Martin (Englewoods Cliffs, NJ: Prentice-Hall, 1971).

Hicks, Granville, Michael Gold, et al. (eds), *Proletarian Literature of the United States: An Anthology* (London: Lawrence and Wishart, 1939).

Hobsbaum, Philip, *Tradition and Experiment in English Poetry* (Basingstoke: Macmillan, 1979).

Hopkins, David, "Questioning Dada's Potency: Picabia's 'La Sainte Vierge' and the Dialogue with Duchamp", *Art History*, 15:3 (September 1992), 317–33.

——, *After Modern Art, 1945–2000* (Oxford: Oxford University Press, 2000).

Hughes, Langston, *The Big Sea* (London: Hutchinson, 1941).

Hughes, Robert, *The Shock of the New: Art and the Century of Change* (London: BBC, 1980).

Hulme, T. E., "Romanticism and Classicism" (1911), *Speculations*, ed. Herbert Read (London: Routledge and Kegan Paul, 1954).

Hussey, Mark, *Virginia Woolf A to Z* (Oxford and New York: Oxford University Press, 1995).

Huxley, Aldous, *Defeat of Youth* (Oxford: Blackwell, 1918).

Hyman, Stanley Edgar, "Nathanael West" (1962); *Modern Critical Views: Nathanael West*, ed. Harold Bloom (New York, 1986).

Jangfeldt, Bengt (ed.), *Vladimir Mayakovsky – Love is the Heart of Everything: Correspondence between Vladimir Mayakovsky and Lili Brik, 1915–1930*, trans. Julian Graffy (Edinburgh: Polgon, 1986).

Jolas, Eugene (ed.), *transition* (Spring 1938).

Jones, E. B. C. (ed.), *Songs for Sale* (Oxford: Blackwell, 1918).

Joyce, James, *Ulysses* (1922) ed. Jeri Johnson (Oxford: Oxford University Press, 1999).

——, *A Portrait of the Artist as a Young Man* (1916), ed. Jeri Johnson (Oxford: Oxford University Press, 2000).

——, *Finnegans Wake* (1939).

——, *Selected Letters of James Joyce*, ed. Richard Ellman (New York: Viking, 1975).

Karl, Frederick R., *Modern and Modernism: The Sovereignty of the Artist, 1885–1925* (New York: Atheneum, 1985).

Kauvar, Elaine M., "An Interview with Cynthia Ozick", *Contemporary Literature*, XXXIV, 3 (1993), 358–94.

——, *Cynthia Ozick's Fiction: Tradition and Invention* (Bloomington: Indiana University Press, 1993).

Kaye, Peter, *Dostoevsky and English Modernism, 1900–1930* (Cambridge: Cambridge University Press, 1999).

Keats, John, *The Letters of John Keats*, ed. Maurice Buxton Forman, 4th edn (London: Oxford University Press, 1952).

Kenner, Hugh, *The Pound Era: The Age of T. S. Eliot, James Joyce and Wyndham Lewis* (1972; London: Faber, 1975).

Kermode, Frank, *The Sense of an Ending* (Oxford: Oxford University Press, 1966).

Kern, Stephen, *The Culture of Time and Space, 1880–1918* (London: Weidenfeld and Nicolson, 1983).

Kernan, Alvin B., "The Mob Tendency: *The Day of the Locust*" (1965), *Modern Critical Views: Nathanael West*, ed. Harold Bloom (New York, 1986).

King, Alex, *Memorials of the Great War in Britain: The Symbolism and Politics of Remembrance* (Oxford and New York: Berg, 1998).

Kolocotroni, Vassiliki, Jane Goldman and Olga Taxidou (eds), *Modernism: An Anthology of Sources and Documents* (Edinburgh and Chicago: Edinburgh University Press and the University of Chicago Press, 1998).

Kornbluh, Joyce L. (ed.), *Rebel Voices: An I.W.W. Anthology* (Ann Arbor: University of Michigan Press, 1964).

Kraus, Karl, *Half-Truths & One-and-a-Half Truths: Selected Aphorisms*, trans. Harry Zohn (Manchester: Carcanet, 1986).

Kumar, Shiv K., *Bergson and the Stream of Consciousness Novel* (London and Glasgow: Blackie, 1962).

L. and R., *Wine and Gall* (Oxford: Blackwell, 1918).

Lamb, Charles, *The Adventures of Ulysses* (London: Juvenile Library, 1808).

Lawrence, D. H., *The Letters of D. H. Lawrence*, vol. I, ed. James T. Boulton (Cambridge: Cambridge University Press, 1979).

——, *The Letters of D. H. Lawrence*, vol. II, ed. Geiorge J. Zytaruk and James T. Boulton (Cambridge: Cambridge University Press, 1979).

——, *Sons and Lovers* (1913; Harmondaworth: Penguin, 1962).

Lee, Hermione (ed.), *To the Lighthouse*, by Virginia Woolf (Harmondsworth: Penguin, 1992).

——, "Notes", *To the Lighthouse*, by Virginia Woolf, ed. Stella McNichol (Harmondsworth: Penguin, 1992).

Lemoine, Serge, *Dada*, trans. Charles Lynn Clark (Paris: Art Data, 1987).

Lentricchia, Frank, *Ariel and the Police: Michel Foucault, William James, Wallace Stevens* (Brighton: Harvester Wheatsheaf, 1988).

——, *Modernist Quartet* (Cambridge: Cambridge University Press, 1994).

Leonard, Tom, *Reports from the Present: Selected Work, 1982–94* (London: Cape, 1995).

Le Queux, William, *The Invasion of 1910, With a Full Account of the Siege of London* (London: Eveleigh Nash, 1906).

Levenson, M. H., *A Genealogy of Modernism* (1984).

—— (ed.), *Cambridge Companion to Modernism* (Cambridge: Cambridge University Press, 1999).

Lewis, Beth Irwin, *George Grosz: Art and Politics in the Weimar Republic* (Princeton, NJ: Princeton University Press, 1991).

Lewis, Wyndham, *Blast*, 1 (1914), ed. Bradford Morrow (Santa Rosa: Black Sparrow Press, 1997).

——, *Blast*, 2 (1915), ed. Bradford Morrow (Santa Rosa: Black Sparrow Press, 1993).

Litz, A. Walton, Louis Menand and Lawrence Rainey (eds), *The Cambridge History of Literary Criticism: Modernism and the New Criticism* (Cambridge: Cambridge University Press, 2000).

Locke, Alain (ed.), *The New Negro: An Interpretation* (New York: Albert and Charles Boni, 1925).

Lodder, Christina, "Lenin's Plan for Monumental Propaganda", *Art of the Soviets: Painting, Sculpture and Architecture in a One-Party State, 1917–1992*, ed. Matthew Cullerne Bown and Brandon Taylor (Manchester: Manchester University Press, 1993).

Lodge, David, *The Modes of Modern Writing: Metaphor, Metonymy, and the Typology of Modern Literature* (London: Longman, 1977).

Lopez, Tony, *The Poetry of W. S. Graham* (Edinburgh: Edinburgh University Press, 1989).

Lowndes, Mary, "On Banners and Banner-Making', *The Englishwoman*, VII:20 (September 1910).

Loy, Mina, *Last Lunar Baedeker: Poems of Mina Loy*, ed. Roger L. Conover (Manchester: Carcanet, 1997)

MacCarthy, Desmond, "The Art Quake of 1910", *The Listener*, 1 February 1945.

——, "The Post-Impressionists", *Manet and the Post-Impressionists*, Grafton Galleries, Exhibition Catalogue (London: 1950).

McHale, Brian, *Postmodern Fiction* (New York, 1987).

McMillan, Dougald, *transition: The History of a Literary Era, 1927–1938* (London: Calder and Boyars, 1975).

McNeillie, Andrew, "Bloomsbury", *The Cambridge Companion to Virginia Woolf*, ed. Sue Roe and Susan Sellers (Cambridge: Cambridge University Press, 2000).

Marinetti, Filippo, "Manifesto of Futurism" (1913), *Modernism: An Anthology*, ed. Kolocotroni et al..

Marsden, Dora, "Philosophy: *The Science of Signs XVII* Truth (continued)", *The Egoist*, VI:45 (September 1919), 49–53, and VI:5 (December 1919), 65–70.

Martin, Jay, *Nathanael West: The Art of His Life* (New York: Carroll and Graf, 1984).

Marvell, Andrew, *Andrew Marvell*, ed. Frank Kermode and Keith Walker (Oxford: Oxford University Press, 1994).

Meisel, Perry, *The Absent Father* (New Haven, CT: Yale University Press, 1980).

Melly, George, *Owning Up* (1965; Harmondsworth: Penguin, 1978).

Menand, Louis, "T. S. Eliot", *The Cambridge History of Literary Criticism*, vol. VII: *Modernism and the New Criticism*, ed. A. Walton Litz, Louis Menand and Lawrence Rainey (Cambridge: Cambridge University Press, 2000).

Moi, Toril, *Sexual/Textual Politics: Feminist Literary Theory* (London: Methuen, 1985).

Moody, A. David (ed.), *The Cambridge Companion to T. S. Eliot* (Cambridge: Cambridge University Press, 1994).

——, *Thomas Stearns Eliot Poet*, 2nd edn (Cambridge: Cambridge University Press, 1994).

Moore, Madeline, *The Short Season between Two Silences: The Mystical and Political in the Novels of Virginia Woolf* (Boston, MA: Allen Unwin, 1984).

Motherwell, Robert (ed.), *The Dada Painters and Poets* (1951), 2nd edn (Cambridge, MA and London: Harvard University Press, 1981).

Murphy, Richard, *Theorizing the Avant-Garde: Modernism, Expressionism, and the Problems of Postmodernity* (Cambridge: Cambridge University Press, 1999).

Nadel, Ira B. (ed.), *The Cambridge Companion to Ezra Pound* (Cambridge: Cambridge University Press, 1999).

Newton, K. M., *Interpreting the Text: A Critical Introduction to the Theory and Practice of Literary Interpretation* (New York: St Martin's Press, 1990).

Nicholls, Peter, *Modernisms: A Literary Guide* (London: Macmillan, 1995).

Nicolson, Benedict, "Post-Impressionism and Roger Fry", *Burlington Magazine*, 93 (1951), 18–21.

Nightingale, M., *Verses Wise and Otherwise* (Oxford: Blackwell, 1918).

Nill, Anegreth, "Weimar Politics and the Theme of Love in Kurt Schwitters' *Das Bäumerbild*", *Dada/Surrealism* 13 (1984): 17–36.

Nordau, Max, *Degeneration* (London, 1895).

Ovid, *Metamorphoses*, trans. Frank Justus Miller [Loeb Classical Library] (London: Heinemann, 1916).

*Oxford Classical Dictionary* (1949).

Pachnicke, Peter and Klaus Honnef (eds), *John Heartfield* (New York: Abrams, 1992).

Peppis, Paul, *Literature, Politics, and the English Avant-Garde: Nation and Empire, 1901–1918* (Cambridge: Cambridge University Press, 2000).

Perelman, S. J., "Nathanael West", *Contempo* 3 (25 July, 1933); *Nathanael West: A Collection of Critical Essays*, ed. Jay Martin (Englewood Cliffs: Prentice-Hall, 1971).

Perloff, Marjorie, *The Dance of the Intellect: Studies in the Pound Tradition* (Cambridge: Cambridge University Press, 1985).

Poe, Edgar Allan, "Philosophy of Composition" (1846), *The Works of Edgar Allan Poe*, vol. v (Philadelphia, PA: Luppincott, 1905).

Ezra Pound, *The Spirit of Romance: An Attempt to Define Somewhat the Charm of the Pre-Renaissance Literature of Latin Europe* (London: Dent, 1910).

——, *Quia Pauper Amavi* (London: The Egoist, 1919).

——, *Selected Poems*, ed. T. S. Eliot (London: Faber, 1928).

——, *Make It New* (London: Faber, 1934).

——, *Guide to Kulchur* (London: Faber, 1938).

——, *The Pisan Cantos* [LXXIV–LXXXIV] (London: Faber, 1949).

——, *Literary Essays*, ed. T. S. Eliot (Norfolk, CT: New Directions, 1954).

——, *Personae: Collected Shorter Poems of Ezra Pound* (London: Faber, 1952).

——, *The Cantos* (London: Faber, 1963).

——, *Pound/Joyce: The Letters of Ezra Pound to James Joyce, with Pound's Essays on Joyce*, ed. Forrest Read (1967; London: Faber, 1968).

Pynchon, Thomas, *The Crying of Lot 49* (1966).

Reed, John, *Ten Days that Shook the World* (1919).

——, *Insurgent Mexico* (1914).

Richardson, Mary, *Laugh of Defiance* (London: Weidenfeld and Nicolson, 1953).

Richter, Hans, *Dada: Art and Anti-Art* (London: Thames and Hudson, 1965).

——, *Virginia Woolf: The Inward Voyage* (Princeton, NJ: Princeton University Press, 1970).

Rickword, Edgell, *Essays and Opinions, 1921–1931*, ed. Alan Young (1974; Manchester: Carcanet, 1979).

Roberts, Matthew, "Bonfire of the Avant-Garde: Cultural Rage and Readerly Complicity in *The Day of the Locust*", *Modern Fiction Studies*, 42, 1 (Spring 1996) 61–90.

Rodker, John, *Poems and Adolphe, 1920*, ed. Andrew Crozier (Manchester: Carcanet, 1996).

——, "Blackwelliana", *The Egoist*, VI:4 (September 1919), 63.

Ross, Robert, "The Post-Impressionists at the Grafton: the Twilight of the Idols", *Morning Post*, 7 November 1910; *Post-Impressionists in England*, ed. J. B. Bullen (London and New York: Routledge, 1988).

Roe, Sue, "The Impact of Post-Impressionism", *The Cambridge Companion to Virginia Woolf*, ed. Sue Roe and Susan Sellers (Cambridge: Cambridge University Press, 2000).

Rosenberg, Isaac, *The Collected Works of Isaac Rosenberg: Poetry, Prose, Letters, Paintings and Drawings*, ed. Ian Parsons (London: Chatto, 1984).

Sachs, Albie, *The Soft Vengeance of a Freedom Fighter* (London: Paladin, 1991).

Scarfe, Francis, *Auden and After: The Liberation of Poetry, 1930–1941* (London: Routledge, 1942).

Scheunemann, Dietrich (ed.), *European Avant-Garde: New Perspectives* (Amsterdam: Rodopi, 2000).

Schwitters, Kurt, *PPPPPP: Poems Performance Pieces Proses Plays Poetics*, ed. and trans. Jerome Rothenberg and Pierre Joris (Philadelphia: Temple University Press, 1993).

——, *Revolution in Revon* (1922), trans. Eugene Jolas, *transition*, 8 (1927; repr. 1967), 60–76.

Scott, Bonnie Kime, *Joyce and Feminism* (Bloomington: Indiana University Press, 1984).

——, *The Gender of Modernism* (Bloomington: Indiana University Press, 1990).

Segal, Naomi, "Sexual Politics and the Avant-Garde: from Apollinaire to Woolf", *Visions and Blueprints: Avant-Garde Culture and Radical Politics in Early Twentieth-Century Europe*, ed. Edward Timms and Peter Collier (Manchester: Manchester University Press, 1988).

Shattuck, Roger, *The Banquet Years: The Origins of the Avant-Garde in France: 1885 to World War I*, rev. edn (London: Cape, 1969).

Showalter, Elaine, "Virginia Woolf and the Flight into Androgyny", *A Literature of Their Own: British Women Novelists from Brontë to Lessing*, (London: Virago, 1982).

Sinfield, Alan (ed.), *Society and Literature, 1945–1970* (London: Methuen, 1983).

Sitwell, Edith, *Clowns' Houses* (Oxford: Blackwell, 1919).

Smith, Stan, *ReReading Literature: W. H. Auden* (Oxford: Blackwell, 1985).

——, *The Origins of Modernism* (Hemel Hempstead: Harvester, 1987).

Sordello, *The Poetry of Sordello*, ed. and trans. James J. Wilhelm (London and New York: Garland, 1987).

Spahr, Juliana, "Introduction" [to Gertrude Stein and George Hugnet], *Exact Change Yearbook* (1995).

Spalding, Frances, *Vanessa Bell* (London: Weidenfeld and Nicolson, 1983).

Speed, John, *A Prospect of the Most Famous Parts of the World* (1627).

Spengler, Oswald, *The Decline of the West*, vol. II: *Perspectives of World History* (1922), trans. Charles Francis Atkinson (London, 1928).

Stansky, Peter, *On or About December 1910: Early Bloomsbury and its Intimate World* (Cambridge, MA: Harvard University Press, 1996).

Stein, Gertrude, *The Autobiography of Alice B. Toklas* (London: John Lane, 1933).

——, *Gertrude Stein: Look at Me Now and Here I Am: Writings and Lectures 1909–45*, ed. Patricia Meyerowitz (Harmondsworth: Penguin, 1984).

——, *A Stein Reader*, ed. Ulla E. Dydo (Evanston, IL: Northwestern Yniversity Press, 1994).

——, *Tender Buttons* (1914).

——, *Writings, 1903–1932*, ed. Catharine R. Stimpson and Harriet Chessman (Washington, DC: Library of America, 1998).

——, *Writings, 1932–1946*, ed. Catharine R. Stimpson and Harriet Chessman (Washington, DC: Library of America, 1998).

——, *A Primer for the Gradual Understanding of Gertrude Stein*, ed. Robert Bartlett Haas (Santa Barbara, CA: Black Sparrow Press, 1976).

Stevens, Wallace, *Collected Poems* (London: Faber and Faber, 1955; 1990).

——, *The Necessary Angel: Essays on Reality and the Imagination* (London: Faber and Faber, 1960; 1984).

Stevenson, Randall, *Modernist Fiction: An Introduction* (Hemel Hempstead: Harvester, 1992).

Swarbrick, Katharine, and Jane Goldman, "The Flowers of Friendship: Gertrude Stein and Georges Hugnet" (unpublished essay).

Szasz, Thomas, *Karl Kraus and the Soul-Doctors: A Pioneer Critic and His Criticism of Psychiatry and Psychoanalysis* (London: Routledge & Kegan Paul, 1977).

Tate, Trudi, *Modernism, History and the First World War* (Manchester: Manchester University Press, 1998).

Terrell, Carroll F., *A Companion to the Cantos of Ezra Pound* (1980).

Thomas, Dylan, *Collected Poems, 1934–1953*, ed. Walford Davies and Ralph Maud (London: Dent, 1993).

——, *Selected Letters of Dylan Thomas*, ed. Constantine Fitzgibbon (New York, 1966).

Tickner, Lisa, *The Spectacle of Women: Imagery of the Suffragette Campaign, 1970–1914* (London: Chatto and Windus, 1987).

Timms, Edward, and Peter Collier (eds), *Visions and Blueprints: Avant-garde Culture and Radical Politics in Early Twentieth-Century Europe* (Manchester: Manchester University Press, 1988).

Tourner, Cyril, *The Revenger's Tragedy* (London: 1607).

Treece, Henry, *How I See Apocalypse* (London: 1948).

Van Wienen, Mark. W., *Partisans and Poets: The Political Work of American Poetry in the Great War* (Cambridge: Cambridge University Press, 1977).

Vrba, Rudolf and Alan Bestic, *I Cannot Forgive* (England: Sidgwick & Jackson and Anthony Gibbs & Phillips, 1963).

West, Nathanael, *Novels and Other Writings* (New York: Library of America, 1997).

Wharton, Henry Thornton, *Sappho: Memoir, Text, Selected Renderings, and a Literal Translation*, 3rd edn (1895).

Williams, Keith, *British Writers and the Media* (Basingstoke: Palgrave Macmillan, 1996).

Williams, Keith, and Steven Mattews (eds), *Re-Writing the Thirties: Modernism and After* (Harlow: Longman, 1997).

Williams, Louise Blakeney, *Modernism and the Ideology of History: Literature, Politics, and the Past* (Cambridge: Cambridge University Press, 2002).

Williams, Raymond, *The Politics of Modernism: Against the New Conformists* (London: Verso, 1989).

Williams, William Carlos, *The Collected Poems, 1909–1939*, ed. A. Walton Litz and Christopher MacGowan (Manchester: Carcanet, 1987).

——, *The Collected Poems of William Carlos Williams*, vol. II: *1939–1962*, ed. Christopher MacGowan (New York: New Directions, 1988).

——, *The Collected Later Poems of William Carlos Williams*, rev. edn (New York: New Directions, 1963).

——, *Imaginations*, ed. Webster Scott (London: MacGibbon & Kee, 1970).

Wisker, Alistair, *The Writing of Nathanael West* (Basingstoke: Palgrave Macmillan, 1990).

Wolfreys, Julian (ed.), *The Edinburgh Encyclopedia of Modern Criticism and Theory* (Edinburgh: Edinburgh University Press, 2002).

Womack, Kenneth, "Russian Formalism, the Moscow Linguistics Circle, and Prague Structuralism", *The Edinburgh Encyclopaedia of Modern Criticism and Theory*, ed. Julian Wolfreys (Edinburgh: Edinburgh University Press, 2002).

Wood, Paul (ed.), *The Challenge of the Avant-Garde* (New Haven, CT: Yale University Press, 1999).

Woolf, Virginia, "Mr Bennett and Mrs Brown" (1924).

——, "Modern Novels" (1919).

——, "Modern Fiction" (1925).

——, *To the Lighthouse* (London: Hogarth, 1927).

——, *Moments of Being* (London: Hogarth, 1985).

——, *A Room of One's Own* (London: Hogarth, 1929).

——, *Between the Acts* (London: Hogarth, 1941).

——, "Professions for Women" (1931), *The Death of the Moth* (London: Hogarth, 1942).

——, *The Moment and Other Essays* (London: Hogarth, 1942).

——, *The Death of The Moth and Other Essays* (London: Hogarth, 1943).

——, *The Letters of Virginia Woolf* (1888–1941), 6 vols, ed. Nigel Nicolson and Joanne Trautman (London: Hogarth, 1975–80).

——, *The Diary of Virginia Woolf* (1915–1941), 5 vols, ed. Anne Olivier Bell and Andrew McNeillie (London, 1977–84).

——, *The Essays of Virginia Woolf*, vols 1–4 (of 6), ed. Andrew McNeillie (London: Hogarth, 1986–1994).

——, *Roger Fry: A Biography* (London: Hogarth, 1940).

——, *The Waves* (London: Hogarth, 1931).

Wordsworth, William, *Poetical Works*, ed. Ernest de Selincourt (Oxford: Oxford University press, 1981).

Wright, Richard, *Native Son* (1940).

Wynne-Davies, Marion, *Sidney to Milton: 1580–1660* (Basingstoke: Palgrave Macmillan, 2002).

Wyrick, Deborah, "Dadaist Collage Structure and Nathanael West's *Dream Life of Balso Snell*", *Studies in the Novel*, 11 (1979): 349–59.

Yeats, W. B., *Collected Poems* (London: Macmillan, 1980).

# Index

SHORT LOAN COLLECTION
WITHDRAWN